D1483422

Content Networking

Architecture, Protocols, and Practice

The Morgan Kaufmann Series in Networking
Series Editor, David Clark, M.I.T.

For further information on these books and for a list of forthcoming titles, please visit our Website at http://www.mkp.com.

Content Networking

Architecture, Protocols, and Practice

Markus Hofmann and Leland Beaumont

AMSTERDAM • BOSTON • HEIDELBERG • LONDON
NEW YORK • OXFORD • PARIS • SAN DIEGO
SAN FRANCISCO • SINGAPORE • SYDNEY • TOKYO
MORGAN KAUFMANN PUBLISHERS IS AN IMPRINT OF ELSEVIER

ELSEVIER

MORGAN KAUFMANN PUBLISHERS

Publishing Director   Diane Cerra
Senior Acquisitions Editor   Rick Adams
Developmental Editor   Karyn Johnson
Assistant Editor   Mona Buehler
Publishing Services Manager   Simon Crump
Project Manager   Justin R. Palmeiro
Cover Design   Yvo Riezebos Design
Composition   Kolam
Copyeditor   Kolam USA
Proofreader   Kolam USA
Indexer   Kolam USA
Interior printer   Maple Press
Cover printer   Phoenix Color

Morgan Kaufmann Publishers is an imprint of Elsevier.
500 Sansome Street, Suite 400, San Francisco, CA 94111

This book is printed on acid-free paper.

Figure credit: Image clips in Figure 6.9 used with permission.

Library of Congress Cataloging-in-Publication Data
Hofmann, Markus.
    Content networking : architecture, protocols, and practice / Markus Hofmann and Leland Beaumont.
       p. cm. — (The Morgan Kaufmann series in networking)
    Includes bibliographical references and index.
    ISBN 1-55860-834-6
    1. Computer networks. I. Beaumont, Leland R. II. Title. III. Series.
    TK5105.5.H63 2005
    004.6—dc22
                                        2005001732

ISBN: 1-55860-834-6

For information on all Morgan Kaufmann publications,
visit our Web site at www.mkp.com or www.books.elsevier.com

Printed in the United States of America
05 06 07 08 09   5 4 3 2 1

Dedicated with great affection to my wife Bettina and our kids Jennifer, Dennis, and Kevin for their love and support, and to my parents for preparing me to take on such an endeavor.
– Markus Hofmann

Dedicated to my parents, who prepared me to write this, and to my wife Eileen, daughter Nicole, and son Rick, for their encouragement and support while writing it.
– Leland Beaumont

Contents

Preface

Why This Book?

People are sociable. They want to stay in touch with each other, share their experiences, and exchange information regarding their common interests. When Markus and his wife moved to the United States a few years ago, the Internet and the Web became their main means to stay in touch with family and friends back in Germany. E-mail, a Web page with guestbook, and instant messaging allowed timely and very effective exchange of the latest gossip. Photos from recent happenings were uploaded to a Web page and shared minutes later. A little later, the first personal video clip found its way from the digital camcorder onto the Web page, allowing even livelier information sharing across the continents.

Soon, however, the limitations of the underlying technology became obvious. Parents and friends back in Germany started to complain about long download times, unavailable Web servers, long playback delays, and the choppy quality of video clips. Knowing our research and work interests, they posed the challenge of helping to overcome these problems: "Hey, you are working on data networking and telecommunications—why can't you produce something useful and help solve these problems?" A team at Bell Labs/Lucent Technologies—our employer at that point in time—took the challenge and worked on designing and developing solutions to overcome the slowdown on the World Wide Web. It is a very exciting effort, which brought Bell Labs Researchers together with system engineers, developers, and sales personnel from Lucent Business Units—working hand in hand, collaborating very closely, and leveraging each other's experiences and strengths. This was also the time when Markus and Lee met, embarking on their very exciting journey into the space of Content Networking.

People are curious. They want to understand and learn about issues that affect and impact them. When we first demonstrated the exciting results of the team's work, people started to ask how it works, what was done, and how it will help improve the scalability and reliability of Internet services. Motivated by this interest, we wrote this book to help people understand the reasons for current problems in the Internet and to explain both the challenges and possible solutions for building a more reliable and scalable Internet. Markus has been working as a researcher in content delivery and related fields for more than 10 years and has gained valuable practical experience, which he would like to pass on to the readers of this book. His colleague, Leland Beaumont, has 30 years of experience in developing data network systems—an invaluable asset when bringing ideas from the research lab into the real world.

Audience

The Internet, and in particular the World Wide Web (WWW), have become an integral part of people's lives. With the increase in popularity, however, users face more and more problems when using the Internet, such as long access delays, poor quality of service, and unreliable services. This book is aimed at helping practitioners and researchers working with network service providers, software and hardware vendors, and content providers to understand the reasons for these problems. It explains the challenges in making content available on the WWW, describes basic concepts and principles for improving the current situation, and outlines possibilities for tapping into the huge potential of custom-tailored services over the Internet. In particular, the book describes the pressures that caused the Internet to evolve from the original End-to-End model to a more complex model that has intelligence embedded within various intermediaries placed throughout the network.

Approach

The book starts with a discussion of fundamental techniques and protocols for moving content on the Internet, followed by an introduction to content replication and Web caching. From there, the book outlines the evolution from traditional Web caching towards a flexible and open architecture to support a variety of content-oriented services. Evolutionary steps include support for streaming media, systems for global request routing, and the design of APIs and protocols that enable value-added services, such as compression, filtering, and transformation. Content navigation, peer-to-peer networks, instant messaging, content services, standards, and future directions are all discussed. The book also explains how the different components interact with each other and how they can be used to build complex content delivery networks.

We hope the reader will learn how the technology evolved from traditional Web caching to more sophisticated content delivery services. The reader will get a better understanding of the key components in modern content delivery networks and the protocols that make the components interact with each other. Various examples are provided to help the reader to better understand how this technology can be deployed and how it could help their business.

The book concentrates mainly on underlying principles, concepts, and mechanisms and tries to explain and evaluate them. While the specific protocols, interfaces, and languages used in content networking will continue to evolve and change, it is expected that the core principles and concepts underlying content networks will remain valid for a long time. As such, the book focuses on principles and attempts to explain and evaluate them. Specific protocols and languages are selected as examples of how the concepts and mechanisms can be incorporated into real-life networks. It uses many examples and case studies for illustration. The book is *not* intended as a reference guide to Web-related protocols, but as a guide providing a systematic and architectural view of the content delivery and content services field. It helps the reader to understand the overall picture and how all the components fit together. The examples are timely and the principles remain timeless.

Much of the design of the Internet is described in freely available documents known as RFC, Requests for Comment. These are relied on heavily as references through the book. RFCs are dynamic. Some classics remain as useful, accurate, and pertinent as they were when they were written a decade or more ago. Others may be superseded before this book completes its first printing. Readers working in the field need to stay abreast of changes as they unfold.

Content

The first chapter serves as introduction to the remainder of the book. It explains the notion of content networking and establishes the key concepts. A brief look at the early days of information access over the Internet establishes the roots of modern content networking—the World Wide Web. The chapter continues with a flashback to the first half of the 1990s, with a history of the Web setting the stage for a discussion of fundamental concepts and principles.

The rest of the book takes us on a journey that follows the evolution of content networks.

Chapter 2 explains the core principles that guided the design of the Internet, leading into a discussion of how content is transported over the Internet. The focus is on the *Hypertext Transfer Protocol (HTTP)* and some of the features that will be important in later chapters of the book.

Chapter 3 shows how Web caching is used to bring static content closer to the users and how this helps in improving content delivery over the Internet. These first three chapters form the foundation for the balance of the book.

Chapter 4 stands alone and extends Web caching to include streaming media such as audio and video. Optimized techniques are introduced that take into account the special characteristics of time-constrained streaming media.

Chapter 5 deals with the question of how user requests actually get to the server or Web cache best suited to serve each user. Different metrics for evaluating closeness in content networks are introduced and different mechanisms for request routing are explained.

Chapter 6 introduces the new concept of peer-to-peer networks, in which the traditional client-server model of the Web is replaced with a federation of end-systems that help each other in delivering content. Chapters 4, 6, and 7 each stand alone and may be reading any order, or skipped entirely at the discretion of the reader.

Chapter 7 extends the notion of content networking to include delivery of interactive media, such as instant messaging. The chapter explains a variety of standards-based and proprietary approaches that enable people to interact with each other in (near) real-time.

Chapter 8 is the centerpiece of the book, describing Content Services. After developing an architecture for content services, two similar approaches are introduced. These are the Internet Content Adaptation Protocol (ICAP) and the Open Pluggable Edge services (OPES), the latter one being standardized in the IETF. The W3C sponsored approach to Web-based services is then described. Finally, the wide range of services made possible by the convergence of Web services and traditional telephony are described.

Chapter 9 brings the various technologies and network elements together, and explains how they can be deployed to build content networks for specific needs.

Chapter 10 provides an overview of the various standards activities relevant to the field on content networking, and explains which efforts are of interest for each specific area.

Chapter 11 finally summarizes our journey through the evolution of content networks and attempts to provide an outlook of what the future might bring.

A glossary at the back of the book includes terms that are unique to this content area.

The focus of this book is on the architectures and protocols specific to content networks. It cannot address every single topic in depth. Therefore, the book does not address other relevant topics such as security issues surrounding content networks or the operation and management of content networks.

A companion Web site for this book exists at http://www.content-networking.com/ or at www.mkp.com/?isbn=1558608346. At this site, you will find additional support material to enhance reading of the book. We suggest that you visit the page for this book every so often, as we will be adding and updating material and establishing new links to content networking related sites on a regular basis.

In this spirit, start the engines, get rolling, and have fun!

Acknowledgments

Clearly, an undertaking such as this book is impossible without the support of others. First and foremost, we thank our families—Bettina with Jennifer, Dennis and Kevin, and Eileen with Nicole and Rick—for their patience, their sympathy, and their continued encouragement during the sometimes stressful period of writing this book. The book was written in addition to the commitments of our daytime jobs, written exclusively on personal time—nights, early mornings, and weekends. It is time now to make up for some of the lost weekends with beach visits, hikes, biking tours and canoe and kayak trips.

Many colleagues and co-workers have given us inspiration—too numerous to mention individually. However, we would like to say special thanks to Wayne Hatter, whose calm, yet determined and highly motivational leadership helped transition some of the concepts presented in this book into real-world products. Wayne represents an entire team of excellent and bright developers that we had the pleasure to work with. We also thank our management at Bell Labs Research, in particular Krishan Sabnani and Sudhir Ahuja, for their encouragement in finishing this book. A special thanks also to Sanjoy Paul, who has been key in starting our efforts around Content Networking.

The book was made possible only by our own excitement and enthusiasm for the Content Networking space, fueled even more by active participation and involvement in several international standardizations efforts—not a trivial task! Our colleague Igor Faynberg provided helpful hints and tips on how to move our work into the respective standards bodies. Guidance from Allison Mankin ensures that the work on content services being done by others and ourselves is sensitive to the existing Internet architecture. Acknowledgments also go to Michael Condry and Hilarie Orman, who inspired much of the work in the content services field.

The thoughtful and detailed comments of our manuscript reviewers—including Mark Nottingham, Alex Rousskov, Michael Vernick, and Martin Stecher—have greatly strengthened the final result. Their critique and suggestions have prompted improvement in the structure of the book and addition of new subjects. A big "Thank you!" for their help.

We also wish to acknowledge the editorial staff at Morgan Kaufman/Elsevier for a great job in giving the book this professional touch. Karyn Johnson has to be thanked for her extreme patience and persistence getting work back on track after deadlines slipped. Rick Adams deserves much credit for having the courage to ask us to write this book.

The content of this book is based on several tutorials and graduate lectures, which Markus gave before and during the preparation of this book. Notably, we thank the tutorial chairs and organizers of ACM Multimedia, NGC Workshop, World Wide Web Conference, and IEEE ICNP for the opportunity to present tutorials accompanying this book. Likewise, we thank the professorship (in particular Martina Zitterbart) and the administration of University of Braunschweig, Germany, and University of Karlsruhe, Germany, for the opportunity to present two 5-day graduate lectures based on the content of this book.

Growing Together

Most of the book was written in the wonderful and vibrant shore region of New Jersey. Other parts were written during trips in places around the world, including Karlsruhe (Germany), Juan Les Pins (France), Yokohama (Japan), San Jose (Costa Rica), London (England), Boulder (Colorado, USA), Los Angeles, San Francisco, San Diego (California, USA), Atlanta (Georgia, USA), and mid-air between several of these places. Hopefully, the technology described in this book will help people in all these places and around the world to grow together even stronger.

Markus Hofmann and Leland Beaumont,
New Jersey, USA, September, 2004

About the Authors

Markus Hofmann is Director of Services Infrastructure Research at Bell Labs/Lucent Technologies. He received his PhD in Computer Engineering from University of Karlsruhe, Germany, in 1998 and joined Bell Labs Research the same year. Currently, he is also an Adjunct Professor at Columbia University in New York, USA. Markus is known for his pioneering work on reliable multicasting over the Internet and for defining and shaping fundamental principles on content networking. He is Chair of the Open Pluggable Edge Services (OPES) Working Group in the IETF since it has been chartered in 2002. More recently, Markus' work has extended into the areas of VoIP and converged communications. Markus is on the Editorial Board of the Computer Communications Journal, has recently been elected chair of the Internet Technical Committee (ITC), and has published numerous papers in the multicasting and content delivery area. His PhD thesis won the 1998 GI/KuVS Award for best PhD thesis in Germany in the area of Telecommunications, and also the 1998 FZI Doctoral Dissertation price awarded by the German Research Center for Computer Science. More information is available at www.mhof.com.

Leland Beaumont consults on quality management and product development. Prior to that, he was responsible for specification and verification of content delivery products at Lucent, including Web caching and content network navigation. After graduating with highest honors from Lehigh University, he received his Master of Science degree in Electrical Engineering from Purdue University. He has worked in the data communications product development industry for over 30 years.

CHAPTER 1

Introduction

Over the last few decades, the Internet has revolutionized our society and our economy. It has changed the way people communicate with each other and the way business is conducted. The Internet has created a global environment that is drawing people from all over the world closer together. Collaboration and interaction of individuals through their networked computers have been main applications on the Internet since the beginning. Electronic mail and Internet chat rooms are just two examples of popular applications. Over the last decade, the Internet has been used ever more as a mechanism for information dissemination and broadcasting, mainly driven by the emergence of the World Wide Web—also referred to as WWW or the Web. The Web forms a universe of information accessible via networked computers, offering *content* in the form of Web pages, images, text, animations, or audio and video streams. This book examines the technical concepts and the challenges of distributing, delivering, and servicing content over the Internet. Business-related aspects are considered when they have impact on the underlying technology. The focus is on fundamental principles and concepts rather than providing a reference for specific communication protocols or implementation details.

The first chapter serves as an introduction, explaining the notion of content networking and establishing the underlying key concepts. A brief look at the early days of information access over the Internet segues to the roots of modern content networking—the World Wide Web. The chapter continues with a flashback to the first half of the 1990s, with a history of the Web setting the stage for a discussion of underlying concepts and principles. These include the *representation, identification,* and *transport* of Web objects, which are most often referred to as Hypertext Markup Language (HTML), Universal Resource Identifier (URI), and Hypertext Transport Protocol (HTTP), respectively. The power of URIs and hyperlinks allows a variety of protocols to link new content types together and add richness to the original WWW. For example, other protocols such as RTSP and RTP allow other object types, such as multimedia streams, to be linked into the WWW. The chapter continues looking at Web applications as a driving force for the evolution of the Web and for adopting new technology. It identifies the shortcomings of today's Web architecture and outlines an evolutionary path toward advanced communication architectures of the future. The technology-focused part is complemented with a description of the various Web beneficiaries and their diversity of interests. The chapter concludes with a tour through the book that outlines the remaining ten chapters.

1.1   **The Early Days of Content Delivery over the Internet**

Until about a decade ago, most of the world knew little or nothing about the Internet. It was used largely by the scientific community for sharing resources on computers and for interacting with colleagues in their respective research fields. When work on the ARPANET—the origin of today's Internet—started in the late 1960s and the 1970s, the prevailing applications were as follows: access to remote machines, exchange of e-mails, and copying files between computers. Electronic distribution of documents soon gained importance, as it became apparent that the traditional academic publication process was too slow for the fast-paced information exchange essential for creating the Internet. When the *File Transfer Protocol (FTP)* [Bhu71, RFC 959] came into use in the early 1970s, documents were prepared as online files and made accessible on servers via FTP. Interested parties used an FTP client program to establish a connection to the server for downloading the document. Over the years, FTP evolved into the primary means for document retrieval and software distribution over the Internet. In the early 1990s, FTP accounted for almost half of the Internet traffic [Mer1].

However, FTP did not solve all the problems related to information retrieval over the Internet—it enabled downloading files from remote machines, but it did not support users facing the daunting task of navigating through the Internet and in locating relevant resources. Retrieving documents via FTP required users to know in advance the exact server to contact and the name of the file to download. Knowing just the title and the authors of a research paper, for example, was not sufficient for retrieving an electronic copy of the paper. Moreover, the user was required to figure out which FTP server was storing the paper and which file name had been used. The Internet worked very much like a library without a catalog or index cards—users had to know where to look to find the content they needed.

Locating relevant files on the Internet was simplified to some extent with the introduction of *archie* in 1991 [ED92]. The archie system made use of a special "anonymous" account on FTP servers, which gave arbitrary users limited access without having to enter a password. Using these "anonymous" accounts, archie servers periodically searched FTP servers throughout the Internet and recorded the names of files they found. This information was used to create and maintain a global catalog of files available for download. Users could use this catalog to search for file names matching certain patterns. When matches were found, archie also indicated the FTP servers on which the files were available.

A major restriction of archie was its limitation to pattern matching on file names rather than the actual content of the files. The *Wide Area Information Server (WAIS)* project [KM91] implemented a more powerful concept by searching through the text of documents in addition to their file names or titles. Suppose you are interested in finding articles on Michael Jordan's second comeback to professional basketball, and you perform an archie search using "Jordan" as your keyword. Even if the file named "NBA-News-September-2001.txt" includes a story covering Jordan's comeback, it would not turn up under an archie search. As WAIS digs through the entire text of the article, that file would appear with a WAIS search. Moreover, the WAIS mechanism provided a scored response, ranking retrieved information based on the quantity of keyword appearances in the text and on how close to the document's beginning they turned up. WAIS was originally developed at the beginning of the 1990s by a consortium of companies that included Thinking Machines Inc., Dow Jones, Apple Computer, and KPMG Peat Marwick. The first version of WAIS was available in the public domain in 1991. By summer 1992, the project had evolved into a separate company called—not surprisingly—WAIS Inc. This company can be considered the first to commercialize technology related to content retrieval over the Internet.

However, the WAIS system was not perfect—the user interface was relatively difficult to use and the search capabilities were initially limited to text documents. Besides, it scored documents based on the absolute number of keyword appearances rather than the density of their appearance. As a result, long documents were more likely than short documents to end up at the top of the list. WAIS further lacked the capability for hierarchical organization of content resources—a feature introduced by the *Gopher* system [RFC 1436].

Gopher was developed at the University of Minnesota in 1991 and named after the school's furry mascot. It let users retrieve data over the Internet without using complicated commands and addresses. Gopher servers searched the Internet using WAIS and arranged the results in hierarchical menus, using plain language. As users selected menu items, they were lead to other menus, files, or images, which might not even have resided on the local Gopher server. References could move users to remote servers or fetch files from distant locations. Gopher significantly simplified information retrieval on the Internet. It handled the details of actually getting requested information, without requiring users to know how and from where to retrieve those resources. Initially deployed only on the University of Minnesota campus, other institutions quickly discovered Gopher's versatility and set up their own Gopher servers. At one time, there were a few thousand Gopher servers registered with the top-level server "Gopher Central" at the University of Minnesota or its counterparts in other countries.

Archie, WAIS, and Gopher emerged in the same era and coexisted for some time. They all had their advantages and disadvantages, and occasionally, they are still used today. Nevertheless, in the course of the 1990s, they all were subsumed into yet another system—the World Wide Web (WWW).

1.2   The World Wide Web—Where It Came From and What It Is

The *World Wide Web* is an Internet facility that links information accessible via networked computers. This information is typically represented in the form of Web pages, which can contain text, graphics, animations, audio/video, and hyperlinks. Embedding hyperlinks in documents is an important feature of the Web and differentiates it clearly from Gopher and other approaches. Embedded hyperlinks connect a Web page to other resources either locally or on remote computers. Users can follow the links and access referenced resources simply by pointing to the hyperlink and clicking a mouse button. This intuitive mechanism allows browsing through a collection of information resources without having to worry about their actual location or their format.

This section will briefly describe the origin of the Web, where it came from and why it has been so successful. A description of the architectural components will help in the understanding of the fundamental design of the Web and, at the same time, motivate the evolution of the Web. A detailed introduction to the Web can be found in [KR01].

1.2.1   The Origin of the World Wide Web

The World Wide Web has its origin at the European Organization for Nuclear Research (CERN) near Geneva, Switzerland. It was initially proposed by Tim Berners-Lee in 1989 to improve information access and help communication within the particle physics community [Ber89]. The community included several hundred members all scattered among various research institutes and universities. Although the groups were formally organized into a hierarchical management structure, the actual working and communication structure looked more like a loosely coupled mesh whose linkages evolved over time. A researcher looking for specific information was typically given a few references to experts who may prove helpful. In order to get the desired information, the researcher used the provided information to contact the respective colleagues. While this communication scheme was principally working fine, a high turnover of people made project record keeping and locating expertise increasingly difficult. A solution was required that would support dynamic, non-centralized interaction and quick access to documents stored at secluded locations.

In this situation, Tim Berners-Lee proposed to his management the idea of using *hypertext* for linking information available on individual computers [Ber89]. The hypertext concept had been envisioned earlier as a method for making computers respond to the way humans think and require information [Bus45, Nel67, EE68]. Hypertext documents embed so-called hyperlinks, which can be represented as underlined text or as icons in any size and shape. By selecting and clicking on a hyperlink, associated information is loaded and displayed. Tim's proposal extended the hypertext concept to allow linking of information not only on a single local machine, but also of information that can be stored on remote computers connected via a network. Retrieving the associated information over the network is transparent to the user, without burdening the user with having to know the resource location and the network protocol to be used for retrieval. This scheme proved to be very powerful as it allows users transparent accesses to documents on remote computers with a click of the mouse.

The CERN management approved the proposal and launched the project in the second half of 1990. Tim started implementing a hypertext browser/editor and finished the first version at the end of 1990. The program was running on a NeXT computer and offered a graphical user interface. It was called WorldWideWeb but later renamed Nexus to avoid confusion with the abstract concept of the World Wide Web itself. At the same time, the implementation was complemented with a separate line-mode browser written by CERN student Nicola Pellow. Other people soon started implementing browsers on different platforms. By 1992, first versions of Erwise, ViolaWWW, and MidasWWW were introduced for the X/Motif system, followed by a CERN implementation for the Apple Macintosh in 1993.

At that time, there were around 50 known Web servers deployed, and the WWW was accounting for about 0.1% of the Internet traffic. It was a promising approach, but the real breakthrough came with the creation of Mosaic, the first widespread graphical Web browser. Mosaic development was started at the National Center for Supercomputing Applications (NCSA) by Marc Andreesen and Eric Bina. They realized that broad acceptance of Web technology would require a more user-friendly interface. Their browser software added clickable buttons for easy navigation and controls that let users scroll through text. More important, Marc and Eric were the first ones to get embedded images working. Earlier browsers allowed viewing of pictures only in separate windows, while Mosaic made it possible for images and text to appear in the same window. The application was trivial to install and the team followed up coding with very fast customer support. Overall, Mosaic drastically simplified the first step onto the Web and even allowed beginners to take advantage of the new, exciting Web technology. The Unix version of Mosaic was available for download from NCSA in early 1993. The software was provided free of charge and within weeks tens of thousands of people had downloaded it. Software versions for the PC and Macintosh followed later the same year, boosting its popularity even further. The Web started eclipsing competing systems, as it subsumed their main features and functionality. Users could conveniently access FTP servers as well as Archie, WAIS, and Gopher from their Web browsers, thus eliminating the need for these specialized applications.

By 1994, Marc and Eric had graduated and headed for Silicon Valley to commercialize their software. Initially called Mosaic Communications Corporation, their company was soon renamed Netscape Communications Corporation—the birthplace of the famous Netscape browser family, also known as Netscape Navigator and Netscape Communicator. The Web's popularity increased, and the number of Web sites grew from approximately 500 in 1994 to nearly 10,000 by the beginning of 1995. Netscape quickly became the dominant browser and by 1996, about 75% of Web users used Netscape. Noticing the growing importance of the Web and Netscape's enormous business success, Microsoft Corporation got into the act and started the development of its own browser software—Internet Explorer.

With Microsoft entering the browser market, a bitter fight began to establish dominance in Web software—often referred to as "The Browser War." While the relentless competition between Netscape and Microsoft pushed rapid innovation and created free commercial browser software, it also created problems and led to incompatibilities in the display of Web sites. Both companies created and integrated proprietary extensions that were not part of official standards. Because some of those extensions did not work together, Web page appearance varied on Netscape browsers and on Internet Explorer. As a result, users and Web page designers alike were plagued by inconsistent page appearance, essentially defeating the main purpose of a Web browser. Incompatibilities between the two browsers quickly extended into different kinds of scripting languages that allowed downloading and running applications locally. After the initial dominance of Netscape, Microsoft eventually crushed Netscape and other competitors. According to global statistics in July 2004, Microsoft accounts for about 80–90% of the browsers used on the Internet, while Netscape and its successor Mozilla musters only about 5–15% [Cou04, W3S04]. While Microsoft and Netscape battled over proprietary browsers, it is interesting that Apache dominates the server world with their open source.

Microsoft's market entry underlined a trend toward increased commercialization of the Web. What started as a way for scientists to better share information has grown to include all kinds of commercial services, from information portals to online shopping malls. People order books, appliances, and even cars over the Web. They use it to access the most up-to-date headline news. The Web has become the center of Internet activity, with many people actually not realizing the difference between the Internet and the Web. Many users are not even aware that some of the most popular Internet applications, such as e-mail or news, have been around long before the Web. Nevertheless, ever since the Web caught people's attention, the amount of information and services available has increased at a staggering rate. The tremendous growth of the Web, however, causes new technical problems—ranging from scalability and reliability problems to unpredictable service quality and high download delays. The remainder of the book illuminates these problems, explains where they come from, and how emerging technology can help solve them. As such, the following section will describe the main architectural concepts and the service model of the Web.

1.2.2 Basic Concepts of the World Wide Web

The World Wide Web forms a large universe linking information accessible via the Internet. The information is represented in the form of Web pages—or, more generally, *Web objects*—and is made available on computers, which are referred to as *Web servers*. A Web object can be anything from a simple text document to

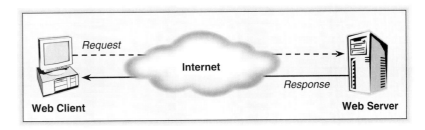

Figure 1.1 The client-server model of the Web.

a multimedia presentation or an audio/video clip. Internet users identify Web objects they are interested in and request them from the corresponding Web server via the Internet. The application initiating the request to the Web server is known as the *Web client*. Figure 1.1 illustrates the client-server–based model of the Web.

Accessing information on the Web usually starts with typing in the address of a *homepage* in a Web browser or clicking on a predefined button. A homepage is a hypertext document, which typically serves as an entry portal to a Web site. It can contain hyperlinks to other Web objects, stored either locally on the same server or anywhere on the Internet. Once the address of the page is typed into the browser, the Web client sends a request over the Internet and receives a response back from the Web server. The response includes either the requested page or an error message.

The Web model involves three elementary concepts: a common representation format for hypertext documents, a scheme for naming and addressing Web objects, and a standard mechanism for transmitting control and data messages between server and client. We will consider each of them in the following paragraphs.

Representing of Web objects—the hypertext markup language (HTML)

Information on the Web can be represented in different formats and media types, stretching from simple text documents to rich multimedia content embedding images and audio/video elements. The lingua franca of the Web is the *Hypertext Markup Language (HTML)*, which is a standard representation for hypertext documents and is derived from the more general *Standard Generalized Markup Language (SGML)* [ISO86]. The HTML language was originally specified by Tim Berners-Lee at the beginning of the 1990s, but has since been developed and extended far beyond its initial form. Standardization of HTML was initially moved into the Internet Engineering Task Force (IETF) [IETF1] and is now carried out by the World Wide Web Consortium (W3C) [W3C1].

HTML defines the layout and the formatting of a Web page, and it allows authors to embed hyperlink references to other resources on the Web. The HTML syntax is relatively simple and is expressed in plain ASCII format. As such, the language is easy to learn and can be authored with any text editor or word processor. Over the years, various document transformation and publishing tools for automated HTML generation have been developed. Many word processors and publishing programs now export their documents directly into HTML, obviating the need for most Web page authors to learn HTML. The ease of page creation has further fueled the growth of the Web.

While HTML is the fundamental representation language of the Web, not all Web objects are necessarily authored and represented in this language. It is possible, for example, to make audio/video clips or unstructured text documents available on Web servers as well. In contrast to HTML, however, plain data formats do not allow embedding hyperlinks, nor is the author able to specify the layout and the fonts to be used for displaying the page in Web browsers.

Identifying Web objects—URNs, URLs, and URIs

The World Wide Web is inhabited by a large number of objects that may reside on any Web server anywhere in the world. To find and access a specific Web object, the user needs some kind of handle that identifies the object in a unique way. There are two fundamental ways for identifying objects in the Web space: a *name* distinguishes one object from another in a globally unique way, while a *location* tells where the object can be found. Historically, the two concepts were reflected in different schemes for identifying objects on the Web—the *Uniform Resource Name (URN)* [RFC 1737, RFC 2141] and the *Uniform Resource Locator (URL)* [RFC 1738, RFC 1808].

A URN provides a persistent name for a Web object, independent of its current location. The name is assigned once and remains unmodified as the location of the object changes. Moreover, URNs are required to remain globally unique and persistent even when the object ceases to exist or becomes unavailable. A URL, in contrast, provides a non-persistent means to uniquely identify an object based on its current location and its access method. A URL tells the user where to find an object and how to access it, which implies that the URL changes when the associated object moves.

To illustrate the difference between these concepts, let us consider how the authors of this book can be identified among all the people in the United States. Each author of this book has a Social Security Number, which has been assigned by the federal Social Security Office. This Social Security Number is guaranteed to be unique and has an institutional commitment to persistence and availability. It can be considered a URN for the author of this book. It identifies and names him in a persistent way, but it does not reveal any information about his current location. The author's location is typically given by his home address or work address, which—at an abstract level—can be considered URLs for him. Obviously, the author's URLs can change when he moves or changes jobs. Moreover, his former URLs can point to other persons in the future, for example, when somebody else moves into his house at the given address. This is quite different from the URN (i.e., the Social Security Number), which will remain the same for his lifetime and will always refer to this person. The mindful reader may have noticed a little discrepancy with this comparison—while a URN is required to stand for an object even when it ceases to exist, Social Security Numbers may be reused after the lifetime of a person. For the sake of this comparison, though, we simply assumed this would not be the case.

It is very likely that most readers have already seen and are quite familiar with URLs, which might look like http://www.content-networking.com/ or http://www.google.de/. Nowadays, it is quite common to find such URLs on business cards and in advertisements. Usually, a URL is made up of three parts: a *protocol* identifier, a *server* name, and a *path*. These parts are represented according to the following syntax:

```
<protocol>://<server>/<path>
```

The protocol part indicates the communication protocol to be used for requesting and retrieving the Web object from the server. Various communication protocols are valid and have well-defined identifiers assigned, for example FTP, WAIS, and Gopher. The most commonly used communication protocol on the Web is the Hypertext Transport Protocol (HTTP) and will be discussed in the following section. The URLs given above, for example, indicate that the protocol to be used for object retrieval is HTTP.

Immediately following the protocol identifier are the characters ":// " and the server name. The server name is a regular Internet hostname (or an IP address) and identifies the Web server where the referred Web object can be retrieved. The server name is terminated by the next forward slash '/' in the URL string. The server part can optionally include a TCP/IP port number at its tail, which is separated from the actual server name by a colon. Briefly, a port number is used to direct messages to the correct application running on the server. If no port number is given, the default port of 80 is assumed for HTTP.

Finally, the path component of a URL specifies the exact file and the location of that file in the server's directory structure. If the path component is not explicitly included in the URL, a default directory location and a default filename are assumed (e.g., index.html). As an example, the URL

http://www.content-networking.com/papers/brochure-webdns.pdf

identifies a Web page that can be accessed using the Hypertext Transport Protocol ("http://") and is on a server named "www.content-networking.com". In the server's directory structure, the file is located in the directory "papers" and is named "brochure-webdns.pdf".

The *Uniform Resource Identifier (URI)* [RFC 1630, RFC 2396] is an abstraction that includes both URNs and URLs—it represents a superset of both schemes. The URI rules of syntax, set forth in RFC 2396, apply for all names and addresses in the Web space. It is a common misconception that URL and URI are the same, and quite often, these terms are used interchangeably. Throughout this book, the popular term URL will be used rather than the more general term URI. An exception will be made whenever the distinction between these terms is important.

Transporting Web objects—hypertext transfer protocol (HTTP)

The World Wide Web is composed of distributed, heterogeneous servers and clients. Its operation depends on the capability to communicate and exchange messages between these components. Just as humans depend on knowing a common language for communicating with each other, the Web depends on having a well-defined mechanism for interaction of servers and clients. The rules, the syntax, and the semantics for this interaction are described in the form of a communication protocol. The protocol specifies a message format and semantic rules indicating how the various parts of the messages have to be interpreted.

The *Hypertext Transport Protocol* [RFC 1945, RFC 2616] is the primary mechanism used to transport objects on the Web. It is an application-level protocol, which has been designed so that it can theoretically run on many underlying communication networks. In practice, however, HTTP runs mostly on top of the TCP/IP protocols of the Internet. HTTP evolved along with the Web in two major phases: from the initial proposal labeled HTTP/0.9 at the beginning of the 1990s [Ber92] to the official HTTP/1.0 specification in 1996 [RFC 1945]. The second phase also lasted about four years and moved HTTP from version 1.0 to version 1.1 [RFC 2616].

HTTP is a request-response protocol, which means that a client sends a request message and the server replies with a response message. The message headers are text-based, which makes them readable by humans and simplifies debugging and extensions. A fundamental design principle of HTTP is that each message exchange is treated separately without maintaining any state across different request-response transactions. Each transaction is processed independently without any knowledge of previous transactions, which is why HTTP is called a stateless protocol. While this design improves simplicity and scalability, it complicates the implementation of Web sites that react based on previous user input such as a username or a location. This shortcoming is being addressed with additional technologies, such as Cookies or JavaScript. Chapter 2 will elaborate on these and HTTP in general.

Later in this book, we will see that the three elementary concepts mentioned in this section are not exclusive. Other representation formats and protocols emerged, for example to transmit audio and video content on the Web. However, most of the newer technology has been derived in some form from these basic concepts.

1.2.3   Applications on the World Wide Web

The growth and the evolution of the World Wide Web are mainly driven and heavily influenced by applications that individuals and businesses use. It is important to understand emerging trends and developments in the applications area to shape the underlying Web technology in the most appropriate way. The initial Web application was to facilitate sharing of online documents. Ever since, the Web evolved into an infrastructure and a development platform for a broad variety of distributed applications—ranging from simple document retrieval all the way to delivery of audio or video and interactive collaboration. This section would fail in attempting to list the diversity of existing and emerging Web applications. Instead, it discusses four fundamental types of Web applications that evolved over time, each of them having significant impact on the evolution of Web technology. New application developments around content services and Web services will be discussed in Chapter 8.

Retrieving static content

The World Wide Web originated as an Internet facility linking static content. Static content comprises stored documents that reside on Web servers for retrieval by users. These documents change infrequently—remaining constant for days or weeks at a time—and require explicit modification by the author in order to change their content. As such, they provide the same combination of text or images to each visitor. Typical applications involving retrieval of static content are access to personal homepages or fetching research papers from a document repository. Both types of Web objects are usually static—they are created once and are served unmodified for an extended time. Although this application model is adequate for many purposes, it allows only limited interaction with the user. Furthermore, it is not suitable for serving frequently changing data such as stock quotes or currency exchange rates. The information transmitted to the user is only as current as the last manual update.

Retrieving dynamic content

Retrieving static content is the most widely used application on the Web so far. More recently, dynamic content made new levels of user interaction possible, which is particularly interesting for e-commerce and content portals. Dynamic content is created only at the time it is requested. Its final form is not stored, but rather it is created by assembling information gathered at the time of the request. When a request for dynamic content arrives, the Web server typically runs a specific program that creates the content immediately. The program may consider user-specific information obtained from the request, such as the user's IP address, her preferred (natural) language or any information the user entered in a Web form when issuing the request. It is also possible that the program queries a database or retrieves additional information from a user profile. This provides the ability to deliver customized content to each user based on her individual preference. Furthermore, dynamic content can be tailored according to the capabilities of the user's end-device or network connection. Use cases of dynamic content include content portals that provide headlines, news, stock quotes, and weather forecasts based on the user's interests and location. Such services can be found, for example, at My Yahoo! (http://my.yahoo.com/) or My eBay (http://www.ebay.com/).

This definition of dynamic content implies that a Web server may deliver differently assembled content to individual users requesting the same Web object at the same time. This is different from frequently changing static content. Such preauthored content is modified in very short time intervals, thus resembling the behavior of dynamic content. However, frequently updated static content still looks the same to different users requesting the content in-between update intervals.

Retrieving streaming content

Streaming is often thought of as the playback of continuously flowing media such as audio and video. A more accurate description, however, considers the distinction between true streaming technology and the simple playback of downloaded audio or video files. Prior to the invention of true streaming technology, users had to download audio and video files in their entirety before starting playback. This is usually not a problem with relatively small text documents or images, either of which can be downloaded very quickly. The large sizes of audio and video files, however, generally translate into painfully long download delays before playback begins. Streaming technology addresses this problem by establishing a steady data flow from the server to the client, allowing the client to listen or view the content as it is downloaded. It is no longer required to fetch the entire audio or video file before playback starts, which significantly reduces the initial playback delay.

While streaming technology is mostly associated with audio and video media, it can also be used in conjunction with other media types such as images. Most modern Web browsers, for example, start displaying embedded images in Web pages before the image is received in its entirety. Nevertheless, this book will refer to "streaming" in the context of time-constrained audio or video playback, if not otherwise noted. It will further distinguish between two main categories of streaming—*on-demand* streaming, which delivers prerecorded content to many users at different times, and *live* streaming, which broadcasts live content to many users at the same time. Example applications include Video-on-Demand systems and Internet radio, respectively.

Interactive collaboration

The Web has traditionally served as a medium for collaboration, as evidenced by the success of applications supporting document sharing and discussion archiving. Most of these applications have been limited to asynchronous activities, whereby users do not interact in real time. Instead, applications provide interfaces for working within a shared workspace over an extended period. User activities are not synchronized and are time-wise decoupled from each other. Recently, the Web has also been used for interactive collaboration, allowing two or more users to interact in real time. Example applications include videoconferencing, networked gaming, instant messaging, and Web-based help desk systems. In these applications, users typically react to previous actions of other users in real time. In the case of videoconferencing, for example, users respond to other participants' questions and comments. Interactive collaboration creates new challenges for the underlying Web technology, as data has to be transferred synchronously with low delay and in real time to a potentially large number of users.

These different types of applications show that the Web has matured to a point where it is valued for more than document sharing and exchanging static content. Businesses and individuals are looking to the Web as a high-quality and reliable vehicle for delivering rich multimedia content. Recent developments around multimedia content, interactive applications, and dynamic content exposed some shortcomings of the traditional Web model and led the industry to turn to enhanced network technologies overlaying the Internet, mostly referred to as *content networks*.

1.3 The Evolution of Content Networking

Over a period of less than ten years, the World Wide Web evolved from an Internet application for scientists and researchers to become the transforming business phenomenon it is today. Companies and businesses depend more than ever on the Web's ability to instantaneously deliver relevant content and services. However, an enormous growth in network traffic, driven by rapid acceptance of broadband access, along with increases in system complexity and content richness, brings new challenges in managing and delivering content to users. A decrease in service quality, along with high access delays, led people to reinterpret WWW as an acronym for "World Wide Wait." User frustration, mainly caused by long download times, has become more of an issue as companies compete for e-commerce over the Web. Recent studies suggest that users abandon slow loading e-commerce sites, which translates into lost sales and dissatisfied customers. As Web-based e-commerce represents a significant business and continues to grow very rapidly, this provides great financial incentive for companies to improve the service quality experienced by users accessing their Web sites.

As such, the past few years have seen an evolution of technologies that aim to improve content delivery and service provisioning over the Web. Entire markets have been created offering novel network appliances, software tools, and new kinds of network services. When used together, these technologies form a new type of network, which is often referred to as *content network* [RFC 3466]. This section examines the problems that led to the emergence of content networks and discusses possible solutions in terms of the technologies and services that comprise a content network.

1.3.1 The Traditional Web Model Comes of Age

The decentralized nature of the World Wide Web—and the Internet, in general—has very much helped its growth and its propagation. The lack of central control and management allows any individual or business to quickly set up a Web site offering content and services. There is no need to go through a central bureaucracy. Easy-to-use authoring tools simplify Web page creation. A new breed of service providers have emerged offering Web site creation and hosting for individuals and businesses. Most Internet service providers even include basic Web hosting services in their Internet access offerings, allowing individuals to set-up their own private Web page without having to deploy their own Web server.

The simplicity of Web site creation results in an ever-increasing variety of content offered over the Web. Almost anything can be found, from personal photos of one's last family reunion to the latest headline news and stock quotes. While the Web offers an almost endless pool of information, its decentralized nature makes navigating and locating relevant content quite a challenge. Search engines support users in finding their way through the unorganized mass of information, while content portals attempt to catalog a relatively small subset of the most popular Web pages. It is interesting to note that although the number of Web pages keeps growing at a breathtaking speed, only a surprisingly small subset of those pages account for the majority of user requests. This fact not only allows content portals to cover a large percentage of requested information, but also provides the opportunity for performance improvements through Web caching—a technology that will be discussed in more detail in Chapter 3.

The Web is highly decentralized and distributed. From the perspective of a single Web site, however, the traditional service model as shown in Figure 1.1 is actually centralized. All user requests for a particular Web page are handled by a single Web server storing the requested content. This approach has serious scalability problems, as illustrated in Figure 1.2. The load on the Web server and on the network link connecting the server to the Internet increases with the number of user requests. This is not a problem for specialized Web sites serving only a small number of interested parties. Highly popular Web sites, however, easily get overwhelmed with a large number of incoming user requests. When more and more users request content from a single Web server, either the server's processing capacity or the bandwidth available on its connection to the Internet can easily be exceeded. If this happens, user requests are dropped, which results in increased access delays or even unavailability of the Web site.

Scalability issues become even more severe when sudden or unique events occur that are of extreme interest to the public. Such events typically trigger an extraordinary, and often unexpected, large number of requests at the Web sites providing relevant information. For example, in September 1998 most Web sites permitting access to the Starr report were overloaded in the days after the report was published. A similar behavior was observed when pictures of the Mars Lander mission became available, or when Victoria's Secret broadcasted its first fashion show on the Web [Bor99]. More recently, the tragic events of September 11, 2001 triggered an enormous interest in the various news sites on the Web, with millions of users requesting the latest news updates and video

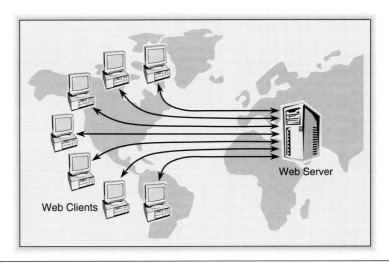

Figure 1.2 Scalability problem of centralized Web servers.

footage. This resulted in extreme traffic peaks at the various Web sites—something that could not be foreseen. It is important for Web site providers to not only protect their mission-critical sites from normal traffic peaks, but also from such unexpected spikes in user interest.

Another problem of the centralized Web service model relates to the distance between a Web server and potential Web clients. This distance can be measured using different metrics such as number of hops, delay, packet loss on the path, or even geographic distance. Even if a Web server has enough resources to handle all incoming requests in a timely manner, the distance between server and clients can lead to noticeable delays. In the example given, clients located in America always have to send their requests to a central server in Europe. This not only increases the load on transatlantic links, but also results in increased transmission delays. More important than the geographical distance, however, is the so-called *network distance* between server and client. Network distance is defined as the number of routers on the path between two hosts. Each router on the path adds to the time required for transmitting data between the hosts. Consequently, it is desirable to minimize the network distance between Web clients and Web servers for improved service latency. Geographic proximity does not necessarily translate into network proximity, though. Users in Germany accessing a Web server in France, for example, quite often have to connect through a major peering point located in Washington, DC, USA. This absurd situation is fairly common and is caused by a lack of local peering agreements between Internet Service Providers (ISPs) in Europe.

Emerging broadband technologies such as cable modem and DSL aggravate these performance and scalability problems by forcing servers, routers, and backbone links to carry even more data traffic. High-speed, always-on Internet access encourages an increase in online time by the average user and makes new resource-intensive applications possible. In addition, it stimulates the development of commercial products for resource intensive playback of streamed video and audio, which makes the slowdown even worse. As a result, consumers often experience low service quality due to high delay, unstable throughput, and loss of packets in the best-effort model of the Internet.

1.3.2 Evolutionary Steps in Overcoming the Web Slowdown

Adding more bandwidth, more processing power and other mechanisms to improve quality-of-service (QoS) to the Internet infrastructure is one potential remedy for performance problems. While this may provide some relief, it does not address the fundamental problem of overloaded servers and data traversing multiple domains and many networks. In addition, deployment of QoS-enabled systems is costly, difficult, and time-consuming. Even when high-quality network services are available, people might prefer to use best-effort services if the cost is lower. Network providers are also concerned with scaling up to meet spikes in data traffic. It is difficult to engineer network capacity for unpredictable spikes, such as breaking news stories, which overwhelm Web sites with unexpected demand. Just throwing in more bandwidth and adding infrastructure support for quality-based services does not solve all the problems mentioned above. Additional and complementary approaches are required for the Web to live up to the higher expectations of today's and tomorrow's users.

Current developments can be seen as evolutionary steps from the traditional Web model toward more dynamic content networks. The first step of this evolution focused on overcoming the server side bottleneck by deploying load-balanced server farms. This approach still assumed a centralized Web site providing content and services. The next step relaxed the centralized model by distributing content and moving it closer to the user. Replication of content in geographically dispersed locations and deployment of Web caching systems have been the main technologies. The second step leads to a model in which static content is distributed at various sites, but services such as e-commerce or creation of dynamic content are still being provided at a central server. The next logical step now is to distribute the services as well, which is currently being worked on in the context of content services and Web services. Each of those evolutionary steps is summarized below, with technical details being provided in subsequent chapters of the book.

Distributing load at a centralized server site

A potential bottleneck in the traditional Web architecture is the Web server itself, which might run out of resources as more requests arrive at the site. The most obvious solution to this problem is improving the server hardware by adding a high-speed processor, more memory and disk space, or maybe even a multi-processor system. This approach, however, is not very flexible and improvements have to be made in relatively big steps. It is not possible to start small and slowly add enhancements as the traffic increases. At some point, it might even be necessary to completely replace a server system.

A more scalable solution is the establishment of *server farms*. A server farm is comprised of multiple Web servers, each of them sharing the burden of answering requests for the same Web site. The servers are typically installed in the same location and connected to the same subnet. Incoming requests first pass through a front-end load balancer. This component dispatches requests to one of the servers based on certain metrics, such as the current server load. This approach is more flexible and shows better scalability, as it can start small with servers being added in incremental steps as they are needed. Furthermore, it provides the inherent benefit of fault tolerance. In the case of a server failure, incoming requests can still be satisfied by the remaining active servers in the farm. For this purpose, load balancers implement failure detection mechanisms and avoid dispatching requests to failed servers. Over time, load balancers have become increasingly sophisticated, adding more features and basing their routing decisions on more complex metrics. These changes are reflected in modern terms describing these devices, such as Layer 4–7 Switch, Web Switch, or Content Switch. The first term is often used to describe on which layer of the Internet protocol stack a device operates. A Layer 4 Switch, for example, bases its switching decision on information included in the TCP protocol (e.g., the port number), as TCP represents Layer 4 in the TCP/IP protocol stack. Content switching will be discussed in detail in Chapter 5.

Deployment and growth of server farms normally go hand-in-hand with appropriate upgrades of the network link that connects the Web site to the Internet. Further performance gains and improved fault tolerance can be achieved by connecting a server farm to multiple Internet Service Providers.

Distributing content and centralized services

A promising approach in overcoming the Web's notorious bottlenecks and slowdowns is distributing and moving content closer to the user where it becomes faster to retrieve. User requests are then redirected to, and served from, these devices. Server replication and proxy caching are examples of such technologies. A proxy cache, preferably in close proximity to the client, stores requested Web objects in an intermediate location between the object's origin server and the client. Subsequent requests can be served from the cache, thus shortening access time and conserving significant network resources—namely bandwidth and processing resources.

A Web cache resides between Web servers (or origin servers) and one or more clients, and monitors requests for HTML pages, images, and files (collectively known as objects) as they come by, saving a copy for itself. Then, if there is another request for the same object, it will use the copy that it has, instead of requesting it from the origin server.

Caching Web objects has been studied extensively starting with simple proxy caching [LNB99], followed by improvements in hierarchical caching and cooperative caching under the Harvest project [CDN+96] and the Squid project [Wes02], respectively. The latter schemes allow multiple caching systems to collaborate with each other, improving scalability and fault tolerance even more. For proxy caching to be effective on a scale required by ISPs and enterprises, it must integrate methods for cache replacement, content freshness, load balancing, and replication. Caching will be discussed in detail in Chapters 3 and 4.

Distributing content and services

As the percentage of dynamic content on the Web increases and users demand more sophisticated services, it is no longer sufficient to distribute just static content. Instead, recent developments extend the idea of a distributed content model to include the services operating on such content as well. Architectures and systems are being developed that move server-side services out to the edge of the network, closer to the user. Such services may include dynamic assembly of personalized Web pages or content adaptation for wireless devices.

Work is also underway to define a framework for distributed Web applications, which is most often referred to as the Web Services architecture. Web services are interoperable building blocks for constructing complex Web applications. Once a Web service is deployed and published, other applications can automatically discover and invoke it. As an example, a digital library application could be realized by combining Web services for searching, authentication, ordering, and payment. The traditional Web model enables users to connect to content and Web applications on centralized servers. The Web Services framework adds open interfaces, which allow more complex applications to be composed of several more basic and universal services, each running on remote servers. Chapter 8 will deal with these approaches in more detail.

The evolutionary steps outlined above illustrate how the Web is currently extending from a centralized model toward an architecture that included distributed content provisioning and distributed applications. The centralized architecture very much facilitated the Web's growth because a Web site in a single location is much easier to setup and to manage. The distributed architecture comes at the cost of increased complexity and higher initial investment, but scales better for large numbers of global users and provides better performance and reliability.

Example: Server-side load balancing and web caching

Figure 1.3 takes up the previous example scenario and shows how Web caches can be deployed together with a load-balanced server farm for improved performance and fault tolerance. In the example, a second Web server has been added to the location of the original server, with a front-end Web switch balancing the server load. Both servers together with the Web switch form a simple server farm. Furthermore, two Web caches have been deployed between the American clients and the Web servers. They watch requests coming from users in America and temporarily store the responses received. Subsequent requests for the same object can then be served directly from the Web cache, without having to contact the servers in Europe. This not only reduces server load and load on the transatlantic links, but also improves access delay and service quality experienced by the American users.

A quick comparison between Figures 1.2 and 1.3 illustrates the added complexity, needed to provide the improved scalability of the extended architecture.

1.3.3   Content Networking Defined

Several different terms and names have been used in the past when referring to the emerging technologies discussed in the previous sections. Terms such as "Content Distribution" and "Content Delivery" are probably among the more popular expressions. Others talked about "Caching Overlays" or "Proxy Networks." The vocabulary used in this book largely follows the terminology as outlined in [RFC 3466]. To facilitate a common understanding and further discussions, this section defines the meaning of "content" and "content networks," followed by an introduction of the functional components that make up a content network.

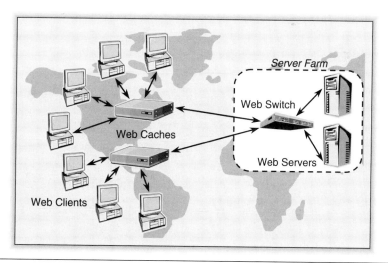

Figure 1.3 Improved scalability through Web caches and a server farm.

Definition of terms

The content of a document—or an object, in general—refers to what it says to the user through natural language, images, sounds, video, animations, etc. This book uses the term "content" in a more restricted way in the following sense:

> *The term* content *refers to any information that is made available to other users on the Internet. This includes, but is not limited to Web pages, images, textual documents, audio and video as well as software downloads, broadcasts, instant messages and forms data.*

In particular, content is not limited to a single media type; it can be represented in various different forms such as text, graphic, or video. Content can also be represented as a combination of multiple content objects, each of them having a different media type. Such content is referred to as *multimedia content*. Examples include video clips with audio or Web pages incorporating text, images, and videos.

Content networks provide the infrastructure to better support delivery of relevant content over the Internet. They utilize and integrate the methods mentioned above, forming a new level of intelligence overlaid on top of packet networks. Whereas packet networks traditionally have processed information at the protocol Layers 1–3, content networks include communication components operating on protocol Layers 4–7. The units of transported data in content networks are application-level messages such as images, songs, or video clips. They are typically composed of many smaller-sized data packets, which represent the basic transport unit of the underlying packet networks. In summary, content networks are defined as follows:

> *The term* content network *refers to a communication network that deploys infrastructure components operating at protocol Layers 4–7. These components interconnect with each other, creating a virtual network layered on top of an existing packet network infrastructure.*

While it might be controversial to include network elements operating on protocol Layer 4 in the above definition, Layer 4 information can give important clues for mapping content to applications. Well-known TCP/UDP port numbers are frequently used for drawing conclusions on the encapsulated application data. TCP port 80, for example, is by default associated with the HTTP protocol, indicating that the encapsulated data is most likely related to a Web transaction.

The necessary ties between overlaid content networks and the underlying packet network infrastructure are enabled via *intermediaries*. Intermediaries are application-level devices that are part of a Web transaction, but are neither the originating nor the terminating device in the transaction. The most commonly known and used intermediaries today are proxies and Web caches.

Functional components of content networks

In general, a content network is built of multiple functional components that work together to accomplish the overall goal of improved content delivery. These components include:

- *Content distribution:* Services for moving the content from its source to the users. These services can comprise Web caches or other devices storing content intermediately on behalf of the origin Web server. The distribution component also covers the actual mechanism and the protocols used for transmitting data over the network.
- *Request-routing:* Services for navigating user requests to a location best suited for retrieving the requested content. User requests can be served, for example, from Web servers or Web caches. The selection of the most appropriate target location is typically based on network proximity and availability of the systems and the network.
- *Content processing:* Services for creating or adapting content to suit user preferences and device capabilities. This includes modification or conversion of both content and requests for content. Examples are content adaptation for wireless devices or added privacy by making personal information embedded in user requests anonymous.
- *Authorization, authentication,* and *accounting:* Services that enable monitoring, logging, accounting, and billing of content usage. This includes mechanisms to ensure the identity and the privileges of all parties involved in a transaction, as well as, digital rights management.

It is not required that a content network embodies all of the functional components listed above. The content network shown in Figure 1.3, for example, includes Web caches for improved content distribution and Web switches for request-routing. However, it is without any component for content processing.

The remaining chapters of the book will follow-up with a thorough discussion on these logical components, as well as a description of how they are combined and work together in building more complex content networks.

1.4 The Diversity of Interests in Content Networking

It seems that these days almost everyone has a stake in the Internet and the World Wide Web. Cable companies and telephone providers are eager to provide high-speed Internet access to a broad audience, while ISPs providing dial-up access are trying to gain market share. Backbone service providers are under pressure to cope with continuing growth in data traffic over the Internet, and e-commerce companies are concerned about the security, the reliability and the performance of their Web sites. All these parties have different stakes and incentives in the Internet business. Understanding the diversity of their interests and their role in the value chain of content networking is an important factor to be considered in the design and deployment of content networks. At a high level, the value chain of content networking beneficiaries begins with the content provider and extends to include the content network provider and the content consumer. This simplified value chain is illustrated in Figure 1.4, with each of the three parties discussed in more detail below.

Content provider

Large organizations may create and author their own Web pages, but the actual Web server storing the content is often housed by separate third-party facilities that provide space and access to the Internet. Such an arrangement is often referred to as server co-location. Small businesses and home users usually do not deploy and maintain their own Web servers, but rather use dedicated or shared hosting options offered by Internet Service Providers. As such, the creator of a Web page can be different from the entity hosting the Web server. Whenever it is helpful to distinguish the different roles, this book will refer to the author of Web pages as the *content creator*, while the provider of Web server space is called the *content host*. If this distinction is not necessary, the term *content provider* may be used as an abstraction for both.

Content providers are increasingly faced with the challenge of providing rich content at consistent, high service levels. They are concerned about response times for their customers and about permanent availability of their Web sites. In the past, the lion's share of content providers have been hosting and managing all their content themselves, but increased difficulty of meeting customer expectations for content delivery makes partial outsourcing more attractive. Still, content providers would like to keep full control of the content and the machines

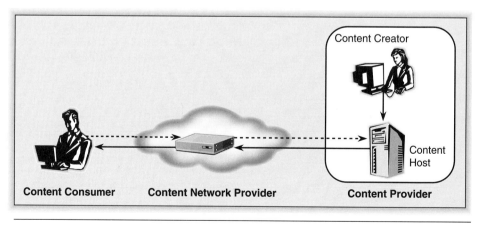

Figure 1.4 The value chain of content networking.

that govern the content, access rights, and policies. Furthermore, content providers rely on insights into content usage through the analysis of usage statistics. As high access rates often translate into high advertisement revenues, content providers are typically interested in attracting as many users as the available infrastructure can handle.

Content networking provider

Content network providers are predominantly in the business of helping content providers deliver content to the users. Their resources typically provide caching and replication of data, as well as request-routing and possibly services for content processing. As their revenue is mainly determined by the amount of data served out of their network, content networking providers aim to attract as many content requests as possible. At the same time, they strive to reduce the aggregate load on their resources and on the network links connecting them, which leads to serving most content from resources as close to the user as possible. In Figure 1.4, for example, the content network provider is likely to be interested in serving most content from the Web cache deployed between the content consumer and content provider. While this allows revenue generation, it also relieves load on the link between the Web cache and Web server, thus reducing the operation costs. As described in the previous section, however, content providers rely on insights into content usage patterns, which is no longer available to them if the Web cache serves requests on behalf of the Web server. In this situation, the diversity of interests requires content networking providers to deliver detailed usage statistics to the content providers. Otherwise, it would be unlikely for content providers to let Web caches deliver content on their behalf.

Enterprises and Internet Access Providers also deploy content networking technology such as Web caches and Web switches. While this puts them into the category of content network providers, their primary interest is not in supporting content providers. Rather, they want to improve the service quality as experienced by their customers and optimize resource utilization in their network. For example, the content networking provider could be seen as an enterprise deploying Web caches for reducing load on the trunk link between the enterprise's Intranet and the Internet. As providers introduce content networking technology they reduce their need for transport pipes, which can create a conflict of business interest between the content networking provider and the providers of the underlying transport infrastructure.

With profit margins for basic access and hosting services getting slimmer and slimmer, content networking providers are seeking to differentiate themselves from the competition and to add new revenue streams. They are highly interested in offering value-added content processing services, which allow them to provide additional customer-tailored services. Akamai is one example of a content networking provider discussed further in Chapter 5.

Content consumer

The *content consumer* is the final destination of the content. Content consumers are typically Internet users requesting information through their Web browsers. With the availability of high-speed cable and DSL Internet access, content consumers increasingly thirst for rich multimedia content delivered with high quality and low service delays. Users of wireless devices, on the other hand, expect content to be tailored according to their devices' capabilities and to the available network connectivity. Furthermore, expectations increase on receiving personalized and location-based content rather than generic content created uniformly for all users worldwide.

This short digression on the value chain of content networking suggests a diversity of interests among the parties involved in content networking, quite often leading to a disparity of interests. Later chapters in this book will discuss such conflicts and explain their impact on the technology to be developed.

CHAPTER 2

Content Transport

Content traverses networks. The World Wide Web is composed of geographically dispersed servers and clients. Its operation depends on the capability to interact and to transport messages between these components. Moving bits and bytes over a network follows certain rules and methods, which are the subject matter of this chapter. As the Web typically transports its content over the Internet, we will begin with a discussion about fundamental design paradigms and protocol architecture. It follows up with a description of the most widely used transport vehicle on the Web—the Hypertext Transport Protocol (HTTP). The discussion centers on fundamental characteristics of HTTP, laying the foundation for a better understanding of HTTP-related content networking issues. Selected HTTP mechanisms and features are described to help illustrate certain problem areas in content networking. The chapter ends with an introduction and some thoughts on multicasting, a network technique often used to transmit data to a large number of recipients.

This chapter is not meant to serve as a detailed introduction or as a reference to the various Internet and Web protocols. It focuses on fundamental paradigms and a few selected technical details insomuch as they will be relevant for the understanding of content networking issues in later chapters. For a more detailed coverage and a reference of Internet and Web protocols, the reader is referred to related books such as [Ste94, Hui95, Com00, KR01].

2.1 Protocol Architecture and Design Paradigms of the Internet

Just as humans depend on knowing a common language for communicating with each other, the Web depends on having a well-defined mechanism for interaction of servers and clients. The rules, syntax, and semantic interpretation for this interaction are described in the form of communication protocols. The protocols specify message formats and semantic rules indicating how the various parts of the messages have to be interpreted, similar to the way foreign languages specify the words and the grammar to be used for human interaction. Communication protocols are typically organized in multiple *protocol layers*, with each of the layers managing a specific task. Every protocol provides a set of services to the next higher layer and requests a set of base services from the next lower layer. Layer interaction takes place via well-defined interfaces. The division and encapsulation of specific communication functions in layers enables each protocol to focus on specific sub-tasks, thus modularizing and simplifying development of complex communication systems. Interoperability between communication components from different vendors is enabled by standardization of the protocols and is discussed in more detail in Chapter 10.

The Internet and the World Wide Web follow this architectural principle and are organized into several protocol layers. The following subsections provide an overview of this architecture, with focus on two fundamental design paradigms of the Internet—the hourglass-like protocol layering and the *End-to-End principle*.

2.1.1 The Internet Hourglass

Internet applications depend on a suite of communication protocols enabling message exchange between computers connected to various networks around the globe. The protocol suite that makes the Internet work consists of five protocol layers, as depicted in Figure 2.1.

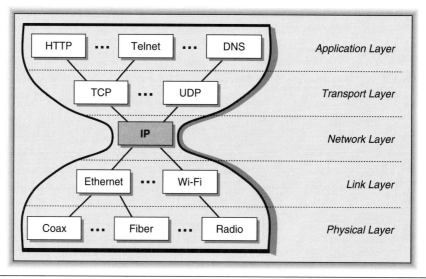

Figure 2.1 The hourglass model of Internet protocol.

The *physical layer* is primarily concerned with the electrical and optical characteristics of the physical medium used to transform bits and bytes into signals, which the medium will propagate. Widely used transmission media include copper (both twisted-pair and coax), fiber optics, or radio transmission. The *link layer* handles the details of interfacing with the physical communication medium. It utilizes the serial bit stream service provided by the physical layer to provide for the transmission of structured data units, such as frames, packets, or cells, along a single network link. Link layer protocols include Ethernet, Token Ring, Token Bus, Fiber Distributed Data Interface (FDDI), and Wi-Fi-compliant protocols based on IEEE standard 802.11. The *network layer* provides the forwarding of data packets through the network, across multiple network links and multiple network segments. Network layer protocols reside both at communication endpoints and at routers inside the network. Some examples include IP, X.25, and Frame Relay. The *transport layer* coordinates the data exchange between endpoints and enhances the service provided by the underlying network layer to meet the needs of the application. Features provided at the transport layer may include error correction, recovery from packet loss, and congestion control. The most important transport protocols on the Internet are the Transmission Control Protocol (TCP), which provides loss-less and ordered packet delivery, and the User Datagram Protocol (UDP), which does not provide any delivery guarantees. Application-specific communication details are handled at the *application layer*, which is typically implemented as part of the application software. Example protocols include HTTP, Telnet, File Transfer Protocol (FTP), and the Domain Name System (DNS).

From Figure 2.1, we see that the Internet protocol architecture has the shape of an "hourglass" [Dee91]. A variety of upper-layer application and transport protocols is supported by a single, pervasive network layer protocol called *Internet Protocol (IP)*. IP itself rests upon a diversity of protocols at the data link layer, which in turn can operate over a variety of physical media. The hourglass design, which derives from the "IP over everything" philosophy, provides the Internet's immense flexibility in accommodating emerging applications and new communication technologies. IP acts as a "protocol unifier," allowing transport protocols to interoperate with IP and not worry about the variety of link layer protocols. Link layer protocols, on the other hand, have only to support IP and do not care about the applications running on top of it.

Protocol layering is an effective design principle, which simplifies development of complex communication systems. In theory, protocol designers have to deal with only two interfaces—one to the protocol layer above, and one to the protocol layer below. If the layering principle is strictly followed, however, certain optimization opportunities can be lost. In practice, popular protocols have been designed making some implicit assumptions about other layers in the protocol stack. Most of these assumptions have not been written down explicitly, but become apparent with recent changes in technology. As such, transport protocols have made implicit assumptions about IP that are affected by the underlying link layer in use. TCP, for instance, implements a congestion control scheme based on the assumption that packet loss is caused by network congestion. While this assumption meets the characteristics of traditional wireline networks, packet loss on wireless and satellite links can very well be caused by bit errors rather than congestion. As a result, bit errors on wireless links trigger TCP's congestion control mechanism to erroneously reduce its transmission rate. Similarly, certain protocol mechanisms built into TCP were motivated by early Internet applications such as FTP and remote login (Rlogin and Telnet). In contrast to these applications, a Web client typically establishes multiple simultaneous transport connections for parallel downloading of Web objects. While this can increase overall throughput for an individual user, it can result in unfairness to other TCP clients and in higher network and server load. Besides, most Web responses involve only a relatively small amount of data, which does not work well with TCP's slow start mechanism [KR01]. These examples make clear that good performance cannot always be achieved by completely abstracting from the remaining protocol layers. Instead, assumptions of all other layers have to be taken into account—whether they have been written down explicitly or not. New protocols should be tolerant and adaptive, having fewer rigid assumptions about the characteristics of other protocol layers.

Protocol designers and network architects also need to understand the impact new mechanisms might have on the existing protocol architecture. This issue is often raised in the context of content networking, wherein solutions have been proposed that achieve performance gains by intermixing layer functionality. Message forwarding, for example, is typically considered a network layer feature. Nevertheless, content networks often use application-specific information (e.g., URLs or application type) for routing user requests to the most appropriate server. The benefits and the risks of such layer intermingling will be discussed in later chapters.

Recent design controversies in the Internet community include a related observation about the progressive fattening of the hourglass waist [Dee91]. Over time, the Internet has grown immensely and has been forced to adapt to changing demands and increased stress. Its original design underwent a number of mutations, and new functionality has been added such as network support for multicast and service differentiation. As a result, the waist of the hourglass is no longer as narrow and elegant as it originally was. Added complexity at the IP layer and the deployment of new types of networking devices (e.g., network address translators, firewalls, or interception proxies) challenges the Internet's core characteristics—mainly the fundamental End-to-End principle, which is explained in the following section.

2.1.2   The End-to-End Principle

The *End-to-End argument* is attributed to Dave Clark and his colleagues at MIT, who identified and named it in a classical paper published in 1984 [SRD84]. The End-to-End argument describes a design principle that organizes and guides the placement of functions within a system. When applied to communication networks, it postulates the sharing of responsibilities between the network and its connected end hosts. In short, the argument is to keep the core network relatively simple and move necessary intelligence as much as possible outside the network into the end hosts. A function or a service should be provided within the network only if it is needed by all end hosts connected to that network. As such, the core Internet provides only for simple forwarding of individual data packets, while the end hosts control and provides sophisticated communication services.

The resulting communication architecture, as implemented by the Internet, is illustrated in Figure 2.2, which depicts the protocols typically involved in a Web message exchange. Routers inside the network implement protocol layers one through three, realizing a simple, best-effort packet forwarding service through the network, across multiple network links, and multiple network segments. Building on top of IP, end hosts implement higher-layer protocols that coordinate the message exchange and organize lower-level network resources to efficiently achieve application-specific design goals. TCP, for example, is often used to add advanced features such as error control, congestion control, and ordered packet delivery on top of the basic IP service. These features enable TCP to provide the underpinning for most application-level protocols such as Telnet, FTP, and HTTP. The Internet architecture allows many different users with different applications to share common, lower-level network resources in an efficient way.

In some sense, the Internet design can be seen analogous to the postal system. Just as IP provides a best-effort packet delivery service, the standard postal service makes its best effort to deliver letters to a given address in a timely

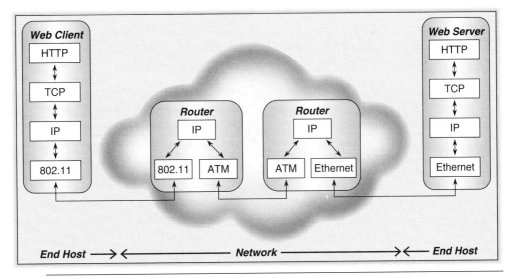

Figure 2.2 Example placement of protocol functionality in the Internet.

manner, but does not give any guarantees for successful delivery. The postal service provides such letter delivery based solely on the information written on the envelope. It does not analyze the content or the purpose of the letter (i.e., the "application") when forwarding the letter to its final destination. It is up to the sender and the receiver of the letter (i.e., the end host) to use the postal delivery service in the most appropriate way for their specific purpose.

The End-to-End principle, which postulates a dumb network with intelligent end hosts, is in sharp contrast to the telephone network. In the traditional telephony world, the network is built of complicated switches, connecting very simple end devices (i.e., telephones). Building complex functions into the network implicitly optimizes the network for a specific set of applications, while substantially increasing the cost for different types of uses. This is not a problem for the circuit-switched telephony network, as its focus is on a single application—transmission of real-time voice. The Internet, however, serves as a unifying transmission medium for a variety of applications—ranging from asynchronous messaging to interactive remote access and real-time distribution of audio and video. If the Internet had been optimized for circuit-switched, telephony-style applications, it would hardly have enabled the experimentation that led to the World Wide Web.

While the End-to-End principle argues that functions be provided within the network only if they are needed by all clients, it does not preclude the idea of building a programmable network [RSC98]. Network programmability per se does not increase functional complexity for all users. It rather allows end hosts to implement the specific services they need inside the network—possibly resulting in improved efficiency and enabling new kinds of applications. This outcome is in line with the End-to-End argument, which is more about *who* should provide and control the code for specific functions rather than about *where* the code should be executed. However, as network designers look into ideas and approaches to provide specific services inside the network, it is important to understand whether the expected benefits outweigh potential architectural costs, such as loss of simplicity and potential costs concerning network robustness and data integrity. Such considerations often lead to highly polarizing discussions, as seen in the context of active networking [TSS97, RSC98] and, more recently, in connection with content services at the network edge [RFC 3238]. We will elaborate on this topic later.

A related concept often mentioned in this context is *network transparency*. It refers to the original Internet concept of a single universal logical addressing scheme and the mechanisms by which packets flow unaltered from source to destination [RFC 2775]. Application messages arrive at their destinations exactly the way they have been sent from the source—no modifications are made during message transport. In other words, the network is transparent to applications. Returning to the postal analogy, the Internet handles data packets just as the postal system handles letters. The postal service might modify the envelope of a letter, for example by stamping the postmark, but it will never alter the content of the enclosed letter. In a different context, postal mail delivery is based on globally unique addresses. It assumes the existence of a single logical address space covering the entire world. The recipient of a letter is unambiguously given by the destination address on the envelope, just as the originator can be identified by the given return address. In analogy, the original Internet design developed a single logical address space covering the whole Internet, which allows using network addresses as unique labels for Internet hosts. Whenever a data packet is sent to a specific network address, the receiving host is unambiguously given. Similarly, receivers can determine the originating host of an incoming data packet based on its source address. It was not envisioned that the source address or the destination address of a data packet would be changed by the network.

The uniqueness and durability of network addresses have been exploited in many ways, in particular by incorporating them in higher layer protocols or application mechanisms. TCP, for example, includes the network address into its checksum, and many Web applications use a message's network address for identification purposes. Nevertheless, driven by the threat of IPv4 address exhaustion and by new business models, new inventions such as Network Address Translators (NATs) and interception proxies now cause non-uniqueness and volitility of network addresses. As a result, many applications will fail, unless they are specifically adapted to avoid the assumption of address transparency. Possible mechanisms to overcome such problems include insertion of application-level gateways, or having the NAT modify message payloads on the fly. In either case, the mechanism is application-specific and, therefore, not universal.

These observations illustrate that the fundamental design principles of the Internet and the resulting dependencies play an important role when introducing new communication mechanisms. This applies in particular to the area of content networking, as several proposed mechanisms touch those fundamental principles. Later chapters will take up these considerations when describing interception proxies or content services provided from inside the network.

The Internet, with its fundamental design principles, is the main vehicle for transmitting content between geographically dispersed sites on the Web. The following section touches on how content is transmitted over the Internet by introducing the application-level transfer protocol of the Web—the HTTP.

2.2 Hypertext Transport Protocol—HTTP

The HTTP is the lingua franca of the Web. It is an application layer protocol used for the transfer of Web resources, whether these are documents, Web pages, or images. Although designed to be usable over any underlying transport-layer protocol, virtually all implementations of HTTP run on top of the TCP protocol. HTTP was originally proposed by Tim Berners-Lee in 1990 and evolved further in two distinct phases—from protocol version 0.9 to version 1.0 over a period of four years, and from version 1.0 to version 1.1 in another four years.

This chapter introduces the key concepts of HTTP based on HTTP/1.0 [RFC 2621]. When extensions of HTTP/1.1 [RFC 2616] are discussed, they will be mentioned explicitly.

2.2.1   HTTP Characteristics

Just as every human language has its own characteristics, communication protocols can be described by their properties and attributes. This section introduces the Hypertext Transport Protocol by discussing some of its key characteristics, with focus on the implemented request-response mechanism, resource identification, protocol statelessness, and its ability to carry metadata information about Web resources.

Request-response mechanism

Like most application-layer protocols on the Internet, HTTP uses a request-response–based communication scheme, as illustrated in Figure 1.1. An HTTP transaction is always initiated by a client sending a *request* to a server. The protocol specifies a set of *methods* that are chosen by the client to indicate which operation has to be executed. Example operations include the creation, modification, or transmission of a Web object. The server generates a *response* and transmits it back to the client. The response, for example, may include a requested Web page. HTTP transactions are always initiated by the client, and a server never generates a response without being asked for it by a client. It is possible, however, that a server chooses to not respond to an incoming request.

Although the request-response mechanism occurs directly between server and client, it is possible that additional systems in the middle participate in the message exchange. Such systems include proxies, Web caches, gateways, or other systems. Although these systems can play an active role in a Web transaction, they do not change the fundamental scheme of a request-response mechanism.

Resource identification

HTTP is used by clients to request specific actions on *resources* that can reside anywhere on the network. A resource in this context is a Web object, a service, or any collection of entities that can be uniquely located on the network. For example, a client could request, via HTTP, transmission of a specific Web page or the execution of a certain service. As such, HTTP relies on a naming mechanism to uniquely identify global resources. This is achieved by using Uniform Resource Identifiers (URIs) in all HTTP transactions, as introduced in Section 1.2.2. Each HTTP request includes a URI, indicating the resource to which the request has to be applied. The server applies the requested method to the given resource and sends the generated response back to the client.

Statelessness

After transmitting an HTTP response back to the requesting client, a server does not maintain any information about the transaction. Subsequent request/ response pairs are completely independent and are not related to past client requests. Each HTTP response is generated independently, without any knowledge of previous requests or responses.

The absence of any state preservation across transactions is referred to as *statelessness*. HTTP has been designed as a stateless protocol to ensure its scalability and robustness. In contrast, *stateful* protocols have to maintain the history of past transactions, which is complex and does not scale well as the number of incoming requests increases. In addition, the state information may be inconsistent if a client or a server crashes, thus requiring complex mechanisms for reconciliation. All these problems have been circumvented by not including any intrinsic support for state maintenance in HTTP.

As the Web evolved, though, the statelessness of HTTP turned out to be a problem for some emerging applications. E-commerce, for example, requires a server to keep track of previous customer transactions. It is important for the server to remember which products a customer has put into her shopping cart, or which shipping option she has chosen during checkout. Such information has to be maintained, even if one of the requests in sequence is aborted. In an approach to overcome these difficulties, *cookies* have been introduced. A discussion of HTTP's cookie mechanism follows in Section 2.2.5.

Support for metadata

In certain scenarios, it is helpful for the client to receive some additional information about the characteristics of a requested resource. For example, the last modification time of a resource can be used in deciding whether a response should be cached locally, or when a response should be considered stale. Likewise, processing is improved with information about the encoding of a returned Web object. Other examples of additional information include the language of a text object or the size of an object. Information describing the attributes of a resource is referred to as *metadata*. HTTP has been designed so that metadata about a resource can be included in the messages exchanged between client and server. Depending on the resource type and the respective situation, different metadata can be included. While indicating the language of a text object might be helpful, for example, the same would not make sense for binary code or photos. The following section on HTTP message formats includes a discussion on how metadata is embedded in HTTP messages.

2.2.2   HTTP Message Format

A message is the fundamental communication unit in HTTP. It occurs either in the form of a *request* sent from a client to a server, or as a *response* sent from a server to a client. Designed with user friendliness and extensibility in mind, HTTP messages are text-based, making them readable by users, simple to debug, and open for extensions.

Each request message starts with a request line, whereas response messages begin with a status line. The request or status line is terminated by a carriage return/line feed (CR/LF), and is followed by zero or more header lines that together make up the HTTP header. Header lines are intended to carry additional information—the metadata—associated with the resource that is referred to in the request. The body of an HTTP message is separated from the last header line by an additional carriage return/line feed (i.e., by an empty line). The message body itself is optional, meaning that HTTP messages do not necessarily have to carry a payload (some HTTP message types *must not* carry a payload per se). An HTTP request asking for delivery of a Web page, for example, does not include any data in its body—all the required information is carried in HTTP headers. In turn, the corresponding HTTP response delivers the requested HTML code in its message body.

The description above focuses on the most common HTTP header structure, but does not provide a complete definition. For example, it is possible for a single HTTP header field to span multiple lines using what is called linear white space (LWS). For a comprehensive reference, the reader is referred to the HTTP standards, RFC 1945, and RFC 2616. More details about the syntax and the semantics of HTTP request and response messages follow.

HTTP request messages

The format of an HTTP request message is illustrated in Figure 2.3. The message begins with a request line that consists of a request method, followed by a URI indicating the requested Web object (i.e., the "Request-URI"), and the protocol version. In the given example, a client is using the GET method to request a file named /index.html via HTTP version 1.0. The request line is terminated by a carriage return/line feed and followed by optional header lines. Each

Figure 2.3 HTTP request message.

header line begins with a header field name, which is separated by a colon from one or more attributes. The example above shows four separate header lines indicating the hostname of the addressed Web server, the date and time the request was issued, the user agent of the client (e.g., the type of Web browser), as well as, the preferred language of the client. The message header is terminated by an empty line (i.e., an additional CR/LF) and followed by an optional message body. In our example, the message body is empty, which is not necessarily the case for all HTTP request messages. HTTP requests using the POST method, for example, typically include a non-empty message body that might carry input from a Web form.

In general, the method included on the first line of a request message tells a Web server what action to perform on the Web object identified by the subsequent URI. In the example given above, the request line tells the Web server to apply the GET method to the resource /index.html. The specification of HTTP 1.0 defined only three methods—GET, POST, and HEAD. Some browser and server developers soon started to implement additional methods such as PUT, DELETE, LINK, and UNLINK. The rarely implemented LINK and UNLINK methods, for example, allowed creation and deletion of Unix-style links between URIs and other resources. They were dropped in the specification of HTTP, while some of the other methods survived and are now part of the protocol specification. The request methods specified in HTTP/1.1 are discussed below.

GET Method

The GET method instructs a Web server to return whatever information is identified by the Request-URI. Most commonly, the URI refers to an HTML document or an image, which the server sends to the requesting client. It is possible, though, that the Request-URI refers to a data-producing program rather than a static Web object. In this case, the server will execute the identified program and return the generated data output to the client. Typical examples include personalized Web pages that are dynamically generated when the HTTP request comes in. GET certainly is the most commonly used method today, since retrieval of information still is the main application on the Web. The previously discussed Figure 2.3 shows an HTTP message carrying a GET request.

POST Method

While the GET method is used for information retrieval, the POST method is used to submit information to a Web server. Use cases include posting to a bulletin board, the submission of a user form, addition of database entries, or providing input parameters for a server-side software program. The information to be submitted is included in the message body of a POST request. The actual function performed by the POST method usually depends on the Request-URI.

Any output generated in response to the submission is sent back to the submitting user. For example, the request

```
POST /phonebook.cgi HTTP/1.0
Date: Sun, 18 Jul 2002 04:28 EST
User-Agent: Mozilla/5.0 [en] (WinNT; U)
Accept-Language: en-us
Content-Length: 14

700-555-4141
```

indicates that the server should execute a program named /phonebook.cgi to look up the phone number 700-555-4141 transmitted in the message body. The example also shows that a POST request usually includes a Content-Length header indicating the length of the message body. In the example, the server would execute the referred program with the given input, and send the search result to the client indicating the name and address of the customer associated with the submitted phone number.

While it would have been possible to transmit the phone number in the above example as part of the URI in a GET request (e.g., in the form of /phonebook.html?number=700-555-4141), using the POST method yields several advantages. First, most implementations limit the length of a Request-URI, thus limiting the number and the length of parameters that could be embedded in a URI. Second, Request-URIs are typically logged on all systems involved in a Web transaction. As such, input parameters would end up in the system log files, which might violate privacy preferences of the user. Data submitted in the body of a POST request, in contrast, is typically not logged.

HEAD Method

The HEAD method is identical to GET except that the server's response will not include a message body. The HTTP headers in the response to a HEAD request are identical to the information sent in response to a GET request. As such, this method is practical for obtaining resource metadata without having to transfer the actual resource, thus reducing network load. It is often used for debugging purposes and for testing hypertext links for validity, accessibility, and recent modification. For example, the HTTP request

```
HEAD /index.html HTTP/1.0
Host: www.content-networking.com
Date: Sun, 18 July 2004 04:30 EST
```

could be used to verify the existence of the resource /index.html, or for checking whether the resource has been modified after a specific time. The message a server would send in response to the shown HEAD request is identical to the message the same server would send in response to the GET request shown in Figure 2.3 except that it has no message body.

PUT Method

The `PUT` method requests a server store the enclosed data under the supplied Request-URI. If the Request-URI refers to an already existing resource, the resource enclosed in the message body should replace the existing one. If the referred resource does not yet exist, it will be created. The `PUT` method could be used, for example, to publish Web objects to a Web server. Due to security concerns, however, most Web servers require the content authors to use other mechanisms, such as FTP, for Web publishing.

DELETE Method

The `DELETE` method is used to remove the Web object identified by the Request-URI from the Web server. It provides a convenient mechanism to remotely delete objects, without having to actually log into a Web server. Obviously, allowing remote delete operations can be very risky, which is why the Web server is free to ignore the request for deletion.

TRACE Method

The `TRACE` method is used to invoke a remote, application-layer loopback of the request message. On receiving a `TRACE` request, a server reflects the received request back to the requestor as the body of its response message. This method allows a client to see what is being received at the server. This knowledge can then be used for testing or diagnostic purposes. By using the `Max-Forward` header in the request, it is possible to limit the number of proxies or gateways that can forward the request to the next inbound server. This can be useful when targeting a specific intermediary, or when attempting to trace a request chain that appears to be failing or looping in mid-chain.

OPTIONS Method

The `OPTIONS` method is used to request information about various communication options available on the server. It allows the client to detect the options and requirements associated with a resource, or the capabilities of a server.

HTTP response messages

The syntax of a HTTP response message is very similar to the HTTP request message format. As illustrated in Figure 2.4 an HTTP response message begins with a status line, which includes the protocol version, a numerical response code indicating the result of an operation (e.g., success or failure), and a phrase explaining the result code (the reason phrase). In the example, the server supports HTTP version 1.0 and uses a result code of 200, indicating that the

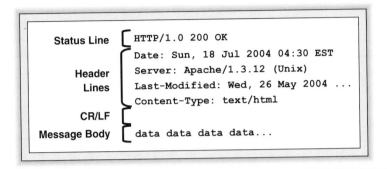

Figure 2.4 HTTP response message.

request succeeded. The status line is terminated by a carriage return/line feed and followed by optional header lines. The example shows four header lines indicating the day and time when the response was generated, the server type, the day and time when the included resource was last modified, and the content type of the resource. The message header is terminated by an empty line (i.e., an additional CR/LF) and followed by an optional message body. In most cases, the message body includes the Web object that was requested by the client using a GET request.

Result Code and Reason Phrase

The result code is a three-digit integer indicating the outcome of the server's attempt to satisfy the client request. The reason phrase is meant to give a short textual description of the result code. The code itself is intended for use by machines and computers, while the reason phrase is intended for human interpretation. The first digit of the reason phrase specifies the class of response. The last two digits do not have any categorization role. The first digit establishes the following five categories:

- 1xx: Informational—Request received, continuing process.
- 2xx: Success—The action was successfully received, understood, and accepted.
- 3xx: Redirection—Further action must be taken to complete the request.
- 4xx: Client Error—The request contains bad syntax or cannot be fulfilled.
- 5xx: Server Error—The server failed to fulfill an apparently valid request.

The following humorous interpretation—found on a web discussion forum as "the real interpretation" of a Web server's response—may be easier to remember.

- 1xx: Informational—Not done yet.
- 2xx: Success—You win.
- 3xx: Redirection—You lose, but try again.
- 4xx: Client Error—You lose; your fault.
- 5xx: Server Error—You lose; my bad.

Web applications are not required to understand the meaning of all specified status codes, though such understanding is obviously desirable. However, applications must understand the class of any result code, as indicated by the first digit, and treat any unrecognized response as being equivalent to the x00 status code of that class.

The individual values of numeric status codes and the corresponding reason phrases are defined in the HTTP protocol specifications RFC 1945 and RFC 2621. Note that the reason phrases can be changed without affecting the operation of the protocol. Hence, automation scripts should strictly parse for the numeric code rather than the reason phrase. An example set of result codes and corresponding reason phrases is given below.

- `200 OK`: The request succeeded and the requested information is enclosed in the response.
- `204 No Content`: Indicates successful completion of the request with no new information to send back. This tells the client that no changes are to be made from his current document view, that is, the browser display will not change.
- `300 Multiple Choices`: Several instances of the requested resource are available, with their location and other relevant information being indicated in the response.
- `301 Moved Permanently`: The requested object has moved permanently to a new location, which is indicated in the response. The client should use the new location from now on.
- `302 Moved Temporarily`: The requested object has moved temporarily to a new location, which is indicated in the response. The client should continue to use the old location in future requests.
- `304 Not Modified`: Indicates that the requested resource has not been changed since the time included in the request. The resource itself is not returned in the response.
- `400 Bad Request`: The server was not able to understand the request due to malformed syntax.
- `404 Not Found`: The server is unable to locate the requested resource. This result is often caused by a user mistyping the request URI in his or her browser, or by requesting a non-existent Web page.
- `500 Internal Server Error`: The server encountered an unexpected internal error and is unable to determine the precise error condition.

There are many more result codes defined. For a complete list and explanation, the reader is referred to RFC 1945 and RFC 2616. Additional result codes will be discussed later.

2.2.3   HTTP at Work—Try It Hands-On!

Now that we have outlined the fundamental format of the HTTP messages, its semantic meaning, and how it is exchanged between client and server, it might be interesting to see it working hands-on. Fortunately, HTTP messages are written in plain text, so it is not necessary to create and analyze complicated binary messages. Instead, all we need to do is open a Telnet session to our favorite Web server, type in a correct HTTP message, and wait for the server's response. Telnet is a terminal emulation program that allows users to connect to a server on the network. Today, Telnet is included in most operating systems.

To illustrate, consider retrieving a page from the Elsevier Web site (www.elsevier.com). Open a Telnet shell and connect to www.elsevier.com at port 80 (i.e., a well-known HTTP port) by typing

```
> telnet www.elsevier.com 80 [return]
```

at the command prompt. (Do not type the '>' character, it just represents the command prompt.) Hit the [return] key as indicated and wait for the connection to be established. The screen typically displays something like

```
> Trying. . .
> Connected to www.elsevier.com
> Escape character is '^]'.
```

It is also possible that the display changes to a blank screen while waiting for further input. When the connection has been established, type

```
> GET /index.html HTTP/1.0 [return][return]
```

and press [return] two times as indicated.[1] Depending on your software, however, you might not be able to see what you are typing. The line you entered represents a simple, but complete HTTP request consisting of a single request line. The request issues a GET method asking the server to deliver the resource at /index.html. The protocol version is indicated as HTTP version 1.0. By hitting the [return] key twice, an empty line is added, terminating the HTTP header and adding an empty message body. On receiving the HTTP request, the server generates the appropriate response, which in turn is displayed in your terminal window. In our example, you can expect a response similar to:

```
> HTTP/1.1 200 OK
> Content-Type: text/html
> Content-Length: 106
> Last-Modified: Tue, 25 Nov 2003 11:14:18 GMT
> Server: Apache/1.3.20 (Unix)
```

---

[1]This assumes that the Telnet software is configured to send CR/LF for each [return], or the Telnet server is robust and accepts bare LF as request line terminator. Both assumptions are usually true, but may vary for some users.

```
> Date: Sun, 18 Jul 2004 16:51:57 GMT
>
><HTML>><HEAD>
> {some text here}
> </HEAD></HTML>
>
>Connection closed
```

The response delivers the corresponding page of Elsevier's Web server. Connect to different Web servers, issue different requests, monitor possible error responses, and experience the difference between a GET and a HEAD request hands-on. It is a great help when learning HTTP to see exactly how a server responds to a particular request. It also helps when troubleshooting, and it will prepare you to understand the more advanced HTTP features discussed in the following sections.

2.2.4 Improvements in HTTP/1.1

Like many communication protocols, HTTP has been evolving over time. Version 1.1 has been redefined over the last few years to address new needs and to overcome some of the shortcomings of version 1.0. Changes were made to improve the average response time, which is achieved by allowing multiple transactions to take place over a single, persistent TCP connection. Delivery of dynamically generated pages has been improved by supporting chunked transfer encoding, which allows a response to be sent before its total length is known. Other additions allow multiple domains to be served from a single IP address, enabling a more efficient use of the existing IP address space. While a few more improvements have been made in HTTP version 1.1, the following section will focus on the improvements just mentioned.

Persistent connections

HTTP messages are typically transferred over a TCP connection. In HTTP 1.0 and earlier versions, the client has to establish a new, separate TCP connection for each resource to be retrieved. Since opening and closing TCP connections causes additional delays and requires a substantial amount of bandwidth, memory, and CPU time, this approach turns out to be problematic in practice. Most Web pages embed several components such as images or banners that are likely to reside on the same server as the page itself. As illustrated in Figure 2.5A, a HTTP 1.0 client has to open and close separate TCP connections for each of those objects, which results in increased access delays and in additional protocol overhead. Much can be saved in HTTP/1.1 with a default behavior allowing multiple requests and responses to be sent through a single *persistent connection*. As shown in Figure 2.5B, HTTP/1.1 default behavior leaves the connection open after a response has been sent. The client can send subsequent requests to the

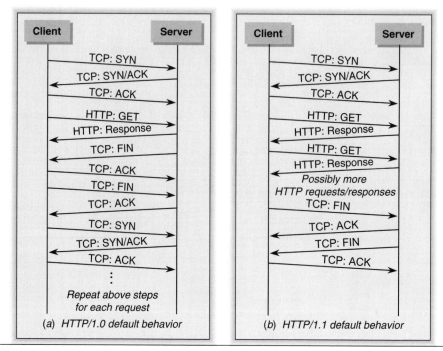

Figure 2.5 Client-server interaction in HTTP/1.0 and HTTP/1.1.

same server using the established TCP connection—without the overhead and delay associated with repeated TCP connection establishment and teardown. Persistent connections, however, also have drawbacks. For example, a busy server has to maintain a large pool of idle connections. Servers also proactively close connections, ending up with unusable connections in a long TIME_WAIT TCP state.

A related concept often used in conjunction with persistent connections is *request pipelining*. Request pipelining allows a client to transmit several requests in a series over a single connection without having to wait for a response. If a client pipelines multiple requests, the server has to send responses in the same order as the requests went out, allowing simple mapping between responses and their corresponding requests.

A persistent connection can be closed by either one of the peers. If a client wants to close a persistent connection, it includes a Connection: close header in the next outgoing request. This indicates that the server should tear-down the TCP connection after the corresponding response has been sent. Clients use this mechanism if they do not want to support persistent connections, or if they know the request will be the last one sent on that connection. Similarly, a server can include a Connection: close header in a response. This indicates that the server will close the TCP connection following that response, and the client should not send any more requests through that connection.

Since a server is allowed to close a connection before all outstanding responses are sent, a client must always keep track of requests and resend them as needed. The teardown of idle persistent connections is typically triggered by a timeout period or by a system reaching its limit on the number of idle connections, causing the oldest idle connection to be closed.

Persistent connections are the default in HTTP/1.1, so no specific indication is required to use them. They help improve performance for delivering conventional, static Web content but introduce a new challenge in supporting dynamically created content. The following paragraph discusses this issue and explains a solution—*chunked encoding*.

Chunked encoding

It is important for a Web client to know when it has received a complete server response. HTTP/1.0 allows servers to indicate the size of a response message through the `Content-Length` header field. The message length can easily be determined for static resources. For dynamic resources, however, a server has to wait until the response is fully generated before being able to compute its length. As a result, if the server wants to keep the underlying TCP connection open, it cannot start sending a response until the resource has been created in its entirety. This is not a problem for short response messages, but it introduces noticeable delay and memory exhaustion for long responses. For these reasons, HTTP/1.0 servers did not use the `Content-Length` header for dynamic content. Instead, a server indicated the end of a dynamically generated message by closing the underlying TCP connection. Since this mechanism does not allow use of persistent connections, an alternative way for indicating the end of a message was required in HTTP/1.1.

The problem is solved in HTTP/1.1 by introducing *chunked transfer encoding*, which allows the sender to break a message body into arbitrary-sized chunks and to transmit them separately. Since the chunks themselves can contain as little as one byte of content, their length can easily be determined and precedes the chunk. The end of the entire message is indicated by adding a zero-length chunk. Receipt of the zero-length chunk indicates to a receiver that the entire message has been transmitted and no more chunks for this message are expected to arrive. Thus, the receiver is ensured that the entire message has successfully been received. Chunked encoding can be used for both HTTP requests and HTTP responses, though it is more commonly used for dynamically created response messages.

As an illustration, consider the response message in Figure 2.6, which is divided into separate chunks. The `Transfer-Encoding: chunked` header indicates that the message is transmitted in several chunks, requiring the receiver to reassemble the full message from separate pieces. In the example, the message is split into three chunks, with the first chunk having a length of 542 bytes (21E in hex), the second one having a length of 97 bytes, and a zero-length chunk to indicate the message end. Each chunk is preceded by a number indicating its size.

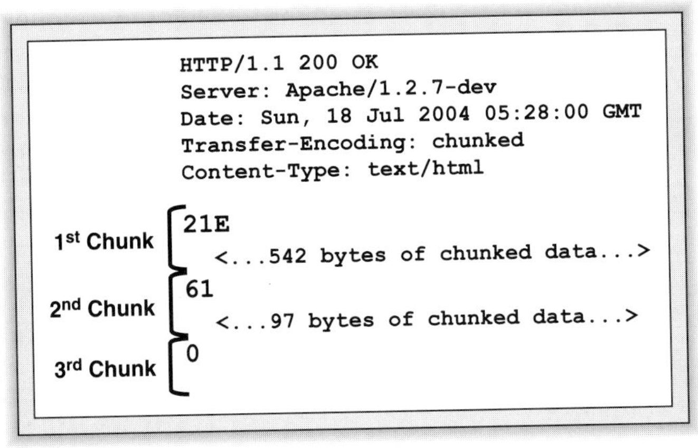

```
                    HTTP/1.1 200 OK
                    Server: Apache/1.2.7-dev
                    Date: Sun, 18 Jul 2004 05:28:00 GMT
                    Transfer-Encoding: chunked
                    Content-Type: text/html

1st Chunk   ⌈  21E
            ⌊      <...542 bytes of chunked data...>
2nd Chunk   ⌈  61
            ⌊      <...97 bytes of chunked data...>
3rd Chunk   ⌈  0
```

Figure 2.6 A chunked HTTP response.

It is important to understand that HTTP chunking has no impact on how the underlying transport layer treats the various data segments. A single HTTP chunk might span multiple IP packets, while it is also possible for multiple chunks to fit into a single IP packet.

2.2.5   Client-Server Interaction

HTTP allows Web clients and Web servers to interact in a variety of different ways, starting from simple page download to complicated e-commerce transactions. The different types of interactions are supported through several protocol mechanisms in HTTP. This section examines two representative examples that are most relevant to content networking—*cookies* and *user authentication*. Additional interaction mechanisms will be discussed in later chapters.

Cookies

HTTP is a stateless protocol, which means that the server does not retain any information across multiple client requests—the server generates a response and forgets about the client and its request (except for considering TCP-level information that needs to be maintained for persistent connections). Although this characteristic proved to be crucial for the scalability of the Web, it also turned out to be a problem for certain applications. A shopping site, for example, needs to keep track of the goods a user has already put into her virtual shopping cart. The provider might also be interested to learn whether a customer has visited the site before, so that appropriate content can be presented. Without alternative mechanisms, the server would have to maintain such state information over an extended period for all of its customers—potentially thousands or millions of users—certainly not a scalable approach.

Cookies are HTTP's way to manage such information, shifting the burden of state maintenance from the server to the client. A cookie is a small amount of state information that a Web server sends to a Web client for storage and presentation with future requests. The mechanism is illustrated in Figure 2.7. When a client contacts a cookie-enabled server for the first time, the server's response includes a `Set-cookie:  <cookie>` header line, whereby <cookie> represents the actual cookie value—an arbitrary string selected by the server. The client does not interpret the cookie string, but simply stores it on the local disk in a so-called cookie file. For all subsequent requests to the same server, the client software checks for previously stored cookies from that server and includes the cookie information in the `Cookie` header field of outgoing requests. This way, a server is presented the previously returned state information with each request coming from the client. For example, a server could assign an ID number to the client on the first access, and return the ID in the `Cookie-set` header. Whenever the client accesses the site again, it presents the previously assigned ID number in the `Cookie` header line of the request, allowing the server to recognize the client and to perform appropriate actions (e.g., a database lookup to retrieve the customer's profile). It is also possible to encode information about previous client actions in the cookie. For example, a server could track a user's browsing behavior by including information about which pages a user has visited in the current session. This is made possible by allowing a server to modify and to add cookies using the

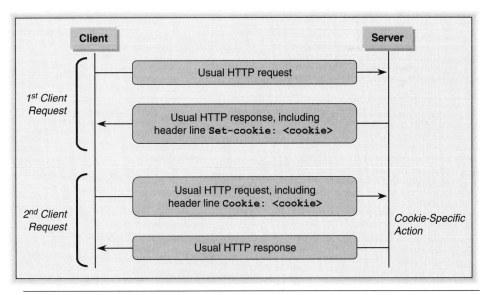

Figure 2.7 An illustration of the HTTP cookie mechanism.

`Set-cookie` header with any response. The cookie mechanism was first introduced in 1994 by Netscape [Net94]. Further standardization moved into the IETF,
which formalized the use of cookies in RFC 2965.

Cookies represent a simple, yet powerful and scalable mechanism to maintain state across multiple HTTP requests. There are many reasons why Web sites
might be interested in using cookies. These range from the ability to personalize
information or to help with online sales and services. Cookies also provide pro-
grammers with a quick and convenient means of keeping site content fresh and
relevant to the user's interests. Cookies are also used to help with back-end interaction, which can improve the utility of a site by being able to store personal
data that the user has shared with a site.

However, cookies are also used for tracking user behavior or demographics,
which caused widespread concerns about user privacy. While cookies themselves
do not act maliciously on computer systems, nor access a machine's disk or
spread viruses, they can be used to learn about user behavior and for tracking a
user's path through the Web. Furthermore, cookies are transmitted in clear text
without any encryption applied to them by the network. An eavesdropper is able
to read and possibly modify the content of a cookie. As such, privacy and security is reduced when personal data is sent as part of a cookie unless a secure
communication channel is used or the server takes precaution and encrypts the
cookie value itself. All these privacy concerns lead many users to disable the
acceptance of cookies in their browser software, making it impossible for Web
sites to use this mechanism to maintain state information. This fact should be
considered when developing Web sites and networking technology for the Web.
It might be a good idea to include cookies for optimization purposes, but a system should also work without relying on users to accept all presented cookies.

The discussion on cookies already touched on the issue of user identification. It was not yet explained, however, how users can be authenticated and what
support HTTP offers—a topic addressed in the following section.

User authentication

There are many reasons why we may want a Web server to control access to certain resources. We do not generally intend for Web pages containing private and
personal information to be viewed by the entire world, but only by our friends
and relatives. Likewise, a company might restrict access to proprietary information to its employees only. Providers of paid-for services want to ensure that only
paying users can actually access those services. These examples illustrate the
need for *access control*, which includes mechanisms for user authentication and
for *authorization*. The former deals with identifying a user who originated a
request, while the latter verifies whether the user is granted access to the
requested resource. Mechanisms for authorization are implemented locally on
the Web servers and have no direct impact on the communication protocol used
between client and server. Therefore, this section focuses on user authentication
and related features built into HTTP.

Users typically authenticate themselves to a system by entering a username and a password. The server matches this input with a password file stored locally and either denies the request or proceeds to establish a session with the user. If the user is accepted, the server remembers the user identity for the duration of the session. HTTP, however, is stateless and does not include the notion of a session. Each user request is handled separately and independently from previous ones. Hence, a Web server must perform user authentication for each individual request, even if the same user has been authenticated before. Since it would be annoying and time-consuming for a user to be required to enter his or her username and password for each individual request, the user's browser software will remember previously entered authentication credentials and automatically include them in the HTTP headers of subsequent requests to the same server. Having the authentication credentials in each request allows the server to treat all requests independent from each other. The browser software typically deletes stored authentication credentials once the browser is closed, unless it is instructed otherwise by the user.

HTTP allows a server to select from different kinds of authentication methods, including basic authentication or digest access authentication [RFC 2617]. Figure 2.8. illustrates the basic authentication mechanism, which follows a simple challenge-response scheme. A user clicks on a Web link pointing to a protected resource on the server. The click results in an HTTP request being sent

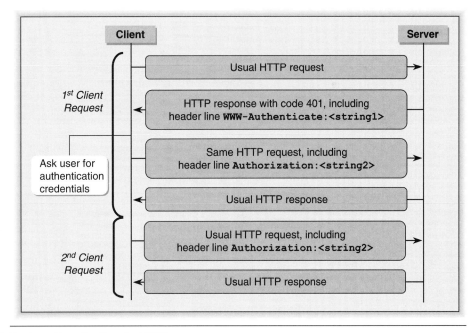

Figure 2.8 Basic authentication in HTTP.

to the server. The server realizes that the requested resource is protected and that it needs to authenticate the user. The server now returns a `401 Unauthorized` response message including a challenge in the `WWW-Authenticate` header field. On receiving the response, a browser prompts the user for his username and password. The client then resends the previously issued request, but includes the authentication credentials in an `Authorization` header field of the outgoing request. If the server is satisfied with the credentials, it will respond with a regular HTTP response message. For all subsequent requests to the same server, the client's browser software will automatically include the appropriate `Authorization` header field, thus eliminating the additional authentication step.

While the basic authentication mechanism of HTTP is a first step towards protecting sensitive data, it needs to be noted that all the authentication credentials are transferred in clear text. Any eavesdropper software capable of intercepting network traffic can be used to learn about exchanged authentication credentials, enabling the eavesdropper to use it for its own purposes. The next section addresses this issue in a more general context when talking about techniques for secured Web transactions.

2.2.6   Secure Web Communication Using SSL

With the growth of e-commerce and the ubiquity of the Internet in everybody's life, people are increasingly concerned about the confidentiality and security of private information traveling the network paths. In the days when the Internet was primarily an academic resource, all content was transmitted in clear text—anyone viewing the data in transit could read it using readily available network tools. With the increasingly sensitive nature of information carried over the Internet (e.g., personal information, credit card numbers, etc.), mechanisms for secured information transfer have become paramount.

Security was taken seriously by the Web community relatively early on. Some security mechanisms were built into HTTP, but attempts were also started to provide secure communication at a protocol layer below the application. The efforts resulted in the *Secure Socket Layer (SSL)* [SSL96] mechanism, which was introduced by Netscape in 1994, and is further developed into the *Transport Layer Security (TLS)* [RFC 2246] standard of the IETF.

The SSL protocol itself is application independent and operates between the application layer and the transport layer. This means application protocols such as HTTP, Telnet, Internet Message Access Protocol (IMAP), Simple Mail Transport Protocol (SMTP), and Network News Transport Protocol (NNTP), are easily layered on top of SSL, with TCP/IP working underneath it. SSL provides data encryption, server authentication, message integrity, and optional client authentication for a TCP/IP connection. When using SSL between a client and a server, everything in their communication is encrypted, including all the HTTP headers and, in particular, the Request URI. This will play an important role when we talk about content switching and interception proxies later on.

An introduction and more detailed discussion of security mechanisms and encryption techniques are beyond the scope of this book. Readers are referred to specialized books on Internet and Web security, for example [KR01].

2.3 Multicast Transport

Web documents have become a very popular medium for bringing information to large numbers of people. As a result, content providers and ISPs are struggling to upgrade their servers and their networks to handle the huge volumes of Web traffic. These scalability problems partially arise from the client-server model of the Web. In this model, information is delivered to clients only when they request delivery—servers themselves never initiate delivery of content to a client. This requires a server to serve each client individually, meaning the data is always transmitted via a point-to-point connection between the client and the server—also referred to as *unicast* communication. As illustrated in Figure 1.2, scalability problems are inherent with this solution, and Web caching has previously been mentioned as a possible remedy. However, more can be done. A networking technique that can be used in conjunction with caching to further improve scalability is *multicast* transport. With this approach, Web pages are delivered to multiple awaiting clients using one server response instance. Although multicast has long been viewed as a promising approach to improve efficiency and scalability of content delivery to a large number of receivers, its practical use is still very limited. This section will briefly introduce multicast fundamentals, and follow up in an attempt to shed some light on why multicast has not yet been deployed successfully.

2.3.1 Multicast Support on Different Protocol Layers

Content can be delivered to a group of receivers by repeatedly transmitting data units using point-to-point transfers to each individual receiver. However, this approach does not scale well with the number of recipients and increases the network load proportional to the group size. Broadcasting, on the other hand, seems an acceptable solution for small networks, but it causes a flood of data packets in global networks such as the Internet. Rather than broadcasting information or using multiple unicast transfers, the better approach is for receivers to subscribe to a multicast group. All data sent to the multicast group is delivered only to those hosts that have explicitly subscribed to the group. All subscribers to a multicast transmission receive a single, shared data stream. The amount of bandwidth saved increases with the number of subscribers. However, efficient support for multicast communication requires special capabilities and appropriate mechanisms on various layers of the protocol stack, as discussed in the following paragraphs.

Link-level multicast

Efficient multicast communication requires appropriate support even below the network layer, which is to say, on the data link layer. Every data packet received by a network interface causes an interrupt and stimulates further processing at higher protocol levels. Therefore, it is desirable that hosts receive and process only those packets that are destined to them. This goal is achieved by adding multicast filtering on the network interface hardware. Multicast filters allow a network interface to receive packets sent to a specific multicast group in addition to broadcast packets and packets sent specifically to the network interface. This enables the use of multicast addresses instead of the all hosts address or multiple unicast addresses. Transmitters connected to a broadcast media (e.g., Ethernet) need to send only one copy per packet without causing further packet processing at non-member host locations.

Network-level multicast—the IP multicast model

The network layer plays a central role in supporting multicast communication, since it is responsible for group addressing and efficient packet forwarding through the network. Network-level multicast services take a single copy of a data packet and deliver it to the receiver group specified in the group address. Replication of data packets is delayed until they have to traverse different links, thus making most efficient use of the network resources. This requires routers and switches to incorporate group management facilities as well as mechanisms to establish and maintain multicast paths.

The Internet multicast model was originally defined by Deering in 1989 [RFC 1112]. It is based on an open service model, which does not restrict users to create or to join multicast groups. It also allows any host to send data to existing multicast groups and to receive data from a group. A sender is not required to be a member of the group, which is referred to as the *open group model*. Membership of a group can change at any time. It is possible that multiple senders share the same multicast address, and there is no way for a sender to prevent other senders from choosing the same multicast address. While the IP multicast model is highly flexible and supports a variety of applications, its openness and loose control causes serious problems, as discussed in Section 2.3.2.

Transport-level multicast

The transport layer is responsible for supporting the end-to-end data exchange between communication partners, typically distinguishing between reliable and unreliable transport services. Current transport protocols, such as TCP, are based on pure point-to-point communication. For error control purposes, the receiver sends an acknowledgment to the sender to signal that data has been received correctly. Simply extending this mechanism to multicast could mean that with large groups the sender would have to process a very large number of acknowledgments—namely, from all the members of the group. This is likely to create an acknowledgment implosion, overwhelming the sender with confirmation messages. Obviously, this approach is not scalable for large groups since the sender can easily create a bottleneck.

Transport protocols are often responsible for providing reliable services between users. Once again, it is important to point out the special problems of group communication that sometimes necessitate the introduction of new reliability classes. The result is that in the future a single transport protocol will no longer be able to accommodate the diverse requirements placed on multicast services. It is rather expected that a pool of multicast transport protocols, each with a specifically designed service, will emerge. Other important aspects include the degree to which group members are known and the dynamic of a group. Multicast transport protocols must address all these aspects.

Application layer

Given the limited availability of network level multicast in today's networks, multicast support is increasingly provided at the application layer. In this approach, application entities provide for multicast delivery, utilizing existing unicast transport protocols such as TCP or UDP for data transmission among themselves. While this approach typically makes less efficient use of network resources, it leverages well-established features of underlying transport protocols, such as congestion control, error control, etc. The emergence of application level multicast is mainly driven by the very limited deployment of network-level multicast, which raises the question about the reasons for this lack of multicast deployment.

2.3.2 Deployment Issues

The deployment of any networking technology is dictated by application needs, user requirements, and business motivation. It is essential to understand these aspects when assessing emerging technologies and evaluating their suitability for practical deployment. For multicast technology being deployed successfully, it will be required to provide at least the same level of reliability and manageability as existing unicast networks. Multicast will become attractive only if it is easy to install, manage, and maintain—for both the network provider and end users. Network providers are less likely to accept and deploy a technology requiring them to train their personnel or even to hire additional experts. Likewise, end users are likely to refrain from using multicast if it requires installation of additional software or complex setup and configuration. Furthermore, end users will expect ubiquitous availability of multicast services, making scalable interdomain communication a must. Furthermore, content providers using multicast for content distribution will expect their transmission to be protected from unauthorized senders to avoid unwanted interference.

Having these requirements and the current IP multicast model in mind, limited multicast deployment might no longer be surprising. As mentioned before, IP multicast does not allow control of which hosts can send or receive multicast data. This conflicts with the content providers' desires for protection from unauthorized senders and receivers. It also turns out that the installation, configuration, and debugging of multicast-enabled networks is by far more complex than managing a unicast network. This discourages network providers and end users equally. Finally, yet importantly, the lack of good business models has prevented network providers from figuring out how to make money out of their investment in multicast technology. Together these aspects have limited the practical deployment of multicast, driving other solutions for scalable content delivery and content networking forward.

CHAPTER 3

Caching Techniques for Web Content

Closer is better. It is faster and easier to use materials stored close by than to retrieve them repeatedly from a distant source. Squirrels gather nuts throughout a large territory to store them near their nest for easy winter access. Dairy farmers collect milk from cows each day. The milk is trucked to various processing plants and distribution points before it arrives on the shelf at the neighborhood supermarket. A few times a week, the family shopper travels a mile or so to the market to buy milk and bring it home. The milk is stored in the kitchen refrigerator, only a few feet away from the kitchen table. Each morning a container of milk is moved from the refrigerator and placed on the kitchen table, only a few inches from the family's breakfast cereal bowls where it is actually used.

Many centuries ago the French used the word *cacher*, meaning "to hide." This became the modern word *cache*, meaning "a hiding place used especially for storing provisions." Computers make good use of caches for storing information close to where it is used. Modern processors include instruction caches to speed up instruction access and memory caches to accelerate data access. Web content moves through many caching mechanisms as it travels from the disk of the origin server to the Web client. The content is stored on the server disk. It is then copied to the server's main memory, then to the processor memory cache on the way to the network. As it reaches the client, it is captured off the wire, and goes through the client processor cache on its way to the client's main memory.

Caches located in several places throughout the network can provide a variety of benefits to content consumers, content producers, and network operators. The benefits of locating a cache within a workgroup, at the network gateway to an enterprise, within an ISP, in the backbone of the network, and as part of a server farm will each be analyzed.

Finally, performance, capacity, network engineering, myths about caching, and some other practical considerations in designing and deploying them will be explored.

3.1 **Local Caching**

Most Internet browsers include a local cache mechanism tuned to the characteristics of Web pages. This local cache mechanism saves time and bandwidth, often unbeknownst to the user. For example, each time you use the browser's back button to view a previously loaded page, the browser retrieves that page from the local cache, rather than requesting it again across the network.

Local caches make lots of sense, and most, if not all, browsers have them. It is easy and instructive to examine the local cache in Internet Explorer (IE). The example given here is for IE Version 6 but is similar for other browsers. Select Tools / Internet Options / General / Temporary Internet Files / Settings and a "Settings" dialog box appears. The first option setting establishes how often the cache should "Check for newer versions of stored pages." This is one *replacement rule* (sometimes also called a *replacement algorithm* or *freshness heuristic*) and is one example of an important cache design decision. This rule is analogous to deciding to discard milk that has passed its freshness date. Replacement rules affect the freshness of the cache content.

The second option adjusts the amount of disk space dedicated to the cache. Obviously a bigger cache can store more objects, but how big is big enough? We will study this question in more depth later in the chapter. The homeowner faces a similar question in deciding how large a refrigerator to buy. Smaller local storage requires more trips to the remote source. This is true for both milk and Web content.

The "Settings" dialog box also includes an option to "view files." This option lists many files with generally cryptic names. Each of these is a single object, either text or a graphic image, which has been part of a Web page recently viewed on the client computer. A typical Web page consists of many such objects. The Yahoo! homepage is a typical complex page. Today it includes the graphic Yahoo! logo, and individual graphics for Personalization, Finance, Shopping, Mail, Messages, and Shopping. The search window and search button are each individual objects. It is not unusual for such a page to include fifty or more objects.

The local cache saves time and reduces the load on the network and the origin server by storing frequently used content close to the user. The design assumption is that if the user has visited a particular page once, they are likely to come back again. It makes sense to store a copy of the Yahoo! logo in the cache, and retrieve this local copy the next time the user visits the page. After all, the logo has not changed in several years,[1] and graphic files are typically large, so this saves time and reduces network traffic.

But the Yahoo! homepage has much more on it than the corporate logo. It has news headlines, weather, sports, and timely financial reports. This information changes often and can be seriously misleading if stale information is

---

[1] Interestingly, the headers of this object show it was last modified in 1994 with an `Expires` date in the year 2010.

mistaken for fresh information. The decision of what to cache, when to refresh, and who gets to decide is a major topic in the design of any Web cache. This will be discussed in detail later in this chapter.

3.2 Motivation and Goals of Web Caching

In taking the Hippocratic Oath, doctors around the world swear to "First, do no harm." This ancient principle is also important in the design of a Web cache. The most important requirement is that a Web cache never silently serves up altered or stale content. Reliability is a related requirement. If a Web cache fails, it must not disrupt the connection to the origin server. Although a perfect cache will not store any content marked as uncacheable, it may decide not to store all objects that are marked as cacheable.

The purpose of a Web cache is to speed up user access to Web content, reduce network load, and reduce origin server load. If the requested object is stored in the cache, the presence of the cache is almost certain to accelerate content access and reduce network load. However, in the case of a cache miss, the extra steps introduced by a poorly designed Web cache can slow down access and even increase network load.

Both hit and miss cases have to be analyzed to determine if access is accelerated, on average, to all users. The size of the cache store, cacheability rules, the speed of the cache's network connection, maximum transaction rate of the cache, the location in the network, and the characteristics of the content requested by the users are all factors that affect the access speed and network traffic impact of a particular installation.

Finally, features to assist with the administration of the Web cache and the management of the network are helpful. These include easy installation, traffic and performance reports, logging traffic through the cache, cacheability analysis of Web objects, and identifying requests that will bypass the cache.

The next sections describe the basic operation of a shared Web cache and expand on the concepts introduced in Chapter 1 and the discussion of Figure 1.3.

3.3 Basic Operation of a Shared Web Cache

During operation a shared cache located in the network has to make a few important decisions for each request transaction it handles. Figure 3.1 helps to illustrate these decisions.

The first client request might look like:

```
GET /index.html HTTP/1.1
Host: www.content-networking.com
User-Agent: Mozilla/6.0
Accept: text/html, image/gif, image/jpeg
```

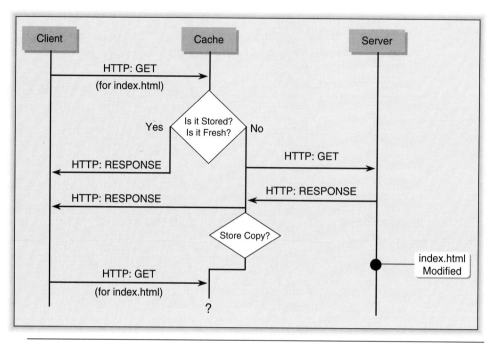

Figure 3.1 Basic network cache operation.

The cache receives the request and promptly determines if the requested object is already in the cache object store by examining the inventory of stored objects. It also has to decide if the stored object is up-to-date and valid for sharing *(fresh)* by examining available information about the object creation date, storage date, expiration date, and client and server preferences. HTTP version 1.1 includes many facilities to help make this decision accurately. If the stored object is fresh, it is retrieved from the local cache object store, and then sent as an HTTP response to the client. In this scenario, there is no need to go all the way back to the origin server, saving time and bandwidth.

If a fresh copy of the object is not in the cache, then it must be retrieved from the origin server. The cache transforms and forwards the original client request to the server, and receives the object in the response. The response may look like this:

```
HTTP/1.1 200 OK
Date: Mon, 29 Sep 2003 04:29:01 GMT
Server: Apache/1.3.12 (Unix)
Last-Modified: Mon, 29 Sep 2003 01:10:42 GMT
Content-Type: text/html

<data>
```

The cache then forwards this object as the response to the client.

The cache now has to decide if it will write a copy of the object into its local object store. This decision is based on the space available in the object store and an estimate of the future value of the object. *Replacement rules* are the general scheme that is used to decide what objects get *ejected* from the local object store when it is full and new objects need to be stored. *Dynamic object rules* are used to examine the characteristics of an object to estimate its future value and determine if it is worthwhile adding to the local object store.

It is possible that the index.html object was modified and a fresh copy is stored on the server some time after the previous version was stored by the cache. To ensure fresh objects are delivered to the client the cache has to decide freshness on each client request.

3.3.1 Replacement Rules

Since an object store has only finite capacity, it will eventually fill up. With fast networks and many clients relying on a shared network cache even a very large cache object store fills, perhaps after a few days of operation. Once the cache is full, deciding to store the current object requires a decision to remove and replace an object that is already stored. Several strategies are used to choose the object to be replaced. Popular strategies are:

- Least Recently Used (LRU)—Replace the object that has gone without a request for the longest time. Under this policy the cache will eventually fill with the most recently requested objects.
- First In, First Out (FIFO)—Replace the oldest object, based on when it was first stored in the object cache. The cache will eventually fill with the most recently refreshed objects.
- Least Frequently Used (LFU)—Replace the object that has had the fewest requests, or lowest request rate, since it was first stored. The cache will eventually fill with the most frequently requested objects.
- Next to Expire (NTE)—Replace the object that is forecast to expire the soonest. The cache will eventually fill up with the most stable (infrequently changed) objects.
- Largest File First (LFF)—Replace the largest object, hoping to free up the most space for new objects. Often both size and age is considered in choosing the object to be replaced. The cache will tend to fill with the smallest objects.

Each of these replacement strategies has its strengths and limitations. They are often combined and augmented with heuristics to provide the most practical solutions.

3.3.2 Dynamic Object Rules

Dynamic object rules work to estimate the value an object may have in serving future requests. Dynamic content, such as news headlines, weather reports, and stock quotes lose their value very quickly. Personal information such as travel plans, journals, and family photos interest only a very small number of potential clients. Private information, such as bank account balances, account numbers, and passwords must not be shared with unauthorized clients. One common dynamic object replacement rule recognizes that URIs containing /cgi or /cgi-bin are usually Common Gateway Interface (CGI) requests. These are requests to run programs on the server to generate individualized responses that incorporate dynamic content. These almost always create responses having dynamic, personal, or private information and typically should not be cached. An algorithm that does not cache responses to CGI requests is conservative but it may not honor the cacheability intent of the content provider. The primary mechanism for identifying what should and should not be cached is the HTTP cache control header, described in the next section.

Caches often use the HTTP Conditional GET feature to determine if an object they already have stored is up to date, and may still have future value. This feature allows the cache to ask the server to only send the object if it has been modified recently. This reduces network and server load, but may not speed up responses, because the requests and responses still have to traverse the network. The request header includes the If-modified-since field and might look like:

```
GET /index.html HTTP/1.1
Host: www.content-networking.com
User-Agent: Mozilla/6.0
Accept: text/html, image/gif, image/jpeg
If-Modified-Since: Mon, 29 Sep 2003 01:10:42
```

If the requested object has not been modified since the specified time, the server responds with only the header. The header specifies response code 304, indicating that the requested object has not been modified "since" and includes the reply date and no body.

```
HTTP/1.1 304 Not Modified
Date: Fri, 01 Oct 2003 04:29:01 GMT
Server: Apache/1.3.12 (Unix)
```

The conditional GET is one example of cache content validation. The next section describes cacheability considerations in more detail, describing when to store an object and when a stored object can be used to respond to a request.

3.4   **Cacheability Considerations**

Section 13 of RFC 2616, the HTTP 1.1 protocol specification, describes caching considerations in detail. The protocol includes a number of features intended to make caches work as well as possible, maintaining content accuracy while speeding up access and reducing network traffic. These features include server-specified expiration times, validation features, and the Cache-Control header directives.

3.4.1 Expiration

Servers can assist cache operation by specifying the expiration times for objects using either the `Expires` header or the `max-age` directive of the `Cache-Control` header. The `Expires` header specifies the time and date when the object is considered stale. This is like the freshness date on a container of milk. The `max-age` directive specifies how many more seconds the object can be considered fresh. They are similar because `max-age` provides a relative time and `Expires` provides an absolute time when the object expires. Because the `Expires` header relies on accurate clock synchronization between the cache and the server, the `max-age` directive is preferred.

Unfortunately content providers don't use the `Expires` header very often. Server administrators may not be aware of the feature, or may not know how to use it effectively. It may be difficult to predict when an object will become obsolete. For example, it is impossible to predict when a news headline will arrive and make the previous information out-of-date. However, some timely objects such as stock quotes or weather reports can have a planned currency period, where they are scheduled to expire and be replaced every 15 minutes, for example. Some content providers always include an `Expires` header set to the current date and time to defeat caches and force requests to always go to the origin server. Later in this chapter we will see how this can be useful in obtaining accurate statistics about each user request.

Since origin servers do not always provide explicit expiration times, caches may assign expiration times using heuristic algorithms that use other header values (such as the `Last-Modified` time) to estimate a plausible expiration time. For example, it is likely that documents that have not changed for a long time are unlikely to change soon. Using a simple 50% rule, a cache may estimate that a document that was last modified 10 days ago will stay current for another 5 days. Heuristic algorithms are not always accurate, and this can cause stale objects to be served from a cache. Attempts to standardize these heuristic rules have not attracted much interest.

Invalidation contracts are a proposed approach to server management of cached object expiration. In this plan, the server provides each cache that stores its content with a specific expiration date and time for that content. The server also keeps track of all of the caches it has contracted with. If the server modifies an object before that expiration date, the server contacts each cache to notify it of the early expiration of the object. Each cache then invalidates the content.

3.4.2 Validation

The validation features of the HTTP protocol allow a cache to determine if a stored object is equivalent to the object with the same URI available from the origin server. The `Last-Modified` entity-header field is the most often used cache validator. This works together with the `If-Modified-Since` request header directive to create the conditional `GET` feature, as was described in Section 3.3.2. Another validator is the entity tag (`Etag`) response-header field. This allows the content of a named object to be uniquely identified (tagged), and is similar to a checksum or version identifier. This allows more reliable validation than the `Last-Modified` field in situations where modification dates are not suitable. The server is responsible for changing the `Etag` whenever the object content changes. The `If-Match` request-header field is used to make the `GET` request conditional on the value of the `Etag`. The server responds with the new object only if the `Etag` has changed.

3.4.3   Cache-Control Directives

The `Cache-Control` header field allows the client and server to provide specific directions to the cache regarding their preferences for storing or retrieving cached objects. Cache *request directives* appear in the header of requests from the client to the cache. They are

- `Cache-Control: no-cache`—Do not use a cached object to satisfy this request before successfully revalidating the content.
- `Cache-Control: no-store`—Do not store any portion of this request or its response object, perhaps because it is private or privileged information. This differs from `no-cache` because it directs that the objects are never to be copied to durable storage media, such as disk or back-up tape.
- `Cache-Control: max-age=delta-seconds`—Indicates that the client is willing to accept a response whose age is no greater than the specified time in seconds. Note that setting `max-age=0` requires the cache to perform an end-to-end revalidation, confirming with the origin server that the object is still up-to-date. This differs from `Cache-Control: no-cache` if the cache confirms locally that the stored object has not yet aged beyond `delta-seconds`.
- The client can use the `Cache-Control: min-fresh` directive when the client wants a response that will still be fresh for at least the specified number of seconds. Using the `Cache-Control: max-stale` directive indicates that the client is willing to accept a response that has exceeded its expiration time.
- `Cache-Control: no-transform`—This directive forbids the cache from responding with an object that was compressed or transformed in any way before it was stored.
- `Cache-Control: only-if-cached`—Return only those responses that the cache currently has stored. Do not reload or revalidate with the origin server. This may be useful in some cases, such as during extremely poor network connectivity.

Cache *response directives* appear in the header of responses sent from the server to the cache. They are:

- `Cache-Control: public`—The cache is encouraged to store this object.
- `Cache-Control: private`—Indicates that all or part of the response is intended for a single user and must not be cached by a shared cache.

- `Cache-Control: no-cache`—Do not use this object to satisfy any future requests before successfully revalidating the content.
- `Cache-Control: no-store`—Do not store a copy of this object, perhaps because it includes private or privileged information.
- `Cache-Control: no-transform`—This directive forbids the cache from modifying the object in any way (such as compressing the object or using any other transformation on it) before it is forwarded or stored.
- `Cache-Control: must-revalidate`—The cache, whether shared or non-shared, must not use the entry after it becomes stale to respond to any request without first revalidating it with the origin server.
- `Cache-Control: proxy-revalidate`—This is important for the operation with shared caches of HTTP authentication applications such as those described in the User Authentication section accompanying Figure 2.8. It has the same meaning as `must-revalidate`, except that it does not apply to non-shared user-agent caches. This allows the user's local cache to operate as described in Chapter 2, while requiring shared caches to revalidate and trigger the authorization mechanism for each new user. When using this directive the server allows the non-shared user agent cache to automatically reconfirm the user's credentials while requiring the shared network cache to reconfirm the validity of the object with the server each time it is used in a response. This is essential to ensure that a shared cache does not deliver content from password-protected sites to unauthorized users. Whenever an origin server distributes such an object, it includes a `Cache-Control: proxy-revalidate` directive in the response. A shared cache is allowed to store the object only if it also includes the `public` cache control directive, but it has to mark it with `proxy-revalidate`. Later, when a request for the object arrives, the shared cache sends a conditional `GET` to the origin server. If the conditional `GET` includes a valid `Authorization` header, the origin server responds with `304 Not Modified` and the cache forwards the object to the client. However, if the conditional `GET` does not include valid authorization, the origin server responds with `401 Authorization Required` which the cache forwards to the client. This forces the client to enter the requested authorization information, such as a valid password. Problems can occur when a cache is installed if the origin server has not properly used the `proxy-revalidate` directive. If the origin server neglects this directive it is possible for password-protected pages to be served from the cache. Users may be quick to blame the cache, even though the error is in the origin server's failure to use this directive.
- `Cache-Control: max-age=delta-seconds`—This provides an alternative to the `Expires` header for allowing the server to specify an object expiration time. The response becomes stale `max-age` seconds after its most recent validation, which may be when it is originally stored, or some later revalidation. A related directive, `s-maxage`, overrides the maximum age specified by either the `max-age` directive or the `Expires` header for a shared cache, but not for a private cache.

3.5   Placing a Cache in the Network

Shared network caches can be located in one of three positions in the network. A *forward proxy* acts on behalf of a specific group of content consumers. A *reverse proxy,* also called a *server accelerator*, acts on behalf of the origin server and helps a specific group of servers deliver content. An *interception proxy* serves the network traffic directed to it. These are each described more fully in the following sections.

3.5.1   Forward Proxy

Most Web browsers support the use of a forward proxy. If your network administrator has installed a forward proxy it is easy and instructive to examine the network proxy settings in Internet Explorer. The example given here is for IE Version 6 but is similar for other browsers. In the browser select Tools / Internet Options / Connections / LAN Settings. In the dialog box that appears, check "use a proxy server for your LAN" and then click on the "Advanced" button. This opens the "Proxy Settings" dialog. In the HTTP row, enter the IP address, either as a host name or numeric IP address, of the forward proxy. Enter the port number (the number assigned by the network operator for proxy use), perhaps 8080 or 8000. Now, every user request will be sent to the forward proxy, rather than directly to the origin server.

Referring to Figure 3.2 we can follow an example forward proxy installation used to improve content delivery for a workgroup or enterprise. In this example the Chemistry Department at State University has installed a forward caching proxy and assigned it the IP address of proxy.stateu.edu.[2] Following the example in the previous paragraph each of the department members has configured their Web browsers to use proxy.stateu.edu as their HTTP proxy.

1. Professor C requests the Web page `index.html` from the Web server www.content-networking.com. Because a proxy is configured, the Web browser creates the HTTP request using the absolute URI form (see RFC 2616, Section 5.1.2). It might look like this:

   ```
   GET http://www.content-networking.com/index.html HTTP/1.1
   Host: www.content-networking.com
   User-Agent: Mozilla/6.0
   Accept: text/html, image/gif, image/jpeg
   ```

   This request is then sent over the workgroup Local Area Network to the IP address of the forward proxy (proxy.stateu.edu), *not* to the origin Web

---

[2]Actual IP addresses are always numeric, in the form of 1.2.3.4. The string "proxy.stateu.edu" is actually a symbolic host name, and not an IP address. However, we use this shorthand form throughout the text whenever the context of the host name is more important than the value of the IP address. Chapter 5 describes in detail how host names are resolved to one or more IP addresses.

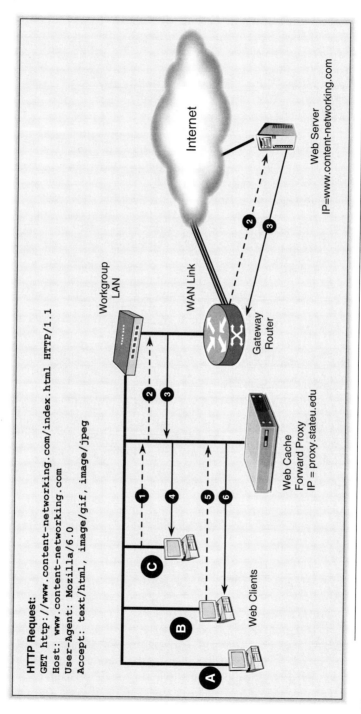

HTTP Request:
GET http://www.content-networking.com/index.html HTTP/1.1
Host: www.content-networking.com
User-Agent: Mozilla/6.0
Accept: text/html, image/gif, image/jpeg

Figure 3.2 State University Chemistry Department. An example of forward proxy installation.

server. When the Web cache receives the request, it examines its object store and determines that the requested object is not stored.

2. The Web cache requests the `index.html` page from the Web server by forwarding the original client request. The request is directed through the gateway router and then across the wide area Internet to the Web server with an IP address of www.content-networking.com.

3. The Web server responds to the Web cache with the requested page. The Web cache then stores a copy of the object, and

4. The Web cache responds to Professor C's workstation with the requested page where the browser displays it and the professor can view it.

5. Some time later Professor B requests the same Web page. As in step 1 above, the request is sent to the forward proxy. This time the Web cache examines its object store and determines that the requested object is stored and up-to-date. The Web cache retrieves that object from its local store.

6. The Web cache responds to workstation B with the requested page. No traffic has to go outside of the workgroup Local Area Network to fulfill Professor B's request.

The forward proxy provides the workgroup members with several advantages. Because they work together, it is likely that they have common interests and visit several of the same Web sites. This increases the probability that browsing by one member of the group will load the cache with content relevant to other members of the group. This increases the probability of a cache hit. In the case of a cache hit, all of the network traffic is on the LAN, where it is fast and inexpensive. This reduces the traffic over the slower and more expensive wide area connection. The forward proxy is easy to install. It can be placed anywhere on the workgroup LAN and assigned an IP address. Once this address is known, any workgroup member who wants to take advantage of it can configure their browser to identify it as the HTTP proxy. The only disadvantage is that the users have to manually configure their browsers to identify the proxy, and non-members who know the address of an unsecured proxy can get a free ride. Security mechanisms should be used to minimize unauthorized use.

3.5.2 Reverse Proxy

Referring to Figure 3.3 we can follow an example reverse proxy (also known as a *server accelerator* or *gateway*) installation used to improve content delivery from a content provider site. In this example the content-networking.com content provider installed a reverse proxy to improve the operation of their server farm. The reverse proxy is assigned the IP address of www.content-networking.com so that traffic over the Internet destined for their Web site will resolve to the proxy, rather than their servers. Each server is assigned an IP address such as s1.content-networking.com so the reverse proxy can directly address it.

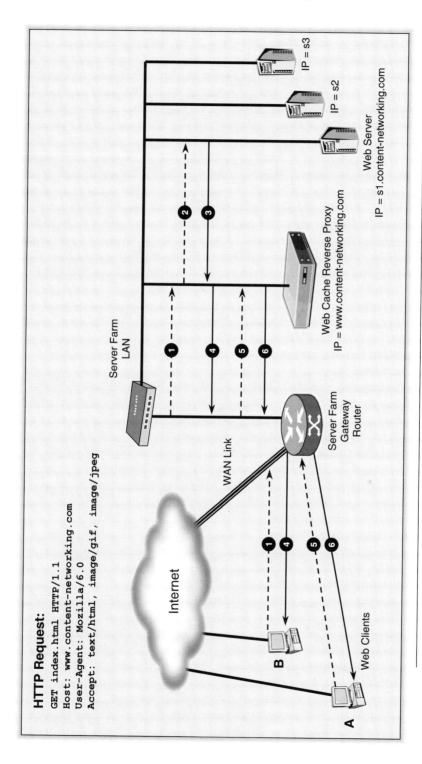

HTTP Request:

```
GET index.html HTTP/1.1
Host: www.content-networking.com
User-Agent: Mozilla/6.0
Accept: text/html, image/gif, image/jpeg
```

Figure 3.3 Content networking server farm. An example of reverse proxy installation.

1. The user at workstation B requests the Web page `index.html` from the Web server www.content-networking.com. The request is routed across the Internet and arrives at the Web cache reverse proxy assigned the IP address of www.content-networking.com. When the Web cache receives the request, it examines its object store and determines that the requested object is not stored.

2. The Web cache requests the `index.html` page from one of the Web servers. The cache can use one of several algorithms to choose the server. These algorithms are designed to balance network or server traffic, speed responses, or segregate content types. Server selection algorithms are covered in depth in Chapter 5. The request is directed across the server farm Local Area Network to a Web server with an IP address of s1.content-networking.com.

3. The Web server responds to the Web cache with the requested page. The Web cache then stores a copy of the object.

4. The Web cache responds across the Internet to workstation B with the requested page where the browser displays it and the user can view it.

5. Sometime later a user at workstation A requests the same Web page. As in step 1 above, the request is sent across the Internet to the reverse proxy. This time the Web cache examines its object store and determines that the requested object is stored. The Web cache retrieves that object from its local store.

6. The Web cache responds across the Internet to workstation A with the requested page. No traffic has to go to the Web server to fulfill user A's request.

The reverse proxy gives the content provider several advantages. The proxy greatly reduces the traffic load on the origin servers. Since the full extent of the content of all the site's origin servers is limited, the probability of a cache hit is quite large. This enables the servers to be optimized for creating and editing content, rather than for serving heavy volumes of traffic to the network. It also improves the scalability of the site. If the traffic to the site increases, more server accelerators can be added to handle the load. This may be more convenient than adding origin servers. Also, the origin servers can be located remotely from the server accelerator. This allows the flexibility of locating the reverse proxy near the customers while locating the origin servers near the content authors. The disadvantage is that the performance savings might not be great. The wide area network traffic is not reduced, and the Web cache has to have good performance to provide a significant advantage over an origin server.

3.5.3   Interception Proxy

Referring to Figure 3.4 we can follow an example interception proxy installation used to improve content delivery from an Internet service provider. In this example the ISP installed an interception proxy to improve service to their cus-

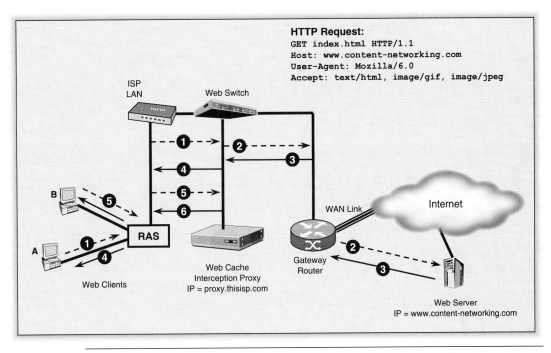

Figure 3.4 Internet service provider. An example of interception proxy installation.

tomers while reducing the traffic they receive across the wide area connection to the Internet. Key to the operation of an interception proxy is the installation and configuration of a Web switch, although some routers can be configured to steer traffic directly to an interception proxy. The purpose of the switch is to direct HTTP traffic to the Web cache. This is done by placing the switch on the LAN between the Remote Access Server (RAS) and the gateway router and configuring the switch to intercept traffic on port 80 and send it to the IP address of the Web cache. Controversy over the use of interception proxies is discussed in Section 5.2.6. The operation of Web switches is discussed in detail in Chapter 5.

1. User A requests the Web page `index.html` from the Web server www.content-networking.com. At the ISP the Web switch intercepts this request and directs it to the Web cache. This request is then sent over the ISP Local Area Network to the IP address of the interception proxy proxy.thisisp.com, *not* directly to the gateway router. When the Web cache receives the request, it examines its object store and determines that the requested object is not stored.
2. The Web cache requests the `index.html` page from the Web server. The request is directed through the ISP's gateway router and then across the

Internet to the Web server indicated by the HOST header, if present. In this case the host is www.content-networking.com.

3. The Web server responds to the Web cache with the requested page. The Web cache then stores a copy of the object, and

4. The Web cache responds to workstation A with the requested page where the browser displays it and user A can view it.

5. Sometime later user B requests the same Web page. As in step 1 above, the request is sent through the Web switch to the Web cache. This time the Web cache examines its object store and determines that the requested object is stored. The Web cache retrieves that object from its local store.

6. The Web cache responds to User B with the requested page. No traffic has to go over the wide area network toward the Internet from the ISP Local Area Network to fulfill User B's request.

The interception proxy gives the ISP operator and their customers several advantages. Cache hits are delivered to the customer quickly, without encountering delays while traveling across the network to origin servers. Customers often choose an ISP located close by, so the total network distance traveled can be significantly reduced. Also, the delays caused by busy origin servers are avoided. Perhaps the biggest savings, however, is the reduced need for wide area bandwidth connecting the ISP with content providers. Figure 3.5 shows a graph of the traffic from an actual ISP running an interception proxy. The graph was recorded using MRTG [OeRa1] and the horizontal axis is labeled with the time of day. The jagged black line shows the ISP traffic delivered to the content consumers. The solid gray area shows the ISP traffic from the content providers. The difference in these two traffic levels is accounted for by cache hits and is a direct measure of reduced network traffic. For example, at 17:00 (5:00 p.m.) the customer traffic was approximately 4 Mbits per second and the WAN traffic was less than 1 Mbits per second. This is significant because it allows the ISP to defer the purchase of additional WAN lines. They have traded the capital expense of the purchase of the Web cache for the ongoing operational expense of leasing a high-speed transmission line.

The disadvantage of an interception proxy is the added expense and complexity introduced by the Web switch and modification of the protocol running between the client and server. The Web switch can complicate certain authorization schemes that rely on the actual IP address of either a client or a content provider. The interception proxy can modify server-generated error messages. Finally, while introducing a single Web switch can introduce a single point of failure, a well-designed Web switching configuration can provide load balancing and increase reliability of the installation. This is discussed further in Chapter 5.

An interception proxy located at the WAN gateway of an enterprise, such as a university campus or office building, combines the advantages of an interception proxy with those of a forward proxy. Combinations of these three basic

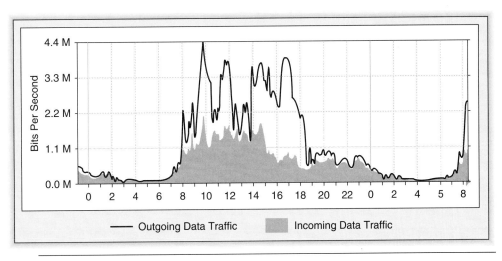

Figure 3.5 An example of ISP traffic.

topologies provide improvements in several areas. The next section explores interconnecting groups of Web caches into chains and networks.

3.6 The Evolution of Caching Systems—Networks of Caches

If you are home baking a cake and run out of milk, you can ask a neighbor for a cup of milk, or you can go to the store to buy some. Depending on how far it is to the store; how far it is to your neighbor's house; and how likely it is that your neighbor will be home, have fresh milk, and be willing to give you a cup; it may be faster to go directly to the store. People who design and configure Web caches face a similar decision between two uncertain options. The first option is to assume no accessible cache has the object, and to go directly to the origin server. The second option is to assume an accessible cache has the object, and to take the time to locate this cache and retrieve the object. Depending on which assumption is true, the networking is either saving time or wasting time.

The network infrastructure of the Internet is primarily hierarchical, as is shown abstractly in Figure 3.6. Local networks connect to regional networks that connect to national networks that are interconnected around the world. Peer connections and high usage routes also interconnect networks at various levels throughout the Internet. Several Web caches are typically located within each network at each level of the hierarchy. With many Web caches operating in the network, it is important when a cache receives a request for an object that it does not have in its store to consider if the cache should request the object from the origin server or from another cache.

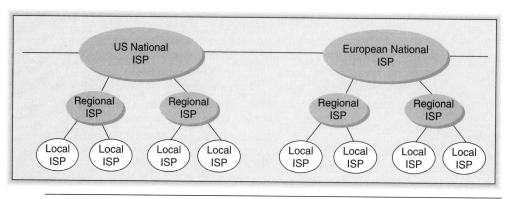

Figure 3.6 Hierarchical structure of the Internet.

In the previous section we have seen that ISP operators may have installed interception proxies in their networks and content providers may have installed reverse proxies in front of their origin servers. Consequently, a cache may obtain content from another cache operating within the network without any management of requests from one cache to another.

3.6.1 Chaining

A cache that supports chaining can be configured to request objects from another cache, rather than from an origin server. Typically these Web caches will be arranged to form a chain up through the network hierarchy. Upon a miss, the local cache will request the object from a regional cache, which might then request from a national cache. This is like asking your neighbor to borrow a cup of milk, who then asks his neighbor, before eventually finding out neither friend has any to lend you. You *might* save a trip to the store, but you will *certainly* spend time talking to your neighbor. This configuration increases the likelihood of a cache hit, but increases the time to serve the client's request. It also does not take advantage of content stored by peer caches.

Arranging caches into a cooperative network may solve these problems, as described in the next section.

3.6.2 Networking

The Internet Cache Protocol (ICP) [RFC 2186, RFC 2187], is intended as a fast way to discover which Web cache has a certain object stored. Caches exchange ICP queries and replies to learn what cache, if any, is most likely to have the object. In a second message a HTTP request is sent to the identified cache to retrieve the object. This simple protocol is typically implemented over UDP to speed queries and minimize traffic.

Although it is not specified by the protocol itself, caches implementing the protocol typically provide several helpful configuration features. Caches can be identified as either *siblings* or *parents*. The essential difference between a parent and sibling is that on a cache MISS from the neighbor the protocol specifies the object may only be subsequently fetched from a parent and not a sibling. As an optimization, caches will only send requests for cacheable objects to its neighbors. The local cache handles requests for non-cacheable objects directly. As a security measure, and to keep from overloading certain caches, caches can implement access control lists to limit the caches it will respond to.

Figure 3.7 illustrates a typical use of the ICP protocol.

1. The client sends an HTTP request to the local cache to obtain a particular object. In this example the local cache does not have the object stored.
2. Using ICP the local cache sends an ICP_OP_QUERY message to each cache configured as its siblings. Another strategy would be to query all of the neighbors, including the parents.
3. Each sibling cache responds with an ICP_OP_HIT message, an ICP_OP_MISS message, some type of error message, or no timely response. If any sibling responds with a HIT message, the local cache would then send an HTTP request message to this cache, requesting the object. It is sensible to choose the *first* cache to reply with a HIT for the subsequent retrieval request. This rapid response may indicate that the cache is close by on the network, the path is not congested, and the cache is not overloaded. In our example, we are assuming that none of the responses indicated a hit. This may be because the response indicated

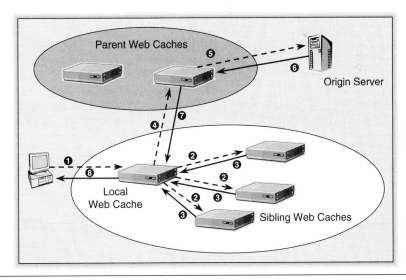

Figure 3.7 Using the ICP protocol.

a `MISS,` or an error, or because the local cache timed out waiting for a response.

4. Because the object is not available from any sibling, the local cache requests the object from a cache configured as a parent. It can make the HTTP request directly to the parent, and expect the parent to retrieve it from the origin server, if the parent does not have it cached already. Alternatively, the local cache could send an `ICP_OP_QUERY` message to each parent in an attempt to identify a parent that has the object stored. This would have to be followed by the actual HTTP request to a parent responding with a `HIT`. Another strategy would be for the local cache to send its HTTP request directly to the origin server. This reduces traffic to the parent, but also denies the parent the opportunity to fetch and store a copy of this object. It is also possible to query the parents at the same time the siblings are queried.

5. If the parent cache has the object stored, it would retrieve it and respond to the local cache. In this example, we are assuming the parent cache does not have a local copy. In this case it sends an HTTP request to the origin server.

6. The origin server replies to the parent cache with the requested object. The parent cache stores a copy.

7. The parent cache replies to the local cache with the requested object. The local cache stores a copy.

8. The local cache replies to the client with the requested object.

It is not guaranteed that use of ICP or any cache networking arrangement results in faster responses to the user or decreased network traffic. Only traffic analysis or careful measurement and experimentation with various network configurations can identify the best configuration for any particular situation.

3.6.3   Satellite-Based Web Caching

Combining the capabilities of satellite transmission with Web caching can turn the network inside out in this innovative architecture.

In this proposed content delivery network, each local ISP has a cache with a conventional Internet connection, huge storage capacity, and a satellite dish for receiving content. The central site has a conventional Internet connection and a satellite transmitter. There are no intermediate regional or national caches in the network.

When a user request generates a miss at some local cache, that local cache obtains the requested document from the origin server using HTTP over a conventional Internet connection. After responding to the user request, the local cache then sends the URL (but not the actual documents) to the master site. The master site uses HTTP to obtain the same document from the origin server, and then transmits (pushes) the document over the satellite channel to all local caches. The local caches each receive the document and cache it. As a result, the user populations at each of the local ISPs are aggregated together to form one very large user population. Each actual request is used to predict the future requests of the other users. The greater the user population, the greater the likelihood of repeated requests, and the greater the hit rate. High hit rates correspond to low response times and less wasted bandwidth in the Internet. This brings the Web directly to the edge of the network, trading network bandwidth for huge storage capacity at the edge. This architecture is only economical if edge storage is cheap compared to network bandwidth.

3.7 Performance

Content consumers want correct content delivered quickly. Network operators want redundant traffic reduced. Content providers want rapid access for their customers without overloading their servers. To meet these goals, it is important to understand Web cache performance when choosing a Web cache or engineering a network that includes Web caches. Relax. Predicting Web cache performance in actual operation is even easier than forecasting the weather or predicting stock market behavior!

3.7.1 Measuring Performance

Throughput is expressed in either *requests per second* or *bytes per second* and measures the total amount of traffic that can pass through a Web cache. Whether it is a hit or a miss, every request and every response passes through the Web cache. If the traffic load exceeds the throughput capacity of the cache, it will become a bottleneck on the network. Throughput measured in requests per second is limited by the processing speed of the Web cache. Throughput measured in bytes per second can be limited by the bandwidth of the network connection. Higher throughputs are better. Consider both the peak throughput numbers and the sustained throughput when selecting a Web cache or engineering a network.

Response time measures the interval from when a client makes a request until the client begins to receive the response from the Web cache. In the case of a hit, this measures the speed of the cache in retrieving and responding with the object. In the case of a miss, this includes the time for the origin server to respond to the request. The miss response time can only be assessed if the response time of the origin server is known. Lower response times are better. When evaluating a cache, consider the distribution of response times, including the lowest, average, and longest times.

Hit ratio measures the fraction of traffic that is served from the Web cache. It can be measured in either transactions or bytes. This is a direct measure of the network traffic savings provided by the cache. The transaction hit ratio compares the number of requests resulting in hits to the total number of requests. For example, if 40 requests out of 100 are served from the cache local store, the hit ratio is 40%. The bandwidth hit ratio compares the total number of bytes from responses resulting from hits to the total number of bytes from all responses from the Web cache. For example, if 40 Mbytes of responses are served from the cache local store out of a total of 100 Mbytes of responses, the bandwidth hit ratio is 40%. The hit ratio is most accurately defined as the ratio of client-side traffic to the server-side traffic measured with a representative traffic mix over an extended period of time. The transaction hit ratio is the probability that the requested object is marked cacheable multiplied by the probability that the Web cache is able to store that object. The first probability varies greatly with the workload. The second depends on the size of the object store and the replacement strategy being used. For a given workload, higher hit ratios are better. For example, if 100 requests are made and only 80 of these requests are for objects marked cacheable, and only 40 of those are stored in the local cache, then the transaction hit ratio is 40%.

Other Web cache selection factors include price, reliability, recovery from failures, and total object store size. Throughput normalized by price, for example hits per second per $1,000, can give a rough estimate of Web cache cost effectiveness. This is important to help assess the tradeoff between spending money for an expensive high performance hardware platform, or for better designed caching software.

Most of these parameters will vary greatly as the workload the cache is subjected to varies. The people of The Measurement Factory (www.measurement-factory.com) have worked for several years to provide tools for accurately measuring Web cache performance with realistic workloads. Their Web Polygraph performance measurement tool (www.web-polygraph.org) provides rigorous performance tests and is freely available. They have organized several industry events, called "cache offs," where Web cache venders have the performance of their products rigorously measured and the results published.

Several performance characteristics are important when evaluating a cache. These include throughput, response time, and hit ratio. The importance of each factor will vary based on user, network provider, and content provider needs. It is also important to consider manageability, reliability, and support in evaluating a Web cache.

3.7.2   Estimating Hit Ratios

In engineering a network, it is important to be able to estimate the savings a Web cache can provide. The actual hit ratio of a Web cache depends on many variables of the workload and of the cache design itself. These factors include the number of objects available on the Internet, the size of the cache object store, the average size of an object, the expiration time of an object, the fraction of objects that can be accurately cached (cacheability), and the popularity distribution of objects on the Internet. Although this list is long, reasonable assumptions can reduce hit ratio estimation to a relatively simple calculation.

Internet content objects vary greatly in size. The smaller an object is, the more objects can be stored in a given cache. Although the average object size on the Internet is not well known, an estimate of 5 KB is reasonable. A cache with an object store of 32GB can store approximately 6.7 million such objects.

The total number of objects making up the worldwide Internet is very large, growing, and not accurately known. In analyzing cache performance what is important is the size of the *interest set*. This is the total collection of objects that the user community will ever request. This is much smaller that the total Internet.

Obviously some Internet objects are requested much more often than others. The Yahoo! logo is requested millions of times a day. Many fewer people visit this author's homepage. Attempts to model this popularity distribution have focused on two probability distributions. The *uniform distribution* assumes that each object is equally likely to be requested. This simple assumption is not accurate. Another distribution, called the *Zipf distribution*, named for Harvard linguistic professor George Kingsley Zipf, can provide a more realistic model. A Zipf distribution is one where the probability of selecting the ith most popular item is proportional to $1/i$ [Li99, Knu73].

The class of Zipf-like distributions model the frequency of occurrence of some event, (P), as a function of the rank (i), as a power-law function $P_i \sim 1/i^\alpha$ with the exponent α close to unity. Studies suggest that the popularity distribution of the Internet can be accurately modeled by a Zipf-like distribution with the exponent α in the range of 0.5 to 0.7. [BCP+98] An approximation of the sum of the first n elements of the distribution can be shown to be

$$\sum_{i=1}^{n} 1/i^\alpha \approx \int_1^n 1/x^\alpha \, dx = \frac{x^{(1-\alpha)}}{(1-\alpha)} = \frac{n^{(1-\alpha)}}{(1-\alpha)} \; for \; \alpha < 1 \, [\text{Bea1}]$$

Taking the ratio of this term to the total number of objects in the interest set gives the probability that an object selected will be one of the n most popular. Note that this collapses to the uniform distribution when $\alpha = 0$.

This provides a simple formula for computing Web cache hit ratio. The probability of selecting any one of the k objects from population of n objects, representing a cache storing k items from an Internet of n objects is simply

$$k^{(1-\alpha)}/n^{(1-\alpha)} = (k/n)^{(1-\alpha)} \; for \; \alpha < 1$$

The formula assumes that all requested objects are cacheable. This is not realistic, and the result has to be reduced by the cacheability fraction. It also ignores the effects of traffic to revalidate objects and refresh expired objects. This formula is relatively insensitive to assumptions about the total number of

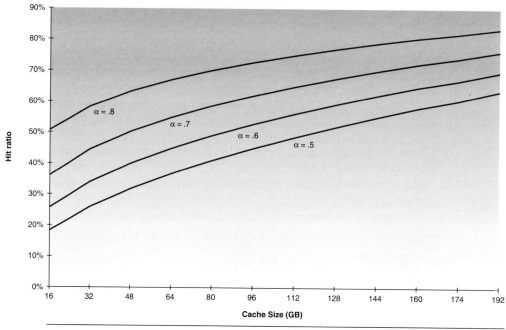

Figure 3.8 Hit ratios for particular Zipf-like distributions.

objects making up the Internet. Figure 3.8 shows the probability of a cache hit as a function of cache object size for several choices of α, assuming that the Internet has one hundred million objects in the interest set, the average object size is 5 KB, and all objects are cacheable. Higher values of α, perhaps 0.7 or 0.8, correspond to users with common interests. Workgroups or people at a particular enterprise location may have this popularity distribution. Lower numbers of α, perhaps 0.5 or 0.6, correspond to less common interest. This may be accurate for ISP users served by a interception Web cache. In any case, the result read from the graph has to be reduced by the cacheability percentage.

3.8 **Caching Challenges and Myths**

The Internet is remarkably diverse and unpredictable. This creates several challenges for people who design and operate caches in real world networks and expect them to work reliably. Dynamic content, secure transactions, encrypted content, cookies, hit counters, on-line advertisements, access control, and privacy-concerned users, are several of the conditions that have to be considered.

3.8.1 **Avoiding Snags**

If content providers were careful to mark all content using accurate cache control directives many problems could be avoided. However, ours is not a perfect world and not all dynamic content is clearly identified by the `Cache-Control` header information. The output of CGI, PHP, and ASP scripts almost always represent dynamic content. However, the server may not have marked it as `no-cache` or `no-store`. To preserve content transparency, the cache has to implement rules that prevent this dynamic content from being cached.

Secure transactions and encrypted content are private. As was described in Section 2.2.6, the URL and the HTTP headers are encrypted in secure, SSL-based transactions. This means that the entire transaction, including the `Cache-Control` header is unintelligible to the cache, and cannot be usefully cached.

Section 2.2.5 described how the cookie mechanism is used to create an association between related transactions of a particular user in a stateless protocol. For cookies to be effective the information in the `Cookie` header field of outgoing requests has to be forwarded to the server. The shared cache cannot reuse the cookie. This makes it difficult or impossible for the request to be terminated by an intermediary, and, therefore, it cannot be completely handled by the shared cache.

For server-side hit counters, pay-per-click mechanisms, banner advertisements, and usage monitoring to work correctly, the origin server has to get accurate information about content requests. Often these counts are used to charge for advertising exposure, or to profile customer interest in particular content. They are important and content providers expect them to be accurate. If the content is cached, the requests will not get to the server, and the counts will be low. Also, information about the source of the request, such as the requesters' network location, time of day, and referring page, is available to the cache but not to the origin server. There are a few solutions to this problem. One simple solution is to mark the pages being counted as `no-cache.` This results in correct counts, but reduces the savings provided by the cache. A refinement of this approach is to include a very small object, perhaps a one-pixel transparent graphic, in each page to be counted. This small object is marked as `no-cache` and the server can accurately count requests for it while the rest of the page is cached.

Unfortunately use of these small uncacheable objects has attracted enough attention to earn the pejorative label of "Web bugs." Many users object to them because they generate traffic and delays primarily for the purpose of gathering user information. Also, some of these bugs are used to collect information users consider private. It is difficult to balance the diversity of interests in every content delivery system design.

An alternative solution is to make use of transaction logs generated directly by the Web cache. Because every request and response goes through the Web cache, it can keep a log of each transaction. This log might include the client IP address, username, time and date, the HTTP request header, HTTP response status code, content length, whether the request was handled from the cache or the origin server, and other pertinent information. The log itself can be transmitted to the content provider for analysis, or the Web cache operator can analyze the log and transmit reports to the content provider. Such a log provides important information to the operators of the Web cache and the network it is a part of. The logs can grow quickly in size. If the Web cache is handling 500 requests a second, and each log entry is 256 bytes, then 7.5 megabytes of information is being logged each minute of operation.

Previously we mentioned the use of heuristics to estimate the expiration time of objects. Other heuristics are used to identify non-cacheable dynamic content. Poor design of these heuristics can increase hit ratio statistics at the cost of delivering stale or private content. It is helpful to keep caching accuracy in mind when evaluating hit ratios advertised by various caching vendors. The Web polygraph, mentioned previously, can help assess Web cache performance under realistically simulated workloads.

Some content providers restrict access to their content based on the client's network address or other client identification. The Web cache masks this information, and the origin server sees the IP address of the Web cache, not the original requester. Moving the access control to the Web cache can solve this problem. An alternative solution, involving programming of the Web switch, is to bypass the Web cache for such traffic. This is discussed more fully in Chapter 5.

Some individuals are especially concerned about their privacy and object to any intermediary that is storing information in the path connecting their client to the origin servers they are accessing. A Web cache may need to implement bypass management features that allow the administrator to exclude these users from obtaining caching services.

3.8.2 Caching Myths

Several fads have swept through the caching industry. Most of them are based on fallacies and readily disputed myths about management of cache operations. These myths include *prefetching, push technology,* and replacement management strategies such as *pin-in-cache* directives.

Prefetching describes a strategy where the cache is loaded with specific content *before* the first user requests it. Push technology is a form of prefetching where the origin server, or some content management system, determines what content to prefetch. The premise of prefetching strategies is that rules can be established to predict what content users will request, before they actually request it. The reality of the Internet is that user behavior is very diverse. More importantly, the potential savings from prefetching are tiny, even if the strategy works as designed. Consider the case where content A is popular, and the Web cache has correctly prefetched it. The key to the analysis is recognizing that prefetching can only improve the response for the *first* user of each Web cache. If 100 users request content A from the Web cache, then only 1 in 100 benefit from the prefetching of content A. The savings diminish further for more popular objects. If the object is not popular, for example it is never requested, then the effort of the prefetching has been entirely wasted, and the cache has stored an object that is never used.

Replacement management strategies are attempts to have human operators improve on the cache replacement rules, such as those described in Section 3.3.1, for particular content. One such strategy, called "pin-in-cache," allows the operator to ensure that a particular object is not ejected from the local object store. The problem is that this feature will make it more likely that stale content is served to the clients. The `Expires` header, the last modified time, and client requests provide the cache the information it needs to effectively manage object replacement. If an object is current, and requested by clients, an up-to-date copy will be retained in the cache local store.

We have seen how storing content closer to the user can speed access and reduce network traffic. The next chapter describes approaches to caching streaming media, where the beginning of a stream needs to be accessed by a client before the entire stream is transmitted, or even created.

Readers interested in learning more about Web caching are encouraged to read *Web Caching*, written by Duane Wessles and *Web Proxy Servers*, written by Ari Luotonen [Luo 97, Wes01].

CHAPTER 4

Caching Techniques for Streaming Media

Streams are continuous. Milk arrives at your home in compact containers; however, water is delivered from the faucet in a continuous stream. Streams are extensive in length, may start and stop at any time, flow at some expected rate, are often expected to be continuous and steady, may combine several sources, and may arrive at several destinations. Important types of content, including audio programs, video programs, and real-time data streams, such as a stock ticker or telemetry monitoring applications, traverse the Internet as streams. This chapter describes protocols and caching techniques suited to the special characteristics of such streaming media.

Important research continues to address the many interesting problems that are associated with caching streaming media. The full scope of this research is too broad to be comprehensively covered in this chapter. However the chapter describes fundamental problems and basic concepts that establish the most practical solutions. Several selected techniques are described in detail because of their practical or promising importance. This background provides the foundation for understanding today's solutions and ongoing research.

After introducing the basic characteristics of streaming media, several protocols designed to meet the special needs of streaming media are described. The real-time transport protocol (RTP), the RTP control protocol (RTCP), and real-time streaming protocol (RTSP) are each described. Also, the Synchronized Multimedia Integration Language (SMIL) and several proprietary protocols are described. With this background, several approaches to caching streaming media are explained. These techniques include *fast prefix transfer*, *object segmentation*, *cache replacement*, and *dynamic caching*. The chapter ends with information from several case studies.

4.1 Streaming Media

Streaming refers to media types with time constraints and continuous data flow, such as audio or video transmissions. Playback begins while the data is being received. This is different from downloading a media file, such as an MP3 audio recording, for later playback. It is also different from a sequence of data, created perhaps by monitoring the performance of automated equipment, which is timely but does not require strict synchronization for playback. The program may be a simultaneous reception such as listening to a live radio broadcast or viewing news or sports video broadcasts. Here the content is not prerecorded and the content consumers tolerate moderate delay before the start of the stream. Live, interactive applications such as teleconferencing, audio, or video phones, and distributed multi-player games, can tolerate only minimal delays to effectively support the flow of the interactive sessions. On-demand applications allow the user to access previously stored programs, such as movies on the Internet, news archives, and video clips published on personal Web pages. Here, moderate delays are tolerated before the start of the stream, but transmission gaps or jitter is not tolerated midstream.

Multicast is often proposed as an effective solution for distributing streaming content to many widely distributed users. Portions of the IP address space known as Class D Internet addresses are dedicated to multicast use [RFC 1112]. Requirements for multicast protocols have been established, used, and refined for well over a decade [RFC 1458]. Chapter 2 describes multicast features available at several layers of the Internet protocols. Let's take a look at one search for this Holy Grail.

In the early 1990s a loosely organized group of people began the development of the MBONE, the Internet Multicast Backbone. Undaunted by the slow deployment of IP-level multicast-enabled routers in the Internet, the MBONE employed a clever workaround. This temporary solution connected islands of multicast-enabled networks by tunneling multicast packets across unicast routers. The MBONE is a virtual network formed by a set of routers that agree to forward multicast traffic on the Internet. The Unix program *mrouted* is a freely available implementation of the Distance Vector Multicast Routing Protocol (DVMRP) [RFC 1075] used by these MBONE routers. The first use of the network was an audiocast from the March 1992 IETF meeting in San Diego where live audio from several sessions was multicast to participants at 20 sites located on three continents [CD92]. Although two-way communications is possible, the network supports only a few session channels so participants have limited program choices available at any one time [Eri94]. By 1996 the network grew to include 3,000 subnets [Dee95]. Since then interest has declined due to the lack of a revenue model, narrow bandwidth of the network, the temporary nature of the workaround, limited session capability, limited administrative support for multicast capabilities in the network, and informal organization of the network administration.

The availability of the MBONE encouraged development of client programs for accessing the multimedia streams. Some of the popular, freely available programs are: [SRL98]

VAT—The Visual Audio Tool.
SDR—The Session Directory Tool is designed to allow the advertisement and joining of multicast conferences on the MBONE.

VIC—the Video Conferencing Tool implements RTP, the real-time transport protocol, described later in this chapter.
WB—the Virtual Whiteboard application used for displaying graphics.

Each of these is available for download from ftp://ftp.ee.lbl.gov/conferencing/vat/ and are described at http://www-nrg.ee.lbl.gov/vic/ except for SDR, which is available from http://www-mice.cs.ucl.ac.uk/multimedia/software/sdr/.

But as we will see in Chapter 9, revenue enables services. For this reason, the world of streaming media is presently dominated by commercial software. These include Real Networks RealOne player and Helix server software, Microsoft's Windows Media Player and NetMeeting products, and Apple's QuickTime Player.

Protocols designed to meet the special needs of streaming media are available. These protocols accommodate the real-time sensitive, packet sequence, packet loss, variable bandwidth, multireceiver, extensive, and continuous nature of various streaming media formats while reducing jitter and monitoring the performance of the network.

4.2   Protocols for Streaming Media

Although the HTTP protocol is well suited for transferring the text and images of Web pages it is not a good choice for streaming media. HTTP running over TCP enforces data integrity without regard to timeliness and is not well suited to meet the time-critical needs of multimedia. Also, HTTP couples the signaling channel with the bearer channel, reducing the flexibility of the signaling. Finally, the signaling capabilities of HTTP do not support random access or time-based access into a stream, nor precise timing control. When HTTP is used to deliver streaming media the data downloads through one application thread while another application thread begins to display what has been received. The user has very little control of the download.

Several protocols have been developed to meet the special needs of multimedia. The real-time transport protocol (RTP) and its companion, the RTP control protocol (RTCP), address the time-critical, high-bandwidth needs of multimedia. With this pair of protocols, RTP is the bearer channel and RTCP is the separate signaling channel. The real-time streaming protocol allows the familiar play, pause, and fast forward functions of a VCR, DVD, or CD player to be transmitted remotely. The Synchronized Multimedia Integration Language (SMIL) is a text-based markup language that allows multimedia streams, text, graphics, and animation to be combined, sequenced, precisely placed on the screen, and synchronized to create a rich multimedia presentation [Aya01]. Each of these protocols is described in more detail.

4.2.1   The Real-Time Transport Protocol (RTP)

Streaming media typically use the real-time transport protocol (RTP) [RFC 1889] in place of HTTP as the application transport protocol. RTP provides end-to-end network delivery services suitable for applications transmitting real-time data, such as audio, video, or simulation data, over multicast or unicast network services. The protocol services include payload-type identification, sequence numbering, timestamping, and delivery monitoring. Applications typically run RTP on top of UDP to make use of its multiplexing and checksum services, but may have to use TCP to traverse certain firewalls. Both the RTP and UDP protocols contribute parts of the transport protocol functionality. However, RTP may be used with other suitable underlying network or transport protocols. RTP supports data transfer to multiple destinations using multicast distribution if that is provided by the underlying network [RFC 1889].

RTP includes sequence numbers to allow the receiver to reconstruct the sender's packet sequence. These sequence numbers might also be used to determine the proper location of a packet, for example in video decoding, without necessarily decoding packets in sequence. The header also includes the M (marker) bit, which is designed to identify significant events in the stream, such as a frame boundary. Although RTP does not provide quality-of-service features, it does provide sufficient information to allow the client to faithfully playback the media stream.

RTP is often used in parallel with its companion signaling protocol, the RTP control protocol (RTCP). RTCP provides the sender and receiver with timely reports on the quality of service and conveys information about the participants in an on-going session. In practice, RTP is sent on an even numbered port, while the associated RTCP protocol runs on the next higher (and therefore odd) numbered port. Many applications choose to omit RTCP and tolerate the performance level and network monitoring capabilities available without it.

In a typical audio broadcast application, the audio data is sent in small chunks, perhaps representing 20 ms of real time. An RTP header precedes each chunk of audio data. This RTP header and data are encapsulated in a UDP packet. The RTP header indicates what type of audio encoding (such as PCM, ADPCM, or LPC) is contained in each packet. This may be useful in selecting the correct codec for the receiver. It may also allow senders or network providers to change the encoding format used during a conference, for example, to accommodate a new participant who is connected through a low-bandwidth link or to react to indications of network congestion.

The RTP header also contains timing information and a sequence number that allow the receivers to reconstruct the timing produced by the source. In this example, chunks of audio are played every 20 ms. This timing reconstruction is performed separately for each RTP packet source in the conference. The receiver can also use the sequence number to determine how many packets are being lost.

As participants join and leave during the conference, it is useful to know who is participating at any moment and how well they are receiving the audio data. For that purpose, the client of each conference participant periodically multicasts (on the RTCP port) a reception report identified by the name of the participant. The reception report indicates how well the current speaker is being received and may be used to control adaptive encoding. In addition to the user name, other identifying information may also be included, subject to control bandwidth limits. Finally a site sends the RTCP BYE packet when it leaves the conference.

If both audio and video media are used in a session, they are transmitted as separate RTP streams. RTCP packets are transmitted for each medium using two different UDP port pairs and/or multicast addresses. There is no direct coupling by RTP between the audio and video sessions, except that a user participating in both sessions should use the same uniquely identifying name (called a CNAME) in the RTCP packets for both streams so that the sessions can be associated. Timestamp information in the RTP packets can be used to provide synchronization when rendering the associated audio and video streams.

The Synchronization Source (SSRC) is an important concept in the RTP protocol. This 32-bit number identifies the source of each stream of RTP packets, and is carried in the RTP header. All packets from a particular synchronization source share a common time base and packet sequence, so a receiver groups packets by synchronization source for playback. Examples of synchronization sources include the sender of a stream of packets derived from a signal source such as a microphone or a camera, or an RTP mixer (see below). A synchronization source may change its data format, such as its audio encoding method, over time. If a participant generates multiple streams in one RTP session, for example from separate video cameras, each must be identified as a different SSRC.

The protocol also provides for *mixers* and *translators* to accommodate a variety of network and receiver configurations participating in a single broadcast session. A mixer resynchronizes incoming audio packets to reconstruct the constant (e.g., 20 ms) spacing generated by the sender. It then combines these reconstructed audio streams into a single stream and forwards the composite packet stream across the link. It may translate the audio encoding format to a lower-bandwidth format. The packets might be unicast to a single recipient or multicast on a different address to multiple recipients. The RTP header includes a means for mixers to identify the sources that contributed to a mixed packet so the receivers can provide the correct talker indication information. Because a mixer acts as a timing source, it writes its own SSRC identifier into each RTP packet header.

In contrast to a mixer, a translator always forwards RTP packets with their SSRC identifier intact. It may transform a stream from one audio or video encoding format to another. It may perform other transformations on the data, requiring it to regenerate packet sequence numbers, payload type, or timestamp. It may replicate from unicast to multicast and provide application-level filters to help transverse firewalls. However, it never resynchronizes packets or acts as a timing source and never regenerates synchronization source information.

Figure 4.1 illustrates an example distribution system employing five endpoints, two mixers, and one translator, each identified by their SSRC. Endpoints E1 through E4 may be microphones used by people speaking at a conference. Endpoint E5 may be the loudspeaker of a personal computer used by a remote

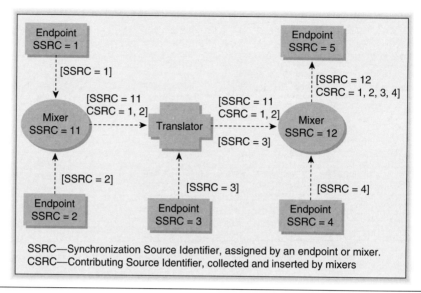

Figure 4.1 RTP mixers and translators.

user to monitor the conference proceedings. In practice, both Synchronization Source Identifiers (SSRCs) and Contributing Source Identifiers (CSRCs) are randomly chosen 32-bit numbers. For simplicity in the figure, small integers were chosen, and will be used to identify each component in the diagram. The SSRC and CSRC of the packets on each stream are indicated in square brackets next to each stream. Mixer M11 combines the streams from endpoints E1 and E2. The mixer introduces its own SSRC, but includes the original synchronization source identifiers of each endpoint as CSRCs. The translator interleaves packets derived from the mixer M11 and endpoint E3. Because the translator does not resynchronize the stream, the SSRC of each of these sources is retained. Mixer M12 combines the streams from the translator and endpoint E4. It establishes its own SSRC and now includes the CSRC from all four sources.

4.2.2   **The RTP Control Protocol (RTCP)**

The RTP control protocol (RTCP) relies on periodically transmitting control packets to all participants in the session. RTCP uses the same distribution mechanism as the related data packets, for example using UDP with separate port numbers. The primary function of RTCP is to provide feedback on the quality of the data distribution. This is an important part of RTP's role as a transport protocol and is related to the flow and congestion control functions of other transport protocols. The feedback may be directly useful for controlling codecs that can adapt to changing network conditions. In addition it is important to get feedback from the receivers to help diagnose faults in the distribution network.

Sending reception feedback reports to all participants allows anyone who is observing problems to evaluate whether those problems are local or global.

The core of the RTCP protocol is the Receiver Report (RR) packet. In addition to identifying information, each packet contains:

- the fraction of lost packets,
- the cumulative number of packets lost,
- the highest sequence number packet received,
- interarrival jitter, (an estimate of the statistical variance of the RTP data packet interarrival time),
- the identification of the last Sender Report (SR) packet received from the sender, and
- the delay since the last SR packet was received.

This information allows calculation of the packet loss rate during the interval between two reception reports. While packet loss indicates persistent congestion, the jitter field provides a short-term measure of network congestion.

With RTP and RTCP providing effective transport of multimedia streams, the work of starting, stopping, and positioning the stream is left to the real-time streaming protocol, described in the next section.

4.2.3 The Real-Time Streaming Protocol (RTSP)

Most people are familiar with using a Videocassette Recorder (VCR) or a DVD player to view movies or other video programs. Here the videotape provides the stream of video and audio information. The controls on the VCR, including start, stop, pause, fast forward, and record, are used to control when the video stream starts and stops playing. In accessing streaming media on the Internet, the RTP protocol is used to deliver the stream, analogous to the videotape. The real-time streaming protocol (RTSP) is used to select and play a stream, pause it, and stop it, analogous to the controls on the VCR [RFC 2326, RTSP].

The RTSP protocol relies on RTP to deliver the actual media streams it controls. RTSP may be transported over UDP or other protocols, but is usually transported over TCP. RTSP is intentionally similar in syntax and operation to HTTP/1.1, and it reuses HTTP concepts where it is logical. However, RTSP introduces a number of new methods and has a different protocol identifier, among other differences.

The base specification of the protocol is supplemented by a *profile* specification document for each particular application. This profile specification document defines a set of payload type codes and their mapping to payload formats (e.g., media encodings). For example, RFC 1890 defines the RTP Profile for Audio and Video Conferences, known as the AV Profile. This specifies payload type definitions for various media including 15 audio formats and a number of graphic and video formats. A profile may also define extensions or modifications to RTP that are specific to a particular class of applications. Typically an application will operate under only one profile.

RTSP provides the methods described below. For each method, its direction, either client-to-server (C→S), server-to-client (S→C) or both (C↔S), is indicated. Also, its need—Required, Recommended, or Optional—is indicated.

DESCRIBE: (C→S, Recommended) retrieves from a server the description of a presentation or media object identified by the request URL. The `Accept` header can specify the format of the description. A common format is the Session Description Protocol (SDP) [RFC 2327].

ANNOUNCE: (C↔S, Optional) The `ANNOUNCE` method serves two purposes: When sent from client to server, `ANNOUNCE` describes to the server an available presentation or media object identified by the request URL. When sent from server to client, `ANNOUNCE` updates the session description in realtime.

SETUP: (C→S, Required) The `SETUP` request for a URL specifies the transport mechanism to be used for the streamed media. This method uses the `Transport` header to specify the transport parameters acceptable to the client for data transmission. The response will contain the transport parameters selected by the server. Typically RTP is chosen and other parameters, such as the RTP profile specification, AV Profile for example, and the port numbers are provided.

PLAY: (C→S, Required) The `PLAY` method tells the server to start sending data via the mechanism specified in `SETUP`. This method, as well as the `PAUSE` method allows a `Range:` header to be included. The `Range:` header specifies the start, and optionally, the stop time, when the stream should begin playing. This can be specified in terms of Normal Play Time (NPT), SMPTE Relative Time, or absolute time. NPT is the stream position relative to the beginning of the presentation, and supports the special constant `now` to indicate the present time in a live broadcast. SMPTE Relative Time is a standard developed by the Society of Motion Picture and Television Engineers for expressing time from the start of the clip in terms of frames and subframes. Absolute time is expressed as ISO 8601 timestamps, using Coordinated Universal Time (UTC) and optionally including fractions of a second. One use of the `Range:` header might be to specify the start and end times of the sports, news, and weather segments of a broadcast stored as a single stream.

PAUSE: (C→S, Recommended) The `PAUSE` request causes the stream delivery to be interrupted (halted) temporarily. If the request URL names a stream, only playback and recording of that stream is halted. The `PAUSE` request may contain a `Range` header specifying when the stream or presentation is to be halted.

TEARDOWN: (C→S, Required) The `TEARDOWN` request stops the stream delivery for the given URL, freeing the resources, including the session identifier associated with it.

GET_PARAMETER: (C↔S, Optional) The `GET_PARAMETER` request retrieves the value of a particular parameter of the presentation or stream specified in the URL. The content of the reply and response is left to the implementation. `GET_PARAMETER` with no entity body may be used to test client or server response, like a `ping` does in ICMP.

SET_PARAMETER: (C↔S, Optional) This method requests setting the value of a parameter for a presentation or stream specified by the URL.

REDIRECT: (S→C, Optional) A `redirect` request informs the client that it must connect to another server location. It contains the mandatory header `Location`, which indicates that the client should issue requests for that URL. It may contain the parameter `Range`, which indicates when the redirection takes effect.

RECORD: (C→S, Optional) This method initiates recording a range of media data according to the presentation description.

OPTIONS: (C→S, Required, S→C is Optional) This is equivalent to the `Options` header in HTTP/1.1. It is used to request information about the communication options available on the request/response chain identified by the Request-URL.

4.2.4 Protocol Layering

Several protocols interact to deliver streaming media. The upper portion of the Internet Hourglass of protocols may look like Figure 4.2 for requesting and delivering a media stream.

Following the example of Figure 4.3 helps to tie these protocols together into a coherent media session. The example illustrates the steps required for a user to load a Web page listing audio tracks, select one track, play the track, and terminate the session.

1. The RTSP Client sends an HTTP `GET` request to a Web server to obtain information about a particular media stream or presentation. This is similar to going to the video store and asking them if they have a copy of a particular movie.
2. The Web server responds with information about the session. There are several options here. One option is for the HTTP response to identify only the URL of the media stream or streams. In this case the client can make an RTSP `DESCRIBE` request to obtain complete session information from the RTSP server. Alternatively, the Web server can respond with the complete session information.

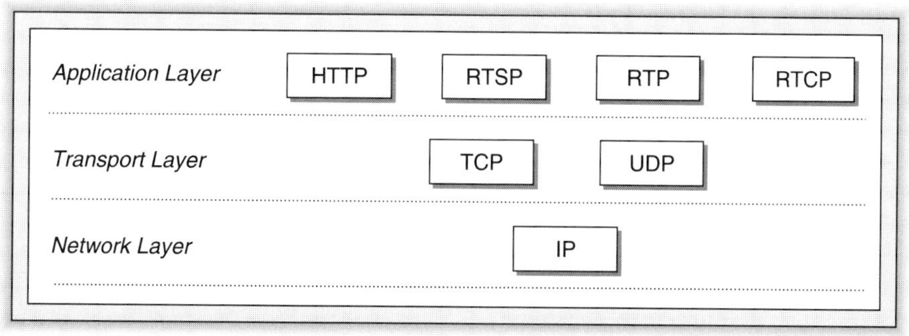

Figure 4.2 Layering of streaming protocol.

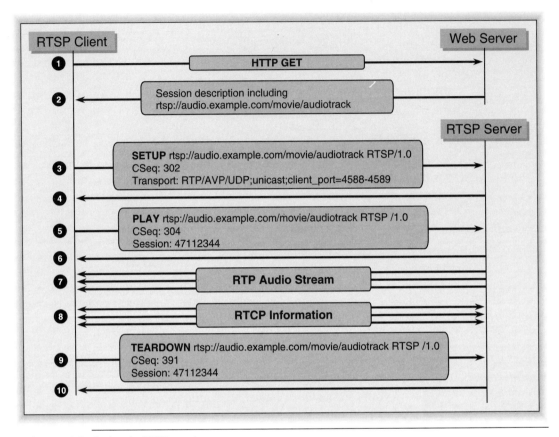

Figure 4.3 A simple RTSP session.

3. The Client sends an RTSP SETUP request to the RTSP server, indicating the URL, sequence number and transport parameters. In this example the transport is RTP, using the AV Profile, unicast over UDP on port number 4588. The associated RTCP session is on port number 4589.

4. The Server sends a response of:

```
RTSP/1.0 200 OK
CSeq:303
Date: 16 Oct 2003 15:35:06 GMT
Session: 47112344
Transport: RTP/AVP;unicast;
        client_port=4588-4589;server_port=6256-6257
```

which indicates acceptance of the request, incrementing the sequence number, assigning a session number, and announcing the server transport parameters.

5. The Client sends an RTSP PLAY request requesting that the stream start immediately from the beginning.
6. The server acknowledges the request with a response message similar to the one described in step 4.
7. The server sends a steady stream of RTP packets. This is the actual media stream.
8. RTCP information providing feedback on the quality of the data distribution are interleaved with the RTP packets. Steps 7 and 8 take place in parallel over an extended period of time, not sequentially as may be implied by the diagram. During this time the user may pause the program or move the slider to fast forward to a particular portion of the stream. In response the client will send PAUSE requests or additional PLAY requests, specifying a particular range of the stream be sent.
9. The Client sends an RTSP TEARDOWN request requesting the termination of the session.
10. The server acknowledges the request.

Freely accessible repositories providing streaming media in purely standard formats are rare on the Internet. Although many video clips are available at sites such as the multimedia archives of www.nasa.gov and www.video.com, they are not in standard formats. These files have a suffix of .ram, which is a Real Networks proprietary file type. However, if the .ram file is opened in a text editor, you can readily see the underlying RTSP request. This stream can then be directly requested using an URL beginning with rtsp://.

4.2.5 Synchronized Multimedia Integration Language (SMIL)

The protocols previously discussed provide effective mechanisms for transporting single streams from servers to clients. However, the problem of sequencing streams relative to a single time base needs to be solved. This is important for synchronizing an audio stream with an associated graphic or animation display, as one example. A presentation may consist of several streams, starting and stopping in some sequence, with some transition between clips. A presentation may include graphics or text that needs to appear and disappear at certain times, perhaps in time with music or other audio background. Finally the problem of placing the rendered image in a particular place on the screen needs to be addressed.

The Hypertext Markup Language (HTML) is the markup language used to lay out and format Web pages consisting primarily of text and static graphics. The Synchronized Multimedia Integration Language (SMIL—pronounced "smile") is an XML-based markup language that provides multimedia screen layout and timing capabilities. SMIL allows users to control spatial layout and timing sequences to create presentations including sophisticated audio, video, image, and animation features using tools as simple as a text editor [Aya01, Bul01].

In its simplest form a SMIL file lists multiple media clips played in sequence. Each media clip is identified by a Media tag, selected from the Table 4-1.

Table 4–1   SMIL media tags

Media Tag	Use
`<animation>`	Animated vector graphics or other animated format
`<audio>`	Audio clip
`<img>`	Still image, such as PNG or JPEG
`<ref>`	Generic media reference used for any clip type not covered by other attributes
`<text>`	Text file, of type .txt
`<textstream>`	Streaming text with attributes such as color, height, and clip start time
`<video>`	Video clip

The media tag identifies the actual media clip by its URL, so a simple reference to an image may look like:

```
<img src=http://www.content-networking.com/smil/hello.jpg/>
```

which is remarkably similar to the corresponding HTML tag. SMIL gets its multimedia power from its precise control of screen layout, regions, and timings.

The background screen or canvas is called the *root-layout* and its size, color and other attributes are set by a `<root-layout>` tag within a `<layout>` `</layout>` container. After defining the root-layout, individual regions of the screen, perhaps each used for a title area, a graphic image area, and a video area are defined using `<region>` tags. Each region is assigned a name, so that subsequent media tags can refer to the region in which they will be displayed.

There are three tags which control the timing of media objects within a presentation.

These timing tags are:

`<seq>`—The *sequential* tag indicates that two or more clips should be played in sequence. This is the default used if the timing container tags are omitted.

`<par>`—The *parallel* tag indicates that one or more clips share a common time base. They should be played at the same time, or begin at some offset from a common reference starting time.

`<excl>`—The *exclusive* tag indicates that only one of the media clips can be active at a time. The active tag is typically chosen using the SMIL event mechanism.

Timing is further controlled for each clip by including beginning (`begin`), duration (`dur`), and ending (`end`) time parameters in each media tag.

Example 4-1 is a SMIL program that presents "hello world" in images and audio. You can copy this example, name it `hello.smil`, and run it using an available SMIL player device. Real Networks (www.real.com) provides a free download of their RealOne Player that can render this file. Also, The Center for

Mathematics and Computer Science (CWI) in Amsterdam makes their AMBU-LANT open-source SMIL Player available from: http://www.cwi.nl/projects/Ambulant/.

```
<smil>
<head>
<layout>     <!–Create the canvas and two display regions –>
  <root-layout width="248" height="300"
              background-color="blue" />
            <region id="a" top="20" left="64" />
            <region id="b" top="120" left="20"/>
</layout>
</head>
<body>
<par>
  <img src="http://www.content-networking.com/smil/hello.jpg"
      region="a"
      begin="0s"
      dur="6s"/>   <!–Display "Hello" image now for 6 seconds –>
  <img src="http://www.content-networking.com/smil/earthrise.jpg"
      region="b"
      begin="2s"
      end="8s"/> <!–Display the "World" image after 2 seconds –>
  <audio src="http://www.content-networking.com/smil/hello.wav"
      begin="4s"/>     <!– Begin the audio after 4 seconds –>
</par>
</body>
</smil>
```

Example 4.1.   A SMIL File to present "hello world" in images and audio.

In addition to the features and tags described above, the SMIL language includes rich features for synchronization, iteration, bandwidth determination, switching between presentation formats, and transition effects between clips, color, layout, and animation.

Although these standard protocols provide many benefits, several major software providers have chosen not to use them. The next section describes why standards are sometimes ignored, and describes the status of several proprietary implementations.

4.2.6 **Proprietary Protocols**

Products based on standards are standard products, not differentiated products. Even when standard protocols provide an excellent technical solution, commercial organizations that depend on profitable revenue may choose not to use them. Product differentiation is often essential for distinguishing a product sufficiently for it to command a price high enough to be profitable. A product based entirely on standards cannot distinguish itself by the protocol features it provides. However, distinguished products based on standards can be built by paying attention to performance, ease of use, reliability, and overall value. Some people follow the bits while others follow the bucks!

Although using standard protocols would allow more rapid improvement of streaming technology, the dominant commercial companies in streaming media software began with proprietary protocols. Real Networks used their PNA—Progressive Network Architecture—in place of the RTSP standard. They used their RDT—Real Data Transport protocol—in place of the RTP standard. Microsoft used their Microsoft Media Server (MMS) proprietary protocol; however, they have included RTSP support in version 9 of their Windows Media Player.

More recently they have moved away from their proprietary protocols to embrace standard, or nearly standard, versions of the streaming protocols described above. Each provider incorporates proprietary extensions to the protocols, or includes proprietary elements in some way.

RealNetworks uses proprietary text-based .ram files to launch the RealOne Player, provide the URL of the actual RTSP file, and set parameters in the Player [Real1]. Their SureStream technology allows encoding for three different transmission bandwidths within a single file. They also support proprietary extensions to the SMIL standard, including RealPix and RealText for annotating graphics and text. Their Helix Universal Server provides support for live and on-demand delivery of major file formats, including Real Media, Windows Media, QuickTime, MPEG 4, MP3, and more.

4.3   Caching Techniques for Streaming Media

We have seen that closer is better and streams are continuous, therefore new approaches for caching streaming media are needed. Streams are generally much larger than text or graphic objects. They have important real-time and time synchronization requirements, and these requirements have led to the use of new protocols for transporting and controlling them. Storing the entire content of several long multimedia streams would quickly exhaust the storage capacity of a cache designed for static Web objects. Therefore a scalable caching solution can only store some portion of each stream. The next sections describe four techniques to enhance caching systems to better support streaming media over the Internet. These techniques are *audio/video smoothing, fast prefix transfer, object segmentation and cache replacement*, and *dynamic caching*. Each of these techniques helps shield the content consumer from the delay, throughput, and loss properties of the network path between the content server and the cache employing these techniques.

4.3.1 Audio/Video Smoothing

Bits arrive in bursts. Multimedia content is inherently bursty, even at the source. Compression techniques increase the variability. As an example, a 23-minute-long video segment of the movie, *The Wizard of Oz* was encoded in MPEG [LeG91] and analyzed frame by frame. The number of bits per frame varied greatly. The sample mean was 41.7 Kbits per frame with a standard deviation of 51.7 Kbits. The smallest frame was only 0.56 Kbits, while the largest was more than 600 times as large at 343 Kbits. Since frames are displayed at a constant rate, the variable frame size corresponds directly to variable bandwidth needs [KH95].

Network channels add delay, packet loss, and congestion and further increase the burstyness. If video frames were displayed immediately as they arrive, this variability would appear as annoying jitter—variable intervals between each displayed frame.

To hide this jitter from the user, multimedia clients typically include a play-back buffer, which acts as an elastic store. The rendering proceeds smoothly, taking frames from the front of the buffer at a constant rate, while the network fills the back of the queue at a variable rate. This buffer may store several seconds of the stream, trading an initial delay for smooth rendering of the stream. This is called *audio/video smoothing*. If the stream arriving over the network is extremely variable, the buffer may empty, and the rendering then must pause until the buffer begins to fill.

Figure 4.4 illustrates the delays that occur. Time is somewhat exaggerated along the vertical scale to better illustrate the sequence of events. The client request traverses the network to reach the server. The server handles the request, fetches the multimedia file, and begins the response by repeatedly sending packets of media to the client at the playback rate. The connection delay is the interval from sending the client request to receiving the first server response. The length of this connection delay depends on the length, congestion, and speed of the network path and on the server response time. The client buffer now begins filling, and introduces a delay until the buffer is sufficiently full to begin playback.

4.3.2 Fast Prefix Transfer

Television viewers and radio listeners often enjoy "channel hopping"—frequently and immediately switching channels. Whether to skip advertisements or just browse the current program—once a consumer gets used to immediate channel switching, she will never accept a system that adds significant delays when changing channels. Likewise, TV watchers and radio listeners expect immediate playback when turning on their TVs or radios.

Internet-based streaming, however, suffers from significant playback delays that are typically in the range of a few seconds. The majority of the delay is caused by buffer delay, with some additional connection delay (see Figure 4.4).

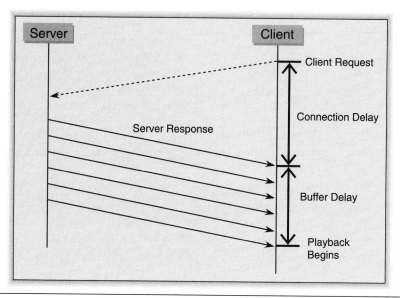

Figure 4.4 Buffered playback.

The question is how to reduce these delays and provide the consumer with a responsive streaming delivery system.

Frazzled software developers have asked their colleagues to please "get started while I go find out what they want." To minimize delay, firefighters begin using water stored in the tanker truck immediately while crews take time to locate a fire hydrant and connect to its steady stream. Similarly, when a cache has previously stored the beginning of a multimedia stream it is able to quickly satisfy user requests while it contacts the server for the remaining portions of the stream. This is the simple essence of prefix transfer mechanisms [SRT99]. Prefix transfer mechanisms help reduce the connection delay, but they do not help with the buffer delay. This is where the *fast prefix transfer* mechanism comes in.

From Figure 4.4, it is obvious that storing less data in the client-side buffer would help reduce the buffer delay. However, this is not a good option because a certain amount of data is needed at the client for audio/video smoothing to absorb network jitter and delay variations. Therefore, the only alternative for reducing buffer delay is to fill the client buffer faster, which translates into transmitting the data to be buffered at a higher rate. This is the idea behind fast prefix transfer.

Figure 4.5 illustrates how prefix caching reduces connection delay and how fast prefix transfer further reduces buffer delay. The client request goes to the cache. The cache begins its response using the previously stored multimedia file prefix. The cache simultaneously sends a request to the server for the remainder of the multimedia stream. If the cache is managed by the client's organization,

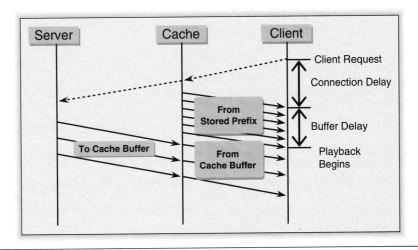

Figure 4.5 Fast prefix caching.

it may be possible to locate the cache close to the client and to employ a fast and lightly loaded connection between the client and the cache. The connection delay lasts only until the first response is received from the cache. This delay can be substantially shorter than waiting for a server response, thus reducing the connection delay. The cache then continues to fill the client buffer while it receives the remainder of the stream from the server. The server stream is buffered in the cache ready for transmission to the client as soon as the prefix is exhausted. The cache has the option of storing any portion of the stream for use in subsequent requests. If this is the first request for this stream, and there is reason to believe additional requests will be made for this stream, the cache will probably decide to store a prefix. If the stream is particularly popular, the cache could decide to store the entire length of the stream for future use. The requests between the cache and the server can run substantially ahead of the playback, but must not lag too far behind. To avoid an interruption in playback, the transfers from server to cache can lag only by the time made available by the playback buffer and stored prefix.

Fast prefix transfer provides an additional advantage. This scheme transmits the prefix to the client at data transfer speeds faster than the playback speed. This fills the client buffer faster and further reduces the delay seen by the client. If several caches are cascaded from the server to the client, fast prefix transfer is especially effective when the client uses the closest cache. In this case the fast transfer is filling the client buffer directly, and directly reducing client delay. If the transfer is five times as fast as the stream playback rate and the prefix is as long as the buffer the delay can be reduced by a factor of five compared to a prefix transfer at the stream rate. A graph showing other results from this technique is shown in Figure 4.6. Here each line represents a different length prefix, ranging from zero to five seconds long. In each case the client buffer was five seconds long. The horizontal axis represents different ratios of fast transfer to playback rate. Note, for example, that a three-second-long prefix reduced access delays to only three seconds when the prefix was delivered four times as fast as the playback speed.

The cache can also be used to replicate (split) a stream to serve many clients while requiring only one connection to the server. Here several clients are served simultaneously from the cache, while only one path is used to the server. If the network connections from the cache to each of the clients are fast and short, the clients will all see excellent service with minimal traffic across the larger network to the server. A cache can even serve as an effective multimedia stream splitter for live broadcasts where prefix caching is impossible. This is analogous to multicast, where the streaming cache is performing the replication.

Streaming media protocols include features that allow a cache to identify and store the initial frames making up the prefix, then request the remaining frames from the server. The RTP protocol includes sequence number and time-stamp information that enables the cache to identify the frames in the prefix and request the remaining frames from the server. The `Range request` header operation in HTTP 1.1 provides a similar capability for Web servers supporting the feature. Finally RTSP supports *absolute positioning* (also known as *seeking*) to request an offset from the beginning of the stream.

For some applications the cache can store several portions of the multimedia stream in addition to the prefix. For example, the stream may be presented to the user as a series of chapters or other logical segments. The cache could then

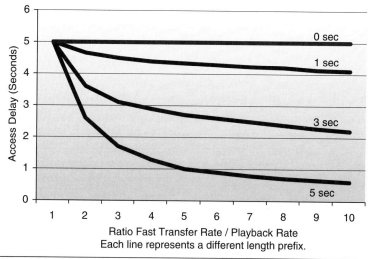

Figure 4.6 Fast prefix delay reductions.

store the beginning of each chapter in anticipation of handling requests for any chapter. However, arbitrary seeking functions, such as fast forward, and seeking to an arbitrary position, are not readily accommodated by this scheme.

Modest cache storage requirements can provide substantial user benefits. For example, a full motion MPEG-2 video stream with a mean rate of 2 Mbits/second requires only 2 Mbytes of buffer space to store an 8-second-long prefix. This is probably enough time to setup and begin transmission of the original stream from the server during most conditions.

The size of the prefix must be chosen carefully. Figure 4.7 illustrates the importance of segmenting a stream in a size that balances delays and traffic from the server with the storage capacity of the cache. Without segmenting the objects, storage limitations cause all of object A to be ejected from the cache after retrieving B. With segmentation, a portion of A can be retained after B is stored. The next section describes an approach to segmentation that increases the caching effectiveness.

4.3.3 Object Segmentation and Cache Replacement

Containerized shipping has improved materials transportation around the globe. The key innovation is a large, rectangular metal container about the size of a tractor-trailer or a railroad boxcar. These containers are built in standard sizes that fit readily onto trucks, rail cars, and ships. Once the containers are filled they can be loaded onto a truck, then moved easily to a rail car and then onto a ship or stored at a warehouse. A single container size is chosen to fit each of the transport vehicles used along the journey. This is shown in Figure 4.8.

Disk storage is allocated in blocks of a particular fixed size. If multimedia streams are segmented into sections the size of disk blocks, then storage, retrieval, and replacement in a local cache store is very efficient. Segments of a

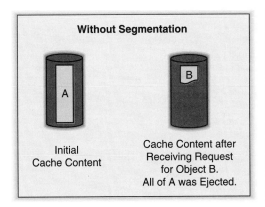
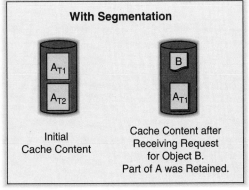

Figure 4.7 Segmenting streaming objects.

Figure 4.8 Containerized shipping.

streaming object can now be cached and replaced independently thereby reducing contention for disk space, and using disk space efficiently [HNG+99].

A drawback of caching and replacing segments independently is that when a streaming request arrives at the cache, it is likely that only a portion of the segments making up the entire stream will be present. Serving the entire stream then requires requests to the origin server, or some cooperating cache, to retrieve the missing segments. This increases signaling and transport traffic. It also increases the probability of losing synchronization in the media stream. A technique for controlling the number of missing gaps (breaks in sequences of adjacent segments) is needed. Increasing the segment size reduces the number of missing gaps, but has the serious disadvantage of increasing contention for disk space. What is needed is a large logical unit for caching, while retaining a fine granularity for disk allocation and replacement.

Figure 4.9 illustrates an effective solution. The streaming object is segmented into logical units called *chunks* for caching. Each of these chunks is further divided into segments corresponding to the disk block size. A chunk is simply a number of contiguous segments within a streaming object. Each chunk is cached independently using the following rules as the replacement policy:

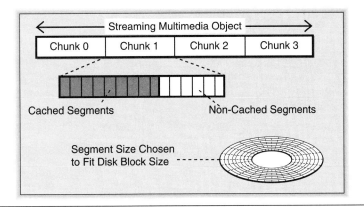

Figure 4.9 Cache replacement for streaming media.

1. The basic unit of caching and cache replacement is a segment. This optimizes disk storage.
2. Segments allocated for a chunk always form a contiguous prefix of the chunk. This captures the advantages of prefix caching described in the previous section.
3. When any segment within a chunk is being accessed, no segment within the chunk can be ejected from the cache. This rule is based on the continuity typical of stream access. The most likely portion of a stream to be requested next is the portion of the same stream that immediate follows.
4. When the replacement algorithm chooses any chunk for ejection, the last segment of the cached prefix is always chosen for ejection. This rule preserves the prefix as much as possible.

Choosing the chunk size allows a design trade-off between the number of gaps and the flexibility in replacing segments. If the chunk size grows very large, the entire stream becomes one chunk, and this becomes the same as prefix caching. If the chunk size is very small, it contains very few segments, and the continuity of the cached stream is lost. Intelligent prefetching may be needed to retrieve missing segments to preserve the timing requirements of the stream. More details, including performance numbers measured from a working prototype, are given in [HNG+99].

4.3.4 Dynamic Caching

The streaming nature of multimedia provides additional opportunities for bandwidth savings. Normally two playback requests require two separate data streams. However, requests from two clients for playback of the same stream differ only in the timing of the request. Playback requests for streaming media are related by their *temporal distance*, the time from the start of playback at one client to the start of playback of the same stream at the second client. If the differences in the timing of the requests can be hidden, then a single stream can serve both requests. This is the basis for *dynamic caching*, illustrated in Figure 4.10.

When a user requests the latest headline news video from CNN, a dedicated stream is started. When a second user requests the same stream five minutes later, it is almost certain that the data currently being sent to the first user will be needed by the second user five minutes later. If a cache shared by both users can provide a buffer to hold those five minutes of streaming media,[1] two users can be served from a single stream. Also, the buffer only needs to be five minutes long, regardless of how long the stream is. The temporal distance of the users determines the buffer size, in this case, five minutes, rather than the length of the stream. It forms a sliding window over the stream. Of course, the first five minutes of the stream has to be retrieved so it can be sent to the second user.

We can formalize the scenario described in the previous paragraph. The client at receiver R_1 requests the streaming object at a particular time t. Some time later the client at receiver R_2 requests the same streaming object. The difference in time, the temporal distance between the two requests, is represented by Δ seconds. When the client at R_2 receives the start of the stream, the first client has already received the first Δ seconds of the stream. However, all of the data being streamed to R_1 will also be needed by R_2. Therefore, by allocating a *ring buffer*, a moving window of Δ seconds of the data stream going to R_1 can be reused to satisfy R_2's request when it occurs Δ seconds later. The ring buffer has hidden or absorbed the temporal distance between the two requests. Now,

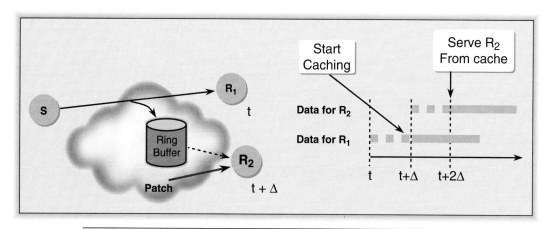

Figure 4.10 Dynamic caching.

---

[1]This assumes that the streaming rate is the same as the playback rate. It is possible for the streaming rate to exceed the playback rate. In that case, the buffer has to be sized according to the playback rate.

R_2 still has to obtain the initial Δ seconds of data that was missed by joining the stream later. This interval of the stream is called a *patch* and can be obtained directly from the origin server, or it may have been stored as a prefix in the cache.

This ring buffer and patching mechanism making up the dynamic cache can be used several places in the network. They can be used in the local client to allow the client to join a broadcast stream already in progress. A network cache can employ these techniques to allow sharing of a stream with several clients, each served by their own ring buffer. If a single cache serves several clients, it can allow multiple taps into a single ring buffer to connect each client with the correct stream delay. Finally, several dynamic caches can cooperate to form a stream distribution mesh in the network. Here each cache requests patches or streams with a particular delay from other caches in the network. It is remarkable that a small ring buffer is sufficient to deliver a complete streaming object to multiple clients, regardless of the length of the stream. The required size of the ring buffer depends only on the time difference Δ between the clients' requests, and not on the length of the stream. This technique is useful when multiple requests occur within a small enough time-span to fill the time difference with the contents of the buffer.

4.4 Case Studies

Proprietary protocols, nonstandard implementations of standard protocols, and the complexities of building a practical system all present challenges in using the techniques presented in this chapter. After describing what was learned from a few surprises, the performance of a practical system is analyzed.

4.4.1 Standard Surprises

Use of open standards is voluntary. They do not come with methods of enforcement or any judicial system. If they help advance influential people's goals, they will be chosen, implemented, promoted, and used. If they are not helpful, they will be selectively implemented, modified, or ignored. Open standards are interesting, but popularly chosen implementations are vital. Chapter 10 discusses the role of standards in more depth.

Previously we mentioned that major software providers have made use of proprietary streaming protocols. To provide acceptable hit ratios, a cache needs to support the protocols used by the most popular clients. Therefore, a streaming cache (at least one built not long ago) probably needs to support proprietary protocols. The specifications of proprietary protocols are trade secrets closely guarded by the companies that expect to profit from them. Implementations of proprietary protocols are not freely available, and are only rarely available as source code. Independently verified conformance tests and performance benchmarking also become impossible. In the arena of proprietary protocols, money talks and secrecy prevails.

Streaming Web cache designers incorporating proprietary protocols have little choice but to pay the licensing fees the owners of those proprietary protocols require. This can add significantly to the cost of each cache device. It certainly precludes any open source or freeware distribution model. The cache has to generate cash; a business model that returns enough revenue to cover the licensing costs of each cache is essential. This business model is typically based on the cache providing additional revenue or cost savings to a collection of users, network providers, or content providers. It may be difficult to convince any of these groups that the financial cost of a cache is less than the additional revenue or network savings. How convincingly can the cost of media streaming delay be put into financial terms?

Failure to adopt standards-based solutions can lead to other problems. In Section 4.2.1 the M (marker) bit was described. This M bit is included in the header so it can be set to identify the start of each frame sequence. A streaming Web cache was designed relying on the M bit to identify frame boundaries. Unfortunately, one of the major suppliers of streaming servers simply failed for an extended period of time to implement this protocol feature. The cache designers had little recourse except to find some other, much less efficient, way to identify the frame boundaries. There is no appeals court set up to hear standards violations.

In another example, attempts to use fast prefix transfer with proprietary protocols failed. The streaming software built around the protocols assumed that the streaming rate was the same as the playback rate. This proprietary software simply could not accommodate the faster data transfers required for fast prefix transfer.

4.4.2 System Performance

A cache device was built incorporating several of the techniques discussed in this chapter. It includes fast prefix transfer, object segmentation, and dynamic caching. After a brief description of the implementation, the performance measurements of the system are presented and described.

Figure 4.11 shows the major components of the streaming cache. As with any intermediary, it must appear as a server to the client and as a client to the server. Because the intermediary terminates the protocols, it must translate header information, including timestamps and sequence identifiers between the server view and the client view of each packet. The following components perform those functions:

- The **RTSP/RTP Client and Server** modules receive and process RTSP requests from the clients, and interact with the RTSP/RTP client module to forward them to the server after appropriate header translation. It also streams data to the clients using RTP. The RTSP/RTP client module contacts media servers or other caches across the network to fetch data for client operations.

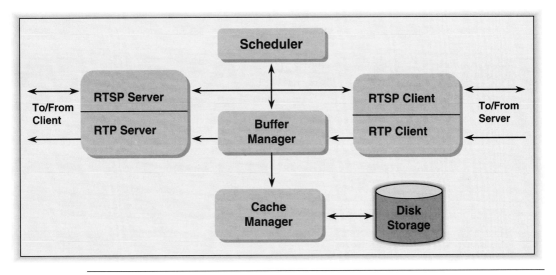

Figure 4.11 Streaming cache implementation.

- The **Buffer Manager** forms a pool of buffers from the available memory. Each buffer is associated with a media object identified by a URL and a time range. It uses the RTSP/RTP client module to fetch data that is not available from disk storage. It works with the cache management module to store and retrieve media objects to and from the disk storage.
- The **Cache Manager** maps URLs to filenames and manages the disk space using a Least Recently Used (LRU) replacement policy. It consolidates non-overlapping time segments of a media object into a single file.
- The **Scheduler** manages a queue of events. This includes client requests, server fetches, and garbage collection.

Many more details of the implementation are provided in [BGH+00].

The performance of this system was measured as a few design parameters were varied. The cache was connected to a server holding 12 video clips, ranging in length from 40 to 70 seconds. Several clients requested whole MPEG video clips from the cache every 15 seconds using a Zipf popularity distribution. The traffic into and out of the cache was measured to derive a traffic reduction ratio, using the formula: R = (Data Out–Data In)/Data In. A perfect cache that never needs to retrieve data from the server has a traffic reduction ratio of one. A cache that retrieves as much data from the server as it presents to the client has a ratio of zero.

Figure 4.12 shows how the traffic reduction ratio improves over time for several choices of prefix cache size. The horizontal axis is the length of time passed since the first client request. The reduction ratio starts out small and increases

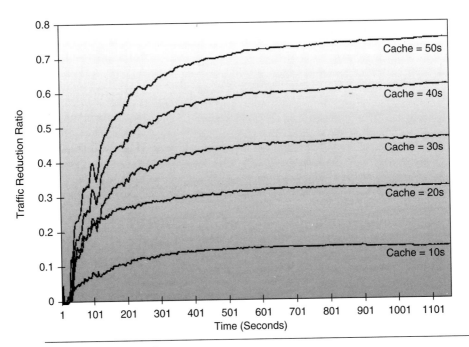

Figure 4.12 Prefix caching benefits.

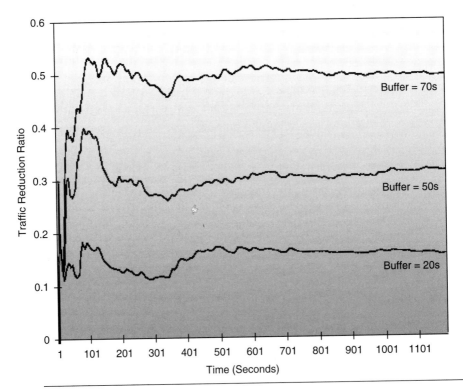

Figure 4.13 Ring buffer benefits.

while the cache fills until it stabilizes. In this case, the total disk store was large enough to store the entire working set of media files, so no cache replacement took place. While caching 10-second-long prefixes provides only a 10% reduction in traffic, caching 50-second-long prefixes provides a reduction in traffic increasing to 75%. Note that the prefix size approaches the entire length of the stream in this example.

The cache incorporates a ring buffer to implement dynamic caching, as described in Section 4.3.4. Figure 4.13 shows how the traffic reduction ratio varies over time for several choices of ring buffer size. Here traffic is reduced by 50% when a 70-second-long ring buffer is used. Smaller buffers provide less traffic reduction.

CHAPTER 5

Navigating Content Networks

Transport requires navigation. Travel is erratic and uncertain until a path toward the destination is known. The mariners of centuries ago who lost countless lives, ships, and cargo because of inadequate navigation understood its essential role in the safety, effectiveness, and efficiency of sailing ships. The danger was demonstrated in tragic human terms on October 22, 1707, when Admiral Sir Clowdisley Shovell made a fatal navigation error. Nearly 2,000 officers and men of the Royal Navy perished when the HMS *Association*, *Eagle*, *Romney*, and *Firebrand* all struck Gilstone Ledge and sunk to the ocean depths. This tragedy led to creation of the British Longitude Act of 1714, which promised an immense prize of £20,000 to anyone who could provide a practicable and useful method of determining longitude to an accuracy of one half degree on an ocean voyage across the Atlantic[1] [Sob95].

Navigation is also essential in content delivery networks. Even the simplest content request requires translating hostnames into IP addresses, routing requests to their destination across the Internet, switching packets to the most effective server, and returning a response to the client.

Navigation refers to the general problem of locating a destination and determining a path toward it. In content delivery networks, the terms *switching* and *routing* are most often used to describe navigation through the network. The terms are sometimes used interchangeably; however, there is often a distinction. *Switching* generally refers to choosing among several local endpoints connected to the switch at Layer 2, the link layer; however, we will see that it is also used to describe selection based on Layer 4–7 (transport through application layer) information. *Routing* is the process of choosing a path over which to send packets. Routing typically refers to path selection at Layer 3, the network layer.

---

[1]After devoting a lifetime to the problem, John Harrison finally received half the maximum award in 1764 for building clocks that retained remarkable accuracy on long sea voyages.

The chapter begins with a description of the Domain Name System (DNS). This distributed directory is used to translate user-friendly hostnames, like www.content-networking.com into the corresponding IP address. Then Layer 4–7 request switching is described, including the use of these switches for server load balancing and Network Address Translation (NAT). Several approaches to *Global Routing* are described. Each of these approaches is designed to locate the server best able to deliver the requested content. The chapter ends by describing a few case studies that illustrate these techniques.

5.1   The Domain Name System

Beginning in 1963, the United States Postal Service (www.usps.com) introduced the Zone Improvement Plan (ZIP) to improve routing mail through the postal system. In this system each local region is assigned a unique 5-digit number, called the ZIP code. In 1983, the Postal Service began using an expanded ZIP Code called "ZIP+4." This consists of the original 5-digit ZIP Code plus a 4-digit add-on code. The 4-digit add-on number identifies a geographic segment within the 5-digit delivery area, such as a city block, office building, individual high-volume receiver of mail, or any other unit that would aid efficient mail sorting and delivery.

When sending a letter to someone at the Veterans Hospital on Elm Street in Fargo North Dakota it will probably arrive sooner if it is addressed using the full ZIP+4 numeric code for that location. The ZIP code is easy to find using a Web page the USPS provides for translating the familiar form of an address to the ZIP+4 code. The ZIP+4 code for that address is 58102-2498. Modern mailing systems, including popular PC-based word processors, write a bar code on envelopes addressed using the full ZIP+4 code. Sorting machines at the post office read this bar code to decide on a route for the envelope and sort it into a bin for transport along the next hop to a post office or regional center closer to the final destination. When the letter reaches the final post office the postal carrier gathers all the mail with his or her ZIP+4 code, and delivers it to the final destination.

The Internet uses a similar system. Endpoints such as hosts and clients are assigned numeric IP addresses, but are addressed by name. The Domain Name System translates hostnames from user-oriented forms such as www.content-networking.com to the corresponding numeric IP address [RFC 1739]. Popular operating systems provide the `nslookup` (Name Server Lookup) command to translate host and domain names into IP addresses. To try this yourself, begin with a command prompt (start / run / cmd if you are using a Windows-based PC, and omnipresent on Unix-based systems) and type:

```
nslookup www.content-networking.com
```

The session will look something like this annotated dialog:

```
> nslookup www.content-networking.com  ← Your request
> Server: ns01.plnfld01.nj.comcast.net  ← Name Server Host Name
> Address: 68.39.224.5  ← Name Server IP Address
> Name: www.content-networking.com  ← Host Name
> Address: 63.219.151.20  ← Host IP Address
```

After entering the `nslookup` command the system responds with the hostname and IP address of the Domain Name Server that resolved the request. It then repeats the hostname and provides its IP address of 63.219.151.20.

Let's take a more careful look at the domain name system, including the structure of the names, the distributed nature of the directory, how requests are resolved, tools for interrogating the directory, and using DNS for load balancing.

5.1.1 Domain Names

Prior to development of the Domain Name System the Internet host name to address mappings were maintained by the Network Information Center (NIC, now called the Internet Assigned Numbers Authority (IANA), www.iana.org) in a single file known as the *host table*. This file, hosts.txt, was obtained using FTP by all hosts in the network [RFC 952, RFC 953]. Remnants of this approach still exist in many of today's operating systems. For example, Windows XP has a text file *hosts* in the \WINDOWS\system32\drivers\etc directory. While the hosts.txt file approach is conceptually simple, it does not scale up to meet the needs of the rapidly expanding Internet. To keep up-to-date, the hosts.txt file had to be modified whenever a new host was added to the network. The file then had to be distributed to each host and installed. A new approach was needed.

In November of 1987, RFC 1034 was published to describe the distributed directory that has become today's Domain Name System.

The DNS has three major components:

1. The *Domain Name Space* and *Resource Records*, which are specifications for a tree-structured name space and data associated with the names.
2. *Name Servers* are server programs that manage information about the domain tree's structure and records. A particular name server has complete information about a subset of the domain space, and pointers to other name servers that can be used to find information from any part of the domain tree.
3. *Resolvers* are programs that extract information from name servers in response to client requests. A resolver is typically a system routine that is directly accessible to user programs.

The Domain Name Space is shown in Figure 5.1. It begins at the root, and extends to a set of top-level domain (TLD) names. These are further organized

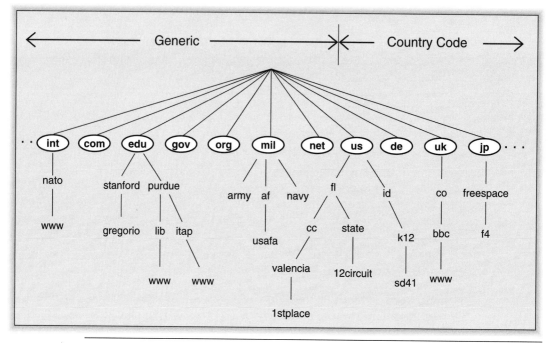

Figure 5.1 The DNS name space.

into country code TLDs (ccTLD) and generic TLDs (gTLD). RFC 1591, published in 1994, discusses these top-level domain names and makes the following prediction that seems quaint in retrospect:

> "There are a set of what are called *top-level domain names* (TLDs). These are the generic TLDs (edu, com, net, org, gov, mil, and int), and the two letter country codes from ISO-3166. It is extremely unlikely that any other TLDs will be created."

At that time the list of gTLDs with their intended use was:

- **com**—for commercial entities, such as corporations
- **edu**—for all educational institutions,
- **net**—intended to hold only the computers of network providers, that is the NIC and NOC computers, the administrative computers, and the network node computers. It has grown beyond that to include many ISPs and other organizations.
- **org**—the miscellaneous TLD for organizations that didn't fit anywhere else, and
- **int**—for organizations established by international treaties, or international databases.

Since then several gTLDs have been added, and more can be expected. The new designations include:

- **aero**—for certain members of the global aviation community,
- **biz**—for businesses,
- **coop**—for cooperatives,
- **info**—intended for use by information portals,
- **museum**—for museums and related persons,
- **name**—for use by individuals, and
- **pro**—for licensed professionals [IANA1].

There are two United States-only generic domains. These are:

- **gov**—used by agencies of the US Federal government and
- **mil**—used by the US military.

This example illustrates some of the political and social consequences of designing the DNS name space and assigning TLDs. Although many countries have militaries, and all have some form of government, these two TLDs are administered by the United States alone.

As an example of a country domain, the US domain provides for the registration of all kinds of entities in the United States on the basis of political geography, that is, a hierarchy of <entity-name>.<locality>.<state-code>.us. An example is "Trenton.nj.us". In addition, branches of the **us** domain are provided within each state for schools (**k12**), community colleges (**cc**), technical schools (**tec**), state government agencies (**state**), libraries (**lib**), and several other generic types of entities. See RFC 1480 for details.

The complete list of country code TLDs is long, presently including 243 entries, and is available at: http://www.iana.org/cctld/cctld-whois.htm.

Descending the name space hierarchy from the root forms hostnames, in reverse order. For example descending from root to **int** to "nato" to "www" corresponds to the hostname www.nato.int. Descending from root to **edu** to "purdue" to "itap" to "www" corresponds to the host www.itap.purdue.edu.

A *domain* is a sub-tree of the domain name space. So **edu** and "purdue.edu" and "itap.purdue.edu" are all domains.

Name server topology reflects the name space hierarchy. The *root* name servers are at the top of the hierarchy and can be queried to begin any name search. Presently there are 13 root name server hostnames worldwide, with each hostname often representing several real servers selected by an anycast mechanism (see Section 5.3.1.4) [Abl03]. Their locations are shown in Figure 5.2. The up-to-date list is available from the Root Server Technical Operations Association Web site at www.root-servers.org. These servers are quite busy, and a surprisingly large fraction of the traffic is nonproductive. For example, one study showed that nearly 98% of the traffic is nonproductive including 12.5% of the queries for non-existent TLDs, such as **.elvis, .local,** and **.localhost** [WF03].

Anyone can run a local name server, and they are typically run by organizations that have several host computers. These include medium to large

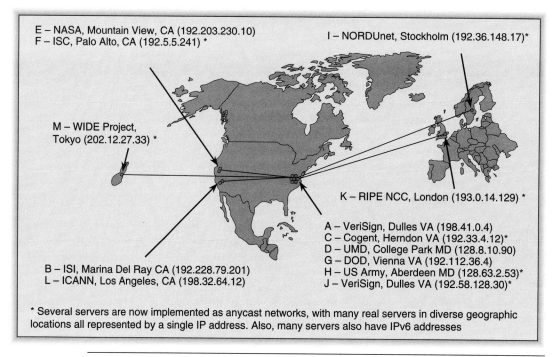

E – NASA, Mountain View, CA (192.203.230.10)
F – ISC, Palo Alto, CA (192.5.5.241) *

I – NORDUnet, Stockholm (192.36.148.17)*

M – WIDE Project,
Tokyo (202.12.27.33) *

K – RIPE NCC, London (193.0.14.129) *

A – VeriSign, Dulles VA (198.41.0.4)
C – Cogent, Herndon VA (192.33.4.12)*
D – UMD, College Park MD (128.8.10.90)
G – DOD, Vienna VA (192.112.36.4)
H – US Army, Aberdeen MD (128.63.2.53)*
J – VeriSign, Dulles VA (192.58.128.30)*

B – ISI, Marina Del Ray CA (192.228.79.201)
L – ICANN, Los Angeles, CA (198.32.64.12)

* Several servers are now implemented as anycast networks, with many real servers in diverse geographic locations all represented by a single IP address. Also, many servers also have IPv6 addresses

Figure 5.2 The DNS root servers.

organizations, corporations, and Internet service providers. Each name server knows the addresses of the root servers. In addition, each name server knows the address of its immediate children in the name tree.

While any name server can learn the IP address of any host, name servers generally only have complete information about some portion of the domain name space, called a *zone*. These name servers are designated as *authoritative* for the domain names in their zone, and are said to have *authority* for that zone. The root name servers know the location of the authoritative name servers for each top-level domain.

For example, Lucent technologies owns the lucent.com domain name, and runs the authoritative name servers for that domain. Because the number of hosts making up the domain is large, it is further subdivided into zones delegated to organizations within Lucent. Individual name servers are then authoritative for their zone within the lucent.com domain. For example, a particular name server may be authoritative for the scportal.lucent.com zone. The administrator of this name server can configure the network making up this zone without further coordination with the authoritative name server for lucent.com. Similarly, the administrator of the lucent.com name server can configure it independently of the .com root name servers.

Most name servers run a program called BIND—the Berkeley Internet Name Domain—which is available from the Internet Software Consortium at www.isc.org. Several other name server implementations are also used.

Efforts to extend the domain name system to include international character sets have led to two approaches. The Internationalized Domain Names (IDN) are based on ASCII and are defined by RFC 3490. The W3C is working to define a system based on Unicode characters called the Internationalized Resource Identifiers (IRIs) [IRI1].

5.1.2 DNS Protocol

The DNS Protocol—the communications protocol that runs between resolvers and name servers—is defined by RFC 1035. Resolvers send messages to name servers to retrieve *resource records*, also called RRs. There are several types of resource records. For the purposes of this book the three most important to understand are:

1. **A records,** or Address records that provide a hostname to IP address mapping,
2. **NS records,** or Name Server records, which list name servers for a particular zone, and
3. **CNAME,** or Canonical Name records, which map an alias (an alternative name) to its canonical (official or non-aliased) name.

The top-level format of each message is divided into the following 5 sections:

1. **Header**—which is always included and contains:
   - a unique identifier,
   - a query/response flag,
   - an operation code specifying a standard query, inverse query (find the name associated with an IP address), or server status request,
   - an authoritative answer flag, indicating the responding name server is an authority for the domain name in question, and
   - a recursion desired flag, requesting a recursive query. This is explained more fully in the following section.
2. **Question**—the question posed to the name server. This includes:
   - the domain name,
   - the query class (usually 1 for Internet (IN) or 255 for any class (*)), and
   - the query type, such as a host address, an authoritative name server, or a request for a transfer of an entire zone.
3. **Answer**—RRs that answer the question, typically an A, NS, or CNAME resource record.
4. **Authority**—RRs that point to an authoritative name server.
5. **Additional**—RRs that provide additional information about the query, but are not sufficient answers.

Resource Records contain *class* and *type* indicators, such as the address of a host or of an authoritative name server, followed by the resource data. This data is often a 4-octet Internet address. Each RR also contains a Time To Live (TTL) field. This specifies how long the resource record may be cached before it should be discarded. If TTL is set to zero, the RR data can only be used for the current transaction before it is discarded.

In the next section we will look at how a name server request is resolved.

5.1.3   Iterative and Recursive Requests

Each name server holds only a small portion of the entire domain name space. Therefore a particular name server will often receive queries that can only be answered by some other server. The two general approaches to dealing with this problem are *recursive*, in which the first server pursues the query for the client at another server, and *iterative*, in which the server refers the client to another server and leaves the client to pursue the query. The domain system requires name servers (other than the root servers) to implement the iterative approach, and allows the recursive approach as an option [RFC 1034].

The two request types are shown in Figure 5.3. In a recursive request, shown in step 1 of Figure 5.3, the local name server is responsible for making successive requests until the name is finally resolved. In an iterative request, such as steps 2, 4, and 6, the name server replies with an NS record identifying the address of a Name Server that is likely to be closer to the authoritative name server. In the example of Figure 5.3 the following eight steps take place:

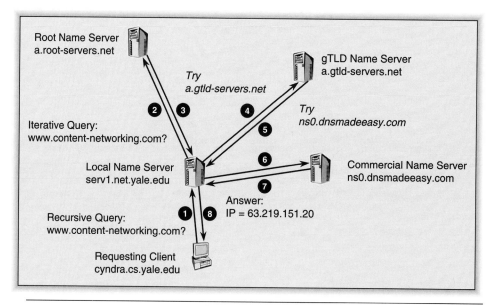

Figure 5.3 Recursive and iterative DNS requests.

1. A client with the address cyndra.cs.yale.edu is preparing to send an HTTP request to www.content-networking.com. The client's resolver is configured to communicate with its local name server at address serv1.net.yale.edu. The resolver sends a *recursive* request to the local name server, asking for the IP address of www.content-networking.com. This is typical because resolvers are often too simple to interpret the responses from iterative requests. Because the request was recursive this local name server is now responsible for resolving the request.

2. The local name server does not know the answer, so it sends an iterative request to the root name server. To reduce their workload, the root name servers are not likely to accept recursive requests. Also, various name server implementations use different algorithms to decide when to query the root DNS servers.

3. The root name server does not provide the answer; however, it provides the additional information suggesting the local DNS try the request at a.gtld-servers.net.

4. The local name server sends an iterative request to the gTLD server, requesting the address of www.content-networking.com.

5. The gTLD name server does not provide the answer, however it provides the address of an authoritative name server for the requested domain. That authoritative name server is ns0.dnsmadeeasy.com.

6. The local name server sends an iterative request to the server at ns0.dnsmadeeasy.com, requesting the address of www.content-networking.com.

7. The server responds with the authoritative answer, identifying the IP address as 63.219.151.20.

8. The local DNS (serv1.net.yale.edu) responds to the client (cyndra.cs.yale.edu) with the answer, IP = 63.219.151.20.

In a recursive request, the queried server either responds with the requested data, (i.e., an A record identifying the IP address of the requested host) or returns an error indicating the information is not available anywhere in the DNS name space. The name server receiving a recursive query that it cannot answer authoritatively will begin with a query to a name server it knows is responsible for the domain or TLD of the hostname being resolved.

When a name server finally receives an answer, it typically caches the answer in anticipation of future requests for the same information. This often saves time and bandwidth, as was discussed in Chapter 3. The cached entry must be purged before the TTL specified in the Resource Record expires. Resolvers often include a similar DNS cache to reduce the number of request they need to make to the local Name Server.

5.1.4   DNS Tools—nslookup, dig, whois, and ARIN

The DNS name space is remarkably accessible through use of the tools *nslookup*, *dig*, *whois*, and the ARIN database. The nslookup tool was introduced briefly in the beginning of this chapter, but it has many more useful features. To examine these, run the tool in an interactive session by typing its name alone on a command line:

```
>nslookup
Default server: ns01.plnfld01.nj.comcast.net
Address: 68.39.224.5
>
```

The system responds with the name of the default name server and its IP address. The particular server will probably be different for you.

Obtain a list of allowed commands and options by typing `help` or `?`. The `set all` command lists all of the options and their current values. Switch to another name server, for example by typing `server serv1.net.yale.edu`. Request a name for which this server is authoritative, for example `cyndra.cs.yale.edu`.

By default the tool makes recursive requests. Iterative requests allow you to explore the series of requests needed to resolve an inquiry. For example type `set norecurse` then request the lookup of an uncommon domain name, for example `fair-haven.us`. As each iterative request suggests a next server, set the `server` to that suggestion and try again.

The *dig* utility provides an alternative to nslookup. It is also distributed with BIND and may be preferable in some cases.

The `whois` tool helps to identify the owner of each registered domain name. Although many operating systems provide a `whois` tool, many do not. Fortunately Web-based access to the database is readily available. Begin at http://www.domainwhitepages.com/ or any one of the many domain registration sites and type in `content-networking.com`. The system responds with:

- the name of the company through which the name was registered,
- at least two name servers that are authoritative for the domain,
- the date the registration expires, and
- other information.

The `whois` database is distributed. The information displayed here was obtained by a query to the server at **whois.godaddy.com**. Further information can be obtained by going to the referral URL listed, in this case http://registrar/godaddy.com. A query here provides the administrative and technical contacts for the domain.

The American Registry for Internet Numbers (ARIN) (www.arin.net) is one of several Regional Internet Registries authorized by IANA. Their database contains information about the owners of particular IP addresses assigned in the Americas. Access the database beginning at: www.arin.net/whois/index.html. As an example, look up the IP address 128.210.11.29 and learn that this address is assigned to Purdue University.

The corresponding registries for numbers assigned in other regions around the world are:

- APNIC—Asia Pacific Network Information Center (www.apnic.net),
- LACNIC—Latin American and Caribbean Internet Address Registry (lacnic.net), and
- RIPE NCC—Réseaux IP Européens Network Coordination Centre (www.ripe.net).

5.1.5 Using DNS for Load Sharing

A Name Server can easily be configured to share a load across several Web servers that share a single hostname. This is convenient for popular sites such as cnn.com that get more traffic than can be handled by a single Web server. In BIND, the system administrator can enter multiple address records, each specifying a different IP address for the hostname. The Name Server then rotates the order of these records when answering each new request. The result is that requests are directed to separate servers in turn. This is called *round robin*. The choice of TTL will determine how long a client dwells on any particular server address. This can be long for sites that get traffic from many newly arriving clients. To allow rotation, TTL may have to be shortened if the site gets traffic from a small number of clients that access the site over an extended period of time. Note that because this simple round robin algorithm distributes requests equally among the available servers, it does not consider the server capacity or load. Also, caching of DNS records by servers at various levels of the hierarchy leads to resolution in an unpredictable pattern. Therefore it is load sharing, not load balancing.

You can see some of this in operation yourself. Begin with an `nslookup` request to cnn.com, or some other very popular site. Note that several IP addresses are returned. Each address corresponds to an individual server sharing the load on the domain. Now `ping` cnn.com and notice the IP address. Wait several minutes (for the TTL to expire.) and `ping` cnn.com again. Note that a different IP address is most likely used. The `setdebug` option of the `nslookup` command will display the actual TTL settings.

Readers interested in learning more about the Domain Name System are encouraged to read AL01.

While DNS load-sharing implementations have the advantages of simplicity and robust support from the existing DNS system, they also have important limitations. First, the DNS system was not designed as a load-balancing system. Its primary purpose is as an address directory and resources spent on load balancing can detract from its primary purpose. It does not scale well; the TTL chosen to optimize the distributed directory may not be a good choice for load sharing, and the DNS may be administered by an authority that is not primarily concerned with load sharing. Second, the DNS only has access to the domain name, it does not have additional context to determine what host may be most suitable for the client's request. Finally, although the DNS *shares* the load, it may not *balance* the load across a variety of disparate servers.

The next section describes how Layer 4–7 request switching provides better solutions for load sharing.

5.2   Layer 4–7 Request Switching

As content becomes more expressive and as more clients request more content, the load on Web servers continues to increase. Using a single bigger and faster Web server to handle the increased load is not an effective solution. A single server may not have the capacity to handle the load. There is no smooth upgrade path; the only way to increase capacity is to replace the existing server with a more powerful one. Also loss of the only server, due to hardware, software, network, or operator failure, will shut down the entire site. The load sharing based on DNS round robin as described in the previous section is also limited. It does not consider server load or capacity, or the activity level of each client, and caching DNS records works against the round robin scheme.

Web switches provide an important solution to these problems of server scaling, load balancing, reliability, flexibility, maintenance, and security. The following sections introduce Layer 4 switching and describe applications for server load balancing, and network address translation. Then Layer 7 switching, server health checks, interception proxies, and other Layer 4–7 applications are described.

5.2.1   Layer 4 Switching

Figure 5.4 shows a typical server-load-balancing configuration. Here the Web switch is assigned an IP address referred to as a virtual IP (VIP). This VIP is the IP address returned by the DNS server to clients requesting the IP address of this particular Web site. Traffic directed to this VIP arrives at the Web switch, where it is then directed to one of the real Web servers, A through D, at the site, based on a particular load-balancing policy.

TCP transmission takes place on a particular protocol port number used to distinguish among multiple destinations within a given host computer. Default port assignments are documented by IANA in http://www.iana.org/assignments/port-numbers, but can be specified by the application to be some other number. For example the default port for HTTP is 80, FTP uses port 20 for data transfer and port 21 for control, and the RTSP protocol uses port 554 by default. Layer 4 switches direct packets according to rules that consider several parameters, including these TCP port numbers. For example, the Web switch can be configured to direct all HTTP (port 80) traffic to a group consisting of servers A and B in our example, while directing all RTSP (port 554) traffic to server C and all FTP (ports 20, 21) traffic to server D.

Because they examine the TCP port number (they are *port aware*) in making switching decisions, they are called Layer 4 switches. Switches that examine IP address information are Layer 3 switches—most commonly called *routers*—and those that look at MAC addresses or ATM addresses are Layer 2 switches.

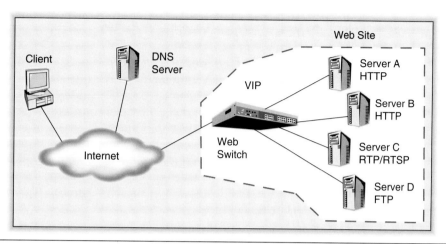

Figure 5.4 Server-load balancing.

Although the VIP in Figure 5.4 is an actual, registered, routable IP address, traffic is not terminated at that address. Instead, the connection is switched through to one of the Web servers. Clients only see the VIP address. The IP addresses of the Web servers never appear across the Internet; they are only used in the network segments between the servers and the Web switch. This allows unregistered or unroutable IP addresses such as those selected from 192.168.*.* or 10.*.*.* [RFC 1918] to be used for the Web servers. This has the advantages of conserving registered IP address space. In the case of unroutable IP addresses, it prevents contact with the Web servers from outside the private network. This can increase security. This is an example of Network Address Translation, which is discussed in more detail—along with its advantages and problems—in Section 5.2.3.

5.2.2 Server-Load Balancing

Layer 4 switches offer a variety of server-load-balancing (SLB) policies. They fall into three broad classes. The first are designed to provide the *best available* server for incoming new sessions. The second are designed to provide *persistence*, always connecting the same client to the same server. The third class *differentiates services* for different user classes (e.g., gold/silver/bronze service levels) providing premium levels of service. These policies can be used in a variety of combinations.

Some examples of *best available* policies are:

- **Random Server Selection**—Connections are assigned uniformly among servers in a group but not in a deterministic sequence.
- **Round Robin**—Connections are assigned sequentially among servers in a group.

- **Weighted Distribution (Static)**—Traffic is directed based on server capacity estimates. The administrator specifies the percentage of traffic to be directed to each of the servers in the group. The switch allocates connections based on these percentages.
- **Weighted Distribution (Dynamic)**—More traffic is directed to the servers with the faster response times.
- **Least Connections**—Assigns the next connection to the server in the group with the least number of connections.
- **Fewest Packets**—Assigns the next connection to the server in the group that has served the fewest packets over a recent time interval.
- **Least Busy Server**—An agent on the server keeps the switch updated on server utilization, health, and capacity. Connections are assigned to the server having the most spare capacity.

There are several circumstances when *persistence policies* are needed. For TCP's protocol acknowledgment mechanisms to work it is essential that all packets within a TCP session be sent to the same server. Ongoing transactions between a client and a server, for example during an online shopping and checkout session, need to be directed to the same Web server for the length of the application session. Also, SSL sessions also typically span multiple TCP sessions. Layer 4 switches have server selection policies to ensure this session persistence. This policy takes precedence over the "best available" server policies described above.

A number of techniques are used in these persistence policies. The most basic approach is to bind a particular server to a particular source IP address, assumed to represent a client. A timer may be set to monitor inactivity over this binding, so the association can be released if the session is abandoned. If several clients are connected through a proxy, for example a Web cache in a forward proxy configuration, they will share a common IP address, as seen from the Web switch. These clients will persist on a single server, as long as any of them are active in a session.

Network Address Translation, or any proxy that terminates TCP, can make this approach less effective. If several clients are behind a NAT device, they appear to the network with the same IP address. Persistence mechanisms will then attempt to direct all of these clients to the same real server. This works against attempts to balance the load.

Session monitoring can improve the persistence policy. Here the binding is valid for the duration of a TCP session. In the case of SSL sessions, the SSL session ID is tracked (at Layer 7) to determine the length of the session and the need for persistence. Interspersing secured and unsecured transactions can make it difficult to determine the length of a session. Finally, it may be possible to track a cookie to identify an application level session, such as a shopping session. This, however, can encounter a number of problems, including the clients' refusal to accept cookies, selecting identifying information from the cookie string, and SSL or application encryption of cookies.

The third class of load-balancing strategies is *differential policies* which attempt to allocate scarce resources to the most important use. These policies identify the most important transaction types or users and provide them with better service. For example, SSL sessions may indicate credit card use, and therefore revenue generation. Cookies may identify some aspects of customers' past behavior and allow an estimate of their revenue potential. The site may provide some form of "pay for premium service" offering gold-, silver-, and bronze-level user agreements at different price levels.

Service can only be differentiated when server capacity is scarce, but not overloaded. Basically the premium clients are moved toward the front of the line at the expense of the other, lower-priority clients. If the line is very short, then the differentiation is meaningless. If the line is growing very long, then the premium customers may be waiting behind many other premium customers, and not get satisfactory service. Therefore, differentiation policies must set a threshold that takes effect when resources begin to become scarce, but are not yet globally overloaded. Elitism has always had its problems.

5.2.3 Network Address Translation

Connecting individual clients to several real servers behind a Web switch that presents a single virtual IP address requires the switch to perform Network Address Translation (NAT) [RFC 1631]. Figure 5.5 illustrates the concept of Network Address Translation in a Web switch. Here the client with IP address X sends an IP packet to the switch using its virtual IP address of SW. The Source IP address field (S IP) and destination IP address field (D IP) of the packet header are shown set to X and SW, respectively, in the block arrow. The switch uses a load-balancing algorithm and chooses real server A for the connection. The switch does not terminate the protocol. Instead, the switch adjusts the header parameters to accommodate the assignment of client to server. Here the source IP address is changed to SW and the destination IP address is set to A. The server responds to destination IP address SW, and the switch translates this to the original destination of Client A. A similar translation (not shown) may also be required for the source and destination port numbers. Assuming this is a TCP/IP connection, the header check sums also have to be adjusted in the TCP header to accommodate the changed IP address and port numbers. Neither the client nor the server is aware of the address translation that has taken place.

The switch needs to keep a table of these translations for each active session. For example, if client Y is connected to server B, then the substitution of Y and B is correct for this session, but not for the previous session. This table, illustrated for associations 1 and 2, is shown within the switch in Figure 5.5. Because of table sizes and processing limits, Web switches that perform NAT are limited in the number of simultaneous associations they can support. The number of supported associations may be very large.

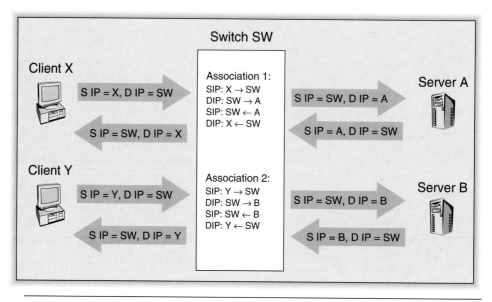

Figure 5.5 Network address translation.

Additional translations are needed to handle FTP and ICMP messages across a NAT switch. Also, none of the fields that carry IP address information can be encrypted. This reduces the number of available security options.

Although NAT provides many advantages by freeing up addresses for local administration, NAT use is controversial because it presents a number of problems [RFC 2993]. Some of these are:

- NATs move connection control away from the endpoints and give some of that control to the NAT device, within the connection path. This violates aspects of the End-to-End design principle [SRD84].
- NATs create a single point of failure in the network. Because the NAT device maintains connection state and dynamic mapping information, all the connections going through it are lost if the NAT fails.
- To increase the reliability of their Internet connectivity, some sites maintain several physical connections to the Internet. This practice, called multi-homing, is made more complicated by NAT.
- Because NAT cannot work with encrypted IP addresses or headers it is incompatible with security techniques based on encryption at the IP level.
- NATs complicate or may even invalidate the authentication mechanism of IP-based authorization schemes such as SNMPv3 [RFC 3411].

Because of their advantages, NAT devices are commonly used and deployed throughout the Internet despite these complications. Newly developed applications and algorithms that consider the implications of NAT can interwork successfully with this installed base.

5.2.4 **Layer 7 Switching**

Examining application layer data provides Layer 7 switches even more flexibility and features than Layer 4 switches alone can provide. Application information examined by Layer 7 switches includes the URL, HTTP Header information, cookies, SSL session identifiers and perhaps other information.

There are several applications for Layer 7 switching. Perhaps the most common is to dedicate certain servers for certain types of content. For example, all URLs requesting images (e.g., ending in ".gif," ".jpg," or ".png") can be directed to a particular server. Other URLs indicating dynamic content, such as cgi-bin scripts or active server pages (".asp") can be directed to a server dedicated to these types of requests. Indications of cacheability, determined, for example, by direct examination of HTTP headers, allow requests for cacheable content to be directed to an interception proxy. In addition, Layer 7 switches can examine cookies, allowing them to identify individual users and Web sites and apply useful policies to each transaction.

Awareness of Layer 7 information helps switches maintain application sessions such as shopping carts, cookie-controlled transactions, and related transactions secured by SSL.

Segregating content by type allows file systems and server hardware and software to be tuned for each particular content type. Also, images may change less frequently than HTML text, which changes less frequently than dynamic applications.

While Layer 4 switches do not terminate TCP connections—they just rewrite header information—the same is not true for Layer 7 switches. Switching decisions based on Layer 7 information cannot be made during TCP session setup, when the TCP SYN packet arrives at the switch. The switch must wait for the HTTP GET request before the decision rule can be evaluated. This requires the switch to terminate the TCP connection. The connection takes place in the three steps shown in Figure 5.6.

In step 1, the client sends a request to the IP address of the switch. The switch accepts the TCP client connection and receives the GET request. In step 2, the switch can examine the Layer 7 information in the GET request and choose a server. The switch then opens a new connection (or uses an existing connection drawn from a pool of open connections to the server) and sends a GET to that server. Finally, in step 3, the switch splices the two connections into a single one connecting the client and the chosen server. Because this final connection began as two independent connections, the TCP packet sequence numbers expected by the client are unrelated to the sequence numbers used by the server. This requires translating sequence numbers and acknowledgment numbers between the client view and the server view of the connection. This splicing is similar to what was described for Network Address Translation, however because the connection is

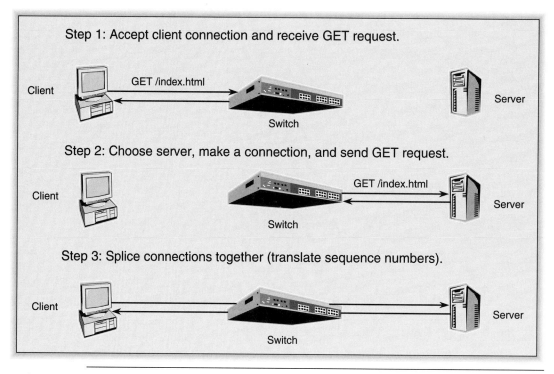

Step 1: Accept client connection and receive GET request.

Client   GET /index.html   Switch   Server

Step 2: Choose server, make a connection, and send GET request.

Client   Switch   GET /index.html   Server

Step 3: Splice connections together (translate sequence numbers).

Client   Switch   Server

Figure 5.6 TCP splicing.

terminated, the sequence number and acknowledgment numbers also need to be translated in the headers.

Now that we have described Layer 4 and Layer 7 switches, you may be curious about Layer 5 and Layer 6 switches. Unfortunately we have been told that protocol Layers 5 and 6 have been delayed in the marketing department indefinitely!

5.2.5   Server Health Checks

Server health checks improve reliability and flexibility of server farms and clusters of interception proxies. As shown in Figure 5.7, a Web switch connects to servers at all seven protocol layers. Coverage increases as the health checks are performed at higher protocol layers. At Layer 3, the switch can initiate an ICMP echo (ping) message to assess connectivity. Observing TCP connections can passively assess Layer 4 connections. If none are set up over some a period of time, the switch can initiate a TCP connection, perhaps to a test port provided by the server for this function. Operation of HTTP at Layer 7 can be assessed passively by observing GET requests or actively by initiating GET requests to the server.

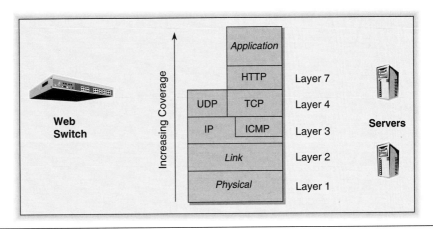

Figure 5.7 Layers of health checks.

Requesting database lookups periodically can monitor back-end servers and dynamic applications, such as databases.

Switches may include health checks for specific applications and protocols. For example the ServerIron Switch, available from Foundry Networks (www.foundrynetworks.com) includes health checks for FTP, HTTP, IMAP4, LDAP, NNTP, POP3, SMTP, Telnet, DNS, and RAD.

Typical Layer 7 switches provide a number of options for setting up these health checks. The request interval, number of retries, and content checks can be specified. The particular servers to be included in each check can be identified. If a health check fails, the switch can be configured to promptly remove the failing server from service. If the failed server is part of a load-balancing cluster, the remaining servers will then carry its load. This allows redundancy sparing of servers within the cluster. It also allows for adding and reconfiguring servers in the cluster. They can be *hot plugged* on and off the network. It can be quite convenient to be able to disconnect servers in live operation and know that no service[2] will be disrupted.

5.2.6 Interception Proxies

Section 3.5.3 described interception proxies. A Web switch is key to their operation. The Web switch can be configured using a Level 4 rule, for example, requesting that all port 80 traffic be diverted to the interception proxy. This will divert HTTP requests that use the default HTTP port. Level 7 rules, examining URLs to identify dynamic content or examining HTTP headers to identify cacheability directives, can improve operation. A cluster of proxies can be arranged in a group and the Web switch can balance the load among them.

---

[2]Except that transactions currently in progress will have to be restarted.

In these arrangements, the servers see the IP address of the Web switch, rather than of the client. This can complicate certain address-based security and authorization schemes.

Use of interception proxies is quite controversial. Basically, the objections are based on breaking the end-to-end nature of the communications by redirecting traffic to a destination other than the one specified in the IP header. Also, proxies alter communications without the knowledge or approval of end users or content providers [Mar00, Moo00]. Despite these concerns, network operators continue to deploy interception proxies to obtain the advantages they offer in managing and reducing Web traffic without requiring browser reconfiguration.

5.2.7   Other Layer 4–7 Switch Features and Applications

Using a Web switch as a server load balancer, as shown in Figure 5.4, introduces the Web switch as a single point of failure. If the Web switch fails, access to the entire server farm is lost. The Virtual Router Redundancy Protocol (VRRP) [RFC 2338, VRRP1] is often implemented by a Web switch to provide protection from such a failure. The protocol was originally developed to improve the reliability of router configurations, but is also used by Web switches. Several of the terms used in the protocol definition describe routers, even though it is being used by Web switches.

This protocol allows a single virtual IP address to identify a *virtual router,* which consists of at least two physical Web switches. The load is shared by these physical switches during normal operation. If a switch fails, the protocol shifts the load onto the remaining switches.

The reliability provided by VRRP and the versatility of Web switch server-load balancing makes them useful in several other applications. For example, a pair of switches sandwiching a cluster of firewalls can balance the load across the individual firewall units [Fou2]. This configuration may be necessary to provide the reliability and capacity required at the gateway to a large enterprise or Intranet.

5.3   Global Request Routing

On August 18, 1910, 15 American retail florists agreed to exchange orders for out-of-town deliveries. Originally called "Florists' Telegraph Delivery," FTD was the world's first flowers-by-wire service. Fifty-five years later, FTD expanded to include international transactions. The company was renamed "Florists Transworld Delivery" to reflect its growing worldwide presence. If you would like to send flowers to someone at the Veterans Hospital in Fargo, North Dakota, you can begin with a visit to your local FTD florist. There you can browse through a catalog or see an actual sample of the flowers that will be sent. After making your choice, your local florist contacts a florist in Fargo, North

Dakota and identifies the flowers you have requested. The North Dakota florist creates the arrangement you chose and delivers it to the local Veterans hospital.

This concept of delegating delivery responsibility to a content source best able to serve the content consumer is also used in Internet Content Delivery Networks. In any case, reaching a destination requires two fundamental decisions. One is deciding where to go; the other is deciding how to get there. We discuss these problems independently. For the same reasons that it is best to learn to sail the ship before navigating the seas, Section 5.3.1, *steering client requests*, first discusses how to get there. Section 5.3.2, *estimating proximity*, then discusses deciding where to go.

5.3.1 Steering Client Requests

Once the destination has been selected, several techniques can be used to efficiently direct client requests to that destination. These include *Global Server-Load Balancing (GSLB), DNS-based request routing, HTML rewriting, Anycasting,* and combinations of these approaches. The next sections describe each of these in more detail. Techniques for identifying the best destination are discussed in Section 5.3.2.

Global server load balancing—GSLB

At least two Web switch manufacturers include a feature called Global Server Load Balancing (GSLB) in their Web switches. This extends their Layer 4–7 switches and allows them to navigate world-wide networks. The scope and operation of this feature is different for the two manufacturers. Figure 5.8 illustrates the approach taken by Nortel/Alteon [ALT1]. Service nodes, consisting of a GSLB-enabled Web switch and a number of real Web servers, are distributed in several locations around the world, or at least in several places throughout the market for this content. Two new capabilities extend these service nodes to allow global server load balancing. The first is *global awareness,* and the second is *smart authoritative DNS*.

In local server load balancing, the Web switch in service node 1 is aware of the health and performance of the real Web servers attached to it, servers A and B in this case. In GSLB, service node 1 also includes the virtual IP address of service node 2 in its list of servers. Similarly, service node 2 is aware of service node 1 and includes its VIP in its list of servers. The result is that the Web switches making up each service node are globally aware, each knowing the addresses of all the other service nodes. They also regularly exchange performance information among the Web switches in the GSLB configuration. This allows each switch to estimate the best server for any request, choosing not only from its pool of locally connected real servers, but the remote service nodes as well.

To make use of this global awareness, the GSLB switches act as intelligent authoritative DNS servers for certain managed domains. Consider an example

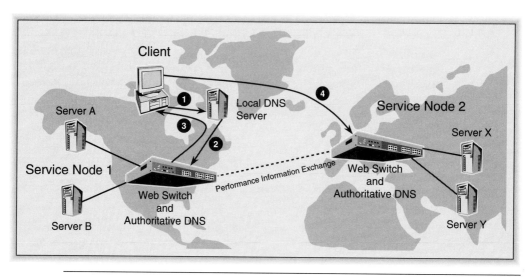

Figure 5.8 Global server load balancing—Approach 1.

of a client in North America requesting content from www.content-networking.
com, which—for the purpose of this example—is assumed to be part of a GSLB
content delivery network (it is not).

1. The client's DNS resolver requests the IP address of www.content-networking.com from the local domain name server.
2. This request works its way through the Domain Name System, until it reaches an authoritative name server for the domain. The system is configured so that the only authoritative DNS servers for that domain are GSLB-enabled Web switches making up this network. These Web switches run the DNS protocol and simple DNS server software to allow them to respond to this request.
3. Since a Web switch is responding to the DNS request, and since each Web switch is aware of the health and performance of each service node, it can respond with the IP address of the service node most likely to give the best performance. For example, because of time zone differences it may turn out that the servers in Europe are lightly loaded during the business day in North America. In this case it may be best for the Web switch at service node 1 to respond to some queries with the virtual IP address of service node 2.
4. The client request is sent to service node 2, and is served by either real server X or real server Y. While this may help to balance the load on the servers, serving a request from a remote site does increase network traffic. Practical GSLB networks are likely to include more service nodes within a smaller geographic region.

Foundry Networks includes estimates of client proximity in their implementation of GSLB [Fou1]. Each Web switch uses the natural traffic flow between the client's browser and itself to measure the roundtrip latency. Periodically, the Web switches report this information to the master switch, designated as the GSLB switch. This GSLB switch is configured as either a DNS proxy, relaying DNS requests to the only authoritative DNS servers, or as the actual authoritative DNS for the managed domains. The system operation is illustrated in Figure 5.9.

1. The client's DNS resolver requests the IP address of www.content-networking.com from the local domain name server.
2. This request works its way through the DNS, until it reaches an authoritative name server for the domain. The system is configured so that the only authoritative DNS servers for that domain are attached through the GSLB-enabled Web switch serving as the master in this network. Alternatively, the GSLB switch itself can act as the authoritative name server.
3. The DNS request is forwarded to the authoritative DNS for this domain. The DNS responds with all IP addresses able to serve this request. This typically includes the virtual IP address of each of the service nodes in this network.

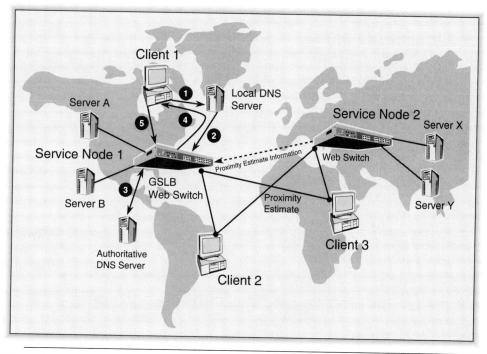

Figure 5.9 Global server load balancing—Approach 2.

4. The GSLB Web switch is aware of the DNS request and analyzes the responses flowing through it. Also, it has been collecting health and performance information for each service node. In addition, the GSLB has been collecting proximity information that estimates the latency between each Web switch and individual clients. This proximity information is indexed by *network neighborhood.* Each network neighborhood is the group of IP addresses sharing the same high order bits. By default, this is configured as the top 20 bits of the client IP address, but can be configured to include a different range. Assessing the performance, health, and proximity information it can respond with the IP address of the service node most likely to give the best service. In this case the virtual IP address of service node 1 is returned. It is likely that requests from client 3 will be directed to service node 2, based on the proximity information.

5. The client request is sent to service node 1, and is served by either real server A or real server B.

The Foundry GSLB implementation uses the following criteria for selecting the best service node:

1. Site, server, and application health checks.
2. The speed of Layer 4 health checks responses, called "flashback" speed by Foundry. Assuming that heavily loaded servers will be slower to respond to a health check request, this is used to estimate server responsiveness.
3. Geography-based site selection. In some cases RFC 1466 and IANA allocates IP addresses based on the continent of origin. The GSLB switch can use this information to direct clients to service nodes within the same continent.
4. Site load conditions are used in GSLB, just as they are in local server load balancing.
5. Configurable thresholds for site load conditions allow administrative limits to be set for including or excluding sites experiencing certain load conditions.
6. Proximity estimates from Web switches to clients. The natural traffic flow between the client's browser and Web switch is used to estimate this round-trip latency. Some fraction of client requests are not directed based on existing proximity information. This allows continuous exploration and gathering of the most up-to-date proximity information.

Although it is difficult to identify one approach as superior to the other, the two approaches can be summarized at a high level. The Alteon approach considers all switches around the world to form a pool it can draw on to share load. The Foundry approach considers proximity information to help direct requests to the closest service node.

DNS-based request routing

To provide an alternative to GSLB, Lucent Technologies briefly sold their WebDNS product [Bea01], which provides a proximity solution based on agents running in reverse proxy Web caches and cooperates with an intelligent authoritative DNS. Agents running in the reverse proxy Web cache in each service node gather client latency information each time a client requests content through the proxy. The WebDNS that acts as the authoritative DNS server collects this proximity data from each proxy. This information is indexed by network neighborhood and is analyzed to identify the service node that is closest to each client. Figure 5.10 illustrates the system, which operates as follows [Bea01]:

1. The client's DNS resolver requests the IP address of www.content-networking.com from the local domain name server.
2. This request works its way through the Domain Name System, until it reaches an authoritative name server for the domain. The system is configured so that the only authoritative DNS servers for that domain are WebDNS.
3. The WebDNS uses its proximity information to choose the service node closest to the client. It responds with the address of that closest service node. This may be the actual IP address of the reverse proxy, or the virtual IP address of the Web switch serving a cluster of reverse proxies, as illustrated in Figure 5.4.
4. Based on the response delivered in step 3, the client request is sent to service node 1, and is served by the reverse proxy Web cache at that service node. If the requested content is not in the cache, the cache requests it from either server A or server B.

Section 5.3.2 discusses proximity-locating algorithms in more detail.

HTML rewriting

The previous techniques routed the client request to a server with capacity and location best able to handle the request. Another technique called *HTML rewriting* responds with content that steers subsequent requests to servers that are close to the client.

Consider a national company that manages the Web site at www.foo.bar [RFC 3092]. Their homepage, www.foo.bar/index.html, includes a graphic corporate logo (logo.jpg), descriptive text (text.html), and another graphic (figure1.jpg). When a request is received from a client located on the East Coast, the foo.bar server modifies the content of index.html by prefixing each URL within the file with "ny.rewrite.net/foo" before responding, as is illustrated in Figure 5.11. This moves the request from the foo.bar address space to the rewrite.net address space. A content delivery network service provider manages the domain "rewrite.net." They have content servers located in many areas around the world. It is assumed that the server ny.rewrite.net is located in New York. Similarly they have a server,

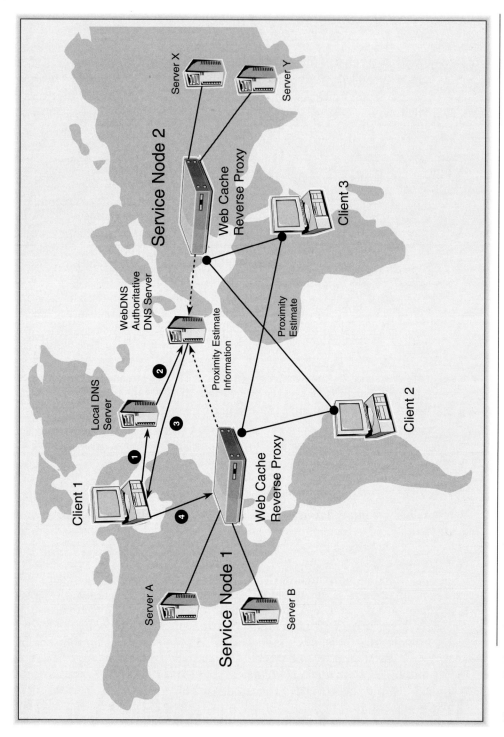

Figure 5.10 WebDNS approach.

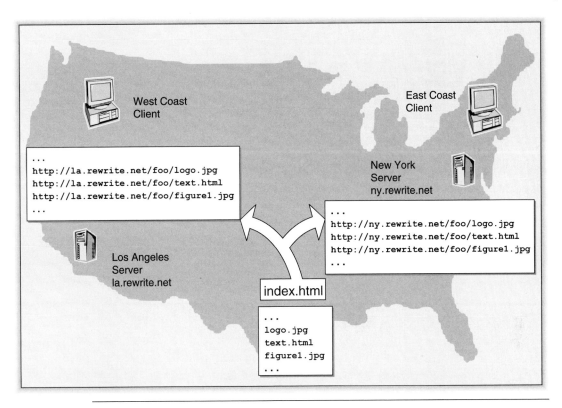

Figure 5.11 HTML rewriting.

called la.rewrite.net, located in Los Angeles. Each of these servers has a file system, named /foo, containing the content of the foo.bar Web site. As the East Coast client's browser reads the (rewritten) file index.html, the URLs it contains direct the client to retrieve the corporate logo and other content from the ny.rewrite.net server. This New York-based server is convenient to the East Coast client. Similarly, if a client from the West Coast makes the same request to www.foo.bar/index.com, the server prefixes each URL in the file with la.rewrite.net/foo. The result is that the West Coast client now retrieves the subsequent content from the Los Angeles-based server of rewrite.net.

With this approach, the first request (e.g., for foo.bar/index.html) is within the foo.bar address space and is served by the foo.bar server. Once the foo.bar server responds with a rewritten request, subsequent requests are served from the rewrite.net address space, using their network. Since these requests are now served by the rewrite.net network, the content delivery network provider, rather than the original server (foo.bar), now controls billing, traffic surveillance, network management, ad insertion, etc., for the content delivery activities.

The HTML rewriting can be done before the content is placed on the Web server (called *a priori* HTML rewriting) or it can be done dynamically as the content is requested (called *on-demand* HTML rewriting) [RFC 3568]. This is a space-time trade-off. The *a priori* approach requires storing several versions of each file, each one optimized for clients of a particular location. The on-demand approach requires processing to analyze and rewrite each page as it is requested.

Several techniques are used to estimate the clients' location. In addition to the techniques described previously on DNS-based request routing, several proprietary techniques are used. These are probably based on laboriously created databases of IP addresses and their physical locations. The whois database and user address information provided as part of e-commerce transactions and other online requests for location information are likely sources of this information.

Akamai is a major provider of content delivery services based on HTML rewriting. To see an example of HTML rewriting, open the source of a Web page of any of their customers, for example www.1800flowers.net. Notice the large number of URL references containing the string "akamai.net". Each of these is a rewritten URL, pointing to content on a server in the akamai.net content delivery network.

Anycasting

The police dispatcher broadcasts the request "will the unit closest to Main Street and First Avenue please respond to assist an accident victim at that location" over the police-band radio. The request is heard by officers in squad cars throughout the city. Several cars near the accident site respond to the dispatcher indicating their location and availability. Finally, after some discussion, the car in the area best able to assist is identified and heads to the accident scene.

In this example the dispatcher is using a simple *anycast* network. Anycast [RFC 1546] is a service that allows a node to connect to one, and perhaps the "best," member of a group able to serve each request. The requesting nodes may be clients, applications, or hosts. The police dispatcher represents this requesting node; however, officers in any of the squad cars could have made a similar request. The group is formed of resources that offer interchangeable services. The various squad cars communicating by radio form such a group because they are all capable of assisting an accident victim. In a computer network, the group may consist of computers with spare CPU capacity, or spare storage capacity. These resources are available to connect to clients needing their processing or storage capabilities. In a content delivery network, the group can consist of the surrogates, either servers or proxy caches, which can deliver the desired content.

Discussions among the police officers helped to identify the squad car best able to respond. It is likely they considered the location of the car, the officers' current activity and assignment, traffic congestion between the squad car location and the accident site, and perhaps other factors to identify the best squad car. In a content delivery network, proximity, capacity, load, bandwidth, congestion, and content availability are all factors that can determine the best server.

Although anycasting was described more than a decade ago, very few practical networks have been built. This is probably because of the technical challenges inherent in efficiently locating the best server. Figure 5.12 illustrates one application-level anycast network that has been described and analyzed [CDK+03]. This figure shows three distinct anycast groups, identified as resource types A, B, and C. These may represent surrogates in a content delivery network each capable of delivering different content types. For example, the nodes labeled A may have news information, the B nodes may have weather information, and the C nodes may have sports information. Each type of node is arranged in a separate tree structure, emanating from the corresponding root node. The group of nodes providing interchangeable services form each network.

Client 1 attaches to the content delivery network at a type C node. The network follows these steps when Client 1 anycasts for type A services:

1. The request is directed toward the root of the A tree at each hop through the combined network.
2. When it arrives at a type A node, the node begins a depth-first traversal of the A tree searching for the best node.
3. Using a variety of criteria, the best node is identified.
4. The selected node responds to the client, and service begins.

The network follows similar steps when Client 2, connected to the network through a type A node, requests type B services.

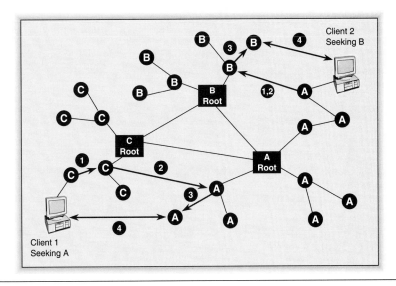

Figure 5.12 Anycast network.

Combined approaches

Local server-load balancing (SLB) complements the global routing algorithms described in this section. The best systems integrate the two approaches. These systems use local server load balancing within the service nodes and use global routing to direct traffic to those service nodes.

When deciding where to serve each request in GSLB networks each switch assesses its pool of local servers before considering remote nodes. In the DNS and HTML rewriting approaches each service node typically consists of a number of servers balanced locally by a Web switch. Global request routing site selection algorithms can be used with a GSLB network. Here the GSLB network is providing a very robust and reliable pool of real servers. The global request routing algorithms then direct traffic to the best starting point in the GSLB network.

HTML rewriting can be combined with any of the techniques discussed here. Once the initial URL rewrite directs the requests to the rewriter's Content Delivery Network, then this network can employ any of these techniques.

Each of the various approaches described have advantages and disadvantages. The GSLB approaches are relatively simple, but may lead to inaccurate and suboptimal routing decisions. The DNS-based approaches assume that clients are close to their local DNS resolvers, but this may not always be true. Also, once a DNS request is served, it persists in the client until the TTL expires. If a bad destination is chosen, it cannot be changed until the TTL expires. The HTML rewriting approach requires that the first request always go to the server, then relies on one of the proximity estimation techniques (described in the next section) to select the rewrite prefix. Anycasting is an interesting concept, but large practical networks are yet to emerge.

5.3.2 Estimating Proximity—Choosing the Closest Service Node

The previous section described how requests can be steered toward a chosen destination. This section describes techniques for choosing the service node closest to a client. This is important information for selecting the best server. There are several sensible measures of the distance between client and service node that can be used to identify the closest node. These distance measures include geographic distance, transfer delay (measured as round trip time (RTT)), the number of router hops, packet loss rate along the path, and congestion along the path.

Standards are not yet available for precisely identifying the geographic location of network elements, measuring network distance, and other measures for selecting the "closest" node. The approaches described here are solutions individual organizations have developed. Some aspects of these approaches are proprietary and not available for publication. Therefore, although the key ideas in each approach are described, some details are left out of the descriptions.

The approaches described include *reactive probing* where, in response to each client request, a specialized DNS probes candidate nodes to estimate their distance. In *proactive probing*, the specialized DNS probes clients in advance of client requests and keeps a record of each of their distances to each well-known network. *Connection monitoring* eliminates probes and relies on the measurement of RTT as connections are naturally made between service nodes and clients.

In each of these examples, the specialized DNS being described has been made the authoritative DNS for the managed content. Also, each service node in the diagram can provide the content the client requests. The service nodes may be Web cache clusters or replicated servers.

Reactive probing

Reactive probing is illustrated in Figure 5.13.

1. The client requests content managed by a reactive probing DNS server. The request goes from the client to its local DNS sever to the authoritative DNS for this site, which is a reactive probing DNS server.
2. In response to this DNS request, the probing DNS server requests that each candidate service node measure its round trip time (RTT) to the

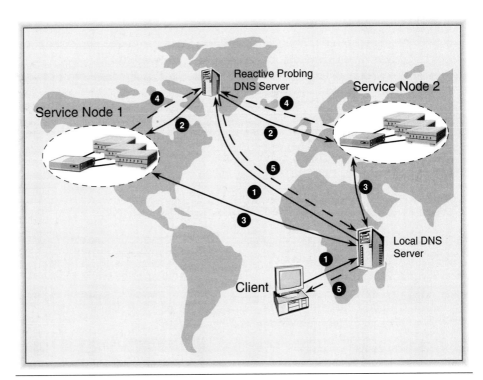

Figure 5.13 Reactive probing.

client's local DNS. This is done assuming that the RTT to the local DNS is a good approximation of RTT to the client. This turns out to be a good assumption in many cases, and a poor assumption in other cases.

3. Each service node pings the local DNS and measures the round trip time.
4. Each service node reports its RTT to the probing DNS, which chooses the shortest RTT.
5. The probing DNS returns the IP address of the service node having the shortest RTT to the local DNS, which returns it to the client.

The client then requests the content from that (closest) service node.

The advantage of this approach is that the RTT measurements are very fresh and therefore likely to reflect current network status. However, network conditions may change before a cached DNS response expires and it may no longer represent the shortest RTT. The primary disadvantage is that the DNS response is delayed significantly while the probing takes place. Other disadvantages are that firewalls often block the ping traffic used by the probe and the quantity of traffic generated by the probes toward the local DNS is often objectionable to the administrators of that DNS.

The primary disadvantage of reactive probing is eliminated by the proactive probing technique.

Proactive probing

In proactive probing, the probing DNS creates a database of round trip times from each service node to a list of Autonomous Systems (AS), representing the universe of known client networks. This is illustrated in Figure 5.14. The data gathering follows these steps:

1. The proactive probing DNS begins with a list of known autonomous systems (As). For each network, the list includes the IP address of some real device on that network. This single IP address is considered representative of the entire AS.
2. The probing DNS server transmits the list of representative IP addresses to each service node.
3. Each service node pings the IP address for each AS. The round trip time (RTT) is measured and recorded.
4. Periodically the RTT measurement results are transmitted to the probing DNS server. The server assembles this information into a table that includes the RTT for each service node to each AS.

This data gathering takes place continuously, keeping the probing DNS prepared to serve DNS requests.

As in the other examples, when a client (not shown in Figure 5.14) requests content managed by the probing DNS, it begins with a DNS resolution request to its local DNS server. This request is eventually handled by the probing DNS which has been made authoritative for this domain. The probing DNS responds with the

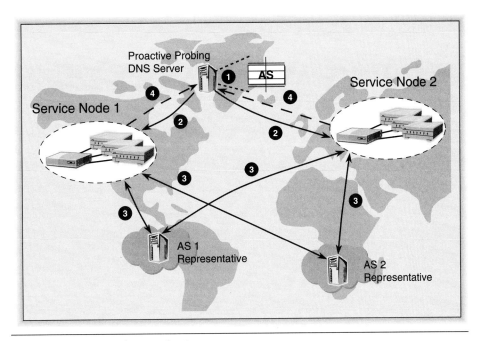

Figure 5.14 Proactive probing—data gathering.

IP address of the service node that has the shortest RTT for the Autonomous System represented by the client's local DNS. Again it is being assumed that RTT to the local DNS is a good approximation for RTT to the client.

Although this approach solves the DNS response latency problem that reactive probing suffers from, it does introduce other problems. It is difficult, if not impossible, to select a single IP address to represent the entire AS. Many ASs are large and diverse. A server in one corner of the network may provide a very poor representation of the distance to a client in another corner of the same network. The same problems of traffic intruding to endpoints that are not part of the managed network, discussed for reactive probing, are at least as bad in this approach.

Connection monitoring avoids the problems of active probing.

Connection monitoring

Connection monitoring eliminates probes and relies on measurements of RTT as connections are naturally made between service nodes and clients. This is an accurate measurement of the transport distance from the service node to the client. Also it requires very little processing overhead and no network overhead. The Web caches making up each service node run kernels that are instrumented to collect this RTT information. The measurement chosen is shown in the inset appearing in the lower left hand corner of Figure 5.15. As each TCP connection is established, it begins with the "triple handshake" of SYN, SYN/ACK, and finally ACK. The elapsed time from when the cache sends the SYN/ACK until the ACK is received from the client is the RTT measurement.

The algorithm learns continuously, gathering more accurate and up-to-date proximity information as it operates.

Operation begins with these steps, illustrated in Figure 5.15:

1. The client begins with a request to the local DNS. This request is eventually handled by the monitoring DNS which has been made authoritative for this domain. If the system is early in its operation, it may not have any information about the proximity of the various service nodes to this client. In this case, it simply chooses a service node at random, or by using some heuristic such as IP address similarity.

2. The DNS replies with the IP address of the chosen service node. Because the system does not yet know if this is a good or bad choice of service node for this client, it uses a very short TTL in the DNS response. This ensures that the client is not stuck with that choice for very long, and it reduces the impact on the client of being assigned to a distant service node.

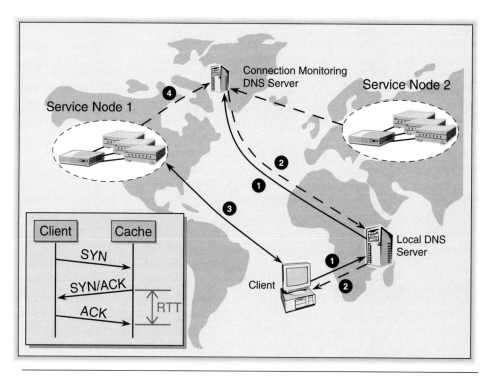

Figure 5.15 Connection monitoring.

3. As the connection is established between the client and the service node, the RTT for this connection is measured by the instrumented Web cache.
4. This RTT measurement information is sent to the monitoring DNS.

The system manages the TTL of the DNS responses it sends to reflect the knowledge it has about the chosen service node. If the service node is chosen at random, the TTL is set very low, so that the DNS response cached by the client will time out soon and the client will have to make other DNS requests. If the RTT is found to be low, then the TTL is set high, so that clients stick with a favorable service node. If RTT is high, then TTL is set low, so the client can soon wander and search for a better service node assignment. Table 5-1 is used to manage TTL values.

When the TTL of the DNS response eventually times out, the client will eventually make another request to the monitoring DNS. If the DNS has not yet found a service node with low RTT to this client, it will choose another service node at random. Again the connection gets set up and the RTT measured, recorded, and sent to the monitoring DNS. If the DNS has located a service node with a low RTT, it returns the address of that node. This design quickly avoids bad choices of service node assignment and quickly converges on good choices even if they are not proven optimal.

The system summarizes client IP addresses by collecting them into network neighborhoods based on the 20 to 24 high order bits of their address. This results in grouping 256 to 4096 IP addresses together in each network neighborhood. This saves table space and helps the learning process. Although the system may not have encountered the specific IP address of your client, it may have learned the best service node for another client in your network neighborhood. The system responds with this close node on your first request. The learning algorithm converges quickly. Analysis of several aspects of a related algorithm is in [ASW+02].

This approach solves the problems faced by probing-type DNS proximity systems, but is still limited by a few factors. These include the assumption that clients are located close to their local DNS, the resolution of network neighborhoods, use of the DNS system in ways that were not anticipated in its design, and learning latency caused by caching DNS responses throughout the network.

Table 5-1   Managing time to live

RTT	TTL
Unknown	Very Short
Low	Long
Medium	Medium
High	Short

5.4   **Case Studies**

Thomas Edison said, "Genius is 1 percent inspiration and 99 percent perspiration." The work required to transform the deceptively simple concepts of global routing described in the previous section into a reliable worldwide content delivery network illustrate the wisdom of Edison's remark. Both Lucent/Bell Lab's WebDNS and Akamai services began as academic challenges.

5.4.1   **Lucent/Bell Labs WebDNS**

Several years ago, Researchers from the Networking Research Department at Bell Laboratories turned their attention to the problem of estimating the network location of clients and finding the most appropriate site for serving a client's Web service request. Recognizing that an efficient solution would involve applied mathematics and algorithms, the networking researchers were joined by colleagues from the Mathematical Sciences Research Center. The joint team designed and evaluated several approaches before refining and prototyping one particularly promising solution. The researchers then approached the development organization to demonstrate the work and to explore how best it could be put to practical use. This is always a critical but highly exciting moment in the life of a research project, since it has to be proven that the elegance and the fundamentally new aspects of the research work can actually be applied to the real world and provide practical value in real networking environments.

To evaluate the practicality of the ideas and begin the design of a useful product, a key question was posed by the development organization: What is the simplest system we can build that will send requests from clients on the East Coast to servers on the East Coast, and will send requests from clients on the West Coast to servers on the West Coast? This simple problem helped focus both the researchers' and developers' efforts on a basic practical system, while also considering more complex and general scenarios in the system design. Requirements for this practical system were written, developers met regularly with researchers, and in a joint effort, a flexible system that could serve this simple scenario, as well as much more complex content networks, was built and ready to be tested.

It was difficult to select a suitable test environment for a content delivery network that extends across the globe. The problem was approached in stages. The first step was to deploy service nodes in labs in two locations within New Jersey. A very small, invisible graphic object (a Web bug, named tiny.gif) served from a domain managed by the WebDNS was then incorporated into the bottom of a Web page that receives modest traffic from around the world (and is owned by one of the developers). The WebDNS network then managed this single object. This provided a small but diverse load on the WebDNS and allowed the developers, testers, business managers, and researchers to monitor, assess, and improve its operation. System failures and reconfiguration activity were invisible to the end users because during a network outage the Web bug simply did not appear on the bottom of the Web page. This was transparent to the users, because the graphic was invisible.

In stages, service nodes were added to this test network. Eventually service nodes were deployed to Germany and California. As the system became more stable, more traffic was moved onto the network. Managed Web bugs were placed onto more Web sites, generating more traffic. Finally there was enough confidence in the system to manage an entire domain. As traffic increased and requests came from more locations, more problems were identified and solved.

The services of Keynote Systems (www.keynote.com) were used to gather more information about the network operations. Keynote measures network performance from the end-user perspective. They have instrumented clients at dozens of locations around the world. These can be set to request content from the network being tested and measure the actual performance. The results are displayed in graphic reports that dramatically reveal the performance of the network. The client requests also create a small load on the system from points all around the globe. Using this performance information we continued to tune the network. Since we knew the location of each Keynote client, and we could monitor the service node it was directed to, we were able to refine the accuracy of the location assignment algorithms.

We could tell when the system made an excellent service node assignment, and when it made poor ones. No amount of willpower was ever sufficient to reduce the RTT of a DNS response once it was delivered to the network!

This phase of the testing demonstrated that the Internet and the content networks that make it up are more diverse than the researchers and developers ever imagined. Many unanticipated conditions occurred. These include regional differences in the administration and use of domain names and hostnames, corporate security procedures for DNS system changes, difficulties in isolating and debugging network problems after a change is made, and sparse coverage areas of the performance monitoring services. Each problem was analyzed and solved, moving the WebDNS closer to a field-ready product.

Network load, service node locations, and monitoring capabilities continued to increase until the system became field ready. Eventually it was used to host a very large and busy Web site of an internationally prominent corporation.

5.4.2 Akamai

Akamai (pronounced AH-kuh-my) is Hawaiian for intelligent, clever, and cool.

Akamai's beginnings lie in a challenge posed by Tim Berners-Lee at the Massachusetts Institute of Technology (MIT) in early 1995. He foresaw the congestion that is now very familiar to Internet users, and he challenged colleagues at MIT to invent a fundamentally new and better way to deliver Internet content.

MIT Professor of Applied Mathematics Tom Leighton, who had an office down the hall from Tim Berners-Lee, was intrigued by the challenge. Leighton recognized that applied mathematics and algorithms could help reduce Web congestion. He solicited the help of graduate student Danny Lewin[3] and several other researchers to tackle the problem.

Together they developed a set of algorithms for intelligently routing and replicating content over a large network of distributed servers—without relying on centralized servers typically used by Web site owners today. Jonathan Seelig joined the founding team and they began building the business plan that would lead to Akamai's inception.

In 1998, the group entered the annual MIT $50K Entrepreneurship Competition, where the company's business proposition was selected as one of six finalists among 100 entries. Akamai obtained an exclusive license to certain intellectual property from MIT, and development efforts began in the fall of 1998.

In late 1998 and early 1999, a group of experienced Internet business professionals began to join this founding team. Together, these computer scientists and experienced Internet professionals founded Akamai, a company dedicated to ending the "World Wide Wait" through intelligent Internet content delivery. The company launched commercial service in April 1999 and announced that one of the world's most trafficked Web properties, Yahoo!, was a charter customer.

Its services are built upon its globally distributed platform for content, streaming media, and application delivery, which is comprised of more than 13,000 servers within over 1,100 networks in 66 countries. The Akamai network handles tens of billions of hits per day. The company has a market capitalization of approximately $1.5 billion [Akam1].

---

[3]Tragically Danny Lewin was killed along with so many others when American Airlines Flight 11 slammed into the north tower of the World Trade Center on September 11, 2001.

CHAPTER 6

Peer-to-Peer Content Networks

Peers are equals. Huge audiences gather to see and hear rock stars, sports heroes, politicians, religious leaders, and other famous, interesting, or powerful people. At the same time, people dialog one-on-one with friends, family, co-workers, and other peers. Similarly, although millions of clients request content from popular sites such as CNN, Yahoo!, and Disney, peer-to-peer communications are symmetric one-to-one relationships.

Although peers are sometimes selfish, greedy, deceitful, malicious, untrustworthy, and unreliable, they are often very helpful and generous and they do make the best friends. The world is full of them, and there is strength in numbers.

Peer-to-peer content networks are formed by symmetrical connections between host computers, which are often the users' own personal computers. Just as you and your human peers exchange roles of speaker and listener during a dialog, here each host computer can act as either client or server in the protocol and takes on these roles alternately as required to complete a request.

There are three situations where peer-to-peer content networks provide unique characteristics compared to client server networks. The first is where content originates with many peers rather than with a central source. This is important in some file sharing applications described in this chapter and it is fundamental to collaboration systems, such as instant messaging, described in Chapter 7. The second advantage is that a peer-to-peer network does not have a single point of failure. While this can increase reliability over client server architectures, the complexity of peer-to-peer networks can lead to an overall decrease in reliability. Also, since the software running on each host is similar, if not identical, a bug in that software is apparent throughout the network and can rapidly lead to a widespread vulnerability. A third characteristic is related to the first two. Because content originates at many peers, and there is no central point of control within the network, the content is more difficult to regulate. Censorship, enforcing editorial policy, imposing political agendas, restricting or focusing distribution, monitoring or charging for access, and identifying content providers and content consumers all become more difficult when content originates with many peers rather than with few servers. Peer-to-peer networks can shift power to the people and reinvigorate freedom of the press and freedom of speech.

This chapter explores how peers can be organized into useful content delivery networks. It begins by characterizing peer-to-peer networks and describes several types. The technical challenges of creating a reliable network from a random collection of unknown peers are discussed. Case studies describe the history and technical aspects of Napster, Gnutella, and Chord. Finally the business and legal aspects of peer-to-peer networks are briefly discussed.

6.1   What Are Peer-to-Peer Networks?

Peer-to-peer networks are distributed systems where the software running at each node provides equivalent functions [SKB01]. A succinct formal definition of peer-to-peer networking is "a set of technologies that enable the direct exchange of services or data between computers" [Int01]. Implicit in that definition are the fundamental principles that peers are equals,[1] and peer-to-peer systems emphasize sharing among these equals. A pure peer-to-peer system runs without any centralized control or hierarchical organization. A hybrid system uses some centralized or hierarchical resources. Peers can represent clients, servers, routers, or even networks.

Figure 6.1 illustrates simple reference architectures for both client-server systems and peer-to-peer systems. Clients are not equal to servers, and they depend on a relatively small number of servers for system operation. Peers are all equal, and they rely only on themselves and their peers.

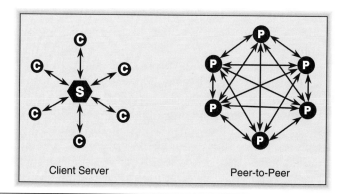

Figure 6.1 Reference architectures.

---

[1]They are equal because they provide equivalent services, but they may have different capacity such as processing power, storage capacity, bandwidth, etc.

The original Internet was designed as a peer-to-peer system. The first Internet applications were remote machine access, e-mail exchange, and copying files between computers. These are all peer-to-peer applications where each host computer can act as either client or server in the protocol and takes on these roles alternately as required to complete a request. For example, to copy a file from host A to host B, A acts as the FTP client and B acts as the FTP server. The roles can be exchanged when a file is copied in the other direction.

Network News, the predecessor of today's news groups, originally propagated content from host to host using UUCP, the Unix-to-Unix copy protocol. In this peer-to-peer system, each host ran the same UUCP program and a symmetrical protocol [RFC 976].

The DNS includes thousands of name servers which all perform the same function of serving DNS requests. This forms a peer-to-peer network in which name servers forward queries to their peers until an answer is found, or it is determined that no answer exists. The root servers and the hierarchical organization of the system does, however, make some peers "more equal" than others.

However, over time the Internet became asymmetrical.

6.1.1 Transparency and Asymmetry in the Internet

Originally the Internet was designed to use a single universal logical addressing scheme and packets would flow unaltered from source to destination. This is called *transparency*—because packets could be retrieved unaltered from their source by knowing only their address [RFC 2775]. This is an important part of the Internet End-to-End design principle as discussed in Chapter 1 [RFC 1958, SM94]. This transparency also enables symmetry (without requiring it) because any endpoint can readily access any other endpoint.

Over time the Internet became asymmetrical. FTP,[2] Telnet, and later HTTP are client-server protocols which allow servers to take on roles different from the clients they serve. Servers typically have wideband connections to the Internet, while many clients dialed up over low speed lines. Clients that have broadband connections often use Asymmetric Digital Subscriber Line (ADSL) modulation or cable modems. Both of these provide substantially more bandwidth toward client than away from it [OMH01].

Asymmetry in access technologies reflects the different roles and resources that are a part of client-server architectures. Limited uplink bandwidth in cable systems and ADSL restricts high capacity servers to the high capacity side of the link.

There are other reasons the Internet has become asymmetrical. RFC 2775 provides a long list of causes that reduce the transparency in the Internet and make it asymmetrical, including:

---

[2]In an earlier paragraph we used FTP to illustrate a peer-to-peer architecture. It is the role of each host, not the protocol it is running, that distinguishes peer-to-peer from client server architectures.

- The Intranet model allows users on the Intranet to access any endpoint on the Internet, but users outside of the Intranet cannot access it.
- Dynamic address allocation, including SLIP, PPP, and DHCP, changes the endpoint address each time it connects to the network. Therefore this transient IP address cannot be used to contact the endpoint after the session is completed and the IP address is released.
- Firewalls, including basic firewalls and SOCKS Firewalls [RFC 1928] act as a one-way gate. They allow anyone inside the internal network to establish a connection to anyone on the Internet, but prevent untrusted hosts on the Internet from initiating connections to the internal network.
- Private addresses known only within a private network [RFC 1597] cannot be used for communication across the Internet.
- Network address translators change IP addresses on the fly and destroy end-to-end address transparency. They also complicate protocols that carry the IP address at the application level.
- Application level gateways, relays, proxies, and caches may alter content in ways that are unknown or uncontrollable by the endpoints.
- Voluntary isolation and peer networks, such as WAP protocol networks, do not use Internet addressing and protocols but connect endpoints to the Internet.
- Split DNS allows an organization to run a DNS on their Intranet that provides hostnames that may not correspond to their Fully Qualified Domain names (FQDN) used outside the firewall.
- Various approaches to load-sharing hide the real endpoint's IP address behind a VPN (see Figure 5.4).

Computer architects have long fought the battle of big Endian vs. Little Endian [IEN 137]. Now network architects are fighting the battle of End to End*ian*! There is no going back.

The symmetry of peer-to-peer network communications cuts across the grain of this trend toward asymmetry in the Internet.

In the early days of the Internet, the peers that were communicating were a small number of large professionally managed computers used by research scientists. Today the peers that are communicating are often large numbers of PCs run by teenagers over networks such as Gnutella and KaZaA. This puts new stresses on the peer-to-peer systems and the underlying network and leads to several important system requirements.

6.1.2   System Requirements

Several ideal characteristics desirable for reliable content management systems are especially interesting in peer-to-peer systems. These include:

- **Availability**—The services of the system can be accessed 24×7×365, any time of the day or night, any day of the year.
- **Durability**—Information stored by the system will be available forever.

- **Access Control**—Information is protected from unauthorized access or alteration. These include restricting read access to private information, and write access to shared information.
- **Authenticity**—The documents are protected against forgery and undetected alteration.
- **Robustness**—The system is resistant to malicious attacks, such as denial of service attacks and other assaults.
- **Massive Scalability**—The system works well with thousands, millions, or perhaps even billions of peers.

In addition, some systems that have been designed to promote free expression and publication have stressed:

- **Anonymity**—The author and publisher of a document are difficult or impossible to identify.
- **Free Expression**—The content cannot be censored or altered after it is delivered to the system.
- **Deniability**—Users are not certain what content is stored on their individual peer machines, so they can reasonably deny responsibility for its ownership.

These free expression characteristics are easier to attain in a peer-to-peer system than in a system with centralized control [Kub03].

6.1.3 Creating Order from Chaos

No doubt your human peers form a diverse group. They may include people who are young or old, rich or poor, fat or thin, ambitious or lazy, arrogant or humble, cautious or reckless, friendly or hostile, reliable or unreliable. Yet despite this diversity, you are able to form groups, work together and accomplish shared goals. Computing peers are also diverse. They differ in processing power, storage space, network bandwidth, network location, connection type, hours of operation, reliability, and user goals. A basic problem is to create a reliable peer-to-peer content network from this diverse collection of peers. This section discusses several characteristics of peer-to-peer content networks [MKL+02].

Whether or not it is a design goal, *decentralization* is a natural consequence of interconnecting a worldwide collection of peers. Decentralized systems are free of bottlenecks and lack single points of failure. Ownership of processing power, storage space, bandwidth, and access to content is shared among the participants in the network. But with no one in charge, it may be difficult to even find the network, let alone the content you seek.

Since there are no centralized resources to exhaust, peer-to-peer content networks have the potential of *massive scalability*. As long as there are peers willing to participate, there is nothing else to run out of as the networks expand and become very large. However, we will see that problems in managing connections to peers and communicating requests and responses require well-thought-out algorithms to provide acceptable performance in large networks. *Organization* can become the scarce resource as the networks grow very large.

Migrating birds such as geese fly in their characteristic V-shaped formation because this is easiest for each goose, not because the lead goose has directed them in this pattern. The same set of instructions is running in each goose [BBC02]. This is an example of *self-organizing behavior.* Similarly, with no central management structure, a peer-to-peer content delivery network must rely on *self organization.* The algorithms must achieve scalability, reliable operation, satisfactory performance, and fault resilience from a collection of unreliable peers with intermittent connections.

Resource *ownership is shared* in a peer-to-peer content network. The cost of obtaining, operating, and maintaining each peer is borne by its owner. The responsibility for creating, publishing, and distributing content is also shared. As the network grows larger, the increasing total cost of the network is shared among the increasing number of participants.

The network is made up of *ad hoc connections* as peers join and leave the network at any time. While it is an exceptional event for resources such as servers to join and leave a centralized network, it is a normal event in peer-to-peer systems. It is difficult to provide service guarantees in this environment.

The potentially massive scale of a peer-to-peer network can either help or hinder *performance.* Aggregating the combined processing power, storage space, and network resources from a large number of peers can provide a huge pool of resources and excellent performance. The SETI@home project harnesses the power of millions of personal computers to gather more processing power than the largest centralized supercomputers. However, the difficulty of communicating to the many peers in a large, distributed, self-organized network can reduce performance. As we will see in Section 6.3.2, performance of the Gnutella network is limited by the large number of organizing messages it generates.

Security is a special concern when you do not trust, or even know, who you are collaborating with. Encryption, isolating processing agents through a technique called *sandboxing,* managing digital rights, firewalls, and relying on reputation and accountability all add to the security of the network. This is discussed in more detail in Section 6.2.2.

Because they lack a single point of failure, peer-to-peer networks have the potential for improved *fault resilience.* However, disconnections, network congestion or failure, unreachable nodes, isolated networks, and node failures create their own set of reliability problems. Also, system maintenance responsibility is distributed across the peers. Redundancy can provide solutions by replicating content, routing paths, and other essential resources across many peers.

In a peer-to-peer network the algorithm running in each peer establishes the character of the network. This leads immediately to *interoperability* problems between various peer-to-peer networks. We will see in Section 6.3.1 that Napster does not use the Domain Name System and instead created its own name space. Peers on network A (e.g., Napster) cannot communicate with peers on network B (e.g., Gnutella). This seems fundamental, because if A is different from B, then they are not equal and therefore not peers. This leads to the very important network effect problem discussed in the next section. Perhaps compatible protocols and gateways can allow interconnection to overcome the network effect, but the nodes still will not be true peers.

6.1.4 The Network Effect

Choose your friends wisely. This time-honored advice is as true for peer-to-peer networks as it has always been for social networks. Peer-to-peer networks are exclusive. The software running on the peer establishes the protocol and algorithm used to communicate with all other peers. When you choose to run the original peer-to-peer Napster software you are interconnecting only to peers that are also running Napster to the exclusion[3] of all the systems running Gnutella and other protocols. You can join only one fraternity, commit to only one religion, and be only at one party when midnight rings in the New Year.

Robert Metcalfe, founder of 3Com Corporation and the designer of the Ethernet protocol, observed that new communications technologies are valuable only if many people use them. *Metcalfe's Law* states that *the value of a network grows as the square of the number of users* [Gil02, NWFE1]. When Alexander Graham Bell invented the telephone in 1876 he had no one to call except his assistant, Thomas Watson. It took another 55 years, until 1931, for enough people to use this new technology that telephone companies put a dial on the instrument. But the idea took off, the telephone network is huge, every phone can connect to any other phone, and competing networks have long since been gobbled up or withered away.

Success breeds success. The best students want to go to the best university to study with the best professors and the best students. The larger an auction site like eBay becomes, the more attractive it is because it provides each member with a larger market.

So the most successful peer-to-peer network is the one that attracts the most, or at least the most valued,[4] users. This emphasizes the importance of massive scalability, while having acceptable performance, reliability, and ease of use. Systems that are unattractive will cause the user base to fragment and reduce the usefulness of the network.

---

[3]While it is true that a wrapper could be created to provide a common user interface to more than one underlying peer-to-peer system, the systems remain distinct and each one manages its own pool of resources.

[4]For example, users that offer the most interesting contributions to the network while consuming few resources and annoying few users may be judged most valuable. Also, a small network dedicated to a special interest topic can be successful if the participants address issues important to the group. The term "valued" can be interpreted according to any set of values shared by the network users.

6.1.5   Types of Peer-to-Peer-Networks

Figure 6.2 decomposes broadly defined peer-to-peer systems into four groups and gives examples of each [MKL+02].

File Sharing systems are the most important for content networking. These are subdivided into pure peer-to-peer networks that don't rely on any centralized resources and hybrid networks that have servers at their core. Multimedia content requires large files. Varied interests demand extensive variety in multimedia content. The resulting storage requirements are enormous. Peer-to-peer file sharing systems, such as Napster, Gnutella, and others, provide the following features:

- *File Exchange Areas* where a peer can retrieve a file stored by another peer in the network. The storage capacity grows as the network grows, bounded only by the number of interested peers and the scale of the network. File exchange is provided by Freenet (www.freenetproject.org), Gnutella (www.gnutella.com), KaZaa (www.kazaa.com), and others.
- *Highly available safe storage* is provided by duplication and redundancy policies in some projects. OceanStore [KBC+00] provides safe storage for nomadic data using an untrusted infrastructure. Chord (pdos.lcs.mit.edu/chord/) provides a bounded search for any document in the system.
- *Anonymity* of authors and publishers is the goal of some specialized systems. Publius [WRC00] is censorship resistant, tamper evident, source anonymous, and deniable. Freenet allows users to publish and obtain information on the Internet without fear of censorship.

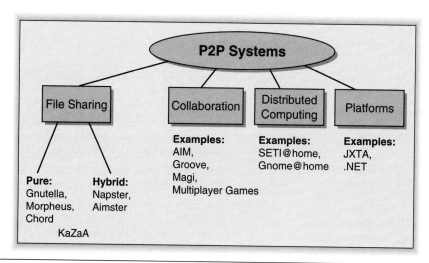

Figure 6.2 Types and example peer-to-peer systems.

- *Manageability* enables easy and fast data retrieval. This is often accomplished by distributing the data to caches located on the edges of the network. Freenet stores data in many locations in the path between the provider and the retriever. Manageability is difficult to achieve when nodes join and leave the network frequently.

Collaboration systems provide real-time interaction allowing users to cooperate toward a common goal or compete in a game. Applications include instant messaging, chat, online games and shared applications for business, education, or home use. Examples include AOL Instant Messaging (www.aim.com), Groove (www.groove.net), Magi (www.endeavors.com), and a number of games such as DOOM and Quake. They can be built using peer-to-peer or client server architectures. Chapter 7 discusses collaborative systems in detail.

Distributed computing creates a huge virtual supercomputer by aggregating the processing resources of a large number of individual personal computers attached to the Internet. Long-running massively parallel computations are best suited to this approach, as the following examples illustrate. In January 1999 distributed.net harnessed the idle CPU time of approximately 100,000 computers around the world and won the RSA DES III challenge when they decoded a message in less than 24 hours that was encrypted using a 56 bit key [MCN99]. SETI@home [ACK+02] harnesses the power of 3 million personal computers to analyze data collected from the world's largest radio telescope in Arecibo, Puerto Rico, in its search for extraterrestrial intelligence. Genome@home (www.stanford.edu/group/pandegroup/genome/) uses a similar approach to design new genes that can form working proteins in living cells.

These are each examples of *grid computing*. Grid computing is defined as "coordinated resource sharing and problem solving in large, multi-institutional virtual organizations" [FKe03]. The Global Grid Forum (www.globalgridforum.org) promotes research and standards related to grid computing.

Because no content is exchanged among the peers, these fascinating applications of peer-to-peer systems are unrelated to content networking and won't be discussed further.

Platforms provide support for naming, discovery, communications, security, and resource aggregation for peer-to-peer systems. The popularity of a small number of widely used operating systems, such as Unix and Windows, has increased the portability of software. The use of browsers with standard capabilities and virtual machines such as the Java virtual machine has increased portability of software distributed over the Internet. Now the creation of peer-to-peer platforms can ease the development of various peer-to-peer solutions.

Example platforms are JXTA (www.jxta.org), sponsored by Sun Microsystems Inc., and .NET (www.microsoft.com/net/), sponsored by Microsoft. Future content networking solutions may be built using these platforms.

6.2   Technical Challenges in Peer-to-Peer Networks

To distribute content to users, a peer-to-peer network must be able to locate content, scale to a useful size, and provide reliable operation. Several approaches to solving these problems are discussed in the following sections.

6.2.1   Locating Content

Bachelors and bachelorettes who move into a new community face the challenge of meeting new friends and romantic interests. They can take several approaches to meeting new and interesting people. One approach is to consult Internet-based information services such as match.com or love.com that hold the names and profiles of millions of people who want to meet others with compatible interests. A single query to this centralized database can provide a list of many peers who claim similar interests.

A more traditional approach might be to quietly let people you meet know you are interested in meeting more people. If a particularly attractive single conveys this information, it can quickly travel through the grapevine. The question "Have you met the hottie that just moved into the neighborhood?" will quickly stimulate many discussions among curious peers. This approach is based on flooding the network with your request and dealing with whatever happens.

Other approaches might involve some form of social referral agent. Trusted friends or recognized matchmakers suggest compatible contacts they believe you would like to meet. Some people join health clubs, ski clubs, or book clubs hoping to meet people with similar interests. New approaches to matchmaking include services such as dinnerintroductions.com which is a social club that arranges small dinner parties to provide their clients interesting social contacts. While these referrals often speed the process of finding Mr./Ms. "Right" they probably only send you in the right direction. You still may end the evening early asking your blind date if she has any sisters or single girlfriends. This approach combines elements of both the centralized and flooding approaches. It uses the special knowledge of the matchmakers to direct the search in a promising direction, and your own networking skills to continue and refine the search.

A similar problem arises in peer-to-peer file sharing systems that need to locate content that matches user requests. Three basic algorithms are commonly used to locate content. These are the *centralized directory* model, the *flooded request* model, and the *document routing* model [MKL+02].

The *centralized directory model* is analogous to people consulting match.com. This approach was used by the original Napster implementations, and is discussed as a case study in Section 6.3.1. Peers connect to a central directory where they publish information describing the content they have to share. When the directory receives a request, it replies with a peer in the directory that matches the request. Several criteria such as closest, highest bandwidth connection, highest capacity, least congestion, or least recently used might be used to select the best peer. The requesting peer then directly contacts the peer it has been referred to and begins the content transfer.

This model depends on a reliable central directory. All the peers share the fate of that directory and the network stops working whenever the central directory is not available. The growth of the network is limited by the capacity of the central directory. This can lead to scalability problems if it is not handled well in a large network. This centralized approach did not limit the growth of the original Napster network, which grew to include as many as 150 centralized servers. It was, however, a fatal element that led to the legal downfall of Napster.

Nearly a decade earlier, archie [ED92], WAIS [km91], and gopher were created to provide centralized directories for locating FTP files located on various systems. MP3 audio files were not exchanged then, so the turmoil surrounding Napster never developed around these systems.

The *flooded request* model is analogous to the buzz speeding through the grapevine when a hottie arrives in town. This approach is used by Gnutella and is discussed as a case study in Section 6.3.2. After connecting to the network, the requesting peer broadcasts a query to its directly connected peers, which each broadcast to their directly connected peers, and so on through the network. This continues until the request is answered, or some broadcast limit is reached.

This approach generates a lot of ineffective network traffic and requires a lot of bandwidth. This network flooding is an important scaling problem and significantly limits the size of the network.

The *document routing* model is analogous to asking a trusted friend for a referral. This approach is used by Chord and is presented as a case study in Section 6.3.3. Each peer has helpful, but only partially complete referral information. Each referral moves the requester closer to a peer that can satisfy the query.

The great advantage of this approach is that the systems can reliably complete a comprehensive search in a bounded number of steps. The resulting systems can grow to be very large and still provide good performance. Section 6.3.3 mentions several systems before presenting a detailed case study of Chord.

6.2.2   Trust, Accountability, and Reputation

Our trust of social peers varies greatly. Although we smile and greet hundreds of acquaintances, most of us have very few friends we fully trust. How many people are you comfortable confiding in? How comfortable are you lending your car to a friend? Yet the Gnutella network is based on sharing everything with 10,000 anonymous strangers!

Content integrity is the primary trust issue in a content delivery network. If the original content is tampered with or altered during storage, transport, or delivery, the requester is misled and the reputation of the author is unfairly and unknowingly tarnished. It is important for both the author and the requester to ensure that the content the requester receives is an exact copy of the content the author originally created. By using a digital signature that is authenticated by a trusted Certifying Agency, such as Thawte [Tha] or Verisign [Ver03], authors provide a way for requesters to verify that the content they receive is identical to the original creation. As requesters continue to use this mechanism to obtain unaltered content, they get an authentic copy of the author's work. This helps build the author's reputation accurately [OWC+01]. Organizations opposed to file sharing deliberately introduced content integrity violations to discourage users from downloading files. They place large files in the network and identify these files as containing popular content, such as a hit movie or song. This encourages users to download the file only to find it is empty or junk, a Trojan horse, or some other waste of time, storage space, and bandwidth.

Limited resources that are freely shared are inevitably overtaxed and often exhausted. Freeways are jammed with traffic, air and water are polluted, and free rock concerts in the park are jam-packed with people. Bandwidth, connections, storage space, processor capacity, and search requests are all in limited supply in a peer-to-peer network. A small number of greedy users can exhaust these resources for the entire community. This is an example of the *tragedy of the commons* [Har68]. The usual solution is to regulate access to the limiting resource. This is the essence of *accountability*; where each user accepts responsibility for the shared resources they consume. Accountable users maintain records of the scarce resources they consume.

We will see later that most of the Gnutella network traffic is caused by so-called *free riders*. Although these free riders do not provide any files for others to share they make up 66% of Gnutella users. This is the inevitable consequence of lack of accountability.

A classic study published in 1842 convincingly argued that the most economically efficient toll to charge on an *uncongested* bridge is zero. This is because the additional cost of one more person crossing the bridge is zero, while the total economic cost of collecting the toll is greater than zero. Some resources may be too cheap to meter. The situation changes considerably, however, when the traffic wanting to cross the bridge exceeds its capacity. In that case tolls should be collected whenever they are needed to manage bridge congestion [Dup2]. Accepting this argument, resources in a peer-to-peer network should be rationed if and only if they are congested or scarce.

Accountability requires each user to pay their share to use each scarce resource. Payment can be in financial form or in some other form that represents a barter or other valuable contribution to the common network. A simple barter system might require users to upload content roughly comparable in value to the content they download. More traditional financial models can be used to pay for bandwidth or any other scarce resource as it is used [ODF+01].

An experimental prototype network, called Mojo Nation, included a flexible micro payment system. This scorekeeping mechanism provided a flexible peer-to-peer credit system and a flexible incentive device. Users earned credits for contributing resources; these credits were used to obtain resources. Free riders contributed nothing and got like in return [Mcc01].

Reputation is the history of accountability and trust behaviors accessible from past transactions. We use reputation to help set expectations for future transactions [OL01]. Reputation information eases exchange of valuables and reduces risk. Online trading sites, such as eBay, help vendors create their reputation by asking customers to rate the quality of every transaction. The resulting reputation information is published. This encourages vendors to continue to provide good service and allows potential buyers to select vendors based on this reputation. Content delivery networks could use a similar technique to establish the reputation of content authors and publishers. In peer-to-peer networks, the reputation of peers could be established based on their contributions to the network, such as the amount of original content authored, the amount of content stored, uploads to the network, the number of connections they support, and the number of transactions they assist in processing. To protect the network, peers who earn a poor reputation can have their participation in the network limited and eventually be cut off.

Now that we have introduced and described the general challenges in building peer-to-peer networks, the next section will take a look at real-life peer-to-peer systems and the mechanisms they use to solve these challenges.

6.3 Case Studies

Several different kinds of peer-to-peer networks emerged over recent years and gained tremendous popularity. The most well-known system was probably the original Napster, which achieved infamy through the legal battles fought in the courtrooms and lively discussion in chat rooms. After Napster was shut down by the courts, other systems such as Gnutella and KaZaA moved into the spotlight. While these systems found immediate popularity, the Chord system was started to research and solve fundamental problems of peer-to-peer networks. This section takes a closer look at each of those peer-to-peer networks, their primary goals, and the mechanisms used.

6.3.1 Napster

The history of Napster is a fascinating example of entrepreneurship during a period of explosive growth and rapid demise of Internet startups. It fundamentally changed the music industry while it focused worldwide attention on peer-to-peer systems for content delivery. Readers may also have some interest in the system architecture.

Company history

In January 1999, 18-year-old Shawn Fanning left Northeastern University after the first semester of his freshman year to work on the Napster software. On July 1, 1999, the software was complete enough to begin offering service. By November

1999 negotiations with major record companies to distribute online music already failed. On December 7, 1999,[5] the Recording Industry Association of America (RIAA) sued Napster for copyright infringement, asking for damages of $100,000 each time a song is copied. On April 13, 2000, the rock band Metallica sued Napster for copyright infringement. To show concern, Napster responded quickly by removing over 300,000 members who had downloaded Mettalica songs from its service. On July 24, 2000, Napster announced plans to work with digital-rights technology company Liquid Audio to try to make its music downloads safe for copyright holders. Two days later U.S. District Judge Marilyn Patel ruled in favor of the record industry and ordered Napster to stop allowing copyrighted material to be swapped over its network. The judge set a deadline of midnight only two days later; however, hours before Napster would have had to shut down, the Ninth U.S. Circuit Court of Appeals ruled that the company should be allowed to continue its operations. The turmoil was enough to get Shawn Fanning's picture on the cover of the October 2, 2000 issue of *Time Magazine* [Mar01].

In an ironic turn of direction on October 31, 2000, German media conglomerate Bertelsmann (www.bertelsmann.com) formed an alliance with Napster, signaling a significant shift in the hostile battle between the major record labels and the start-up. The plan was to support Napster in creating a legal, paid subscription service. Bertelsmann had been party to the lawsuits that shut down Napster; however, they promised to drop its lawsuit once the subscription service successfully launches [HHa00].

While courtroom battles continued, Napster put in place a file screening system designed to block users from downloading music files specified by an initial list provided by record company attorneys. However, on July 11, 2001, a district court judge issued an order prohibiting Napster from enabling file transfers unless it reaches a 100% success rate identifying and screening out music copying abuses they were notified of. This order essentially shut down the Napster file sharing service [Mar01].

The alliance with Bertelsmann, however, was not enough to solve Napster's financial crisis. They were on the verge of bankruptcy on May 17, 2002, when Bertelsmann agreed to purchase Napster's assets and save them from bankruptcy. Under terms of the deal, Shawn Fanning was reinstated as its chief technology officer and Bertelsmann agreed to provide $8 million to repay Napster's creditors [Chm02].

The road to legal respectability and financial solvency was long and hard. On October 29, 2003, the Napster 2.0 music service, now a division of Roxio (www.roxio.com), went live. Under the new pay-to-play model Napster 2.0 offered consumers downloads for 99 cents a song or $9.95 per album. The service includes CD burning, transfer to portable devices, decades of *Billboard* charts, shared playlists within the Napster community, exclusive and original content, interactive radio, music videos, and access to what was then the

---

[5]Ironically this was the 58th anniversary of the infamous Japanese attack on Pearl Harbor.

world's largest music store with more than half a million tracks and growing [NAP03].

The network was at least as busy as the court room. During this time the original Napster had more than forty million client downloads [MKL+02]. In terms of users, the Napster site was the fastest growing in history, passing the 25 million mark in less than a year of operation [Tar00].

The new Napster is a client server system, without peer-to-peer elements. It was quickly overshadowed by the Apple iTUNES system, which was named one of Time Magazine's "coolest inventions of the year" for 2003 [Tay03]. iTUNES is also a client server system. The rapid growth, short life, and commercial failure of the original Napster symbolize both the opportunities and business challenges faced by peer-to-peer networks.

System architecture

The Napster protocol design is everything you would expect to get from a sleep-deprived teenager. The protocol was never published by Napster, but was eventually reverse engineered by the OpenNap project (opennap.sourceforge.net) who published their interpretation of the protocol specification [Ope00].

Napster uses the centralized directory model to locate content.

Napster communicates using TCP but does not use the DNS namespace to name the peers. Instead it created its own namespace based on nicknames chosen by the client. Several messages are used between the clients and server to establish a nickname. Within the protocol descriptions, the nickname appears in messages as `<nick>` when referring to another client and as `<mynick>` when referring to this client.

Each message to and from the server is in the form of `<length>` `<type><data>` where both `<length>` and `<type>` are 2 byte binary numbers and `<data>` is an ASCII string `<length>` bytes long. Fields in the data portion are separated by a single ASCII space character, and some fields are enclosed in double quotes. The following text names each data field in `<angle brackets>`, after specifying the value and meaning of the `<type>` field.

The client uses message code 100 to announce to the server the files it is willing to share. The message has the following format:

Code 100—Client notification of shared file—`"<filename>"` `<md5>` `<size>` `<bitrate>` `<frequency>` `<time>`

In addition to the filename, an MD5 message-digest hash [RFC 1321] computed over approximately the first 300,000 bytes of the file is used to identify each content file. This hash can be used to ensure that two files, perhaps having the same artist name and song name, have identical content.

The recording characteristics of each file are described by the parameters `<size>` in bytes, `<bitrate>` in kbps, `<frequency>` in hertz, and `<time>` in seconds.

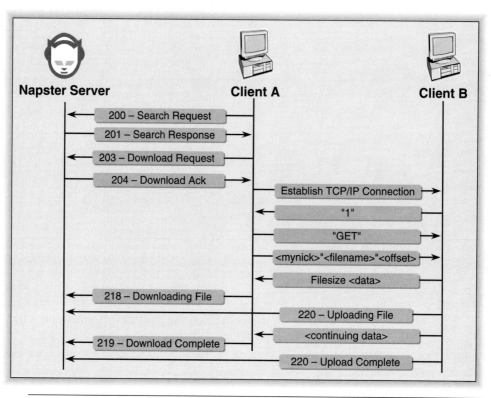

Figure 6.3 Napster protocol session.

The messages required for a typical session to search the server and transfer a file are illustrated in Figure 6.3. They are explained below, where each message includes the numeric code, descriptor, and format.

The sequence begins with the client A request to the server for a particular song file:

200—Search request—`[FILENAME CONTAINS "artist name"] MAX_RESULTS <max> [FILENAME CONTAINS "song"] [LINESPEED <compare> <link-type>] [BITRATE <compare> "<br>"] [FREQ <compare> "<freq>"] [WMA-FILE] [LOCAL_ONLY]`

The server responds with a list of records each including the filename, recording parameters, source client's nickname, and IP address. This list has at most `<max>` records. The `LOCAL_ONLY` parameter limits the results to only the one server, rather than searching other servers. Each response in the list has the following format:

201—Search response—`"<filename>" <md5> <size> <bitrate> <frequency> <length> <nick> <ip> <link-type> [weight]`

The client then requests the server allow the download of the particular file from the client with the supplied nickname:

203—Download request—`<nick>` `"<filename>"`

The server grants this request by providing the IP address, port number, filename hash and line speed of the source client to the requesting client:

204—Download ack—`<nick>` `<ip>` `<port>` `"<filename>"` `<md5>` `<linespeed>`

The role of this 203, 204 sequence is not entirely clear. It does separate the search and download portions of the exchange. It is probably used for flow control and load balancing, to allow the server to throttle download requests to any particular client. Keep in mind that the protocol was never standardized or officially published, and the implementation varied as conditions changed.

The requesting client A establishes a TCP/IP connection to the source client B on the indicated port. The source client responds with the single ASCII character "1". The requesting client begins with "`GET`"—*not* an HTTP `GET`—this is the Napster application protocol, not HTTP—then sends `<mynick>` `"<filename>"<offset>`. The source client responds with the file size immediately followed by the data of the file itself.

Once the data transfer begins, the requesting client sends a 218—downloading file message to the server. Similarly, the source client sends a 220—uploading file message to the server. The transfer continues between the two clients. The `<offset>` parameter allows the transfer to be resumed at any place in the file. Finally, when the transfer is completed, the sending client sends a 219—download complete message and the source client sends a 220—upload complete message to the server. Since the data transfer is peer-to-peer, the messages to the server seem nonessential and only serve to track system usage.

The protocol includes other features to retrieve files from behind a firewall, browse another client's file directly, obtain server statistics, ignore particular users, and manage chat sessions.

The legal challenges to Napster focused on the central server. To delay such legal challenges, the Gnutella protocol allows peer-to-peer file sharing without any centralized structure.

6.3.2 Gnutella and KaZaA

While Napster was clogging the courtrooms, a pure peer-to-peer system called Gnutella was clogging the networks. After providing a brief history, the Gnutella architecture and protocol are described and the traffic is analyzed. A newer system named KaZaA that was derived from Gnutella and takes steps to reduce traffic is then briefly described.

History

Justin Frankel developed Winamp (www.winamp.com), a PC-based audio player that became very popular after its launch in January 1998. His team then founded Nullsoft (www.nullsoft.com) to continue the development and commercialization of Winamp. The Winamp brand and services were acquired by America Online, Inc. in May 1999 [Lau00].

As Napster was under legal attack, developers at Nullsoft turned their attention to peer-to-peer file sharing. Gnutella was developed in only 14 days as a quick hack, reportedly for sharing cooking recipes. In March 2000 a prototype was published on the Nullsoft Web site under a GNU General Public License. After only a few hours, surprised AOL executives recognized the potential of the development and the likely conflicts of interest it could lead to and demanded it be taken off the Web site immediately. The Internet is fast. They were too late. The software was already downloaded several times. The protocol was reverse engineered and published [Clip2] and many systems were built to use that protocol [AHA02].

Gnutella architecture

We have seen that Napster is an implementation based on a centralized directory without a published protocol specification. In contrast, Gnutella is a published protocol specification without any implementation or any centralized elements. The lack of a centralized structure delayed legal attacks, and generated lots of network traffic.

The software running in each Gnutella peer is called a *servent*. These peers use TCP/IP to communicate only with each other. Servent software was developed and distributed by several companies including BearShare (www.bearshare.com), LimeWire (www.limewire.com), and ToadNode (www.toadnoad.com).

A typical session using the Gnutella protocol is shown in Figure 6.4. The session proceeds along the following steps [Clip2]:

1. Because each Gnutella network is fully decentralized it takes some work to find a servent on the network. This problem is not addressed by the published protocol, but workable solutions were quickly put into place. Several of the companies that develop and distribute Gnutella servent software run specialized hosts that cache the IP address of servents that recently joined their network. A servent wanting to join the network contacts one of these well-known *host-cache servers* and receives a list of prospective addresses.

2. The joining servent begins the session by choosing a servent that is likely to be connected to the network. The joining servent sends a `Gnutella Connect` message to one of the addresses on the list of prospective servents it received from the host-cache server. This also makes the joining servent address available to the host-cache server.

3. If the contacted servent is running and on the network, it replies to the `Connect` message with a `Gnutella OK` message. If there is no reply, the joining servent tries another prospective address until it finds an online peer. Note that it is quite likely that a prospective servent is not

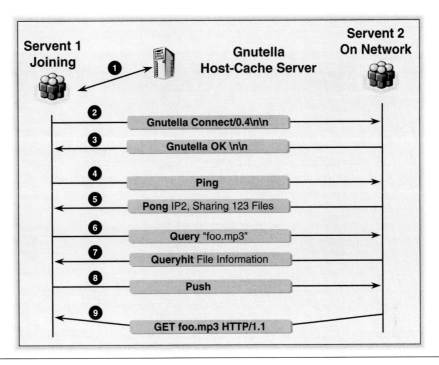

Figure 6.4 Gnutella protocol.

available. Since the servents run on PCs they may be powered down, off line, or using a dynamic IP address newly acquired from DHCP.

Once a servent is connected to the network, it communicates with other servents by sending and receiving Gnutella *descriptors*. Each descriptor is preceded by a descriptor header with the following fields:

Descriptor ID	Payload Descriptor	TTL—Time to Live	Hops	Payload Length

The descriptor ID is a 16-byte string uniquely identifying this descriptor message in the network. Since the `ping` and `query` descriptors (see below) do not include the servent's IP address, or any other identification, and the servents are communicating across several hops (see Figure 6.5), this descriptor ID is the only way to associate `pong` and `queryhit` reply messages with the requesting servent.

The payload descriptor is a code identifying the type of message:

0x00 = `ping`—Please respond with `pong` if you can accept my connection.
0x01 = `pong`—I can accept your connection at this IP address and port number.

0x04 = push—Push the file to me through the firewall.

0x80 = query—If you have a file matching this description, please respond with queryhit.

0x81 = queryhit—The file you requested is here, at this address and port number.

The TTL field is used to limit the maximum number of hops for this message. The default is seven hops. Each servent receiving a message is responsible for decrementing the TTL count and incrementing the Hop count before the message is forwarded. When TTL reaches zero, the message has expired and is no longer forwarded in the network. This creates a network horizon fully connecting nodes within seven hops and isolating nodes farther away. The TTL is the only mechanism for expiring descriptors in the network. It is important for servents to examine this field, decrement it, and expire descriptors when TTL reaches zero.

The joining servent continues by sending these descriptors:

4. The joining servent sends out a ping message to probe the network for other servents.

5. Servents respond to ping messages with their own pong message, indicating their IP address and port, and providing information on the amount of data it is sharing on the network. At this point in the protocol, the joining servent is aware of several servents on the network, but does not know what files are being shared.

6. To locate a particular file,[6] the servent sends a query message with search criteria, such as the file name, to each of the directly connected servents.

7. Servents sharing files that meet the search criteria respond with a queryhit message. This message includes the IP address and identifier of the responding servent, the connection speed and the result set which includes the file index, file size, and file name for each hit.

8. Once a servent receives a queryhit, it may begin downloading a file in the result set. The file download protocol is HTTP. In the simplest case the requesting servent sends this HTTP request to the source servent:

```
GET/get/<File Index>/<File Name>/HTTP/1.0
Connection: Keep-Alive
Range: bytes=0-
User-Agent: Gnutella
```

If the source servent is behind a firewall that blocks incoming connections to the Gnutella port, the requesting servent sends a push

---

[6]Within a Gnutella network each servent only knows about its own content. Servents do not advertise their content and there is no central directory. The query mechanism described here is the only way to discover which servents have the content you seek.

request. The servent receiving this request opens a new connection to the requesting servent. Since this originates from inside the firewall it is likely to succeed. The requesting servent then initiates an HTTP GET to the servent behind the firewall.

9. The file transfer continues between the two servents using HTTP. The range feature of HTTP allows interrupted transfers to be restarted midstream.

The protocol includes several rules for routing descriptor messages. Figure 6.5 begins to illustrate how servents use this protocol to meet peers and generate traffic. The routing rules are described along with the example shown in Figure 6.5.

A servent will forward incoming ping and query descriptors to all of its directly connected servents, except for the one that delivered the incoming ping or query. We see A's ping going first to servent B, then B forwarding it to C and D, and then finally C and D each forwarding the pings to E.

Each servent decrements the descriptor header's TTL field, and increments its Hops field, before it forwards the descriptor to any directly connected servent. If, after decrementing the header's TTL field, the TTL field is found to be zero, the descriptor is not forwarded along any connection. In the example, we are assuming the TTL reached zero after it was decremented at Node E, so the forwarding stopped there.

To avoid loops in the network, a servent receiving a descriptor with the same Payload Descriptor and Descriptor ID as one it has received before, should avoid forwarding the descriptor.

Pong descriptors may only be sent along the same path that carried the incoming Ping descriptor. This ensures that only those servents that routed the

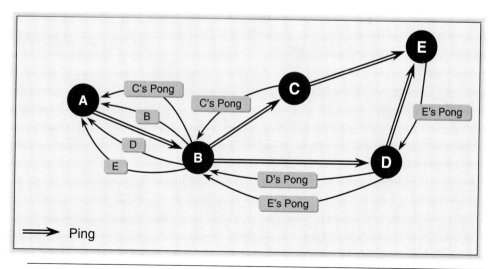

Figure 6.5 Gnutella—meeting peers.

`Ping` descriptor will see the `Pong` descriptor in response. To help enforce this rule, a servent that receives a `Pong` descriptor with a Descriptor ID that does not match a previous `Ping` Descriptor ID should remove the `Pong` descriptor from the network. Following this rule in the example, we see B's pong descriptor going directly to Node A, C and D's `pongs` routing through B to A, and finally, E's `pong` routing through D to B and finally to A. Note that E sends only one `pong`, because the `ping` it receives from C has the same Payload Descriptor and Descriptor ID as the `ping` it has received from D, which is assumed to arrive first in this example.

In Figure 6.6 we see the `query` and `queryhit` descriptors following similar rules. Node A sends a `query` for file foo.mp3 into the network. It gets forwarded until it reaches Node E. Both Nodes C and E respond with `queryhit` descriptors to tell Node A they have the requested file. Both Nodes B and D are silent because they do not have the requested file. Node A chooses to retrieve the file with an HTTP `GET` to Node C. Node C transfers the file using HTTP.

This approach results in a depth-first comprehensive search of the nodes within the horizon created by the TTL. If each peer connects to 3 others, the default TTL of 7 hops creates a horizon including approximately 10,000 nodes.

Traffic analysis

Network traffic resulting from this protocol has been analyzed theoretically and experimentally. For example, if TTL is set to the default of 7 hops and each node

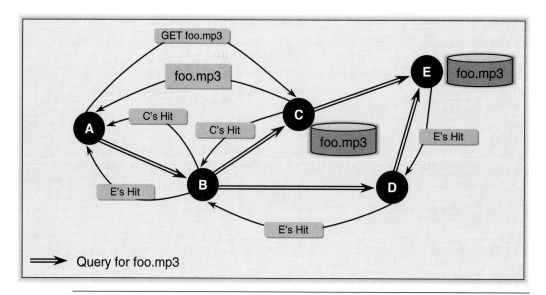

Figure 6.6 Gnutella—searching.

averages 4 connections to other nodes (C=4), each node forwards each ping to 3 other nodes. This results in:

$$2 \times \sum_{i=0}^{TTL} C \times (C-1)^i = 2 \times \sum_{i=0}^{7} 4 \times 3^i = 26240 \text{ messages, including the responses,}$$

resulting from a single `ping`. The number of messages resulting from a `query` is somewhat fewer, because only a few of the nodes reply with a `queryhit` [AHA02].

On June 1, 2002, a research team from the University of California at Riverside captured a five-hour-long sample of Gnutella messages. This sample exceeded 56 million entries. Of these 63% were `ping` or `pong` descriptors. Another 33% were `query` messages and 4% were `queryhit` messages. Nearly two-thirds of the network messages in this sample were simply to discover other peers. When the `query` and `queryhit` messages were analyzed, 19,069,700 `query` messages resulted in 2,296,800 `queryhit` messages. `Querys` outnumbered `queryhits` by more than eight to one [ZYF02].

Another study found that most of the network traffic is caused by free riders. Free riders do not provide any files to share yet they make up 66% of Gnutella users. Nearly 37% of all responses are returned by the top 1% of sharing hosts [AHu00].

One study examined the effectiveness of caching popular content within servents in a Gnutella network. The study concluded that caching does significantly reduce the amount of traffic seen without using a large amount of memory [Sri01].

KaZaA

KaZaA (www.kazaa.com) is a proprietary system based on Gnutella that uses *SuperNodes* to improve searching and reduce network traffic [MKL+02]. SuperNodes are powerful processors with high bandwidth connections. Peers connect to their local SuperNodes to upload information about files they are sharing and to search the network. This creates a hybrid system, intermediate between the centralized Napster approach and the fully decentralized Gnutella approach. It has similarities to the DNS system, where peer nodes are arranged into a hierarchy, and not all peers are created equal.

While this approach reduces network traffic, it still generates substantial traffic. According to a study done at Cornell University in February 2002, if everyone on campus turned off the outbound KaZaA traffic, approximately 50% more bandwidth could be freed up for other Internet traffic [Lee03].

6.3.3 Chord

While so much of the world's attention was focused on Napster, Gnutella, and their derivatives, several researchers found the quiet time they needed to study fundamental problems of peer-to-peer networks. Several projects established a firm theoretical basis for meeting their goals of providing reliable, robust, and massively scalable peer-to-peer networks.

These projects include Pastry [RDr01], Tapestry, CAN [RPH+01], P-Grid [AHP+02], Random Walker [LCL+02], Farsite [BDE+00], OceanStore [RWE+01], FreeNet [CMH+02, CSW+01] and Chord [SKB01]. This section will focus on Chord as an example of these types of document routing systems. The discussion is more advanced and specialized than previous material in the book. Readers uninterested in the details of the Chord algorithms may wish to skip this section.

Chord can comprehensively search the content of a peer-to-peer network in a bounded number of steps. The complexity of the search grows only as the logarithm of the number of nodes in the network [SKB01, LBK02, AHa01].

Figure 6.7 begins to illustrate the Chord search algorithm. The IP address of each node participating in the network is hashed into a fixed-length binary string m bits long, called the *Node Key*. In the example m is chosen as 6, allowing for a total of $2^6 = 64$ nodes. In practice, a much larger value of m is used so that the 2^m possible identifiers are much greater than the number of actual nodes expected in the network. The result is that most of the possible identifiers are not used.

The hash is done using the SHA-1 algorithm [FIPS93] and produces a 160-bit output called a *message digest* which is the node key. The algorithm results in a *consistent hashing* which tends to balance the load because each node receives roughly the same number of keys [LLP+97].

Similarly a description of each file available for sharing in the network (such as the title and author) is hashed using the same algorithm. This provides the *Data Keys*. Note that the Node Key and the Data Keys are both binary strings of the same fixed length, so they share the same number space.

The universe of possible node keys can be represented as a circle, with the key value increasing clockwise. On this circle each node has a *successor* defined as the next populated node clockwise around the circle. Mathematically, the successor to each populated node is defined as the populated node with the next higher node key (calculated modulo 2^m). Data tables are maintained such that each populated node knows its successor node.

Each node is also responsible for storing all of the *Data Keys* that have values falling within the interval of *Node Keys* represented by the arc beginning one past the predecessor node and ending with this node. For the example shown in Figure 6.7, the predecessor of Node 56 is Node 44. Therefore, Node 56 stores all of the Data Keys that have (hash) values falling between the hash values for Node Key 45 (one past predecessor Node 44) and Node Key 56. This is possible because the Data Keys share the same number space as the Node Keys.

Consider how Node 56 can use this structure to search for a particular file. Node 56 begins by hashing the file description information into a Data Key. In this example we will assume the result is a Data Key of 19. The search begins on the node requesting the search. In this case, Node 56 has the data keys for the interval 45–56, but not for Node 19. So Node 56 contacts it successor, which is Node 0. Node 0 does not have the requested key, so it contacts its successor,

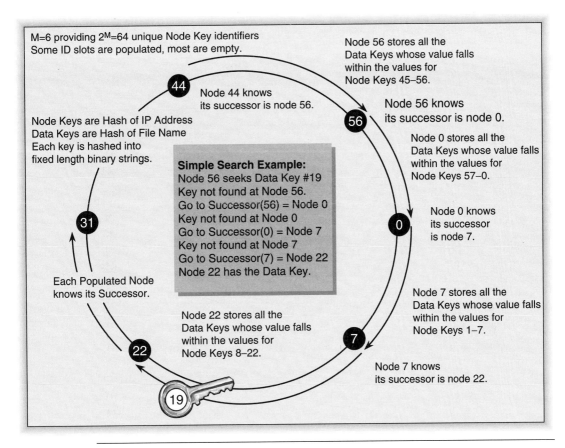

Figure 6.7 Chord search preliminaries.

which is Node 7. This continues until Node 22 is reached. Node 22 has the data keys for the interval 8–22, which includes Node 19.

Stored with Data Key 19 is additional information needed to retrieve the requested file. This includes the IP address of the node where it is stored, the file name, and perhaps other information. This allows Node 56 to directly contact the node where the actual file is stored, which is probably *not* Node 22.

This works well in examples where the number of nodes and keys is small. However, the goal is to handle perhaps billions of files on a network of perhaps millions of nodes. Clearly this linear and exhaustive search will take too long. Chord solves this problem by introducing intermediate routing information called *fingers*.

Figure 6.8 illustrates the finger table entries from Node 0. To improve the clarity of the example, Nodes 1, 2, 4, and 8 have also been populated in this network. Each node stores a finger table with entries pointing to the first

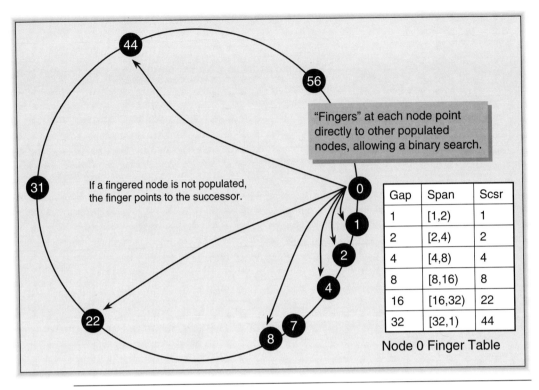

Figure 6.8 Chord routing table.

populated peer that is a successor to each Node Key that is 2^{i-1} greater than its own, for i=1, 2, 3 ... *m*. The finger table for Node 0 is shown in the figure. In this case, Node 0 stores a finger table with pointers to the nodes that are the populated successors to 1, 2, 4, 8, 16, and 32. These indices are the numbers in the "Gap" column of the table. Their successors are Nodes 1, 2, 4, 8, 22, and 44, as listed in the "Scsr" (Successor) column of the table. The finger table also includes—in the "Span" column—the key values that pertain to each finger entry. The notation represents an interval beginning with the Key Value after the square bracket and ending before the Key Value preceding the closing parenthesis. For example, the finger pointing to Node 22 is chosen when searching for key values 16 through 31.

What is particularly clever about this choice of finger entries is that it allows for a binary search of the network. The finger tables have detailed information for nodes near the present node, but also include entries halfway around the circle. This allows a rapid binary search of the network.

The search proceeds by selecting the finger entry in the table that spans the Key Value being searched for. So in searching for key #19, Node 0 would forward the request to Node 22 which has the requested information. The search converges very rapidly.

Nodes join and depart a dynamic peer-to-peer network any time at random. This is a normal condition rather than any exceptional condition for such networks. Chord plans for these joins and departures and handles them easily. It preserves two important conditions as nodes join and depart:

- Each node's successor is correctly maintained, and
- For every key, the successor node to that key is responsible for it.

In addition, the finger tables are adjusted to account for the node addition or loss. Note that the finger tables are a performance optimization and are not needed to ensure a correct lookup. Each Chord node maintains a predecessor pointer to simplify these operations. These important aspects of the protocol are beyond the scope of this book, but are described fully in [SKB01].

6.4 Business Aspects

The business prospects for peer-to-peer networks remain elusive. It is ironic that while Napster drew the most popular attention to peer-to-peer networking, it always used a substantial central directory and re-emerged as a purely client server network. Nonetheless, several business models are described here, and more is said in Chapter 9.

6.4.1 Business Models and Commercial Prospects

Let's follow the money. Bertelsmann poured $85 million into Napster before Roxio agreed to pay $5 million for Napster's patent portfolio and other intellectual property [Kin02, Tar00]. The executives at AOL were upset when they learned that Gnutella was released for free as open source. Chord is a research project funded by DARPA and the Space and Naval Warfare Systems Center. How can the potential of peer-to-peer networks lead to a sustainable profit for a well-run business?

In a sustainable business, users pay for value. In peer-to-peer systems, value comes from the client software, client hardware, network bandwidth and interconnections, search and brokering services, and the authors and publishers of the content being shared.

In most cases clients purchase the hardware the client software runs on. They also typically pay an Internet service fee to cover their share of network bandwidth, interconnections, and access. This is the established client-network infrastructure that exists independent of peer-to-peer networks, and there is nothing new here. There are several models that are candidates for capturing payment for the peer-to-peer elements.

Altruism, including youthful enthusiasm, unfunded projects, ambition, pride, spite, open source contributions, basic research, freeware, donations, philanthropy, and wishful thinking got several peer-to-peer projects started. These include the early days of Napster, Gnutella, and several of the projects originating in research or special interest communities. But we all need to eat to live and altruism does not often last long without reciprocation.

Once systems are developed, they may be inexpensive enough to support by integrated advertising systems. KaZaA offers an *advertising supported* version of their client software.

Client software for any number of client applications, including word processing, spreadsheets, graphics, databases, personal organizers, money management, and entertainment is profitably sold by established software development and publishing companies. The client software used in peer-to-peer systems can also be sold to users at a fair price. KaZaA, BearShare, and LimeWire offer this option as an alternative to their advertiser-supported version. Note that charging for client software may create a barrier to users deciding to join the system. This reduces the number of clients, and according to the network effect, it diminishes the value of the network. To offset this effect, network operators often give away the clients for free to establish a large network, and then begin charging later on when the value of the network is established.

It is technologically possible for network providers to charge usage-sensitive fees for bandwidth and connections. Since popular peer-to-peer systems use substantial bandwidth, users could be charged their fair share for the resources they consume. Users expect to pay more for broadband access than for dial-up. A T3 data transmission line costs more than a T1 line because it provides higher bandwidth.

Real estate agents, auction houses, stock brokers, and eBay are all information brokers that charge a fee for matching up buyers with sellers. The basic location services of peer-to-peer systems perform a similar service. Peer-to-peer networks could charge for the brokering services they provide. However, this may require some centralized accounting system.

Authors create value when they create content. Publishers create value when they bring content to the marketplace. They deserve to be paid fairly for their work. Authors and publishers get fair pay for their work throughout the creative industries, including movies, books, television, theatre, art, photography, and music. Helpful and internationally recognized copyright laws and digital rights management can potentially turn peer-to-peer networks into a valuable and profitable distribution channel for many types of content. This is especially true when the content originates from very many sources, rather than from a few large publishers. However, the lack of a successful business model seems to have prevented peer-to-peer networks from sustaining profitable commercial operation so far.

6.4.2   Legal Aspects

Copying files between computers is legal.[7] Infringing copyrights is illegal. Peer-to-peer systems have made headlines because they are widely used to share copyrighted music and video files.

---

[7]This section is based primarily on US copyright law and the status of the legal actions RIAA has taken to protect their current interests as of the time of this writing. Extension of these principles internationally, or into the future is pure speculation.

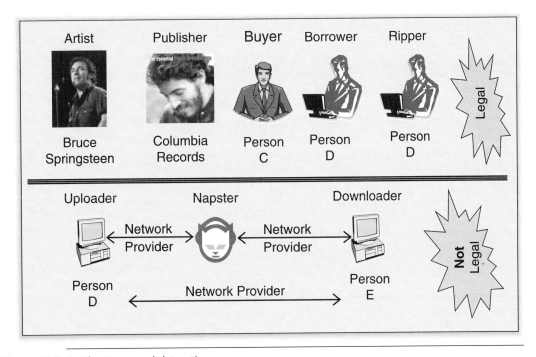

Figure 6.9 Parties to copyright action.

Peer-to-peer systems fragment the operations and disguise the parties responsible for the theft, as shown in Figure 6.9.

1. Person A, an artist such as Bruce Springsteen, creates music and gains a copyright for it, perhaps in partnership with a producer and publisher.
2. Person B, a publisher such as Columbia Records, sells the music on a Compact Disk.
3. Person C buys a copy of the CD, and
4. Lends it to a friend, D.
5. Person D "rips" a song from the CD and copies it to their computer as an MP3 file. Now person D can use audio software like Winamp or Windows Media Player to play the song from his PC.
6. Person D runs a Napster client on his computer and allows the description of the MP3 file to be uploaded, over a network owned by some network operator, to the Napster server. At this point it is likely the "fair use" provision of the copyright law has been exercised and that no laws have been broken; however,
7. Now Person E is also a Napster user and requests a copy of the song, the server identifies Person D as having it, and the song is copied from Person D to Person E.

The courts have maintained that the law has now been broken. In fact, it has been broken by person D who uploaded the file, Napster who brokered the transaction, and person E who downloaded the file. Removing the central directory by substituting Gnutella for Napster only makes it harder to prosecute; it does not change the law.

Copyright law, in section 17 U.S.X. § 106, gives the copyright holder several important rights. The first and most important is the right to "reproduce the copyrighted work in copies of phonorecords." This law goes on to define "copies" in a broad, detailed, and forward-looking way [Vich1, Copy00].

The defense of computer-network aided music file sharing relies on several provisions of the copyright laws. The defense argues:

- Napster is a "service provider" and is protected by provisions of the Digital Millennium Copyright Act.
- The MP3 files are not copies of the original music.
- Napster is a recording device and is protected by laws that allow manufacture, importation, or distribution of digital audio recording devices.
- The "Fair Use" of copyrighted material allows for noncommercial recording by consumers.

The courts have ruled against these arguments [RIAA].

The Digital Millennium Copyright Act [DMCA98] limits the liability of service providers for the intermediate transmitting, routing, or connection of material that they do not originate or terminate. The case of *A&M Records Inc. v. Napster Inc.* ruled this did not protect Napster.

Ripping music to an MP3 file significantly changes the file format and slightly changes the audio quality. The case *UMG Recordings, Inc. v. MP3.COM, Inc.* ruled that this transformed file is a copy of the original and is protected by the copyright law, despite these differences.

The Audio Home Recording Act (A.H.R.A.) bars infringements based solely on "the manufacture, importation, or distribution of a digital audio recording device." This law resulted from the case of *Sony Corporation of America v. Universal Studios Inc.*, which ruled that manufacturing and selling a VCR is legal, even though the manufacturer knows the product can be used to infringe copyright [SAM04]. The court held the manufacture and distribution of recording devices does not constitute infringement so long as it "is capable of substantial non-infringing uses." The Napster-type provider finds no help in either the A.H.R.A. or *Sony,* because Napster is not a "recording device."

The A.H.R.A. provides protection for noncommercial recording by consumers. This is the so-called "fair use" provision of the copyright laws. The users of a Napster-type service, it is argued, are not covered by this protection because their use cannot be considered noncommercial. First, each of the many recipients[8] of the MP3 file are receiving, for free, a product which ordinarily they

---

[8]While copying songs from your friend's CD is probably covered under "fair use" and is legal, the Napster network allowed copying on a huge scale. It is argued that this *large scale* copying exceeds "fair use."

would have to purchase. The courts held that "The global scale of Napster usage and the fact that users avoid paying for songs that otherwise would not be free militates against a determination that sampling by Napster users constitutes personal or home use in the traditional sense." This also applies to the individual who gives her MP3 files away on Napster. This person is not merely taking an album they purchased and giving it away to someone, which would be perfectly legitimate. What she is doing is effectively making millions of copies of the music and giving those copies away.

It is also argued that the user's transaction does not fall under the "fair use" exception. There are four factors to be considered in determining whether copying is fair use. These four factors are: (1) the purpose and character of the use, including whether the use is of a commercial nature or is for nonprofit educational purposes; (2) the nature of the copyrighted work; (3) the amount and substantiality of the portion used in relation to the copyrighted work as a whole; and (4) the effect of the use upon the potential market for or value of the copyrighted work.

Napster was determined not fair use because: (1) The downloaded files are used commercially because users obtain songs for free rather than purchase them; (2) The entire song is typically downloaded; and (3) record company sales have declined as a result[9] [Fine 1].

In short, the participants in Napster-type transactions were found guilty of copyright infringement.

The move to decentralized Gnutella-type architectures has not yet stopped the RIAA's court actions. They settled with the parents of a 12-year-old who was accused of sharing more than 1,000 copyrighted songs on KaZaA [Dea03]. In a recent dispute with Verizon, the courts found that the RIAA can't subpoena Internet providers for subscribers' personal information without going through the court system [Phi03]. In response RIAA began proceedings against 532 people, identified only as "John Doe" and their IP address, alleged to be violating copyright laws [Dea04].

---

[9]Keep in mind that correlation does not prove causality. Although the sales did decline, it is not proven that Napster was the cause.

CHAPTER 7

Interactive Content Delivery—
Instant Messaging

Conversations are interactive. Spoken dialogs, whether face-to-face or over a telephone system, benefit from a characteristic known to psychologists as *interactional coherence*. This refers to the expectation that speakers take turns and their comments "belong together" with each turn intended as a timely response or follow-up to a previous turn. Speakers' comments relate to the particular discussion topic, and changing topics is well managed by the speakers. The greater the time lag between speakers' turns, the more difficult it becomes to identify what comment each response relates to.

So far the book has described content flowing primarily one-way, from a content producer responding to a request by a consumer. This request-response model is not truly interactive. Even in peer-to-peer systems the roles of consumer and producer remain largely fixed throughout a session. In contrast, *instant messaging* is real-time, interactive content delivery. Users alternate roles rapidly taking turns as content consumer and content creator. The resulting communication is a bidirectional and symmetrical dialog. The users benefit from the interactional coherence of the sessions.

Research on spoken conversations highlights the importance of simultaneous feedback on signaling when to listen, the effective timing of taking turns, and maintaining a continuous interaction. Spoken conversation approaches the ideal model of *precisely alternating turns*. Here, the transition from one speaker to the next occurs quickly, without an undue gap or interruption. The speakers alternate roles taking turns speaking and listening.

Although text-only interactive systems provide users less feedback than face-to-face meetings, well-designed interactive systems can achieve interactional coherence, and also allow types of language play that are not common in face-to-face interactions [Her99].

Interactive systems engage users in ways that are impossible with communications requiring a significant time lag, such as letter writing or even e-mail. Interactive systems often rely on the rapid exchange of short messages.

Short messaging has a rather long history.

On September 2, 1837, Samuel Morse sent a telegraph message over a distance of 1,700 feet. Encouraged by the potential of transmitting messages over longer distances, in 1843 the U.S. Congress approved $30,000 for Morse to build a telegraph line from Washington, D.C., to Baltimore, Maryland. On May 24, 1844, Morse sat in the Supreme Court chamber of the Capitol and sent the first official telegraph message: "What hath God wrought!" Not long afterward brokers on Wall Street used the telegraph to gain quick access to important financial information, such as the current price of gold. In 1867, the New York Stock Exchange introduced *stock tickers*—telegraph devices that reported the purchase and sale of stocks. The effects of short messages quickly became far reaching [Bro04].

On May 10, 1869, a crowd gathered at Promontory Summit near Brigham City, Utah, to witness the completion of the world's first transcontinental railroad. The event was distinguished by setting the Golden Spike—joining the western span of the railroad built by Central Pacific Company to the eastern span built by the Union Pacific Company. People gathered in telegraph offices around the country to hear news of the event. A telegraph wire was attached to the Golden Spike and another to the sledgehammer. Closing this circuit would send a single bit of information to many telegraph offices around the country and signal completion of this cross-country gateway. Leland Stanford swung the hammer and hit the rail, missing the spike. The telegraph operator quickly closed the circuit, and then transmitted the short message "Done," and the era of transcontinental railroad travel began [Amb00].

On March 10, 1876, Alexander Graham Bell spoke the first words over a telephone. He was about to test a new transmitter. In another room, his assistant Thomas A. Watson waited for the test message. Suddenly, Bell spilled some acid from a battery onto his clothes. He cried out "Mr. Watson, come here. I want you!" Watson heard every word clearly and rushed into the room, and this short message began the era of interactive telecommunication that continues today [Brod04].

On December 14, 1903, when Wilbur and Orville Wright sent a telegraph to their parents, the short message ". . . success assured keep quiet" foretold manned flight [Dem03, Jay03].

In 1921, the Detroit Police Department started alerting its officers simply by transmitting a signal that made a portable device beep. In 1959 Motorola introduced the term "Pager" to refer to a small radio receiver that delivered a radio message individually to those carrying the pager device. The first pager, as we are familiar with them today, was Motorola's Pageboy I, introduced in 1974. It had no display and could not store messages, but it was portable and notified the wearer that a pager message had been sent [CEA1].

By 1980, there were 3.2 million pager users worldwide. Pagers had a limited range, and were used in on-site situations such as by medical workers within a hospital. By 1990, wide-area paging was practical and over 22 million pagers were in use. By 1994, pagers became popular for personal use and 61 million were in service. Short messages came a long way and were immediately connecting millions of people [Page].

Most of these short messages were not interactive, but by mid 2002 more than 140 million registered users were exchanging messages on the AOL instant messaging system [Woo02].

This chapter begins by defining instant messaging and exploring various types of collaboration. It then introduces a reference model for instant messaging and presence and describes some basic requirements for such systems. Standard IETF models for presence and instant messaging are described. Various Internet-based instant messaging and presence systems are described in detail. These include SIMPLE, based on SIP, and XMPP, based on Jabber. The presence, pager mode, and message mode approaches of the SIMPLE standard are each described. SIMPLE and XMPP are briefly compared. Popular IM systems, including AOL Instant Messenger, MSN Messenger, and Yahoo! Messenger are introduced. Finally, the wireless Short Messaging System (SMS), and the Multimedia Messaging Service (MMS) are briefly introduced and convergence of interactive content delivery systems is discussed.

7.1   Instant Messaging Defined

Instant messaging is real-time, interactive content delivery.[1] IM encourages collaboration and engages participants in ways that one-way, delayed, asynchronous communications like e-mail cannot. It can provide immediate feedback and allows true dialog, not a serial monologue.

Collaboration can take many forms, and the IETF created a standard reference model to describe it.

7.1.1   Collaboration

Face-to-face dialog is the prototype for collaboration. Dialog is a cooperative exchange of ideas, information, questions, or opinions between peers. It is characterized by timely and symmetrical exchange of short messages communicating the interaction among the participants. The participants are present and focus their attention on the dialog. Dialog includes both primary (e.g., verbal or text-based semantics) and supplementary (e.g., non-verbal or other expressions of status and mood) information related to the semantics of the discussion, the nature of the relationship, and the emotions of the participants.

Figure 7.1 illustrates various forms of collaboration that comprise interactive content delivery. A simple dialog between two people is shown in A. They may be separated by some distance and use an instant messaging service to

---

[1]IM is most often associated with text-based messaging. Voice messaging is typically referred to as VoIP, and multimedia messaging is typically referred to as MMS. This chapter describes text-based and multimedia messaging, including voice.

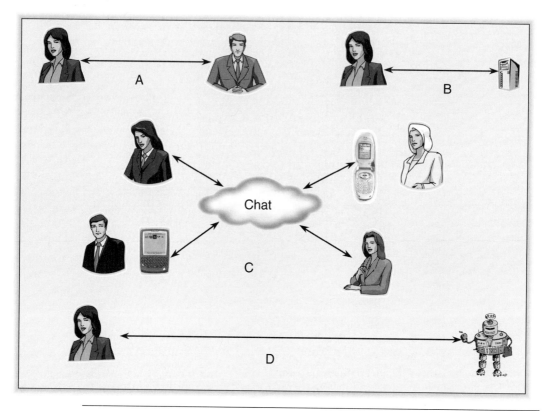

Figure 7.1 Collaboration.

communicate with each other. It is also possible for a human to communicate with an intelligent agent or database, as shown in B. Here an instant messaging system allows the human to exchange information with the agent rather than with another person. In the spirit of interaction and fun, the agent may simulate natural language and a playful personality. The agent may be a simple database responding to queries, or it may be an expert system or game. The expert system poses questions or provides guidance based on the semantics of the dialog to help solve a problem or entertain the human peer. Several people may join in a chat session as shown in C. Here each person sees or hears the contribution of each session participant. The people may participate in the conversation using a variety of client devices. These may be IM clients on personal computers, wireless instant messaging devices, PDA-based clients, or cell phones using text messaging, text-to-voice, or picture messaging. The chat participants may also be engaged in a multi-player game. Instant messaging can be used as the human interface to telemetry; monitoring and controlling remote equipment; or controlling semi-autonomous robots, such as unmanned rovers, aircraft, and space craft as illustrated in D.

7.1.2 A Reference Model

RFC 2778 presents an abstract model for a presence and instant messaging system. This model describes a very general and universal system, and does not prescribe any particular implementation. The model introduces vocabulary that is useful in discussing various approaches and implementations of presence and instant messaging systems. The basic components of the model are shown in Figure 7.2.

People must be present before they can interact by sending messages; therefore presence information is important for interactive messaging. Presence information can be useful alone, without messaging; it can send the simple but often reassuring message "I am here." Also, messages can be sent while the receiving principal (e.g., person) is absent. In this case the message waits for the principal to return and read it. To accommodate these loosely coupled dependencies, the model describes the presence service independent of the instant messaging service. The figure shows these systems related through *principals* that make use of the two systems simultaneously.

To help make this abstract model more concrete, we will use an example of two friends communicating over the AOL instant messaging system (AIM). Here, each of the friends is a principal in the system.

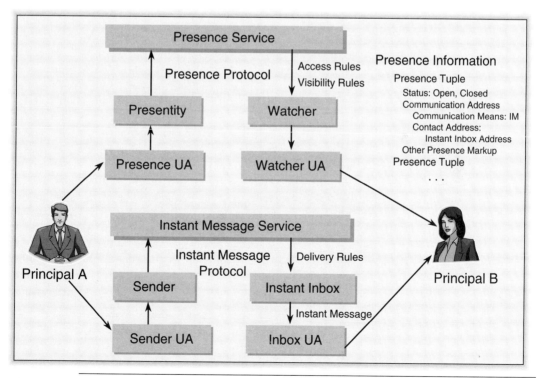

Figure 7.2 Presence and IM model.

The *principal* is the system user and may refer to a human, a group of people working together, or a program that appears to the system as a single actor. Each principal accesses the service through user agents. There are four such agents shown in the figure, labeled *Presence UA, Watcher UA, Sender UA,* and *Inbox UA.* These user agents are often combined into instant messaging clients such as AIM, Microsoft Windows Messenger, Yahoo! Messenger, and the many others mentioned throughout this chapter.

The *presence service* accepts, stores, and distributes *presence information.* The *instant messaging service* accepts and delivers *instant messages* to *instant inboxes.* Instant messages are typically defined as small identifiable units of data. As we will see, the model extends to include audio and video conferencing and other modes of interaction.

The presence service has two distinct sets of clients, called the *presentity* and the *watcher*. The authors of RFC 2778 graciously apologize for coining the term *presentity.* It refers to the entity (e.g., principal) that is having its presence watched and reported. The presentity provides the presence information that the service stores and distributes. The watchers receive the presence information from the service.

AIM clients display presence information. The icons in the buddy list illustrate who is online and who is not. Friend A (the watcher) can easily see if his Friend B (the presentity) is online or not. The system is symmetrical so Friend B can watch the presence status of Friend A. The presentity is separate from the principal in the model because while the presentity *represents* the principal it is *not* actually the principal. For example, a person can be present at their PC and have their presence status represent them as offline.

Although it is not shown in the figure, there are two kinds of watchers, called *fetchers* and *subscribers.* A fetcher requests the current presence information; however, a subscriber is sent notifications of changes in presence information. A fetcher that periodically requests presence information is called a *poller.*

The presence information is formed from a number of *presence tuples.* Each tuple includes status information, the communication address, and other optional presence markup information. The status can be either *open,* representing an instant inbox that is ready to accept messages, or *closed,* representing an instant inbox that is unable to accept messages. The communication address consists of a *communication means,* which can have the value of *instant messaging service,* and a *contact address.* The contact address provides the address of an *instant inbox* of an instant messaging service.

A *presence protocol* carries presence information between the presentities, the presence service, and the watchers.

Similarly, the instant messaging service has two types of clients. A *sender* provides *instant messages* for delivery by the instant messaging service. Each message is addressed to a particular instant inbox address, and the service attempts to deliver the message to the corresponding instant inbox.

An *instant message protocol* carries instant messages from the sender through the service to the instant inbox.

AIM clients allow sending and receiving instant messages. When Friend A acts as the sender he types an instant message that gets sent using an instant messaging protocol to Friend B who receives it in his instant inbox.

The model includes several features designed to protect principals' privacy. *Access rules* determine how presence information is made available to watchers. This allows presentities to hide their presence information from some or all watchers. *Visibility rules* similarly determine how watcher information is made available. They allow watcher information to be hidden from some or all watchers. Together, these rules are important to prevent unwanted *stalking* which refers to using presence information to infer the location of the principal. *Delivery rules* allow the receiving principal to decide how instant messages are filtered from the instant inbox.

RFC 2779 uses this model to recommend general requirements for instant messaging and presence protocols. These requirements include the following:

1. Support for mobile wireless access devices with low bandwidth, high latency, intermittent connections, modest computing power, battery constraints, and small displays and keyboards.
2. The presence service can exist independent of the messaging service, and vice versa.
3. The namespace can be partitioned into an arbitrary number of domains.
4. The entities in one domain can interoperate with entities in other domains.
5. The system can scale to serve millions of entities within a single domain, and millions of domains within a single namespace.
6. A watcher can subscribe to hundreds of presentities, and hundreds of subscribers can watch a single presentity.
7. Access controls provide principals with control over who sees presence information and who can send or read instant messages.
8. The network topology supports intermediate proxies and allows or disallows communication through commonly deployed firewalls.
9. The protocol supports encryption and authentication of instant messages.
10. Presence information must be accessible even when a presentity is out of contact.
11. The protocol must allow presence information to be cached, updated, and replicated.
12. Instant messages must identify the sender and the intended recipient, and include a return address.
13. Instant message transport must be rapid enough to allow for comfortable conversational exchanges of short messages.
14. Delivery or non-delivery of a message is reported to the sender.

7.2   Internet-Based Instant Messaging

Not long ago, the IETF had three separate working groups dedicated to Internet-based instant messaging. Two of those groups have successfully finished their charter and are no longer active. The result of their work is crystallized in the form of several RFCs and is finding deployment in today's instant messaging systems. The first concluded working group is the Instant Messaging and Presence Protocol (IMPP) Working Group, which has defined a general model for IM. Its work on presence data formats and interoperable instant message formats has been adopted by two other IM-related working groups, namely SIMPLE and XMPP. SIMPLE, which is short for SIP for Instant Messaging and Presence Leveraging, is defining use of the Session Initiation Protocol (SIP) for instant messaging. The Extensible Messaging and Presence Protocol (XMPP) protocol is based largely on the previously implemented Jabber systems. The results of each of these groups are described below. The many popular instant messaging systems that use proprietary protocols are also described.

7.2.1   Presence and IM Protocols

To progress from the abstract reference models described in Section 7.1.2 toward architecture and protocols, the Instant Messaging and Presence Protocol (IMPP) Working Group of the IETF has provided several Internet RFCs. These include the Common Profile for Presence (CPP) [RFC 3859], the Presence Information Data Format (PIDF) [RFC 3863], and Common Profile for instant messaging (CPIM) [RFC 3860]. Each of these is briefly described below. The relationship of these protocols is illustrated in Figure 7.3.

Common profile for presence

The Common Profile for Presence (CPP) specification defines common semantics and data formats for presence so that gateways between presence services can be built. This includes the semantics of *subscribe*, *response*, and *notify* operations. CPP also introduces the presentity URI (pres URI) to uniquely identify presentities and watchers. An example of a pres URI is `pres:fred@example.com`.

The *subscribe* operation is a request from a watcher to a presence service to subscribe to the presence information of a particular presentity. The subscribe request includes the watcher, target, duration, subscription identifier, and transaction identifier, each described below.

- **Watcher**—the watcher requesting the subscription, identified by a pres URI, such as `pres:watcher@example.com`
- **Target**—the presentity to be watched, identified by a pres URI

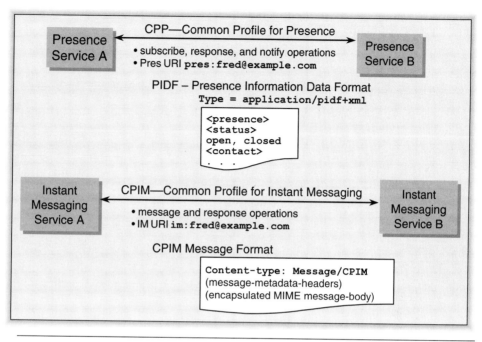

Figure 7.3 Presence and IM protocols.

- **Duration**—the maximum number of seconds that the subscription should be active. This is set to zero to implement a one time "fetcher" request rather than to establish a subscription.
- **Subscription Identifier (SubscriptID)**—a unique reference to this subscription instance, used to unsubscribe
- **Transaction Identifier (TransID)**—a unique identifier used to correlate the subscribe operation with the response operation

When a presence service receives a subscribe operation, it immediately responds with a *response* operation. This includes the status, TransID, and duration:

- **Status**—indicates if the subscription request succeeded or failed
- **TransID**—the same transaction identifier used in the subscription request
- **Duration**—the number of seconds for which the subscription service will be active. This may differ from the value in the subscription request.

If the response operation indicates success, the service immediately sends a *notify* operation to communicate the presence information to the watcher. The notify operation includes the watcher, target, and TransID. The values of watcher and target are identical to those given in the subscribe operation that triggered this notify operation. The TransID is a unique identifier for this notification.

The notify operation also has content, namely *presence information*. This presence information supports the Presence Information Data Format, described below.

The presence information data format

The Presence Information Data Format specification defines the format (PIDF) used for expressing presence information. This is a specification for an XML-based common presence data format and a set of operations and parameters to achieve interoperability between different instant messaging and presence protocols that meet RFC 2779. It defines the new content type `application/pidf+xml` for an XML MIME [MIME] entity that contains presence information.

PIDF is a common presence data format for CPP-compliant presence protocols that allows presence information to be transferred unmodified across CPP-compliant protocol boundaries. This provides benefits for both security and performance.

PIDF defines the base presence format and extensibility required by RFC 2779. It defines a minimal set of presence status values defined by the IMPP Model document [RFC 2778]. However, a presence application is able to define its own status values using the extensibility framework provided by PIDF.

Readers unfamiliar with XML may wish to read the Appendix before continuing. Briefly, XML provides type identifiers for data elements. Each type identifier begins with the name of the type in angle brackets (e.g., `<type>`) and ends with the same type name preceded by a slash (e.g., `</type>`). The information delimited by such a pair is called an *element*. Elements are often nested. XML also allows namespaces to be defined for particular applications. The XML namespace `impp` is defined for PIDF with the corresponding URN of `urn:ietf:params:xml:pidf`.

The presence information is contained in an `application/pidf+xml`-type document. The specific XML identifiers for each element are included here with the name and description of each element:

- *Presence element* `<presence>`, which is the root element of every presence document. It includes the `entity` identifying the pres URI of the presentity and the namespace declaration `xmlns` indicating the namespace on which the presence document is based.
- List of *Presence Tuples* `<tuple>` including
  - *Identifier*: token to identify this tuple within the presence information.
  - *Status* `<status>`—the `<basic>` value `open` indicating the person is accepting messages or `closed` to indicate absence, and/or some extension status value.
  - *Communication Address*: the *Communication Means* and *Contact Address* `<contact>` of this tuple. This is the URL of the contact

address. This is optional because the presentity may wish to hide its communication address, or there might be tuples not related to any communication means. This element can also include the optional field, *Relative Priority*, providing a numerical value specifying the priority of this *Communication Address* relative to other addresses for this presentity.

- ○ *Timestamp* `<timestamp>`—the date and time of the status change of this tuple (optional)
- ○ *Human Readable Comment* `<note>`—a free text memo about this tuple (optional)
- ● *Presentity Human Readable Comment* `<note>`—a free text memo about the presentity (optional)

Here is a simple PIDF presence data example using a default XML namespace:

```
<?xml version="1.0" encoding="UTF-8"?>
<presence xmlns="urn:ietf:params:xml:ns:pidf"
   entity="pres:someone@example.com">
<tuple id="sg89ae">
   <status>
     <basic>open</basic>
   </status>
   <contact priority="0.8">tel:+ 09012345678</contact>
  </tuple>
</presence>
```

This declares that the presentity `someone@example.com` is open to receive messages at her telephone number +09012345678 with a contact priority of 0.8.

Common profile for instant messaging

Analogous to the common profile for presence, the common profile for instant messaging provides a means for preserving the end-to-end features (especially security) as messages pass through instant messaging interoperability gateways. The specification also provides recommendations for instant messaging document formats that can be employed by instant messaging protocols.

CPIM specifies the semantics of two operations. Applications use the *message* operation to send a message to an instant inbox. The message service responds using the *response* operation.

The *message* request includes the source, destination, maximum number of forwards, the transaction identifier, and content as follows:

- **Source**—the originator of the instant message, identified by an instant messaging URI. An IM URI is similar to a pres URI, for example: `im:fred@example.com`
- **Destination**—the destination of the instant message, identified by an instant messaging URI

- **Maximum number of forwards (MaxForwards)**—a hop counter used to avoid loops through gateways. The count is decremented by each IM gateway and the message is discarded if the count reaches zero.
- **Transaction Identifier (TransID)**—a unique identifier used to correlate the message operation with the response operation
- **Content**—the instant message itself. As a minimum, the service must support the mime type `Message/CPIM` format described below.

When the service receives a message operation, it immediately replies with a *response* operation. This includes the TransID, and status:

- **TransID**—the same transaction identifier used in the message operation
- **Status**—an indication of whether the message delivery succeeded or failed. Status values are "success," "failure," or "indeterminant" if the service is acting as gateway or proxy.

CPIM message format

The Common Profile for instant messaging (CPIM) described above specifies the operations required for interworking diverse instant messaging protocols. The intent is to allow a variety of different protocols interworking through gateways to support cross-protocol messaging that meets the requirements of RFC 2779 as previously described in Section 7.1.2.

Meeting the security requirements of RFC 2779 requires a common message format so that end-to-end signatures and encryption may be applied. The common profile for instant messaging describes a common message format that must be used by any CPIM-compliant message transfer protocol. This allows signatures to be calculated for end-to-end security.

Existing formats, such as those specified in RFC 2822 and [MIME] have several shortcomings for this application. For example:

- Optional encodings and a variety of ways to encode a particular value lead to variability that can invalidate an end-to-end security signature.
- Use of 7-bit ASCII in the header causes problems for encoding international character sets.
- Changes to header information can invalidate the security signature.

The mime type `Message/CPIM` is defined to overcome these problems.

A `Message/CPIM` object has multiple parts where the first part contains the message metadata and the second part is the message content. The two parts are separated by a blank line, to keep the message header information separate from the MIME message content headers.

The complete message looks something like this:

```
MIME Overall Header  [ Content-type: Message/CPIM

     Blank Line       [

  Message Header      [ (message-metadata-headers)

     Blank Line       [

Encapsulated MIME     [ (encapsulated MIME message-body)
```

The end of the message body is defined by the framing mechanism of the transport protocol used.

Here is a simple example, adapted from RFC 3862, of a complete message employing MIME security features described in RFC 1847:

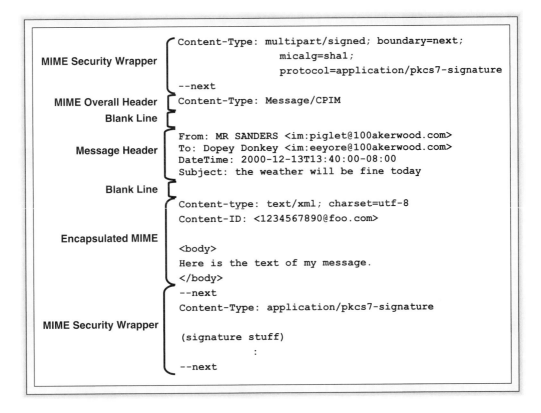

```
MIME Security Wrapper   Content-Type: multipart/signed; boundary=next;
                                      micalg=sha1;
                                      protocol=application/pkcs7-signature
                        --next
MIME Overall Header     Content-Type: Message/CPIM
    Blank Line

 Message Header          From: MR SANDERS <im:piglet@100akerwood.com>
                         To: Dopey Donkey <im:eeyore@100akerwood.com>
                         DateTime: 2000-12-13T13:40:00-08:00
                         Subject: the weather will be fine today
    Blank Line

                         Content-type: text/xml; charset=utf-8
                         Content-ID: <1234567890@foo.com>

Encapsulated MIME        <body>
                         Here is the text of my message.
                         </body>
                         --next
                         Content-Type: application/pkcs7-signature

MIME Security Wrapper    (signature stuff)
                                   :
                         --next
```

7.2.2 SIMPLE

The Session Initiation Protocol (SIP) [RFC 3261] is an application-layer control and signaling protocol for creating, modifying, and terminating *sessions* with one or more participants. Here a session is considered an exchange of data between some number of participants. These sessions may be voice phone calls that take place over the Internet (VoIP), multimedia distribution, multimedia conferences, or many other types of sessions.

An IETF working group is defining extensions to the SIP protocol [RFC 3261] for instant messaging and presence. The group is named SIMPLE, short for SIP—for Instant Messaging and Presence Leveraging [SIMPLE]. It might seem odd to extend a signaling and control protocol to carry actual bearer data in form of instant messages. But SIP features used to initiate a session have a lot in common with the needs of instant messaging and presence services, such as those described in Section 7.2.1. This commonality makes it a good choice for extending to these applications.

A complete description of SIP is beyond the scope of this book, and is unnecessary for understanding the work of the SIMPLE group. To provide an introduction to SIP and provide the background needed to understand its use in presence and instant messaging, the next section describes a few basic elements of SIP.

The SIP protocol is used to invite users to participate in sessions. The signaling messages sent by the protocol are called *invitations*, and they carry session descriptions that allow the invited participants to agree on a set of compatible media types, such as audio or video, and the specific encoding used. SIP uses network elements called *SIP proxy servers* to help route requests to each user's current location. These proxies also play a role in authenticating users, authorizing them to use services, implementing call-routing policies, and providing features. SIP also provides a *registration* function that allows users to announce their current locations to the system. SIP runs on top of a variety of transport protocols, notably TCP and UDP.

During or between sessions the participants may move between endpoints. The participants may be addressable by several means, corresponding to fixed voice phones, mobile phones, computer-based softphones or other terminals, and they may communicate using several different media. SIP enables Internet endpoints, called *user agents*, to discover one another and to agree on session characteristics that will best allow them to communicate. SIP is independent of the underlying transport protocol, the type of media, or the type of session that is being established.

SIP supports five facets of establishing, managing, and terminating multimedia sessions:

1. **User location**—determining the address of the end system used for the communication
2. **User availability**—presence—determining the user's willingness to participate in a session at this time and place
3. **User capabilities**—determining the media types and characteristics the user can support
4. **Session setup**—ringing—altering users and establishing session parameters at both the calling and called party

5. **Session management**—transfer and termination of sessions, modifying session parameters, and invoking services

SIP is based on an HTTP-like request-response transaction model. Like HTTP, SIP consists of a request that invokes a particular *method* on the server to carry out a particular function. The INVITE method is illustrated in the example in Figure 7.4. Later we will introduce the REGISTER method and then the SUBSCRIBE and NOTIFY methods and illustrate their use in a presence server.

Figure 7.4 illustrates a simple example of a SIP message exchange between two users, named Alice and Bob. Here Alice uses a SIP application running on her PC (called a softphone) to call Bob on his SIP phone over the Internet. Two SIP proxies, atlanta.com and biloxi.com, are used to help establish the session. This typical arrangement is called a *SIP Trapezoid* because of the shape formed by the dotted line connections between these four elements. The session follows these steps:

1. Just as a caller rings your voice phone to invite you to join the conversation, Alice invites Bob to join her in a session. She addresses him using his SIP identifier, analogous to the pres URI, called a SIP URI. In this example it is sip:bob@biloxi.com, where biloxi.com is the domain

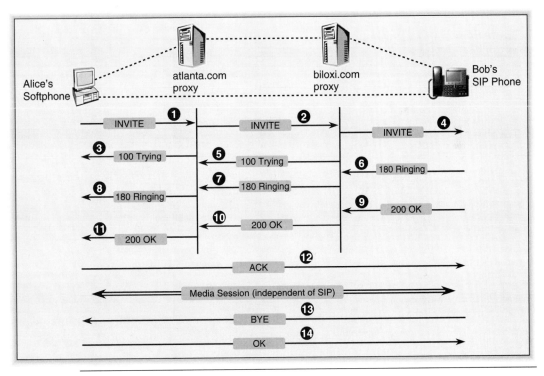

Figure 7.4 SIP session setup.

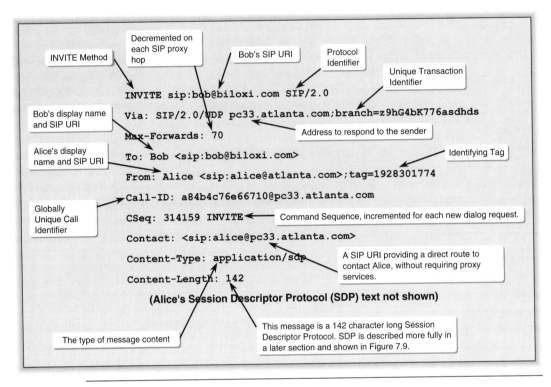

Figure 7.5 SIP invite message.

of Bob's SIP service provider. The annotated text of this message is shown in Figure 7.5. Alice's softphone sends the invitation to the local SIP proxy at atlanta.com. It is interesting to note that Alice addresses Bob himself (in form of the SIP URI), rather than the device Bob will use to communicate with Alice. This is different from the traditional telephony world, where users dial the number of a particular phone rather than a number that identifies the actual user.

2. The atlanta.com proxy receives the `INVITE` message. It consults a location database and determines the IP address of the biloxi.com SIP proxy, and forwards the `INVITE` request to the biloxi.com proxy.

3. Upon receipt of the `INVITE`, the atlanta.com proxy sends a code `100 Trying` message to Alice's softphone using the same `To`, `From`, `Call-ID`, `CSeq`, and `branch` parameter as the `INVITE`. This allows Alice's softphone to correlate this `Trying` response with the original `INVITE` message sent and indicates the original `INVITE` message was received, and has been forwarded.

4. The biloxi.com proxy receives the `INVITE` and consults a location service database to obtain the IP address of the device at which Bob can be

reached. It then forwards the INVITE to Bob's SIP phone. Bob's SIP phone receives the INVITE and alerts Bob to the incoming call, perhaps by ringing.

5. The biloxi.com proxy responds to the INVITE with a 100 Trying message to the atlanta.com proxy.

6. Bob's phone responds with a 180 Ringing message to the biloxi.com proxy, using a path based on the updated VIA field parameters.

7. This 180 Ringing message is forwarded to the atlanta.com proxy where

8. It is forwarded to Alice's softphone, and it can be used to initiate ringback to the caller.

9. Bob decides to answer the call. He picks up the handset and his SIP phone sends a 200(OK) response to indicate the call has been answered. The body of this OK message includes a SDP media description of the type of session Bob is willing to establish with Alice.

10. The 200(OK) is forwarded to the atlanta.com proxy.

11. The 200(OK) response is forwarded to Alice's softphone, which stops the ringback tone and indicates that the call has been answered.

12. Finally, Alice's softphone sends an ACK (acknowledgment) message directly to Bob's SIP phone, without involving any SIP proxies. The media session can now begin communicating directly between the two endpoints. The media session proceeds.

13. Bob decides to terminate the call and hangs up his phone which sends a BYE to Alice.

14. Alice responds with an OK and the session is terminated.

Although this example is of a very simple call setup, the SIP protocol accommodates much more complex situations including session parameter negotiation, security, conferencing, etc.

One might wonder how the correct IP address of Bob's device gets into the database that is used in step 4 of the above example. After all, users are mobile and can roam about different locations using different devices. How does the network learn about devices that can be used to reach a certain user? Figure 7.6 provides the answer by illustrating the *registration* method of the SIP protocol. Here Alice has three separate phones that she uses in SIP sessions at various times. Upon initialization, and then periodically, each of her phones sends REGISTER messages to the SIP registration server. The registration server is addressed within the atlanta.com domain and it may or may not be co-resident or co-located with the atlanta.com SIP proxy. Each REGISTER message associates the IP address of her phone with her SIP URI. This association between a SIP URI and an IP address is stored by the Location Server, and is accessible by the SIP proxy. Alice may have a single SIP URI, in which case, the most recent phone to be activated will be bound to that URI; or she may have several SIP URIs, allowing her to maintain the association between each SIP URI and a particular device. The signaling protocol also allows for serial or parallel forking where her several devices can be alerted sequentially or simultaneously.

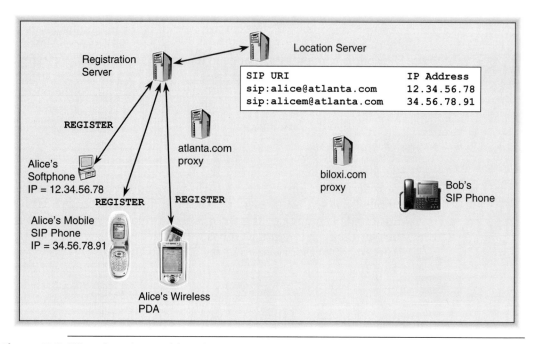

Figure 7.6 SIP registration and location servers.

In the next section we will see how particular SIP methods are used to implement a presence service.

Presence

SIP is well suited as a presence protocol. As we saw in the previous section, the SIP location services contain presence information in the form of registrations. Also, SIP networks can route requests to the registration server having the information for any particular user. This ability allows SIP networks to be reused to provide connectivity for presence subscriptions and notifications.

RFC 3265 and the presence event package for the session protocol [RFC 3856] combine to define the SIP SUBSCRIBE and NOTIFY methods. As defined by the presence event package, these methods allow SIP to be used for subscriptions and presence notifications. This system complies with the common presence profile (CPP) framework described previously and can interwork with other CPP compliant presence systems. The scheme is illustrated in Figure 7.7.

Key to the operation of this event package is the newly defined *presence agent*. The presence agent accepts subscriptions, stores subscription state, and generates notifications when there are changes in the presence information. The presence agent must know the presence state of each presentity within its scope. A presence agent is always addressable by using a SIP URI that uniquely identifies the presentity. There can be multiple presence agents for a particular presentity. The presence agent is a logical entity that can reside within the physical presence server, or within the presence user agent, or elsewhere. It is shown in the figure as a dotted box, to highlight this flexibility. The presence server is shown as a host computer to emphasize that it is a physical entity.

Figure 7.7 illustrates the actions involved in subscribing and receiving presence information. Each step is described below:

1. When a subscriber (watcher) wants to learn about the presence information from some user (a presentity) it creates a SUBSCRIBE request. This request identifies the presentity using a SIP URI, a SIPS URI, [RFC 3261] or a presence URI. More will be said about this choice later. The SUBSCRIBE request is carried along by SIP proxies, as any other SIP request. It arrives at a presence server which forwards it to the presence agent serving the identified presentity. If the presence server hosts the presence agent, this connection is trivial. If the presence agent is hosted

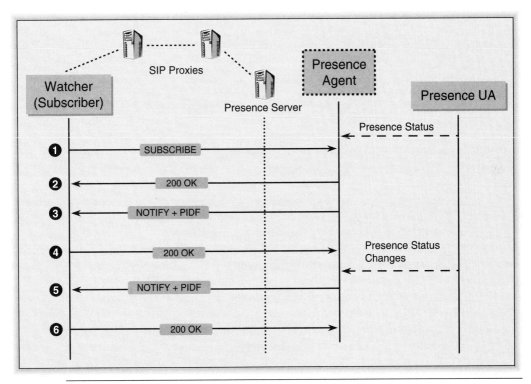

Figure 7.7 SIMPLE presence events.

elsewhere, then the presence server proxies the request to the physical host of the presence agent. The presence agent first authenticates the subscription, and then authorizes it. The methods used for this authentication and authorization are not specified by the protocol, and can take many forms. Authentication and authorization by the presence agent is mandatory.

2. If authorized by the presence agent, a 200 OK response is returned.

3. A NOTIFY message is also sent immediately. This message contains presence information in PIDF format, as described earlier. As a minimum, this contains the presentity state of either open or closed.

4. The watcher acknowledges receipt of the NOTIFY message with a 200 OK.

5. At some later time the presentity state may change. Presence status changes are communicated, outside this protocol, from the presence user agent to the presence agent. In response to this status change, the presence agent uses a NOTIFY method to send updated presence information in a PIDF message.

6. The watcher acknowledges receipt of the NOTIFY message with a 200 OK.

Subscribed watchers will receive additional NOTIFY alerts informing them of subsequent changes in presence information.

The subscription persists for a length of time negotiated in the original request through use of the EXPIRES field in the SUBSCRIBE and OK messages. The subscriber can refresh or terminate the subscription by sending subsequent SUBSCRIBE requests at any time. The presence agent can also terminate the subscription at any time by sending a NOTIFY request with the Subscription-State header field set to terminated. A SUBSCRIBE request with EXPIRES set to zero results in a one-time fetch of the information.

It is common for a user to have both a SIP URI and a presence URI to identify them. This raises questions about how to use these different identifiers and how they relate. Using the presence URI has the advantage of supporting interoperability through gateways to other CPP-compliant systems. It has the disadvantage of requiring resolution to a SIP URI within this network. The SIMPLE working group addresses this issue in RFC 3861.

The interested reader may wish to study many more protocol details that are described in the protocol documents RFC 3265 and RFC 3856.

As Figure 7.2 illustrates, a presence server is only one half of the solution. It needs to be accompanied by an instant messaging service to be complete. The SIMPLE working group describes two solutions for implementing an instant messaging service. The *pager mode* is intended for exchanging a small number of short messages without the overhead of establishing a SIP dialog. The *message mode*, in contrast, is intended for exchanging longer messages and first establishes a SIP dialog. These two approaches are described in the following sections.

Pager mode

RFC 3428 introduces the MESSAGE method, which is an extension to SIP that allows the transfer of instant messages. MESSAGE requests normally carry the instant message content in the message body, in the form of MIME body parts.

Using this method each message stands alone, and no SIP dialog is created by the messages. This is similar to using a two-way pager or SMS text messaging, described more fully in Section 7.3. This approach is most sensible when a small number of short messages are sent to one or only a few recipients over a short period of time. This is contrasted with the message mode approach, described in the next section.

A SIP *dialog* is a peer-to-peer SIP relationship that persists for some time between two user agents (UAs). A dialog is established by SIP messages, such as a 2xx response to an INVITE request. A call identifier identifies a dialog, local tag, and a remote tag. A dialog was previously known as a *call leg* in RFC 2543. Each message in a dialog is routed over the same network path. The MESSAGE method does not establish a SIP dialog and avoids this routing constraint.

SIP also defines the User Agent Client (UAC) and User Agent Server (UAS). A user agent client is a logical entity that creates a new request, and then uses the client transaction state machinery to send it. A user agent server is a logical entity that generates a response to a SIP request. The response accepts, rejects, or redirects the request.

Figure 7.8 illustrates use of the MESSAGE method. The UAC acts as the Sender UA in the instant message model illustrated in Figure 7.2.

1. The UAC for the principal Alice begins the session by sending a MESSAGE method to the local SIP proxy. An instant inbox is most generally identified by an instant message URI, for example im:user@domain.com. To allow routing through the SIP network, the UAC resolves this into a SIP URI which appears in the Request-URI of the message request before it is sent. In this case it is sip:Bob@domain.com. The actual message, "Watson, come here." is transmitted as MIME type text/plain with a length of 18 characters. The message can be any MIME type, including message/cpim, as described in Section 7.2.1. In most cases, the message is restricted to a maximum of 1300 bytes.

2. The proxy receives the request and recognizes itself as the server for domain.com. It looks up Bob in its location database (which has been built up from registrations) and finds a binding from sip:Bob@domain.com to a specific client with the address sip:Bob@Bobpc.domain.com. It forwards the request to Bob, which is the UAS acting as the instant inbox. The message "Watson, come here" is received by Bob, and displayed.

3. An OK response is generated by the UAS and sent back to the proxy. Note that most of the header fields are simply reflected in the response.

4. The proxy receives this OK response, strips off the top VIA, and forwards it to the address in the next VIA, which is Alicepc.domain.com in this

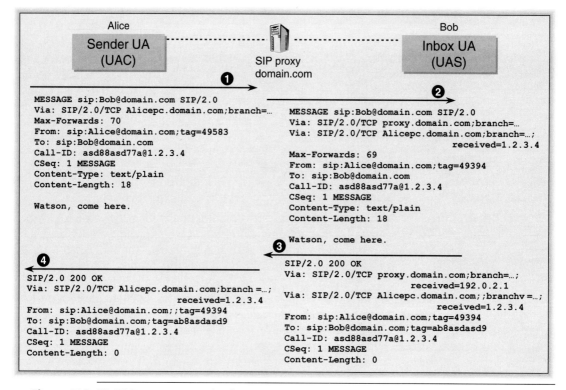

Figure 7.8 SIMPLE message method.

case. The UAC receives this OK response, and is assured the message has been delivered.

Message mode

While the pager mode described above is useful and efficient for sending a small number of short messages, an effective approach to establishing longer dialogs of more complex messages is also desirable. The SIMPLE approach to providing this *message mode* is to use the Session Description Protocol (SDP) over SIP to describe the session, and then use the Message Session Relay Protocol (MSRP) over TCP to transmit the series of messages. This protocol stack is illustrated in Figure 7.9.

The Session Description Protocol [RFC 2327] is described before describing the Message Session Relay Protocol [CMJ04].

The Session Description Protocol is intended to describe multimedia sessions for the purpose of the session announcement, session invitation, and other forms of session initiation. The protocol was developed prior to its application in instant messaging and is used to describe sessions in a variety of environments, including establishing voice phone calls. The purpose of SDP is to

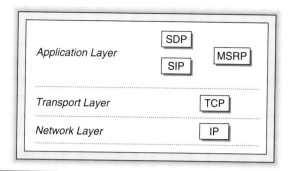

Figure 7.9 Message mode protocol layers.

announce information about media streams in multimedia sessions with enough detail to allow interested parties to participate in the session. SDP is purely a format for describing a session and it can be used over a variety of transport protocols. We focus on its use over SIP.

SDP includes this information:

- the session name and purpose,
- times the session is active, such as start and stop times, or periodically recurring times, such as every Wednesday at 10 a.m.,
- the media used for the session, including:
  - the type of media, such as video, audio, text, etc.,
  - the transport protocol being used. Although SDP allows for a wide range of protocols, including RTP, H.320, and others, we will focus on its use with MSRP over TCP, and
  - the format of the media, such as H.261 video, MPEG video, audio, and others.

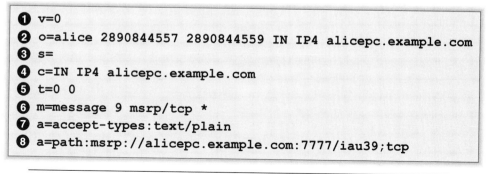

Figure 7.10 SDP example.

- communications information needed to receive those media, including network addresses, ports, formats, etc., and
- optional information about bandwidth used and contact information for the session sponsor.

An SDP session description consists of several lines of text, each having the form `<type>=<value>`. The `<type>` field is always a single character. Figure 7.10 shows an example SDP message used to establish an MSRP session initiated by Alice. Each line is described below.

1. Type `v` specifies the protocol version; in this case it is version 0.
2. Type `o` specifies the originator, owner, or creator of the session. It includes:
   - the `username` of `alice`,
   - the unique `session identifier`. Here an NTP-formatted time stamp is used, but other unique identifiers can be chosen.
   - the `version` of this session announcement. Again an NTP time stamp was used.
   - the `network type` is `IN`, indicating the Internet,
   - the `address type` is `IP4`, indicating Internet Protocol, version 4, and
   - the network `address`, which is the hostname `alicepc.example.com`, which can be resolved by the DNS to an actual IP address.
3. Type `s` specifies the session name, which is left empty in this example.
4. Type `c` is an optional field specifying the connection information. It includes:
   - the `network type` of `IN`, indicating the Internet,
   - the `address type` of `IP4`, indicating Internet Protocol, version 4, and
   - the `connection address` set to `alicepc.example.com`
5. Type `t` specifies the time the session starts and stops. Setting the session start and stop times both to zero, as in this example, establishes a permanent session.
6. Type `m` specifies media announcement. It includes:
   - the `media` type, which must be `message` when using MSRP,
   - the `port` number, which is not used by MSRP but is set to 9 in this example. The actual port used is determined by the session URL which is explained later as part of MSRP,
   - the transport `protocol`, which is MSRP over TCP in this example, and
   - the `fmt lists` describing the allowed media formats, which are typically specified as a media payload type. In MSRP this field is ignored and is set to `*` in the example.
7. Type `a` is an attribute, used to extend SDP. Here the first attribute defines the MIME body types accepted. In this case it is plain text.
8. The second attribute describes the `path` with a particular temporary, session-specific MSRP URL.

Although this example shows only one particular use of SDP, the full protocol specification allows for powerful and flexible expression of session types. This enables rich instant messaging sessions, which may include audio and video components, text, graphics, and file transfers.

The MSRP protocol is being developed to provide message sessions. These can offer advantages over pager-mode messages. For example, any pager-mode message exchange that involves more than two MESSAGE requests will generate more SIP requests than the minimal MSRP session initiation sequence. Also, once the session is INITIATED, the session-mode messages never cross the SIP proxies themselves. Any SIP feature that can be applied to other types of media sessions can also apply to MSRP sessions. This includes conferencing, third-party call control, call transfer, quality of service integration, and privacy. The MSRP protocol is currently described by a rapidly evolving series of Internet Drafts. The following description is based on the most recent Internet Draft available at press time. Updates are expected and must be consulted for current information.

In contrast to the pager-mode MESSAGE, MSRP transactions do establish a SIP dialog.

MSRP uses the following two methods:

- SEND, which is used to deliver a complete message or a chunk (a portion of a complete message), and
- REPORT, which sends a report on the status of an earlier SEND request.

Each endpoint in an MSRP session is identified by a URL. This URL is used with the SIP INVITE method and specifies the host address, port, transport, and security protection level. After inviting[2] a new SIP session, the sender creates a unique transaction identifier and uses this and the SEND method to create an MSRP request start line and begin a new request. Next, the sender places the target path in a To-Path header, and the sender's URL in a From-Path header. An MSRP transaction consists of exactly one request and one response. The response matches the request if they are bracketed by the same transaction identifier and arrive on the same connection the request was sent.

Figure 7.10 shows an example MSRP session. Here Alice is a principal and her softphone is used as a Sender UA in the terminology of Figure 7.2 and as a *sender* in the terminology of MSRP. Bob is another principal and his SIP phone is an Inbox UA in the terminology of Figure 7.2 and as a *receiver* in the terminology of MSRP. In this session pure SIP messages are intermingled with MSRP messages. Several of the SIP messages carry payloads in SDP format.

Each message shown in Figure 7.11 is described here in more detail:

1. Alice constructs a local URL of msrp://alicepc.example.com:7777/ iau39; tcp, and then sends it through the SIP proxies using SDP embedded in a SIP INVITE message. She then begins to listen on TCP port 7777. The

---

[2]Traditionally when using a voice phone the invitation rings the called party phone and the conversation does not begin until the called party answers the phone. In contrast, most IM systems send the first text message simultaneously with the alert. MSPR implementations should support both modes of operation.

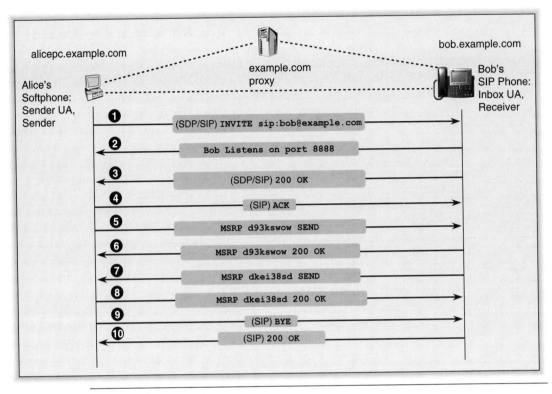

Figure 7.11 MSRP session example.

session is described using SDP and corresponds to the SDP example described above and shown in Figure 7.10. The actual message sent is:

```
INVITE sip:bob@example.com
v=0
o=alice 2890844557 2890844559 IN IP4 alicepc.
example.com
s=
c=IN IP4 alicepc.example.com
t=0 0
m=message 9 msrp *
a=accept-types:text/plain
a=path:msrp://alicepc.example.com:7777/iau39;tcp
```

2. Bob listens on TCP port 8888
3. Bob sends a SIP OK, and includes the negotiated SDP parameters
```
v=0
o=bob 2890844612 2890844616 IN IP4 bob.example.com
s=
c=IN IP4 bob.example.com
```

```
t=0 0
m=message 9 msrp *
a=accept-types:text/plain
a=path:msrp://bob.example.com:8888/9di4ea;tcp
```

4. Alice replies with a SIP ACK. This is analogous to step 12 in Figure 7.4. The endpoints are now ready to begin a media session.

5. Alice opens a connection to Bob and uses the MSRP SEND method to transmit the first text message to Bob. The To-path identifies the target path and the From-Path includes the sender's URL. The message being sent is "Hi, I'm Alice!" A transaction identifier of d93kswow is included at the start and end of the message and the MIME content type is plain text. The message text is:

```
MSRP d93kswow SEND
To-Path:msrp://bob.example.com:8888/9di4ea;tcp
From-Path:msrp://alicepc.example.com:7777/iau39;tcp
Message-ID: 12339sdqwer
Content-Type:text/plain

Hi, I'm Alice!
-------d93kswow$
```

6. Bob acknowledges receipt with an MSRP OK message, bracketed by the transaction identifier. The message text is:

```
MSRP d93kswow 200 OK
To-Path:msrp://bob.example.com:8888/9di4ea;tcp
From-Path:msrp://alicepc.example.com:7777/iau39;tcp
-------d93kswow$
```

7. Now Bob sends text to Alice using the MSRP SEND method. His message is "Hi Alice! I'm Bob!" bracketed by the transaction identifier. The message text is:

```
MSRP dkei38sd SEND
To-Path:msrp://alice.example.com:7777/iau39;tcp
From-Path:msrp://bob.example.com:8888/9di4ea;tcp
Message-ID: 456
Content-Type:text/plain

Hi, Alice! I'm Bob!
-------dkei38sd$
```

8. Alice acknowledges receipt with an MSRP OK message bracketed by the transaction identifier. The message text is:

```
MSRP dkei38sd 200 OK
To-Path:msrp://alice.example.com:7777/iau39;tcp
```

```
From-Path:msrp://bob.example.com:8888/9di4ea;tcp
--------dkei38sd$
```

9. Alice sends a SIP BYE to terminate the dialog.
10. Bob responds with a SIP 200 OK and terminates the session.

This example begins to illustrate the advantages of the MSRP protocol mentioned in the beginning of this section. Fewer SIP requests are needed, the proxies have dropped out of the path, session parameters are managed, and richer communications are possible using a variety of media types.

7.2.3   Jabber and XMPP

Readers who find SIMPLE too complex may be interested in Jabber and the Extensible Messaging and Presence Protocol (XMPP) protocol it has led to.

Most of the core aspects of the Extensible Messaging and Presence Protocol were developed originally within the Jabber open-source community in 1999. In 2001, the Jabber Software Foundation (www.jabber.org) was formed to manage extensions to that protocol in the form of Jabber enhancement proposals. In late 2002, the IETF formed the XMPP working group with the mission of adapting the base Jabber protocol as an IETF-approved instant messaging and presence technology. The Working Group recently concluded its work after publishing four RFCs.

XMPP core features

RFC 3920 defines the core features of the Extensible Messaging and Presence Protocol (XMPP), an open protocol for streaming Extensible Markup Language (XML) elements to exchange structured information in near real time between any two network endpoints. While XMPP provides a generalized, extensible framework for exchanging XML data, it is used mainly for the purpose of building instant messaging and presence applications that meet the requirements of RFC 2779, as described in Section 7.1.2.

The standards documents defining XMPP consistently use examples from Shakespeare's play, *Romeo and Juliet*. We retain this playful context to simplify reference to the original standards documents.

The basic elements of the XMPP network architecture are shown in Figure 7.12. Basic elements of the architecture include *clients*, *servers*, the *Jabber Identifier*, and *gateways* to *foreign networks*.

The network relies on servers to manage connections and sessions for clients, servers, and gateways. The figure shows two servers, named example.com and example.net. These servers route XML elements, organized into *stanzas* and *streams*, over TCP among the network elements. These servers also usually store persistent data, such as contact lists, used by clients. Servers typically intercommunicate using TCP on port 5269.

Clients typically connect directly to a server over a TCP connection on port 5222. The figure shows six clients, with three belonging to the ever popular Juliet, and one each to Romeo, Mercutio, and Benvolio.

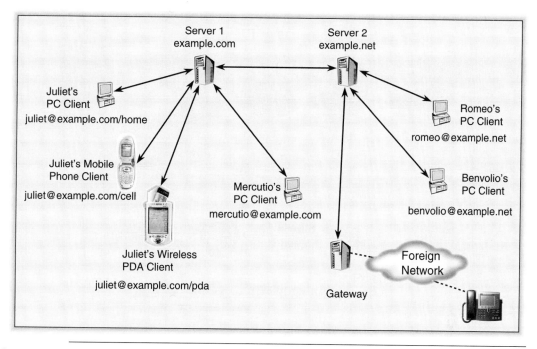

Figure 7.12 XMPP network architecture.

Each network endpoint is identified with a Jabber Identifier, called a JID. JIDs identify instant message users, servers, and the particular client device, called a *resource*. JIDs can also be used to identify a service, such as a particular chat room. They have the general form of `user@host/resource`. In the example, Juliet is a principal who has three JIDs—each one corresponding to one of her three client devices. Her home PC client is identified by `juliet@example.com/home`, her mobile phone is `juliet@example.com/cell` and her personal digital assistant is `juliet@example.com/pda`. She can be reached at any of these devices through the server named example.com.

A *gateway* is a special-purpose service whose primary function is to translate XMPP into the protocol used by a non-XMPP messaging system on a *foreign network*, as well as to translate the return data back into XMPP. Examples are gateways to Internet Relay Chat (IRC), Short Message Service (SMS), SIMPLE, SMTP, and legacy instant messaging networks such as AIM, ICQ, MSN Messenger, and Yahoo! Instant Messenger. The mapping between XMPP and CPIM is described in RFC 3922. This and other gateway issues are outside the scope of this book.

XML-based communications in XMPP

Communication takes place in the form of XML elements exchanged over TCP between network elements. These XML elements are organized into *streams* and *stanzas*.

An XML stream is a container for exchanging XML elements between any two network entities and it corresponds to an ongoing session. The stream extends from an initiating client or server to a receiving entity (usually a server), and corresponds to the initiating entity's session with the receiving entity. The XML stream begins with an opening XML `<stream>` tag (with appropriate attributes and namespace declarations), and ends with a closing XML `</stream>` tag. An XML stream is unidirectional. To enable bidirectional information exchange, the initiating entity and receiving entity must establish one stream in each direction (the *initial stream* and the *response stream*), normally over the same TCP connection.

An XML stanza is a unit of information that is sent from one entity to another over an XML stream; it can be sent completely within a single session. There are only three defined XML stanzas—`<presence/>`, `<message/>`, and `<iq/>`.

Table 7-1 introduces each of the three stanzas and illustrates the relationship of stanzas to streams.

A basic XMPP instant message session

With these basic concepts introduced, Figure 7.13 illustrates a basic instant message session, involving the following exchanges:

1. Juliet wants to begin a session. She initiates a `<stream>` toward her XMPP server by opening a TCP connection and sending the request to example.com. The `<stream>` request includes the `to` address of the server, the XML Namespace used by clients called `jabber:client` and the XML Namespace reserved for streams called

Table 7-1   An XMPP stream

`<stream>`	Open a stream in one direction with a `to` or `from` JID, and optional session identifier, type, language attribute, and protocol version.

`<presence>`
  `<show/>`
`</presence>`
	Publish the initiating client presence status information contained in the `<show>` element. Broadcast this information to all subscribed clients, unless a `to` attribute identifies a single recipient.

`<message to='foo'>`
  `<body/>`
`</message>`
	Send the message in the `<body>` element to the entity identified by the `to` attribute. In this case send the message to foo.

`<iq to='bar'>`
  `<query/>`
`</iq>`
	This Info/Query stanza provides a request-response mechanism. This is used to get a result, set data to a particular value, or report an error. In this example a particular roster is requested by the `<query>` element.

`. . .`	A stream may contain any number of stanzas and remains open indefinitely.
`</stream>`	The stream is closed and the session is ended.

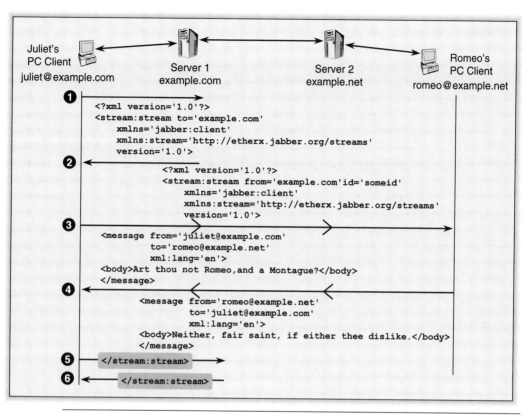

Figure 7.13 A basic XMPP session.

`http://etherx.jabber.org/streams`. It also announces support for XMPP version 1.0.

2. Her server responds by opening a stream toward Juliet. This specifies the `from` attribute as the server JID of example.com, and includes an arbitrary session `id` of `someid`. It also includes the namespace and version declarations.

3. The adventuresome Juliet sends a `<message>` to Romeo. She sends the `<message>` stanza over the connection to her local server example.com. She includes her JID in the `from` field and his JID in the `to` field. She also indicates that the text is in the natural language English by specifying `xml:lang='en'`. She encloses the text of the message "Art thou not Romeo, and a Montague?" inside the `<body>` element of the stanza. Juliet's server forwards the stanza to Romeo's server, example.net, which forwards it to his client `romeo@example.net`.

4. The enamored Romeo responds with his own `<message>` stanza to his local server, example.net. He includes his JID as the `from` address and her JID as the `to` address, and again notes the text is in English. His

artful message is "Neither, fair saint, if either thee dislike." and is enclosed inside the `<body>` element of the stanza. His server forwards the message to example.com which sends it to Juliet's client `Juliet@example.com`.

5. Wary of curious onlookers, Juliet terminates the stream and closes the session by sending `</stream:stream>` to her local server.

6. Her local server responds with `</stream:stream>` to her client, and terminates the stream.

XMPP contact list management

XMPP allows users to manage contact lists, called *rosters*. These are similar to the buddy lists of various legacy IM systems. A user's roster is stored on the server and can be accessed by the client from any resource.

Rosters are managed by `<iq>` stanzas using the `<query>` child element. Here is a simple example of a client request for `roster_1` sent from Juliet's PC client, directed to her server example.com:

```
<iq from='juliet@example.com/home' type='get'
  id='roster_1'>
  <query xmlns='jabber:iq:roster'/>
</iq>
```

Her server's response may look like the stanza shown below, where each of her three contacts are identified by the JID, name, and subscription status within an `<item>` element, and is assigned to the group `Friend` by the `<group>` element:

```
<iq to='juliet@example.com/home' type='result'
  id='roster_1'>
  <query xmlns='jabber:iq:roster'>
  <item jid='romeo@example.net'
     name='Romeo'
     subscription='both'>
  <group>Friends</group>
</item>
<item jid='mercutio@example.org'
     name='Mercutio'
     subscription='from'>
  <group>Friends</group>
</item>
<item jid='benvolio@example.org'
  name='Benvolio'
  subscription='both'>
  <group>Friends</group>
</item>
</query>
</iq>
```

XMPP provides *blocking lists* to control message or presence contact from particular users or lists of users. This implements the access rules, visibility rules, and delivery rules shown in Figure 7.2. These blocking lists are managed using the `<iq>` stanza in a way that is somewhat similar to managing rosters. Among other parameters, the `<item>` element can contain child elements to specify granular control over the types of stanzas to be blocked. The allowable child elements are:

- `<message/>`—blocks incoming message stanzas,
- `<iq/>`—blocks incoming IQ stanzas,
- `<presence-in/>`—blocks incoming presence notifications, and
- `<presence-out/>`—blocks outgoing presence notifications.

XMPP includes several security features. These include use over the Transport Layer Security (TLS) protocol [RFC 2246] and incorporation of the Simple Authentication and Security Layer (SASL) [RFC 2222]. When these services are used, the protocol stack looks like Figure 7.14.

This layering is sensible because TCP is the base connection layer used by all of the protocols stacked on top of it. TLS is often provided at the operating system layer, SASL is often provided at the application layer, and XMPP is the application itself.

This concludes the discussion of instant messaging services of XMPP, and we will move on to discuss presence services.

XMPP presence services

Presence stanzas are used in XMPP to implement presence services. The `<presence>` stanza includes attributes for `type`, and child elements of `<show/>`, `<status/>`, and `<priority/>`, described below [RFC 3921].

The `<type>` attribute describes the client's presence status. If it is omitted, the client is signaling to the server that it is online and available for communication. Otherwise, it can be set to anyone of these values:

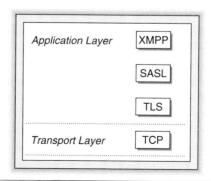

Figure 7.14 XMPP protocol stack.

- **unavailable**—signals that the entity is no longer available for communication,
- **subscribe**—the sender wishes to subscribe to the recipient's presence information,
- **subscribed**—the sender has allowed the recipient to receive their presence information,
- **unsubscribe**—a notification that an entity is unsubscribing from another entity's presence,
- **unsubscribed**—a previously granted subscription has been cancelled or the subscription request has been denied,
- **probe**—a server's request for an entity's current presence, and
- **error**—an error has occurred regarding processing or delivery of a previously sent presence stanza.

The protocol describes how to use these parameters to exchange presence information with a single user (called a *directed presence*); probe for presence information; broadcast the information to all subscribers; and establish, manage, deny, and terminate subscriptions.

The optional `<show/>` element supplements the presence information within the `type` attribute. If it is used, it takes on one of these values:

- **away**—the entity or resource is temporarily away,
- **chat**—the entity or resource is actively interested in chatting,
- **xa**—eXtended Away—the entity or resource is away for an extended period, and
- **dnd**—Do Not Disturb—the entity or resource is busy.

If no `<show/>` element is provided, the entity is assumed to be online and available.

The values of the `<show/>` element are not designed to be read by humans. Instead, the `<status/>` element contains text, such as "busy in a meeting now" that can be displayed and read by humans. Finally the `<priority/>` element can be used to guide stanza routing to preferred resources.

Here is a simple example, incorporating many of the allowed elements, indicating that although Romeo is available for communications, he prefers not to be disturbed because he is wooing Juliet:

```
<presence xml:lang='en'>
  <show>dnd</show>
  <status>Wooing Juliet</status>
  <priority>1</priority>
</presence>
```

Because of the large number of different implementations based on the Jabber protocols, it is difficult to estimate the number of users. However, Peter Saint-Andre (Executive Director of the Jabber Software Foundation) estimates that there are at least 7–10 million end users of various jabber deployments.

7.2.4 Comparison of SIMPLE and XMPP

The debate comparing the benefits and limitations of SIMPLE and XMPP rages on [Moo03]. Although we hesitate to add fuel to that fire, the two approaches can be compared based on their compliance with the requirements of RFC 2779, their ease of implementation, their efficiency, deployment experience, flexibility, and feature richness.

Although these two working groups have taken two different approaches to similar end goals, it is interesting that they were both chartered by the IETF. The SIMPLE group was chartered on March 12, 2001, and the XMPP group was chartered more than a year later on November 6, 2002, long after the first Jabber systems were available in open source. Apparently the IETF did not want to prejudge which approach would be more useful, so they allowed the work to proceed in parallel. Eventually, technical, business, and popular forces will determine the long-term future of each approach.

The charters for both the SIMPLE and the XMPP IETF working groups both include goals for compliance with the requirements of RFC 2779 and RFC 3860, the CPIM specification. The SIMPLE charter expresses a clear goal to comply with each while the XMPP charter says they will be consistent as much as is practical. The XMPP group has recently completed work on RFC 3922 having the descriptive title "Mapping the Extensible Messaging and Presence Protocol (XMPP) to Common Presence and Instant Messaging (CPIM)" and describing the detailed mapping and extent of compliance. The SIMPLE group is beginning similar work.

Section 4.1.10 of RFC 2779 states that the common message format should be based on the IETF-standard MIME. SIMPLE uses MIME for its messages, while XMPP relies on XML.

Implementations of Jabber clients and servers have been freely available since 1999. There are thousands of Jabber server deployments on the Internet today, and millions of people use Jabber clients for instant messaging. With the recent publication of the RFCs defining XMPP, many of these implementations are moving to support for the XMPP standard. Jabber is used for text conferencing of IETF meetings and working group discussions [XMPP1]. SIMPLE clients do not have as long a usage history, although they have the backing of IBM, Microsoft, and AVAYA [Moo03, Sau04]. SIMPLE relies on SIP networks.

The pager-mode of SIMPLE requires a minimum of five SIP messages through SIP proxies to deliver an instant message less than 1300 characters long. However, the message mode allows peer-to-peer media sessions to be established. These sessions may involve text, graphics, file transfer, audio, and video. The XMPP protocol provides excellent support for text messages, but does not now support richer multi-media sessions.

In summary, SIMPLE is an up-and-coming system for sharing presence information, sending a few short messages, or establishing a richer interactive media session. XMPP is a well thought-out up-and-running system for exchanging text messages and presence information.

While the standards battle rages on, millions of people from all walks of life use instant messaging to gossip with friends, keep in touch with extended family, and sometimes even exchange important information with coworkers. The next section describes these popular systems.

7.2.5 Popular Systems

Internet relay chat began in Finland in late August 1988, and instant messaging got an important boost [Oika]. In May 1993 RFC 1459 published a standard description of the system. The IRC protocol is a text-based protocol, with the simplest client being any socket program capable of connecting to the server. IRC itself is a teleconferencing system based on a distributed system client server model. A typical setup involves a server forming a central point for clients (or other servers) to connect to, performing the required message delivery/multiplexing and other functions. Connections are typically TCP/IP.

In 1997 AOL introduced AIM (AOL Instant Messenger), which allowed its members to talk with non-members for the first time.

A small Israeli company, named Mirabilis had 12 million registered users of its free instant messaging software ICQ (I seek you) when AOL purchased the company in June, 1998 for approximately $287 million. By February 1999 the number of users grew to 27 million and AOL was ready to showcase its newest service, called ICQ99 to those ICQ users [Atn99]. Instant messaging quickly became a household word. By late in the year 2000 AIM claimed to have 80 million registered users and this grew to more than 140 million registered users by mid 2002 [Gre00, Woo02].

AIM and ICQ use a proprietary client server protocol called OSCAR. It is officially unpublished, but is documented in an unofficial protocol specification [Fri00]. The protocol has changed and expanded since this analysis and publication.

The proprietary nature of these instant messaging clients quickly causes a network effect, as described in Section 6.1.4. Users of one proprietary IM system cannot communicate with users on other systems. The value of the AIM network grows as the number of users grows. In January 2001, AIM had grown so large that as a condition of approving their merger with Time Warner, the FCC restricted AIM from offering advanced instant messaging features, including videoconferencing, largely because of its dominant market share [MH03].

Microsoft and Yahoo! did not stand idly by while the AIM network grew in size and value. They each launched their own services. Microsoft introduced MSN Messenger in late July 1999 and Yahoo introduced Yahoo! Messenger. When MSN Messenger was launched it could interoperate with AIM. AOL immediately responded by changing its protocols, and Microsoft adapted to the change. The interoperability wars between AOL and Microsoft continued through 1999 when Microsoft finally retreated [DPT03]. Microsoft distributes their closely related Windows Messenger product with their Windows XP operating system.

Although they had virtually zero market share at launch MSN Messenger grew to 23.1 million unique users and Yahoo messenger reached 19 million unique users by March 2003. By then AIM had dropped to 31.9 million users and ICQ had 28.3 million. The FCC lifted its ban on AIM advanced features [MH03]. Now each of these systems offers voice and videoconferencing in addition to text messaging.

Cerulean studios (www.ceruleanstudios.com) offers their Trillian client to help IM users intercommunicate. Working toward the goal of universal IM connectivity, a single Trillian client connects to the major chat networks, including AIM, MSN, ICQ, Yahoo! and IRC. Unfortunately, recent versions of the AIM terms of service agreement prohibit using third party clients such as Trillian [AIM1].

Instant messaging fun and games are not restricted to the courtrooms and boardrooms. Popular IM clients allow users to play interactive games, and converse with *bots* (short for robots) having distinct personalities. AIM users can play checkers and many more modern interactive games with their buddies. The bot ZolaOnAol will chat with AIM users any time and provides calculator, dictionary, games, horoscope, movies, news, polls, sports, stocks, thesaurus, and weather information using an interesting interactive natural language interface. Development systems from Conversagent (www.conversagent.com) enable creation of customized interactive bots to provide customer service, employee services, or many other types of services.

These popular IM clients and services are generally free or advertiser supported. They are fun and useful for chatting with friends and family. However, they are not well suited for use within a business setting. Multiple clients make them cumbersome to use. More importantly lack of security features opens enterprises to liability and potential loss of trade secrets.

Substantial business potential lies with Enterprise IM systems, which are gaining in popularity and acceptance. These systems run on private networks and provide interoperability, security, scalability, integration with other business platforms, logging, and tracking. In addition to the enterprise offerings from major public IM providers and products from other established SW suppliers, such as Lotus SameTime (www.lotus.com), other companies are entering the enterprise IM market. One example is the Professional Online Desktop (POD) from Omnipod (www.omnipod.com) which offers secure instant messaging and file transfer, interoperation with other IM networks, broadcast, search, flexible access, and integration with wireless SMS services described in Section 7.3.1.

7.3 Convergence

Interactive content delivery solutions are not limited to the Internet. In response to the popularity of pagers, the alerting and messaging features of wide area paging were combined with cell phone technology to develop the Short Messaging System. This system allows text messages (no longer than 160 characters) to be exchanged between properly equipped wireless clients such as cell phones and personal digital assistants [SMS1], [IEC1]. Gateways, such as the Bigfoot Web SMS service (www.bigfoot.com), use HTTP to connect Internet users directly with wireless SMS clients using their cell phones or PDAs.

The Multimedia Messaging service (MMS) allows users to send and receive messaging using a whole array of media types, including text, images, audio, and video while supporting new wireless client types [3GPP1].

The road from SMS to MMS involves an optional evolutionary path called EMS (Enhanced Messaging System). EMS is also a standard accepted by the wireless industry 3rd Generation Partnership Project (3GPP at www.3gpp.org). For MMS to be deployed the network operators have to upgrade their infrastructure and devices supporting MMS must be available. Unlike MMS, EMS can be used over the existing infrastructure—although the features provided by EMS are not nearly as advanced. EMS can support relatively simple media such as melodies, simple pictures, sounds, and animations [Mobi1].

Wireless clients, such as the BlackBerry handheld (www.blackberry.com) and the Nokia 3300 music phone (www.nokia.com) now integrate voice, text, Web browsing, and e-mail into a single handheld device. The Nokia 3300 music phone also includes a mobile music player for MP3 and AAC music files, a stereo FM radio receiver, a digital recorder from the integrated FM radio and audio line-in, as well as MMS features such as sending, receiving, and storing images.

If you use AIM as your IM client, and you have some friends who use Windows Messenger and other friends who use SMS text messaging, you want a single system that can easily interconnect to all these users. This is why the network effect exerts pressure on networks of successful services to interwork with other networks offering similar services. Gateways are defined as part of both the SIMPLE and XMPP standards. Despite resistance from the promoters of proprietary solutions, gateways inevitably emerge to interconnect services. If the proprietary operators do not accommodate this interconnection, they will be left with their own island of users, disconnected from what quickly will become the majority of users. Eventually the survivors in this type of network battle become interconnected, and the pattern is well established. Railroads have long used a standard gauge of track throughout large geographic regions so trains can travel across territories once owned by competing operators. Western Union integrated more than fifty separate telegraph systems to allow intercommunication. Phone systems around the world interconnect using standard interfaces and gateways to allow voice communication between any two people in the world. Some day, even AIM and Windows Messenger will either interoperate, or disappear.

CHAPTER 8

Beyond Web Surfing— Content Services

Service is personal. Every individual has his or her own interests and preferences. Dad might enjoy a cup of plain milk in the morning, while his teenage boy prefers chocolate milk, and his little girl likes the sweet taste of artificial strawberry milk. In Chapter 3, we learned that a few times a week the family shopper travels a mile to the market to buy milk and bring it home. Every family member has quick access to the milk in the refrigerator. Every morning, the kids prepare their favorite mug of milk by adding three spoons of chocolate syrup or pink strawberry powder. Mom and Dad are not required to travel back to the store and get each kid's favorite drink. Instead, the kids process the plain milk and "adapt" it to their individual preferences—right at the kitchen counter, only a few feet away from the kitchen table.

Just as our family members each prefer a different flavor of milk, computer users prefer to consume information in different forms. While a European traveler might prefer reading about New York's current temperature in the Celsius scale, her American friend is most likely more comfortable with the same temperature being provided in Fahrenheit. The information presented to both travelers is the same; the content is just being processed and presented differently. *Content processing services (content services)* are the functional components of content networks developed to solve the problem of customizing services. These processing services include creation, modification, conversion, or filtering of either content or requests for content. While such services have typically been provided at Web servers, newly defined elements, called *service engines,* allow these content processing services to be provided on components within the network. Moving not only content closer to the user, but also the services operating on it, is a next logical step in the evolution of content networks.

This chapter describes several approaches that are emerging to provide content processing services. It begins by describing the technical and business forces that stimulate the creation of value-added service offerings in content networks. It then describes an overall architecture for distributing services, using intermediaries to steer selected requests and responses to service engines. Two examples of the distributed services architectures, the Internet Content Adaptation Protocol (ICAP) and the Open Pluggable Edge Services (OPES) are described. The Web services approach to announcing, discovering, describing, and making use of Web services is then introduced. The Universal Description, Discovery & Integration (UDDI) specification, the Web Services Description Language (WSDL), the Simple Object Access Protocol (SOAP), and the XML backplane they rely on are described. The chapter ends by describing the convergence of a variety of information sources that enable creation of very convenient, useful, and powerful services. The chapter illustrates how content services provide important functions for instantly delivering rich relevant content—anytime, anywhere.

A word of caution: Solutions for providing content services continue to evolve rapidly. Alternative architectures are proposed by on-going work in standards organizations. Several of the protocols described here are still under discussion and development. Some of the solutions are quite extensive in scope. The chapter introduces the fundamental problems solved by content services, describes alternative approaches, identifies requirements for functions within content service architectures, and gives selected details and examples of existing mechanisms. For more detailed, up-to-date, and emerging information, the reader is referred to the actual protocol specifications and the work of the IETF and W3C as they continue to create content services solutions. References are given in each of the subsections.

8.1   What Is Driving Content Services?

Powerful forces, both technical and business related, drive the evolution of content networks beyond Web caching and toward an infrastructure that—in addition to distributing content—also migrates the services operating on content from centralized servers to distributed application servers. Consumers are no longer content with plain Internet access, but expect a more exciting and personalized communications experience—as witnessed by the popularity of personalized Web portals such as My Yahoo! or My eBay. At the same time, network providers are eagerly looking for new value-added services to offer, since basic data transport is quickly becoming a commodity service with minimal revenue opportunities. The following sections explore both the technical and the business motivation for developing content services.

8.1.1   Technical Drivers

The previous chapters described architectures, protocols, and mechanisms for distributing static content across the network. Moving content closer to the consumer allows for faster content delivery and improves overall scalability of the Internet. It assumes, however, that the content is static and changes infrequently—maybe daily, weekly, or monthly—providing the same combination of text or images to each visitor. This assumption is inconsistent with recent trends, as consumers increasingly demand a personalized Web surfing experience. When visiting a Web site with news headlines, for example, users prefer to read about stories relevant to their personal interest, rather than being served with a general mix of headlines that are the same for all visitors. Such personalization requires additional processing and dynamic creation of the Web page for each individual user, which is typically being done at the origin Web server. As a result, individual user requests have to be sent to, and be served by, the origin server, eliminating the basic benefits of Web caching and content distribution. The next step beyond distributing static content, therefore, is to distribute services operating on and creating personalized content.

For example, while sitting at your desk you would like to get a local weather report. Typically, this requires the user to manually type in her current location, perhaps in the form of a ZIP code. If the content delivery system knows your current location, this step can be made automatic and the system can give you a report for your local area. If it knows your preferred use of text, graphics, audio, and video, it can customize the content and format of the information display to meet these preferences. The language you prefer to speak may be different from the predominant language spoken at the weather site being reported. What language should the report use and how will it be translated? Perhaps an enhanced service, providing more accurate, up-to-date or detailed information is available. Have you subscribed to the service, or can you pay for a single use of it? On another day you have moved away from your desk and are traveling internationally. You request a local weather report from your PDA. The same request of "give me a local weather report" now refers to a different geographic region, and also needs to be adapted to fit the PDA capabilities.

The architectures, protocols, and mechanisms we will discuss in this chapter are aimed at bringing such services to the network edge, close to the consumer—just as Web caching brings the static content closer to the consumer.

8.1.2 Business Interests

Services generate revenue. And business organizations rely on profitable revenue for their continued success. As transmission speeds and reliability increase and costs decrease, plain transport of bits and bytes quickly becomes a commodity with little profit opportunity. To increase profit levels, business organizations naturally migrate toward providing value-added services. An open infrastructure allowing creation of new content services in cooperation with the network provides attractive opportunities to content providers, the network or service providers, and the content consumers. An architecture has to be designed that allows for quick and easy development and deployment of new services to meet the ever-evolving needs and expectations of the content consumer. This leads to separate, complementary, and attractive arenas for content providers, network providers, and content service providers.

Furthermore, content services make it possible to isolate content processing and adaptation from content delivery and storage—activities requiring different expertise and having different optimization goals.

8.2   An Architecture for Content Services

So far, we have seen an architecture where the content is distributed, for example, in Web caches, but the services creating or modifying the content are still provided at centralized servers, if at all. As the Internet grows, so does the need for content services that scale with both the number of users and the resources required. As users understand the increased value of personalized, dynamically created, and custom-adapted content, the next logical architectural step is to distribute the services. In the weather report example, identifying the user's location, identifying and interpreting user preferences, translating the report into the user's preferred language, and adapting the content to suit the display device are each services that can be distributed throughout the network. Providing these services separately from the function of serving static content and close to the consumer can yield significant benefits.

Figure 8.1 illustrates the network evolution. As we have seen in previous chapters, Web caches are used to move content closer to the user. It is a logical next step to also move the services that transform or create the content in the same way and to provide them on network elements close to the user. Enhancing

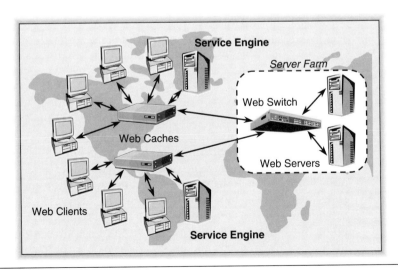

Figure 8.1 Distributing content and services.

Web caches to run additional services, for example, filtering of Web messages, is a first step in this direction. However, Web caches are typically specialized devices, highly tuned for efficient and high-performance file storage and Web retrieval. Running other kinds of processing-intensive services on the same network component is likely to degrade the cache's performance. Processing intensive services such as virus scanning or multimedia content transformation are better provided on separate elements, called *Service Engines* (also called *Callout Servers*, as we will discuss later). Having the option to provide these services on separate elements allows for the separation of content service providers from providers of other services (e.g., network service providers). Provision of an open interface between Web caches/proxies and service engines allows content service providers the required integration with the network. It further allows service engines to make use of the value added by Web caches by operating on the locally cached copy of the content. A general example of Content Services Architecture is shown in Figure 8.2.

This architecture introduces an open standard interface to service engines, creating the content service providers' arena. The Web caches or proxies call out to the service engines when services are needed. The service engine can be co-located with the callout proxy, or it can be located across the network from it. A service engine could even be integrated on the Web cache or proxy itself, assuming the network service provider is also acting as content service provider. Service engines can be added to the network as the need for their particular services is recognized and they become available.

An example illustrates how this architecture works to present the same information to content consumers using two different types of client devices. This is an example of a *content adaptation* service. The content consumer requests a Web page from her PC-based client. The request is routed to a cache in the network, which requests the content from an HTTP content server, stores it in the cache, and forwards it to the PC client. Later on, a PDA user requests the same page. The request goes to the Web cache, which already has the page stored. Recognizing the need to adapt the content to a PDA-type client, the cache sends the content to a service engine and gets back a version adapted for a PDA display. This adapted page is then forwarded to the PDA-based client. Here, the entire request has been completed locally, without the need to access the origin server across the network. This reduces server load, network load, and response time. It is like adding chocolate syrup to the milk from the refrigerator, rather than going back to the store for chocolate milk (or searching for a chocolate cow). This saving becomes more important as the number of different client device types that have to be served increases. Finally, the Web cache has the option of storing this adapted page, or not, representing a typical space vs. processing time trade off.

How does the Web cache decide which services to invoke for which messages? For example, how does the Web cache know that an adaptation service has to be invoked for Web pages that are delivered to PDA users? How does the Web cache select and communicate with the service engine? Who should the

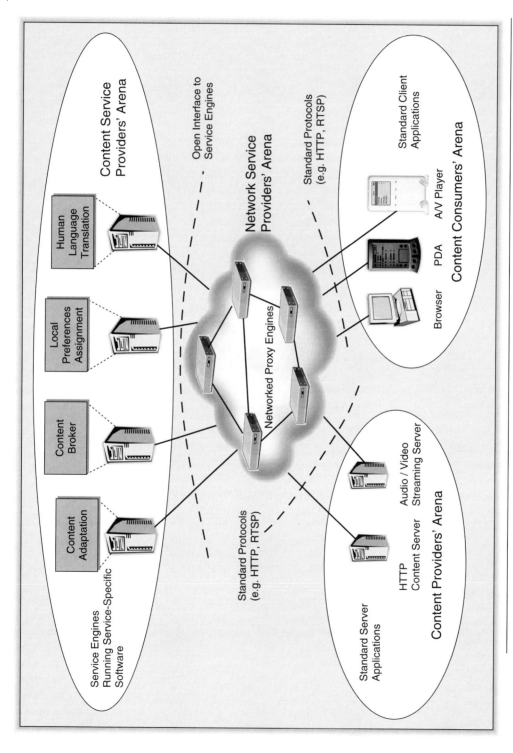

Figure 8.2 Generalized content services architecture.

content consumer and content provider trust to provide services? What other requirements are important to address in this architecture? We will see how the architecture provides answers to each of these questions. We will do this by considering in more detail the key elements of this architecture, including service activation points, callout servers, callout protocols, and authorization and trust issues.

8.2.1 Service Activation Point

In the previous section, we were talking about "Web caches" or "proxies" forwarding messages to service engines. We can generalize this by saying that some kind of *intermediary* is required in the path between content consumer and content provider. It is a network element aware of, and able to interpret, the application-level protocol used between content consumer and content provider (here, HTTP). In the Web world, the intermediary can take the form of a Web cache or a simpler Web proxy, for example. The intermediary analyzes incoming messages and decides whether any service has to be invoked or not. We therefore refer to such an intermediary as a *Service Activation Point*.

Figure 8.3 shows more detail of the architecture, focusing on the service activation point acting as an HTTP intermediary between client and origin server. It hands received messages off to the local data dispatcher, which is responsible for examining them, executing filtering rules, enforcing policies, and invoking services applications. In short—the data dispatcher decides whether any service has to be performed on an incoming message and what that service will be. Services may be provided locally, if the service application is running on the

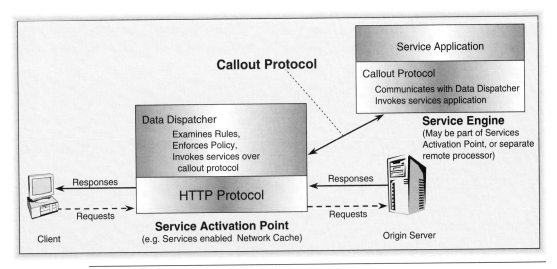

Figure 8.3 Service activation point and service engine.

service activation point, or through a callout protocol, if the service application is running on a remote service engine. The *ruleset* is the collection of individual rules or filters, indicating what services need to be executed on messages. For example, it might include rules such as "if this is a binary download for Markus, perform a virus check" or "if this request is from Lee for the site www.tagesschau.de, then translate it to English." The rules, which are operating within a data dispatcher, can be created by a local administrator, downloaded to the dispatcher over the network, or can be configured in any secure and reliable way that establishes consistent, authorized, and unambiguous rules.

8.2.2 Callout Servers

A dedicated, separate service engine provides better scalability and flexibility for providing several types of content services than does executing the services on the service activation point itself. A dedicated processor is the best design alternative for processing intensive services such as virus scanning and natural language translation. Distributed services, proprietary services, or other services with special security requirements also benefit from a separate processing engine. To clearly indicate the existence of a separate, remote service engine, we will refer to these elements as *callout servers*. Callout servers improve the scalability of the solution by simplifying the addition or the replacement of servers. Partitioning the server and the activation point functions into separate elements also allows separate authorities to operate the server and the service activation point. This encourages more diversity and innovation in the types of services that are available. A callout protocol is used for the communication between the service activation point and callout server, as shown in Figure 8.3.

8.2.3 Callout Protocol

The primary task of the callout protocol is to transfer portions of application messages, such as HTTP requests and responses, between the service activation point and the callout server. For example, a service activation point might determine that the Web page returned from a content provider has to be translated into a different (natural) language before delivering it to the content consumer. The service activation point uses a callout protocol to encapsulate and transfer the relevant parts of the Web page to the callout server. The callout server performs the requested translation and returns the modified Web page to the service activation point, again using the callout protocol.

Why is a separate callout protocol needed when application protocols such as HTTP already support proxying between network elements? After all, one might look at a callout server as just another proxy on the path between content consumer and content provider, forming a proxy chain with the service activation point. No separate callout protocol would be needed, since application messages flow through both elements. The advantage of having a separate call-out protocol is that it does not require both the request *and* the response of a Web transaction to pass through the callout server. It is possible to have only one of the two messages serviced. For example, a virus scanning service provided on a callout server does not need to see HTTP requests. It only needs to receive HTTP responses. In the proxy model, both requests and responses would have to flow through the callout server, while a callout protocol allows forwarding only the responses to the callout server. This provides better performance and more efficient resource utilization. Similarly, a request filtering service only has to examine HTTP requests and does not have to see the corresponding responses coming back from the server.

More optimizations can be designed into a separate callout protocol. For example, it may allow transmitting only the relevant parts of an application message to the callout server, rather than having to always send the entire application message. This capability supports *message preview* and *short-circuit* operations, which allow callout servers to terminate a callout transaction early, thus improving response times and resource utilization (discussed later).

We will discuss two example callout protocols later in this chapter, when we describe the Internet Content Adaptation Protocol (ICAP) and the OPES Callout Protocol (OCP).

8.2.4   Authorization and Trust

While the basic content services architecture outlined above provides many exciting opportunities and promises appealing benefits to both content consumers and content providers, it also has the potential for misuse. Concerns center around the possibility of intercepting a message flow between a content consumer and a content provider without their knowledge. Interception of a message flow for executing services can cause problems similar to the ones described in Section 3.5.3 in the context of interception proxies. Furthermore, consumers and content providers can lose trust in a network that modifies content without either of the endpoints being aware of it.

To maintain a trusted network and awareness of the services being executed, each content service has to be authorized by either the content provider or the content consumer, following a *one-party consent model. Surrogate services* are content services provided on behalf of the origin server. These services might include dynamic assembling of Web pages, watermarking, or content adaptation. The elements making up the surrogate services form a *surrogate overlay* and are logically part of the authoritative domain of their respective origin servers. Similarly, *delegate services* are services provided on behalf of the content consumers or by the applications they are running. These services might include virus scanning or content filtering. The elements making up the delegate services form a *delegate overlay* and are logically part of the authoritative domain of the content consumer applications.

Policy information, describing what types of services are authorized for various types of transactions, has to be securely delegated and transmitted from the authorizing party to the policy enforcement function in the data dispatcher.

8.3   Example Content Services

The architecture previously outlined enables different kinds of content services, ranging from simple filtering of Web requests to complex services that provide content adaptation considering a user's preferences, location, and client device.

Services for Web content can be performed on both HTTP requests and HTTP responses. Services performed on HTTP requests may occur when a request arrives at or leaves a service activation point. The services performed on requests can further be divided into two cases: those that intend to modify requests and those that do not.

A content service may modify a service request on behalf of the content consumer for various reasons, such as:

- Parents might want control over what Web sites their children can access, or a corporate policy may require blocking or redirecting a service request.
- Organizations may restrict or redirect access to certain Web services based on various criteria such as time of day or employee access privileges.
- Hiding the content consumer's identity, user's browser software identifiers (user agent), or referrer may be important in conducting a survey, collecting anonymous feedback, or even in a dating service.
- Adding user preferences or a device profile to the service request to get personalized or adapted services. The weather report example described earlier demonstrates how this can be important.

Content services may also modify a service request on behalf of the origin server in several ways, such as redirecting the request to a different server to reduce the server work load or redirecting image requests to improve access time.

Useful services can also be provided by monitoring requests without actually modifying them, for example:

- administrative functions for the content provider, such as service monitoring activity or tracking usage for billing purposes
- customization services for the content consumer, such as analyzing and profiling their usage patterns (with their consent) to shape adaptation services later on

Content services may be performed on an HTTP response when a response arrives at a service activation point or when it is about to leave the service activation point. In the case of a caching proxy, to ensure the privacy of the stored data, the first service may be an encoding operation before the content is stored in the cache, while the latter may be a decoding operation before the content is returned to the data consumer.

There are several reasons why responses from the content providers might be modified before delivery to the content consumer:

- The content provider may not have all the device profiles and templates necessary to transform the original content into a format appropriate for a variety of mobile devices of limited screen size and display capabilities. Therefore, this content adaptation is an important content service.
- The content provider may not have all the natural language translation capabilities needed to deliver the same content in multiple languages spoken around the world. A single content server may perform the language translation or it may invoke different callout servers to perform different language translation tasks.

A content service may be performed on the responses without modifying them. Examples include:

- examining and recording each response for monitoring, logging, or debugging purposes
- a content server may record the usage information and resource requirements of each service request for accounting or billing purposes

Content services may dynamically assemble Web pages to create a response. In the weather-reporting example the content server could choose information from a variety of content providers to customize and assemble a report to meet the user's preferences.

Figure 8.4 shows another example that illustrates how the various architectural components are leveraged in providing a content adaptation service at the network edge. In step 1, a PC-based Web browser requests a Web page at www.content-networking.com. The Web cache fetches the page from the origin server in step 2, stores it on its local disk, and forwards the page to the requesting PC in step 3. A few minutes later, another user requests the same page using the embedded Web browser on her cell phone in step 4. When the request reaches a Web cache, the cache recognizes that the PC version of the page is available in the local store, but that it will have to be adapted for delivery to the cell phone. Rather than going back to the origin server to request a version for display on a cell phone, the cache acts as a service-activation point and forwards the previously stored PC version of the page to a callout server in step 5. Communication with the callout server is done using a callout protocol. The callout server performs the requested adaptation and returns the modified version to the cache, which forwards it to the cell phone user in step 6. The same actions will be performed when a PDA user requests the same Web page later.

It can be seen that the adaptation for the cell phone user and the PDA user take place locally at the network edge. There is no need to contact the origin server again, thus reducing server load, network load, and service latency.

A comprehensive list, more detailed discussion, and more examples of services can be found in [RFC 3752, BHC00]. The following sections will discuss in

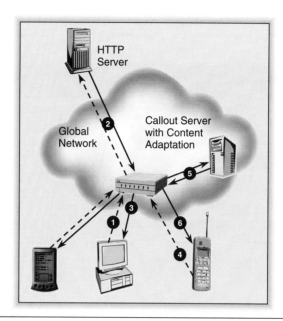

Figure 8.4 Adapting Web pages.

more detail two example callout protocols, the Internet Content Adaptation Protocol (ICAP) and the OPES Callout Protocol (OCP).

8.4   **ICAP—The Internet Content Adaptation Protocol**

Recognizing the need for a standard interface between Web proxies and application servers, several companies got together at the end of the last century to work out and publish an open interface specification. Since the primary focus was on enabling adaptation services for Web content, the protocol being worked on was named the *Internet Content Adaptation Protocol (ICAP)*. The name, however, does not do justice to the capabilities of the protocol. ICAP use is not limited only to the context of adaptation and transformation services. It also facilitates the implementation of filtering, tracking, and other types of services. It is limited, however, to enabling services that operate on HTTP messages.

When efforts to carry out the work in existing standards organizations failed, the decision was made to form a separate industry consortium for specifying the protocol—and the ICAP Forum was born. The ICAP Forum (www.i-cap.org), initially spearheaded by Network Appliance and Akamai Technologies, had its kick-off meeting in February 2000 in Sunnyvale, California, USA. A large number of representatives from a variety of companies showed up for the meeting, ranging from network infrastructure vendors to manufacturers of application servers, and application developers. Encouraged by the turnout at the meeting, a small group of protocol architects from different organizations continued to refine the initial protocol specification proposed by John Martin and Peter Danzig. The work was driven forward through e-mail discussions and phone conferences and resulted in the specification of ICAP versions 0.9 and 0.95. Experience with different implementations and first deployments in the field resulted in a modified version 1.0.

Over time, the desire grew to have the protocol specification documented through a widely accepted standards authority. As a result, the ICAP specification was submitted to the IETF as an individual submission in October 2001— not on the standards track, but for consideration as an informational RFC. During this time, the IETF community discussed creating the Open Pluggable Edge Services (OPES) Working Group, which would be chartered to produce a standards track specification for a protocol providing a superset of the ICAP functionality. After chartering the OPES WG, the IETF decided in April 2003 that, given ICAP's use in production networks, it would be appropriate to document the existing specification as informational RFC 3507. It should be noted that RFC 3507 is *not* the result of an IETF Working Group and is not endorsed by the IETF, but rather an individual submission intended to document current practice.

Today, the ICAP Forum evolved more into a business and marketing vehicle rather than a technology forum. Webwasher joined Network Appliance and Akamai Technologies as co-host of the ICAP Forum to take care of most of the remaining activities such as checking Web page feedback and organizing a mailing list (also see Section 10.2.2 for information on the ICAP Forum). When technical issues come up, they are discussed via a mailing list. However, no new developments or enhancements to ICAP are being considered, since development of a next-generation callout protocol is now being worked on in the IETF/OPES Working Group.

8.4.1 Motivation and Design Goals

ICAP is designed to provide simple dispatching of HTTP messages for obtaining content services. It allows *ICAP clients* to pass HTTP messages to *ICAP servers* for some specified type of processing. The ICAP server executes the requested service and sends the (possibly) modified message back to the ICAP client. Putting this interaction into the context of our general content services architecture, ICAP clients act as service activation points and ICAP servers act as callout servers. For example, a Web proxy might use ICAP to send binary downloads it received to another server for virus checking. The server checks the data, removes detected viruses, and uses ICAP to return the cleaned-up data back to the Web proxy. The interaction is similar to executing a remote procedure call on the message encapsulated in ICAP. These messages can be either HTTP requests or HTTP responses. Though ICAP has recently been used to exchange content other than HTTP, this is beyond the original design of ICAP.

The ICAP design was guided by simplicity and ease of implementation. The goal was to develop an easy to understand, easy to implement, and easy to debug protocol—as simple as possible, but no simpler. Since the protocol evolved to enable services to act on HTTP messages, it is a fair assumption that ICAP developers would be very familiar with HTTP, its syntax, and its semantics. As such, it was a logical choice to make ICAP look very similar to HTTP. In fact, it was initially considered that ICAP would be implemented as either an extension to HTTP or as an application-layer protocol built to run on top of HTTP. This was desirable for a number of reasons. HTTP is well understood in the community and has enjoyed significant investments in software infrastructure, including clients, servers, parsers, etc. The idea was to leverage that existing work and to make it easy for developers to implement ICAP.

But as so often happens, the devil proved to be in the details. Certain features that were considered important for ICAP were difficult to implement with HTTP or caused problems when running ICAP over HTTP. For example, HTTP allows a client to pause the transmission of a message only between the message header and the message body. The client sends the message header and waits to receive a `100 Continue` response from the server before transmitting the message body. With ICAP, however, a different semantic was required. A client should be able to pause the transmission in the midst of a message body and wait for a response from the server before transmitting the remainder of the body. This behavior allows an ICAP server to examine the beginning of a message body and then decide if it wants to terminate the transaction early instead of receiving the remainder of the message body. Such *previewing* can yield significant performance improvements in a variety of situations, as we will see later in this section when we discuss the ICAP preview feature. Moreover, the existence of Web proxies or Layer 4–7 switches between ICAP client and ICAP server needs to be allowed. And certain transformations of HTTP messages by Web proxies are legal—and harmless for HTTP—but caused problems with ICAP's "header-in-header" encapsulation and other features. In the end, it was decided that the tangle of workarounds required to fit ICAP into HTTP was more complex and confusing than moving away from HTTP and defining a new (but similar) protocol.

The ICAP specification describes how to ask for a certain content service and how to transmit the messages to be serviced to the callout server. This is referred to as the *transaction semantics* and specifies the "service invocation" part of the data dispatcher in our general architecture. However, the ICAP specification does not indicate at all "when to ask for a content service, what specific service should be asked for, and from where." This is referred to as the *control policy*, specifying the rules and policy functions of the data dispatcher. Absence of the control policy is an important limitation of the ICAP specification, and makes vendor interoperability and end-user control more difficult. There are workarounds for this limitation, however. For example, manual configuration can be used to define rules and policy. This includes establishing the rules for recognizing messages that require processing, the URIs of available content services, what transactions are authorized to receive services, and so on. For ICAP clients and servers to interoperate, the exact method used to define policy does not have to be consistent across implementations, as long as the policy itself is consistent.

After introducing the general design philosophy of ICAP in this section, the following one will explore the protocol's operation in more detail. The following section is not intended as a protocol reference, but rather attempts to strengthen the general understanding of the protocol by giving selected details. The reader is referred to RFC 3507 for a comprehensive ICAP reference.

8.4.2 Protocol Details

ICAP is a request-response protocol similar in semantics and usage to HTTP/1.1. Despite the similarity, ICAP is *not* HTTP, nor is it an application protocol that runs over HTTP. Instead, it is an application protocol similar to HTTP that runs over TCP. The default port is 1344, but other ports may be used. An ICAP transaction is always initiated by the ICAP client, which sends a request to a passively listening ICAP server. The server performs the requested service and returns a response to the ICAP client. ICAP requests and responses are in text format and use the generic message format of RFC 2822—that is, they are made up of:

- a number of header fields (also known as "headers"), including a start-line (either a request line or a status line),
- an empty line (i.e., a line with nothing preceding the CR/LF) indicating the end of the header fields, and
- a message body.

The start-line, or, more precisely, the Request-URI in the start-line, identifies the ICAP resource requested (i.e., the service to be performed). The headers can include additional metadata, such as cache control information. The message body of an ICAP request contains the (encapsulated) HTTP message that is being processed. As in HTTP/1.1, a single transport connection may be reused for multiple request-response pairs. Specifically, requests are matched up with responses by allowing only one outstanding request on a transport connection at a time. Multiple parallel connections may be used as in HTTP.

Figure 8.5 illustrates how ICAP encapsulates HTTP messages by adding ICAP specific headers. The example shows an HTTP GET request from a Web client arriving at the ICAP client (step 1). The ICAP client encapsulates the original Web request into an ICAP message; the original Web request becomes the message body of the ICAP request (step 2). The service to be performed on the encapsulated HTTP request is indicated by the URI on the first line of the ICAP

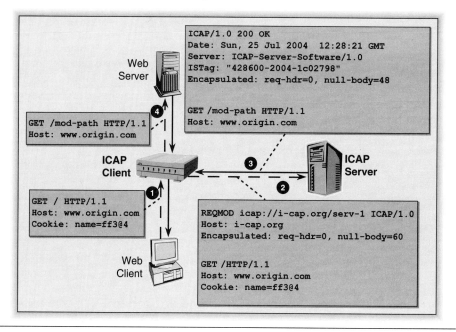

Figure 8.5 Example ICAP messages.

request. Here, a service labeled "serv-1" on server "i-cap.org" is requested. The example assumes that this specific service removes the cookie from the original Web request and also changes the path of the requested Web object to "/mod-path." After performing the requested service, the ICAP server encapsulates the modified Web request in an ICAP response and sends it back to the ICAP client (step 3). The ICAP client than extracts the modified Web requests and forwards it to the Web server (step 4).

The above example illustrates how ICAP is used to modify an HTTP request. Similarly, ICAP can be used to request the modification of an HTTP response. Depending on what kind of message is encapsulated, there are two different ways in which ICAP can work—*Request Modification* and *Response Modification*.

Request modification

The scenario shown in Figure 8.6 is an example of ICAP *request modification* (reqmod). In this situation, an ICAP client encapsulates an HTTP *request* and sends it to an ICAP server, as illustrated by request 2.

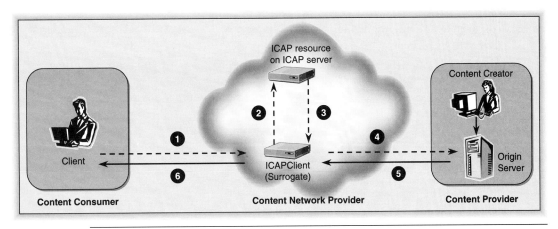

Figure 8.6 ICAP request modification.

The ICAP server may then:

- Return a modified version of the request 3. The ICAP client may then perform the modified request by contacting an origin server 4; or, relay the modified request to another ICAP server for further modification, or
- Return an HTTP response to the request (by creating transaction 6 without contacting the origin server 4 or getting its response 5). This is used to provide context information to the user in case of an error. A request filtering service, for example, can send an error message saying "you are not allowed to see this Web page," or
- Return an ICAP error that the ICAP client has to handle.

Also a response coming back from the origin server can be forwarded directly to the client without having the ICAP server in the path.

ICAP clients must be able to handle all three types of responses. However, ICAP client implementations do have flexibility in handling errors. If the ICAP server returns an error, the ICAP client may (for example) return the error to the user, execute the unmodified request as it arrived from the client, or request the specific service again, perhaps from another ICAP server.

Request filtering or URL blocking is a good example of request modification. Consider an intermediary that receives a request from a client for a Web page on an origin server. The intermediary, acting as an ICAP client, sends the client's request to an ICAP server that performs URI-based request filtering. If access to the requested URI is allowed, the request is returned to the ICAP client unmodified. However, if the ICAP server chooses to disallow access to the requested resources, it may either:

- modify the request so that it points to a page containing an error message instead of the original URI, or
- return an encapsulated HTTP response that indicates an HTTP error.

This method can be used for a variety of other applications, such as masking the identity of the requester, modification of the `Accept:` headers to handle special device requirements, and so forth.

The specific ICAP method used for an ICAP transaction is indicated by the first word in the first line of an ICAP request message. In Figure 8.5, for example, the ICAP requests starts with `REQMOD`, indicating that the client is encapsulating an HTTP request.

`RESPMOD`, in contrast, indicates that the ICAP client is working in Response Modification mode, as discussed in the following section.

Response modification

Not all services have to process HTTP requests. A large number of services operate on HTTP responses, instead. *Response modification* (respmod) has been defined for this purpose. Here, an ICAP client sends an HTTP *response* 3 to an ICAP server as illustrated by request 4 in Figure 8.7.

An origin server typically has generated this response. The ICAP server may then:

- send back a possibly modified version of the response, or
- return an error.

The response modification method is intended for post-processing performed on an HTTP response before it is delivered to a client. Examples include content adaptation, human language translation, and virus checking.

Figure 8.7 illustrates a typical data flow for ICAP response modification.

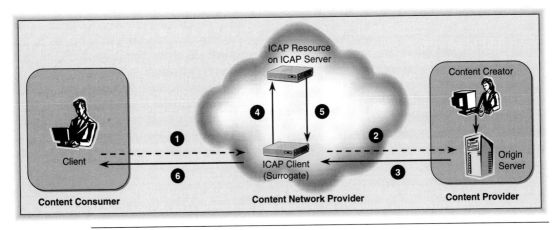

Figure 8.7 ICAP response modification.

1. A client makes a request to an ICAP-capable intermediary (an *ICAP client*) for an object on an origin server.
2. The intermediary sends the request to the origin server.
3. The origin server responds to the request.
4. The ICAP client sends the origin server's response to the ICAP server.
5. The ICAP server executes the ICAP resource's service on the origin server's response and sends the (possibly) modified response back to the ICAP client.
6. The ICAP client sends the response, (possibly) modified from the original origin server's response, to the client.

Early drafts of the ICAP specification included a third method, named "Request Satisfaction." Consider a scenario in which an ICAP client receives an HTTP request and sends it to an ICAP server, for request filtering, for example. But in this case, the ICAP server actually carries out the request. It fetches the requested page directly from the origin server or creates an error page, returning the HTTP response to the ICAP client for relay to the end user. Later revisions of ICAP removed this method, since it was felt that request satisfaction scenarios can also be implemented using request modification without major drawbacks.

Message preview

A separate callout protocol between intermediary and callout server has the big advantage of offering optimizations for specific interaction scenarios. The message preview feature defined in ICAP is an important example of such optimization.

The message preview feature allows an ICAP server to receive only the beginning of an application message and to decide whether it wants to continue receiving the remainder of the message or if it wants to opt-out of the transaction early. Such message previewing can yield significant performance improvements in a variety of situations. For example, by looking at just the file type and the first few bytes of a file, virus-checkers can quickly determine whether a thorough virus check is needed or not. If the specific type of file does not pose any virus threats, it is not necessary to transmit the complete file to the callout server. Only files potentially carrying viruses need to be transmitted to the virus-checking ICAP server in their entirety. Other services that can benefit from the preview feature include content filters and any media transformation services.

The ICAP client makes use of the preview feature by adding a `Preview:` header in its outgoing ICAP request. This header indicates the length of the preview in number of bytes. The ICAP client then sends all of the headers of the respective application message and the beginning of the application message body, if any, up to the number of bytes advertised in the Preview (possibly 0).

After the Preview has been sent, the client pauses and waits for instructions from the ICAP server before continuing. The ICAP server can request the remaining data, in which case the ICAP client continues to transmit the message in its entirety. Alternatively, the ICAP server can indicate that the remaining data is not needed, which terminates the callout transaction early.

8.4.3   Limitations and Shortcomings

Although ICAP provides a useful capability, it has serious limitations. It defines a method for forwarding only HTTP messages, and it does not support other application protocols. A relevant omission is the lack of support for e-mail-related protocols. ICAP also does not support streaming media protocols for audio and video. Furthermore, as was discussed in Section 8.4.1, it defines the transaction semantics, but not the rules or control policy. Presently, ICAP relies on encryption provided by the link or network layer protocols for security. It has no security mechanisms of its own.

The Open Pluggable Edge Services (OPES) Working Group has been chartered in the IETF to produce a standards track protocol specification intended to perform similar functions as ICAP, while addressing these and other shortcomings.

8.5   Open Pluggable Edge Services (OPES)

With the increasing need to provide value-added services on network intermediaries, a growing number of different approaches and solutions emerged—most of them designed for a specific purpose. Some of the developed solutions were open, such as ICAP, but several vendors started to implement their own proprietary mechanisms, making interoperability a real problem. It became desirable to have a standardized, open, and extensible services architecture, which would enable network intermediaries to provide a variety of services for mediation, modification, and monitoring of application messages.

Driven by a small group of people from different companies, a so-called "Birds of a Feather" (BoF)[1] session was held at the 49th IETF meeting in San Diego in December 2000. The BoF was named *Open Pluggable Edge Services (OPES)* and aimed at forming an IETF Working Group for developing the protocols and mechanisms for an open content services architecture.

The meeting started a long, very controversial, and heated discussion in the IETF community—less about technical details, but more about fundamental design principles of the Internet and how they would be affected by the

---

[1]BoF sessions are typically held before an IETF Working Group is officially created. The purpose of a BoF is to determine whether there is enough interest in a specific topic and whether the proposed work is within the scope of the IETF.

proposed architecture. The discussion again focused attention on several architectural and policy issues about robustness and the end-to-end integrity of data—both had been long cited as the overriding goals of the Internet architecture (see Chapter 2). An architecture that would allow modification of messages by elements inside the network was considered to have the potential of eroding these goals. For example, it was feared that at some point in the future some OPES service will perform inappropriately (e.g., a virus scanner rejecting content that does not include a virus), or some OPES element will be compromised either inadvertently or with malicious intent. The discussion was very helpful in identifying potential threats and in helping to focus the proposed OPES work. But at times the debate degenerated into a more philosophical and very dogmatic argument, with several participants crossing the line into truly abusive behavior. It was not until three more BoFs took place, and a series of intermediate workshops hosted by Intel and Bell Labs/Lucent Technologies, before the OPES Working Group was finally chartered in February 2002.

Given the high stakes at play, the Internet Architecture Board (IAB) took the unusual step of issuing RFC 3238 with comments and recommendations on the architectural and policy issues related to chartering the OPES Working Group. The RFC does *not* recommend specific solutions for OPES, nor does it mandate specific functional requirements. Instead, it brings to the fore issues on integrity, privacy, and security that any OPES solution standardized in the IETF is required to address in one way or another, either directly by demonstrating appropriate mechanisms or by making a convincing case that there are no integrity or privacy concerns. The OPES Working Group has responded to this request by producing RFC 3914, which describes how OPES solutions address those considerations.

The documents produced by the OPES Working Group introduce an architectural framework along with a set of requirements to guide standardization of needed protocols and interfaces. At the time of this writing (November 2004), the OPES Working Group has finished its initial charter and has put forward a specification for a next-generation callout protocol. The following sections will examine the OPES architecture, the callout protocol, and initial work on a rules language in more detail.

8.5.1 The OPES Architecture

The OPES architecture [RFC 3835] defines a framework for distributing, authorizing, and invoking networked services at the application level that both offload origin servers and improve the user experience. It extends the notion of Web intermediaries, which are commonly deployed to provide services such as Web caching, request filtering, and virus scanning. While the main focus of OPES was initially on HTTP-based applications, the architecture has been designed to enable support for other applications such as e-mail or multimedia streaming, as well. It follows, in great parts, the generic content services architecture outlined in Section 8.2 and illustrated in Figure 8.3. Details of the OPES architecture and its architectural elements are given in the following section.

Architectural elements

The various architectural elements and their interactions are illustrated in Figure 8.8. The *OPES Processor* is an application-level intermediary on the path between *Data Consumer* (e.g., Web Client) and *Data Producer* (e.g., Web Server, Origin Server). The OPES processor analyzes incoming application messages and invokes the appropriate applications, such as a virus scanning service, for example. The specific component responsible for this message analysis and application invocation is called a *Data Dispatcher* and is an integral part of every OPES processor. The Data dispatcher bases its decisions on a *ruleset* that specifies what applications to invoke on which messages and how. For example, a rule might specify that all binary HTTP response messages have to be scanned for viruses before being forwarded to Markus. The function of handing messages off for further processing is sometimes called *vectoring* of messages. The services that are invoked by an OPES processor are referred to as *OPES Service Applications*. They can reside on the OPES processor itself or be executed remotely on a *Callout Server*. A single OPES processor can communicate with multiple callout servers (indicated by A and B in the figure), just as a single callout server can receive requests from multiple OPES processors. Communication between OPES processors and callout servers is governed by the *OPES Callout Protocol (OCP)*. Looking back at the generic content services architecture illustrated in Figure 8.3, the OPES processor defines a service activation point, while the callout servers represent remote service engines.

The architecture is not limited to a single OPES processor between data consumer and data producer. It is possible that a message traverses through multiple OPES processors on its way between the two endpoints. It is required, however, that the first OPES processor in such a chain is explicitly addressed at the IP layer. This policy prohibits deploying OPES processors in the form of interception proxies, thus ensuring that the originating endpoint is always aware of the first OPES processor its message travels through. This is a first step towards controllability, as we will see in the next section.

Controllability, integrity, and security considerations

A major focus of the architecture is on features intended to provide controllability as content is transformed en route between the endpoints. Learning from the problems introduced by interception proxies (see Chapter 3), the intent is to ensure that endpoints are aware of, and in control of, the services being performed inside the network. Following this principle, OPES requires that either the data consumer or the data producer must consent to each

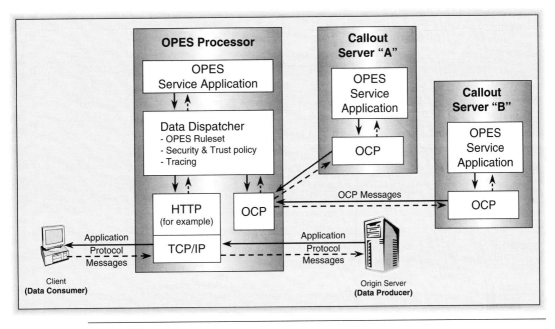

Figure 8.8 The OPES architecture.

content service that can take place. This approach is known as the *one-party-consent* model.

In an OPES system, each message flow must follow policies set forth by the data consumer or the data producer. It is expected that the OPES system implements a mechanism to resolve possible conflicts. The endpoints communicate their policies (i.e., what parties are authorized to perform what services) to their immediate and trusted service provider. This step represents a delegation of authority—the endpoint allows the service provider to act on its behalf, according to the policies it has set forth. For example, a residential customer might authorize her DSL service provider to perform virus scanning on all binary downloads. The service provider can configure the network elements accordingly by activating the appropriate rules on its OPES processors.

Delegation of authority can continue to move to more distant entities in a "stepwise" fashion. Stepwise means that entity A delegates to entity B, and entity B delegates to entity C, and so forth. The entities thus "colored" by the delegation are said to form a trust domain with respect to the original delegating party. In this context, "colored" means that if the first step in the chain is the data producer, then the stepwise delegation "colors" the chain with that data "producer" color. The only colors that are defined are the data "producer" and the data "consumer." Delegation of authority (coloring) propagates from either the content producer, start of authority or from the content consumer, start of authority to create a trust domain (trust chain) of either the producer or the consumer.

User-authorized policies typically extend to include encryption require-ments on the various network links, including possible communication with callout servers. Callout servers must not violate trust policies by transmitting information to servers or processes outside of the trust domain. Customer data identified as private must be kept private throughout each OPES flow, including transmission to callout servers and processing by those servers. To enable selec-tion of trusted callout servers, they must be able to announce their privacy capa-bilities and ability to enforce privacy policies.

To allow verification of its operation, the OPES architecture requires each OPES system to provide tracing functions. Together with strong end-to-end integrity checks, such as digital signature techniques, and other safeguards, this ensures that control over the services provided in the network remains with the endpoints.

Policy enforcement

The policies described in the previous section are typically compiled into a set of rules and downloaded onto the relevant OPES processors. The essential feature of this ruleset is that it is unambiguous. It must enable the OPES processor to clearly determine which service applications, if any, to invoke for each incoming message. As a result, the OPES processor—and more precisely, the data dis-patcher—is a policy enforcement point where policy rules are evaluated and service-specific data handlers and state information is kept up-to-date.

To enable interoperability, the OPES architecture envisions an open, stan-dardized language for specifying and interpreting the ruleset. Although the rule syntax and semantics are precisely specified, the methods for loading the ruleset into the OPES processor are out of scope of the current OPES charter and may be chosen by the implementers.

The OPES rules consist of a set of conditions and related actions. The OPES ruleset determines which service applications will operate on which messages, and is described more fully in Section 8.5.3. But first, let us have a closer look at the OPES callout protocol, which is used for exchanging messages between OPES processors and callout servers.

8.5.2   The OPES Callout Protocol

The OPES callout protocol is close to being published as a proposed IETF standard as of this writing. While this indicates the finalization of the design phase, the protocol details still have to prove valid in practice and are subject to possible modifications. As such, we will not attempt to provide a detailed description or definitive reference to the protocol, but only provide an overview of its workings and some of its features, and refer to the Internet Drafts for more details.

The protocol specification process began by identifying and describing the requirements the protocol needs to meet. This was used as a basis for selecting between alternate design choices. These include functional, performance, and security requirements and are described in RFC 3836.

The primary purpose and value of the protocol is to enable an OPES processor to forward an application message to a callout server so OPES services can process the message. The result of the service operation may be a modified application message. The protocol then enables the callout server to return the result—possibly including a modified message—back to the OPES processor. While the initial goal of the Working Group focused on supporting the exchange of HTTP messages only, it was soon decided to specify a generic, application-agnostic protocol core that would be supplemented by application-specific protocol profiles. The protocol core does not make any assumptions about the characteristics of the application-layer protocol used in the data path between the data producer and the data consumer. This approach has the advantage that features commonly needed for all application protocols have to be implemented only once in the protocol core. Features specific to each application protocol will be developed in separate protocol profiles.

The resulting protocol architecture is shown in Figure 8.9. The OPES Callout Protocol (OCP) Core implements application-agnostic features needed in support of different application protocols [Rou04]. It is assumed to run on top of a reliable transport protocol such as TCP. In particular, OCP relies on the underlying protocol to maintain packet ordering and to provide congestion control mechanisms in conformance with RFC 2914. OCP does not require separate transport connections for each individual callout transaction. Instead, it allows multiple transactions over an established transport connection; similar to the way HTTP/1.1 uses persistent connections. OCP even allows transactions on a single transport connection to overlap. This is a big difference compared to how HTTP handles persistent connections! The OCP Core is

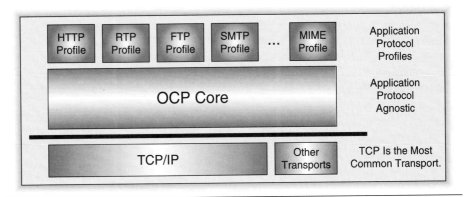

Figure 8.9 OPES callout protocol architecture.

augmented by protocol profiles that are specific to the application protocol used between the content consumer and the content producer. The Working Group has written a specification of a profile for HTTP [RoS04], which allows transmission of Web messages and fragments between OPES processors and callout servers. Specification of a SMTP profile is currently being considered to start as a next step.

The OPES Callout Protocol offers a variety of interesting features, including:

- **Asynchronous Message Exchange**—allows multiple outstanding callout requests on a single transport connection to be issued and provides a method to correlate callout responses to callout requests.
- **Message Segmentation**—allows the OPES processor to forward an application message to a callout server in a series of smaller message fragments. Provides a method to reassemble these fragments into the original message.
- **Keep-Alive Mechanism**—allows both endpoints to detect a failure of the other endpoint even in the absence of callout transactions.
- **Capability and Parameter Negotiations**—support for negotiation of capabilities and callout connection parameters between an OPES processor and a callout server. These parameters may include callout protocol version, fail-over behavior, heartbeat rate for keep-alive messages, security-based parameters, and others.
- **Metadata**—provides a mechanism for the endpoints of a callout transaction to include instructions for the OPES processor and callout server in callout requests and responses. For example, the OPES processor is able to include an ordered list of OPES services to be performed on the forwarded application message. Instructions on keeping a local copy of the application message and tracing are also provided. The OPES processor is further able to include information about the forwarded application message in a callout request. This may be done to specify the type of forwarded application message or to specify what parts of the message are forwarded to the callout server.
- **Premature Termination**—allows a callout server to abort an ongoing transaction at any time. This is helpful in situations where the callout server determines that no further actions are required and that it is not necessary to transmit the remaining parts of the application message. Virus scanners, for example, can use this feature to stop data transmission after detecting that the transmitted application message is a text file and, therefore, not in need of virus scanning. This feature is similar to ICAP's message preview, but offers more flexibility and a more fine-grained control over when to terminate a transaction.

Details on these features and on how they are used can be found in the protocol specifications [Rou04, RoS04].

An example OCP session is illustrated in Figure 8.10. The session begins when the OPES processor establishes a transport connection with the callout server. This is typically done using TCP. A connection start (CS) message requests the callout server to begin monitoring the connection state. The OPES processor must then make a negotiation offer (NO). Requiring one of the parties to initiate the negotiation process avoids possible deadlocks, as when each side would be waiting for the other to make an offer. The negotiation mechanism allows the OPES processor and callout server to agree on a mutually acceptable set of features, including optional and application-specific behavior, as well as, OCP extensions. For example, transport encryption, data format, and support for a new message can be negotiated. Sending a negotiation response (NR) completes the initialization portion of the session. A transaction start (TS) message begins the original data flow, and the callout server begins monitoring the transaction state. An application message start (AMS) notifies the callout processor to begin processing the application message. The OPES processor sends the application data as the payload portion of one or more data use mine (DUM) messages and indicates the end of the applications message with an application message end (AME). The callout processor receives the application data, and performs the requested content services. The callout processor then begins the adapted data flow with an application message start (AMS), followed by one or more data use mine (DUM) messages, including the adapted application data. It then sends an application message end (AME) message to inform the OPES processor that there will be no more data for the corresponding application message and indicates the end of application message processing. Any number of application messages can be adapted in a single session. This is indicated by the second series of AMS, DUM, AME, AMS, DUM, and AME messages. Furthermore, although it is not illustrated in this example, the callout server can initiate a session with an AMS message. Messages can be sent asynchronously and overlap requests and responses. Finally, either side can send a transaction end (TE) message to end the OCP transaction.

8.5.3   The OPES Rules Language

As transactions proceed through an OPES processor, *rules* determine what content gets dispatched to OPES service applications for service processing. These rules determine if processing is required, what flows are intercepted for processing, what OPES service application instance to invoke, and the specific processing required. The rules must be executed quickly and securely. In addition, secure mechanisms are needed for establishing, modifying, and storing the rules.

Performance is critically important in an intermediary like a caching proxy whose main purpose is to accelerate Web access. Introducing a rules engine into such an intermediary must not penalize those who do not want to use the additional services. It must have good performance for all users. The rules engine should be optimized for performance so that user requests for which no service

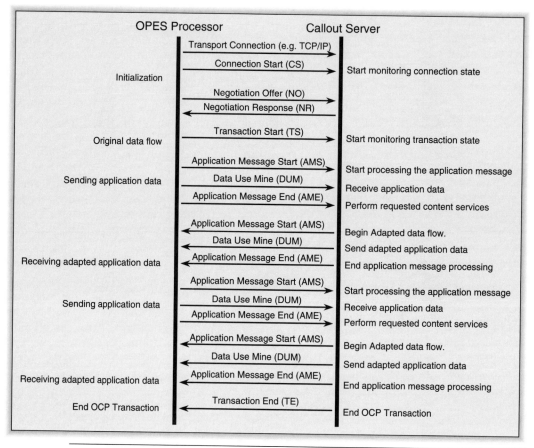

Figure 8.10 Example OCP session.

modules are executed are not slowed down, compared to a non-OPES environment.

Trust and security needs establish another primary requirement. The rules must ensure that services are only invoked under the request and (delegated) authority of a content producer or content consumer. Logging, authorization, and collecting accounting information for billing purposes are also required to establish trust and maintain security.

Rule authors need to be able to specify trigger conditions at a fine level of detail. This may include specifying conditions based on fields in the header, body, or trailer of the application message, for example. Other conditions, such as the time of day, client address, or client device type may also be considered. Separate rules may be needed for each of the various application protocols, such as HTTP or SMTP, being used.

Because a single intermediary will execute many individual rules derived from input by several authors, the execution order and interaction of these rules must be clear. This requires consideration of the dynamic adaptations that can take place as data flows from one service application to the next.

The rules engine must allow for service modules to be executed at different points in the round-trip message flow. This allows, for instance, for services to operate only on messages from the origin server and not from the cache or client. Figure 8.11 illustrates the various execution points. This figure has been adapted from Figure 8.8 to emphasize the ruleset portion of the data dispatcher. It identifies the following four execution points.

Point 1—Client Request. A request from a client has been received. A possible cache lookup (or other value-added service of the intermediary) has not yet occurred.

Point 2—Intermediary Request. The requested Web object cannot be served from the cache and the origin server is about to be contacted for the HTTP response.

Point 3—Origin Server Response. The response from the origin server has been received. It has not yet been stored in the cache.

Point 4—Intermediary Response. The response from the cache or the origin server is about to be sent back to the client.

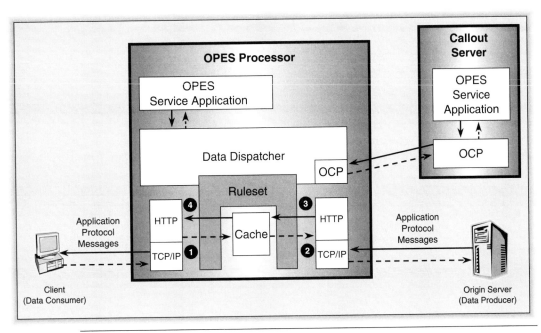

Figure 8.11 Execution points for OPES rules.

Initially, the OPES Working Group has debated two alternative concepts for the syntax of the rules language. One approach, called the *Intermediary Rule Markup Language (IRML),* is an XML-based language that can be used to specify rules for the execution of OPES services [BeH03]. A later proposal dubbed *P: Message processing language* is based loosely on the syntax of object-oriented languages such as Java, C++, and JavaScript. It is a simple configuration language designed for efficient and compact specification of message processing instructions at application intermediaries [Rou03]. After some discussion, the OPES Working Group decided to follow the "P" approach, but at the same time, decided to postpone standardization of the rules language until after the protocols were established. At the time of this writing (November 2004), the OPES Working Group is proposing a new charter that will include specification of the rules language as one work item.

Open Pluggable Edge Services (OPES) extends the notion of Web intermediaries. The next section describes another Web-based approach to services and applications.

8.6   The Web Services Paradigm

The previous sections on ICAP and OPES summarized efforts centered around the IETF community. The World Wide Web Consortium (W3C) has taken a different approach to solving a slightly different but related problem. While the focus of OPES is on rule-based, inline transformation of a data flow between two Internet hosts, the W3C approach to content services targets on-demand invocation of remote services (e.g., in a business-to-business environment). Given the nature of ICAP/OPES style callout transactions, performance and fine-grained control is of the utmost importance for these protocols. We will see in this section that the W3C approach to Web services could be used to implement callout transactions as well, but that its associated overhead is considered an important drawback for scenarios targeted by ICAP/OPES.

The stated goal of the W3C is to develop interoperable technologies—including specifications, guidelines, software, and tools—to lead the Web to its full potential. They are active in defining standards for Web services having a slightly different character than the standards being worked on in the IETF. These include traditional business services, such as submitting a purchase order or finding a plumber, in addition to services automatically invoked by software programs. These Web services can interwork with intermediaries, but are focused on communication and information exchanges between application endpoints. OPES, on the other hand is optimized for communications between an application server and an intermediary, such as an HTTP proxy.

The goals of the overall Web services architecture are to promote

- interoperability between Web services,
- integration with the World Wide Web,

- reliability of Web services,
- security of Web services,
- scalability and extensibility of Web services, and
- manageability of Web services.

The W3C defines a Web service as a software system designed to support interoperable machine-to-machine interaction over a network. The interface to a specific Web service is described in a machine-processable format called Web Services Definition Language [WSDL]. Other systems interact with the Web service using the Simple Object Access Protocol (SOAP)-messages in XML format, which are typically conveyed using HTTP [BHM+ 04].

The specifications that interwork to make up this Web-based paradigm for announcing, discovering, describing, locating, and exchanging messages to use the services are introduced in Table 8-1.

8.6.1   SOAP—The Simple Object Access Protocol

When comedian Lou Costello wanted to know the names of the players on the baseball team, he engaged his partner Bud Abbott in this famous dialogue:

Table 8-1   Components of the web services architecture

Language / Protocol	*Role*
UDDI—The Universal Description, Discovery & Integration specification provides a platform-independent way of discovering and describing Web services and Web service providers.	**Discover Services and their High Level Description**—What services are available?
WSDL—The Web Services Definition Language is a format for precisely describing network services in terms of ports, operations, message exchanges and data formats	**Describe Services Precisely**—What services are provided? What operations can be performed? What service ports provide access to those operations? What messages can be exchanged? What is the data format for each operation?
SOAP—The Simple Object Access Protocol is a lightweight protocol intended for exchanging structured information in a decentralized, distributed environment.	**Exchange Messages**—Exchange information between service ports described by WSDL.
XML—The Extensible Markup Language is a very general and extensible language for identifying the structure of data, including documents.	**Define Data Structures**
HTTP, TCP/IP, and other transport mechanisms.	**Transport Data**—Move information to and from the service.

Costello: So you go ahead and tell me some of their names. . .

Abbott: ... Now let's see. We ... have Who's on first, What's on second,
        I Don't Know's on third.

Costello: That's what I wanna find out.

Abbott: I say Who's on first, What's on second, I Don't Know's on third.

Costello: You know the fellows' names?

Abbott: Certainly!

Costello: Well then who's on first?

Abbott: Yes!

Costello: I mean the fellow's name!

Abbott: Who!

Costello: The guy on first!

Abbott: Who!

Costello: The first baseman.

Abbott: Who is on first! ...

Messages can be easily misunderstood and communication becomes impossible if the structure of the message and the type of the data are not conveyed. If Abbott had tagged the information to show its structure and type:

```
<FirstBase>
  <PlayerName> Who </PlayerName>
</FirstBase>
<SecondBase>
  <PlayerName> What </PlayerName>
</SecondBase>
<ThirdBase>
  <PlayerName> I Don't Know </PlayerName>
</ThirdBase>
```

his meaning would have been immediately clear to Costello.

SOAP—The Simple Object Access Protocol is a lightweight protocol designed to exchange structured information in a decentralized, distributed environment. It is an application of XML that defines an extensible messaging framework and provides a message construct that can be exchanged over a variety of underlying protocols. The message framework is designed to be independent of any particular programming model or other implementation-specific semantics. Appendix A—XML Basics provides an introduction for readers who are unfamiliar with XML.

Two major design goals for SOAP are simplicity and extensibility.

8.6.2   Example SOAP Message

The following example shows a simple message expressed in SOAP. This message may be sent as part of a pager alerting service requesting the service call a pager number to deliver a message at a specific time. SOAP messages contain an *Envelope*, an optional *Header*, and the *Body*. This message contains two pieces of data defined by the "alertcontrol" application. The first is a SOAP header block with a local name of `alertcontrol`. The second is a body element with a local name of `alert`. In general, SOAP header blocks contain control information that might be useful to SOAP intermediaries, as well as the ultimate destination of the message. In this example an intermediary might use the `<priority>` information in the SOAP header to prioritize the delivery of the message. The body contains the actual message payload, in this case the alert message text.

```
<env:Envelope xmlns:env="http://www.w3.org/2003/05/
  soap-envelope">


<env:Header>
  <n:alertcontrol
    xmlns:n="http://example.alertservices.org/
    alertcontrol">
  <n:priority>1</n:priority>
</n:alertcontrol>
</env:Header>


<env:Body>
  <m:alert xmlns:m="http://example.alertservices.org/
    alert">
    <m:msg>Pick up Mary from school at 2pm</m:msg>
  </m:alert>
</env:Body>


</env:Envelope>
```

Example 8.1.   SOAP message containing a SOAP header block and a SOAP body.

The ultimate recipient of this SOAP message sent from the client application is the alert service application, but it is possible that the SOAP message may be *routed* through one or more SOAP intermediaries that act in some way on the message. Some simple examples of such SOAP intermediaries might be ones that log, audit, or possibly, amend each alert service request.

8.6.3   WSDL—The Web Services Description Language

It is difficult to describe exactly how to access a business service. The first time Lee contacted a particular plumbing supply store, I called the wrong phone extension, parked in the wrong lot, waited in the wrong line, filled out the wrong forms, did not bring enough cash, and drove away with the wrong part. WSDL is designed to describe the operation of Web-based services precisely enough to allow automated computer-to-computer business transactions to complete successfully.

WSDL—the Web Services Description Language—describes how machines interwork to access a service. It is an XML grammar for describing network services as collections of communication endpoints that exchange messages. WSDL documents specify precisely how messages are used to access the services provided by distributed systems. This provides a prescription for automating the details involved in communicating between the applications that request service and those that provide services.

A WSDL document defines *services* as collections of network endpoints, or *ports*. Note that these ports are different from the protocol ports used by TCP. In WSDL, the abstract definition of endpoints and messages is separated from their concrete network address or data formats. This allows the reuse of abstract definitions called *messages*, which describe the data being exchanged and *port types*, which are collections of *operations*. The association of concrete protocol and data format specifications for a particular port type establishes a reusable *binding*. A *port* is defined by associating a network address with a reusable binding. A collection of ports defines a service. Refer to Figure 8.12 for an illustration of the following elements used in a WSDL document to define a network service.

- **Service**—a collection of one or more related port specifications. An example service might be online book sales. Individual ports might correspond to the operations of searching, price inquiry, inventory inquiry, purchase order submittal, payment submittal, and problem reporting.
- **Port**—a single endpoint defined as a combination of a binding (identified by name and referring to an operation) and a network address. For example, the search port named "SearchPort," may refer to binding "SearchBinding," and exist at network address http://soap.amazon.com/schemas3/Amazon WebService.wsdl
- **Binding**—concrete protocol and data format specification for a particular port type. This consists of a name for the binding; the port type (identified by name); the transport protocol (e.g., SOAP over http); and the specification of the action, input, and output data format for each defined and named operation. For example, the binding might be named "SearchBinding" and include the transport protocol http://schema.xml soap.org/soap/http and the operation named "KeywordSearchRequest."
- **Port Type**—an abstract set of operations supported by one or more endpoints. This consists of a name for the port type (linking it to the binding) and a specification for each operation comprising it. Each of these

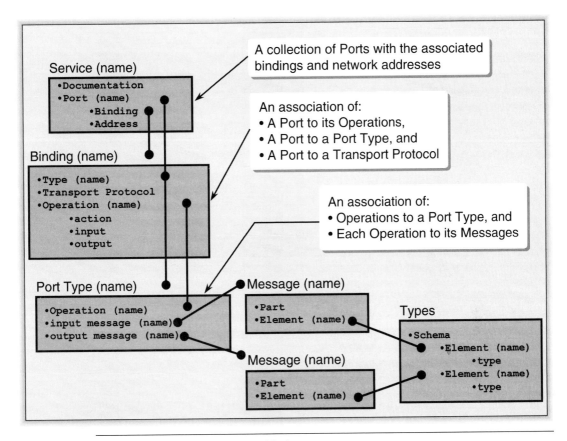

Figure 8.12 WSDL document elements and linkages.

operations is named, providing linkage to the corresponding binding. For example, the port type might be named "SearchPort," and include the operation "KeywordSearchRequest."

- **Operation**—an abstract description of an action supported by the service. This begins with a name for the operation linking it to the binding. Each operation then identifies the input and output messages, by name, that it requires. For example, the operation "KeywordSearchRequest" requires input message "KeywordSearchRequest" and creates output message "KeywordSearchResponse."

- **Message**—an abstract, typed definition of the data being communicated. This consists primarily of the message name linking it to the operation and an element name linking to the data type specification for each element of the message. For example, a message named "KeywordSearchRequest" contains a complex element type of `<KeywordRequest>`.

- **Types**—A container for data type definitions (i.e., schema) correspon-ding to the elements of each message using a type specification system (such as XSD). Each element is linked by name to the corresponding ele-ment in the message it defines. The inquiry message in our example may have the complex type of `<KeywordRequest>`, which contains an ele-ment of type `<keyword>`, which is of the elementary type `string`.

WSDL does not introduce a new type definition language. Instead, WSDL is an XML application and relies on the XML Schema Specification (XSD) as its canonical type system.

In addition to the core service definition framework, the WDSL specifica-tion introduces specific *binding extensions* for the following protocols and mes-sage formats:

- SOAP 1.1,
- HTTP GET/POST, and
- MIME.

These language extensions are layered on top of the core service definition framework. Additional binding extensions could be defined for WSDL at a later time.

8.6.4 UDDI

Web search engines, such as Google, Altavista, and Excite, have helped us locate content on the World Wide Web for many years. If we are interested in shop-ping for a dining room table, we enter "table" and get a long list of pages that contain the search word "table." In fact, the list includes approximately 250 mil-lion pages containing the word table. Unfortunately, the search does not distin-guish between tables as charts, tables as furniture, people selling tables, people collecting tables, people designing tables, people buying tables, and all the other concepts and activities involving a table. The information the search engines use is unstructured, so they cannot determine the particular sense to which a table is referred. Furthermore, these search engines are oriented toward Web content, not Web services. They are examples of unstructured Web content directories.

UDDI is an example of a structured Web services directory. UDDI—The Universal Description, Discovery & Integration specification provides a plat-form-independent way of describing, publishing, and discovering Web services and Web service providers. The UDDI data structures provide a framework for describing basic service information, and an extensible mechanism to specify detailed service access information using any standard description language [C.K03].

In the context of UDDI, the term "Web services" describes a broad range of business functions made publicly know as an invitation to other people, busi-nesses, or software programs to make use of the business function. This may include the ability to send a purchase order or invoice, search a product catalog, or calculate shipping charges.

Central to UDDI is a registration database used by businesses to publish services information. This database can be searched by people and programs to find particular services. The Web services offered by the UDDI Business Registry's nodes can be found at http://uddi.org/register.html (for publication of business services) and http://uddi.org/find.html (for inquiry and discovery of business services). The goal of this registry is to allow information to be registered once and published everywhere [UDD00].

The registry consists of specification documents written using the XML-based UDDI information model and accessed using the UDDI Applications Program Interface (API). The information model is based on four major information structures illustrated in Figure 8.13. They are:

1. Business information, the "yellow pages," is described in the `businessEntity` structure. This is the top-level information related to the business unit. Searches of this information can be performed to locate businesses serving a particular industry, product category, or within a particular geographic region.

2. Business descriptions of Web services, part of the novel "green pages," is described in the `businessService` structure. Groups of related business services, such as purchasing, shipping, and billing are described.

3. Technical information binding the services to more detailed descriptions in the `bindingTemplate` complete the "green pages" section. This includes the network address or the service in the `accessPoint` element and a pointer to the details of the technical model.

4. The technical model of the services is called the `tModel`. Each distinct specification, transport, protocol, or namespace is represented by a distinct tModel. These descriptions may be based on Web Service Description Language (WSDL), XML Schema Definition (XSD), or other documents that describe how to access the Web service. Each `tModel` is referenced by its unique `tModelKey`. This allows a single `tModel` to be referenced by any number of `businessServices` and `bindingTemplate` structures. The use of `tModels` is essential to how UDDI represents data and metadata.

The specific mapping of WSDL elements to UDDI structures needed to capture a WSDL document in a UDDI registry are described in detail in [CoKo3]. This allows queries of many useful types, including these examples:

- If a developer needed to learn the *specific methods to access a service over a particular WSDL port type*, the developer could use the name of that `wsdl:portType` in a UDDI query to find a tModel representing that `portType`.
- If a developer needed to learn all of the *services related to a particular WSDL port type*, the developer could use any tModel representing a

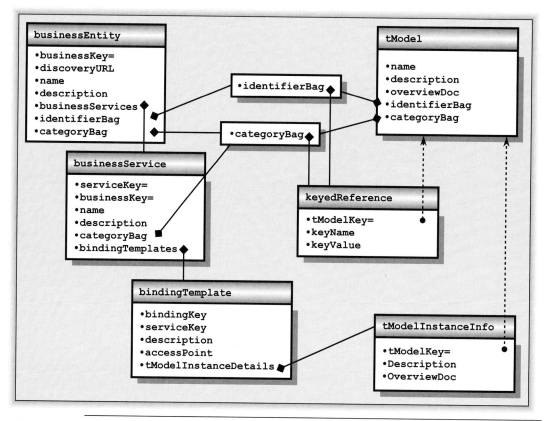

Figure 8.13 The UDDI information model.

particular `portType` in a UDDI query to find all tModels representing that `portType`.

To allow software programs to access Web services, the UDDI specifications include an API. This API is divided into two logical parts, one for searching and interrogating the registry and the other to publish information to the register. The complete specification is given in [UDDI V3] and is summarized in the Table 8-2.

Only allowing authorized individuals to publish or change information within the UDDI business registry is the approach that is taken to ensure security of the information. This principle is enforced by each individual implementation of the business registry.

8.7 Service Personalization and Service Convergence

Several forces provide information users a proliferation of choices, while simultaneously driving the convergence of services. Users typically want rich relevant

Table 8-2   UDDI application program interface functions

Inquiry API Functions	*Publisher API Functions*
Find Things:	**Save Information:**
● find_binding	● save_binding
● find_business	● save_business
● find_relatedBusinesses	● save_service
● find_service	● save_tModel
● find_tModel	**Delete Entries:**
Get Details:	● delete_binding
● get_bindingDetail	● delete_business
● get_businessDetail	● delete_publisherAssertions
● get_operationalInfo	● delete_tModel
● get_serviceDetail	**Manage Publisher Relationship Assertions:**
● get_tModelDetail	● add_publisherAssertions
	● get_assertionStatusReport
	● get_publisherAssertions
	● get_registeredinfo
	● set_publisherAssertions

content instantly delivered anytime, anywhere. This content can include a variety of information, such as news, weather, sports, stock quotes, reports, ratings, opinions, and assessments. It can include entertainment such as high-fidelity audio, or high-resolution video of prerecorded music or movies, or of current or personal events from a Web cam. The content may be important for learning new technologies, procedures, new recipes, or new skills.

The convergence on digital representation of information, whether in text, audio, graphics, pictograms [WAP 01], animation, or video form, provides the user with a wide variety of choices for accessing, retrieving, and representing information. The success of radio and satellite transmission allows the mobile user access to information, and also provides a choice of access media when stationary. The miniaturization of display devices, energy storage devices, information storage devices, sound transducers, input devices, and processors allows powerful hardware devices to be easily carried. These portable devices include radio receivers, two-way radios, pagers, mobile phones, audio players, PDAs, digital cameras, television receivers, wireless laptop computers, and GPS receivers. Increasingly, the functions of several of these devices are integrated into a single device. Cell phones now include digital cameras, text and multimedia messaging, push to talk, GPS, and other features. Wireless PDAs that include MP3 playback are another example.

People want information customized and personalized. High-resolution graphics, full motion video, and high fidelity audio generally improve the user's experience. This requires representing information in ways that make full use of the capabilities of the client device hardware, while not exceeding its limitations. It also requires accommodating the user's personal preferences, geographic position, presence (i.e., focus of attention), and payment options while respecting their privacy. As the user moves away from the desktop PC, they may use a classic telephone to access information using only voice over the Public Switched Telephone Network (PSTN). At some other time they may use a wireless device with limited display capability and limited bandwidth. Services can better meet the user's needs if profiles describing preferences, status, limitations, and capabilities are available.

8.7.1   Types of User Profiles

The Wireless Application Protocol (WAP) is a series of standards describing the use of a wide variety of wireless devices to access the Internet [WAP02, WAP00]. The WAP User Agent Profile (UAProf) specification, which is related to CC/PP [W3C CCPP], is concerned with capturing classes of device capabilities and preference information [WAP UA]. These classes include the hardware and software characteristics of the device, as well as information about the network to which the device is connected. The user agent profile contains information used for formatting content. A user agent profile is distinct from a user preference profile, described more fully in the next section.

Table 8-3 lists examples of the information in the fields of the user agent profile.

Table 8-3   WAP user agent profile (UAProf) example fields

Display Characteristics

Whether the device supports display of images

The display screen size

Whether the device display supports color

Bits per pixel

Characteristics of the browser being used

Input Device Characteristics

The type of keyboard supported

Whether the device supports text entry

A list of video input encoders supported by the device

A list of audio input encoders supported by the device

Whether the device supports any form of voice input, including speech recognition

Audio Characteristics

Whether the device supports sound output

Continued

Table 8-3—cont'd

Security Features

A list of security or encryption mechanisms supported by the device

Language Preferences

A list of preferred document (natural) languages

Pictogram classes supported

Transmission Channel Characteristics

A list of bearers (wireless carrier protocols) supported by the device

Push preferences

Hardware device manufacturers and software applications providers can supply this user agent profile information. However, no broadly accepted standards for user profiles exist. They may be very application specific; however, here are examples of the types of information that may be included in a user preferences profile:

Language

Natural language preferences and limitations

Format

Preferences for audio, text, graphics, pictograms, and video representations

Preferences for trading off speed for detail, resolution, and fidelity

Interests

Favorite news topics

Favorite sports and sports teams

Stock quotations and other financial interests

Hobbies, favorite movies, books, and music

Local weather, other weather locations

Horoscope

Accessibility Capabilities and Limitations

Visual acuity

Auditory acuity

Speech characteristics

Payment Options

What services are authorized for payment

How to pay for them

Privacy Options

What information can be revealed to what services

What must remain private

Example 8.2. Example user preference profile information.

In addition to user preference and presence information, providing information about the user's current status is useful in customizing services. Here are examples of the types of information that may be included in a user status profile:

Presence Information

Entity Identification

Status (open, closed, or extended status)

Communication address (with optional relative priority)

Time stamp

Human-readable note

User Location

Latitude and longitude

Indoors or outdoors

Home, work, or away

Moving or stationary

User Network Addresses

Client IP Address

Caller and Called PSTN number or mobile phone number

Example 8.3. Example user status profile information.

This information changes often. Also, precise location information may be unknown to the user, especially while traveling. Therefore, it is best if the user status profile information is obtained automatically by the client device or network services. The presence information data shown above has previously been introduced in Chapter 7 as the "Common Profile for Presence."

8.7.2 Location Services

Several approaches to determining the location of wireless devices are available. These systems use information from the Global Positioning Satellite System, from the cell towers in the Radio Access Network, or both. The least accurate system, cell identification (Cell-ID), identifies the cell site with the strongest signal. Therefore, the distance between cell sites determines the position accuracy. This approach has an uncertainty of 150–500 meters in an urban environment, and the uncertainty may increase to more than 2000 meters in a rural area. One of the most accurate systems, *uplink time difference of arrival* (U-TDOA), uses signal timing information from many cell sites to compute client location to within approximately 50 meters [TPC].

For any of these systems to work, the network has to communicate with the client to determine and report the location. This location determination function is part of the wireless access network that forms a gateway to the Internet.

The list of services that could be provided using accurate location information is quite interesting. Some examples are tracking packages or other assets during transport, providing emergency services to people in distress, tracking a fleet of vehicles, navigation, tracking people or animals, recovering stolen vehicles or other property, identifying restaurants or service stations in the area, advertising opportunities in the area, and providing local weather forecasts. Privacy is a huge concern in this context, and research is ongoing to protect the user's privacy while still enabling location-based services.

8.7.3 Voice Services

VoiceXML, the Voice Extensible Markup Language, is designed for creating audio dialogs that feature synthesized speech, digitized audio, recognition of spoken and DTMF key input, recording of spoken input, telephony, and mixed mode conversations. It allows users to access Web content and services using a voice interface over wireless or wireline telephones. A VoiceXML implementation platform includes a Voice XML interpreter and a gateway to the Public Switched Telephone Network (PSTN) to provide telephone access. This gateway interprets VoiceXML documents, provides text-to-speech synthesis, voice recognition, digital audio file rendering, and provides connections to the telephone network and the Internet.

The following VoiceXML document instructs such a gateway to synthesize the phrase "Hello world!" [TellB, VoiceXML].

```
<vxml version="2.0">
<form>
     <block>
          Hello, world!
     <exit/>
     </block>
</form>
</vxml>
```

Example 8.4. VoiceXML example to say "Hello world!" in synthetic speech.

Some location information can be inferred from the calling number, which is available to the VoiceXML application. Domino's Pizza makes use of this feature to direct customers calling 1-800-DOMINO to the nearest Domino's Pizza Shop [TellA].

TellMe Networks, Inc. provides several useful services that can be accessed by calling 1-800-555-TELL.

8.7.4 Examples

A few examples will help to show how these various components work together to complete service requests. Refer to Figure 8.15, "Services Transformations," and begin with scenario A, where a PC-based client requests a local weather forecast. The request goes through these steps:

1. The client generates an HTTP message, requesting a local weather forecast from a well-known, global weather Web page. The request is transported along with the User Status Profile to a Service Activation point, running on a proxy within the Internet.

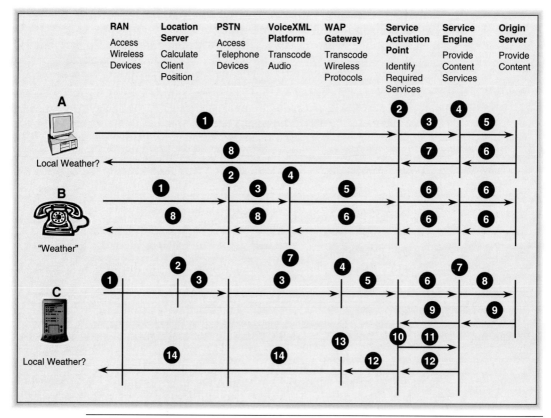

Figure 8.15 Services transformations.

2. The rules engine within the service activation point examines the request. Using the User Status Profile it determines the user's locality to be New York City (NYC). It also selects a callout server to perform the requested service.

3. Using the OPES Callout Protocol, the service activation point forwards the request to the selected service engine.

4. The service engine chooses an origin server to provide a forecast for NYC weather. It may extract information from the User Status Profile, or the User Preferences Profile (if it is available) to request a forecast report customized to these preferences.

5. The service engine generates an HTTP request to the selected origin server requesting a weather forecast for NYC.

6. The origin server responds with the requested report.

7. The service engine relays the response to the service activation point.

8. The service activation point forwards the response to the PC client, where the user can view the weather forecast.

In scenario B, the user requests a local weather forecast by speaking the word "weather" into a traditional voice telephone. The request goes through these steps:

1. The user dials the phone number of a VoiceXML implementation platform.

2. The PSTN connects the caller to the VoiceXML platform.

3. The user speaks the word "Weather."

4. The Voice XML platform recognizes the audio, and transcodes it into text. It also uses the calling phone number to estimate the location of the caller (which we assume to be NYC in this example).

5. Following the instructions of the VoiceXML document controlling this session, it generates an HTTP request for a weather forecast for NYC and forwards that request to the service activation point.

6. Actions similar to steps 3 through 7 of scenario A are completed to obtain the relevant forecast information, which is returned to the VoiceXML platform.

7. The VoiceXML platform transcodes the text of the weather report into speech.

8. The synthesized speech report is voiced to the user through the PSTN.

In scenario C, the American-born user has traveled to Munich, Germany, and requests a local weather forecast from a wireless PDA. The request goes through these steps:

1. The wireless PDA connects through the Radio Access Network (RAN) to the Internet. The client generates an HTTP request for a local weather forecast. The three profiles describing the user agent, user preferences, and user status are sent along with this request.

2. The location server examines the uplink signals from the PDA to determine its location within Munich. This location information is inserted into the user status profile.
3. The PSTN routes the request to a WAP Gateway.
4. The WAP gateway uses the Device Profile to transcode the wireless PDA protocols into general Internet protocols.
5. The transcoded request is forwarded on a service activation point.
6. Using the OPES Callout Protocol, it forwards the request to the selected service engine.
7. The service engine chooses an origin server to provide a forecast for Munich Germany.
8. The service engine generates an HTTP request to the selected origin server requesting a weather forecast for Munich.
9. The origin server generates the requested (German language) response and returns it to the service engine which replies to the service activation point.
10. Using the language preference information in the User Preferences Profile the rules in the service activation point select a service engine to translate the weather report from German to English.
11. The German language report is forwarded to the selected service engine for translation into English. Note that this is probably a different service engine than the one providing the weather information in step 7.
12. The translated report is returned to the service activation point and forwarded to the WAP gateway.
13. Using the Device Profile, the WAP gateway transcodes the report into formats suitable to the Wireless PDA.
14. The translated and transcoded report is transmitted to the PDA through the PSTN and RAN.

These examples illustrate how the various components and features of different approaches to content services can be used to provide a personalized experience for the consumer. The following chapter will expand on how the various components of content networks work together and how they are deployed.

CHAPTER 9

Building Content Networks

Purpose shapes networks. Each of the network elements described in the previous chapters can be combined in many ways. The variety with which the elements are combined into networks depends on the purpose and the goals of its owners. This chapter explores three distinctly different network examples.

The first example is a campus or enterprise network. Here, the same organization that uses the network owns it and pays to build and run it. The goal is to provide adequate network services to all users at the minimum overall cost.

The second network is owned and operated by a network service provider. Here the goal is to generate revenue by providing useful services to both content consumers and content providers. The network spans a large geographic area and offers a variety of attractive services for each of its customers.

The third network is run by a content distribution company. Their primary goal is to generate revenue by providing premium content distribution services to the content providers subscribed to their service. The network also has a large geographic span, and includes features that ensure rapid content delivery to a very large number of content consumers. This particular company does not own the wide area transmission facilities, such as the SONET links they use. Instead they rent bandwidth from companies that own and operate these transmission links.

Revenue enables services. Network equipment is expensive to purchase, install, operate, and maintain. The network can only exist if it provides significant cost savings or revenue-producing services for the content consumers or the content providers, unless, perhaps, it is subsidized.

Services enable revenue. Network operators are in a very competitive business. Unless they provide good value compared to their competitors they cannot expect to attract customers and generate the revenue they need to sustain their businesses. The Internet bubble has burst. Do not expect business people to soon repeat the investment mistakes made at the start of this millennium.

The examples used in this chapter are fictitious. The names "State University," "Global Links Networks," "*New World Times*," and "Kala" do not represent existing organizations. However, the examples are very real because they represent problems and solutions typical of so many organizations like the hypothetical ones described here.

9.1   Campus and Enterprise Network Example

In this section we follow a hypothetical example illustrating how a typical university campus or enterprise grows its network to include Web caching, streaming caches, and Web switches.

The campus network of State University is illustrated in Figure 9.1. The chemistry department houses an Ethernet switch that is used to interconnect each of the several desktop PC Web clients used by the professors in the building. A Web server and gateway router are also connected to that switch. The university has a single T1 wide area link connecting the router to the Internet, providing a maximum of 1.544 Mbits/second raw bandwidth. Overhead for framing, TCP headers, and HTTP headers reduce the actual bandwidth available for transmitting content.

The math department is located in a separate building across the campus, nearly a half a mile from the chemistry building. The math professors also want connectivity to the server and Internet. The network administrators install an optical fiber gigabit Ethernet link between the two buildings. The system works well and the professors are able to store course materials, research materials, and other content on the server. At this point the network has grown large enough that responsibility for managing it has shifted from the chemistry department to the University's information technology department.

To provide Internet access to the students, the network has grown to connect two separate residence halls to the network. These are also linked to the switch in the chemistry building using gigabit Ethernet links. The network designers consulted Table 9-1 [Tech1] summarizing Ethernet LAN characteristics to choose the media for the local network.

The network administrators use simple network management tools to monitor the traffic in the network. The Ethernet switches come equipped with Web-based traffic monitoring tools that display traffic measurements for each port. To automate the traffic monitoring they have installed MRTG (as described in Section 3.5.3) running on the Web server. This produces traffic level graphs like the one previously shown in Figure 3.5.

With the growth in network use, the T1 wide area link has become overloaded. The network administrators considered several solutions. They consulted Table 9-2 of Trunk-carrier characteristics to help identify their alternatives. These include:

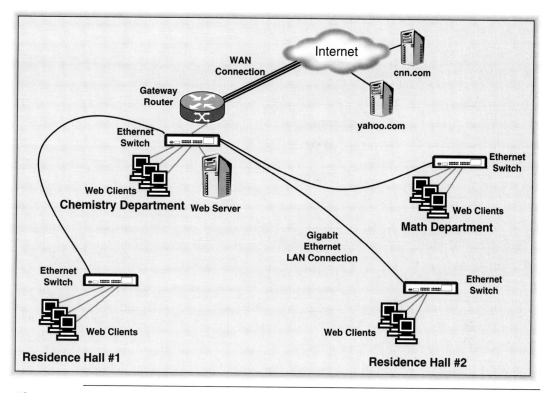

Figure 9.1 Campus network.

Table 9-1 Ethernet LAN characteristics

Designation	Media	Distance	Standard
Ethernet: 10 megabits per second			IEEE 802.3
10Base-T	Twisted Pair	100 Meters	Clause 14
Fast Ethernet: 100 megabits per second			
100BASE-T	One of the following:		Clauses 22, 28
100Base-TX	Cat-5 Twisted Pair	100 Meters	Clause 24
100Base-FX	Two optical fibers	400 Meters	Clause 26
Gigabit Ethernet: 1000 megabits per second			
1000Base-SX	Duplex multimode optical fibers	550 Meters	Clause 38
1000Base-LX	Duplex single mode or multimode fibers	5 km	Clause 38
1000Base-CX	Two pairs of shielded jumper cable	25 Meters	Clause 39
1000Base-T	Cat-5 Twisted pair	100 Meters	Clause 40

Table 9-2   Trunk-carrier characteristics

Designation	Data Rate
North American Digital Carrier (T Carrier)	
T1	1.544 Mbps
T3	44.736 Mbps
European Digital Carrier	
E1	2.048 Mbps
E3	34.368 Mbps
Japanese Digital Carrier	
J1	1.544 Mbps
J3	32.064 Mbps

- purchase a second T1 link,
- replace the T1 link with a T3 link, providing approximately 45 Mbits/second raw bandwidth, or
- install a Web cache to reduce the WAN traffic and improve response time.

After considering the costs and other factors, the administrators chose the Web caching solution. The resulting network is show in Figure 9.2.

The Web cache is configured as a forward proxy. Notices are sent to the students and faculty instructing them to configure their browsers to identify the Web cache as their forward proxy. Those users who follow the instructions enjoy faster Web access and help reduce the load on the WAN link. Other users ignore the instructions, or have difficulty following them.

Because of the many shared interests of the university community members, the cache hit ratios are high, often approaching 30% or more.

Network use continues to grow, and the WAN link is again approaching overload. To reduce the WAN traffic the network administrators decide to increase the capacity of the Web cache by introducing a Web switch (also known as Layer 4–7 switch) and creating a Web cache cluster. This network configuration is shown in Figure 9.3. Here, as previously illustrated in Figure 5.4, the Web switch translates its single VIP into a balanced load spread across the several real Web caches attached to it. Users configure their Web browsers using the Web switch VIP as the proxy address. The Web switch is configured to partition the URL address space across the various Web caches. This increases the total cache store capacity, and processing power, and increases the hit ratio. For example, if all images are directed to cache #1 and all HTML files are directed to cache #2, then the cache storage space is additive and the probability of a hit increases, as previously illustrated by the graph in Figure 3.8.

To improve security the network administrators also install a firewall between the gateway router and the WAN connection. The first application of

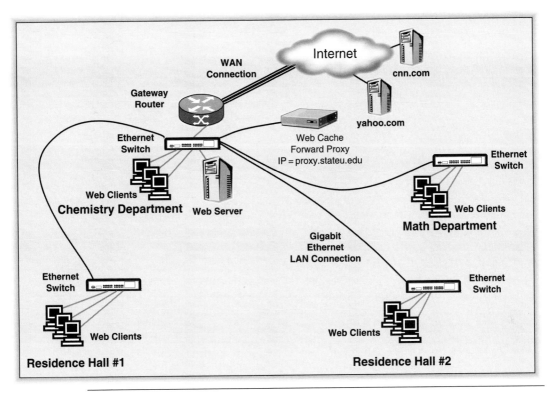

Figure 9.2 Web cache reduces WAN traffic.

the firewall was to block incoming traffic on port 80. This prevents access to the content of the Web server from across the Internet, while allowing free access from within the university. Soon the firewall was put to another use. Despite repeated reminders, a significant fraction of the university community failed to configure their Web browsers to use the Web cache as the forward proxy. This increased WAN traffic unnecessarily. The network administrators took steps to enforce use of the proxy. Their plan was to block all port 80 (HTTP) traffic through the firewall, except for the traffic that passed through the Web cache. First they configured the Web cache proxy to use port 8000 for HTTP traffic rather than port 80. They announced this change, and after the grumbling died down, many users changed their browser configurations to specify port 8000 rather than the default port 80. But of course, many did not. Next they configured the firewall to block port 80 traffic in both directions, except for the traffic to and from the Web cache. Now the only way university members could access the Internet is through the forward proxy Web cache. This forced users to configure their browsers and use the Web cache. After a sharp drop in

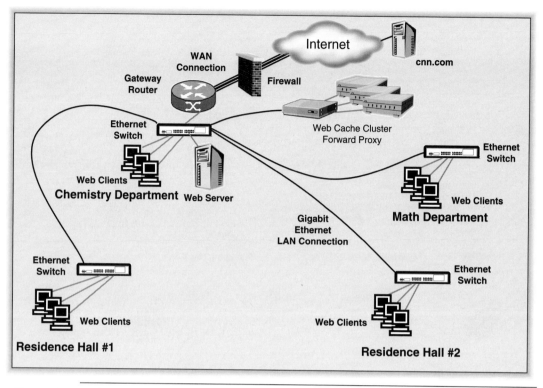

Figure 9.3 Web switch and cache cluster increase capacity.

popularity, the network administrators' reputation eventually improved as all the users enjoyed better network performance.

The chemistry department wanted to broadcast live streaming video of classroom lectures to students in their residence halls. In addition, students and faculty were viewing streaming multimedia content available over the Internet. This put a significant strain on the network bandwidth.

The solution the network administrators chose was to install streaming caches as forward proxies in the chemistry department and each of the residence halls. The math department uses streaming video only occasionally so it is satisfactory for them to share the streaming cache located in the chemistry building. This is illustrated in Figure 9.4. Many people enjoy these local Webcasts and the multimedia streams available from the Internet. The streaming caches give enough of a performance improvement that users readily configure their browsers to use them.

University officials were becoming increasingly concerned about the number of students using file sharing programs to download MP3 and other types of audio files. This uses substantial bandwidth, causing network congestion, and

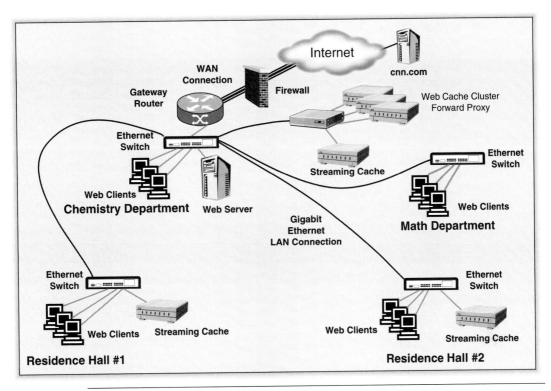

Figure 9.4 Streaming caches enable multimedia.

could lead to lawsuits from copyright owners. The first solution the network administrators implemented was to use the firewall to block access to the TCP/IP ports used by the popular file sharing programs. However, students outnumber the network administrators by a large margin, and they began to find ways to circumvent this barrier. The next solution was to use the Layer 7 features of the Web switch. The router, firewall, and Web switch were configured to pass all the WAN traffic through the Web switch. The switch was configured to block access to any files of type .mp3, and other popular audio file types, from the WAN link. There is no way to predict how long this deterrent will last, however. For a longer term solution the network administrators are investigating an OPES service engine that can implement more sophisticated rules and policies for fine grained, user-specific content filtering that will initially be used to prevent audio file downloads. This scalable OPES solution will also allow the university to implement virus scanning and content adaptation. The first planned content adaptation will be used to deliver Web content to the increasing number of WiFi-connected PDAs becoming popular across the campus.

As the network continues to grow, it needs more WAN bandwidth. As more people depend on the network for more services the reliability and availability of the network has become very important. The network administrators decide to obtain several additional WAN links, purchased from at least two different service providers. They use VRRP (see Section 5.2.7) and multiple gateway routers, in some cases connected through load balancing Web switches, to improve reliability. Now the network can continue operation even in the case of a WAN link failure, a router failure, or a Web switch failure.

Figure 9.5 provides an alternative view of the State University network evolution. The dashed line shows the ever increasing demand over time for bandwidth connecting content users to content consumers. The stepped solid line shows the actual network capacity. Each step increase in capacity is identified with the network improvement responsible for providing the increase. The university network administrators keep this chart up-to-date and use it to forecast and plan future network improvements.

Although this example is described in a university setting, the principles illustrated here apply to enterprise networks of many types. This includes office buildings, branch offices, manufacturing plants, shopping malls, libraries, and any of the many types of organizations where people in close proximity need to share information and access the Internet.

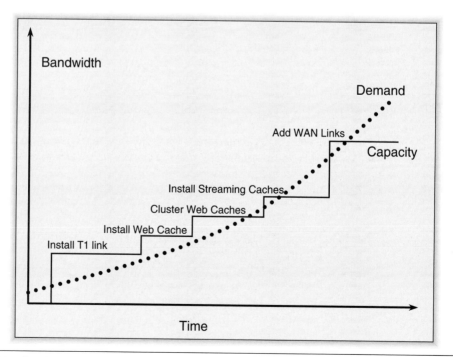

Figure 9.5 Meeting increasing bandwidth demands.

Because this network is managed as a cost center, the network administrator constantly needs to balance overall network performance with overall network cost. The caches are a good choice because they help to reduce WAN costs and increase performance.

9.2 **Content Network Provider Example**

In this section we follow the hypothetical example of Global Link Networks illustrating how a network provider configures its network and evolves to provide content services.

Global Link Networks provide a variety of Internet services to content providers and content consumers over a very large geographic region. Their high level network map is shown in Figure 9.6. They have backbone nodes in several of the largest cities across their service area. These are interconnected using SONET OC48 optical links. Each of these OC48 optical connections provides a 2.488 Gbps link directly between each backbone node router.

SONET is an American National Standards Institute (ANSI) standard (T1.105:1988) for optical digital transmission at hierarchical rates from 51.840

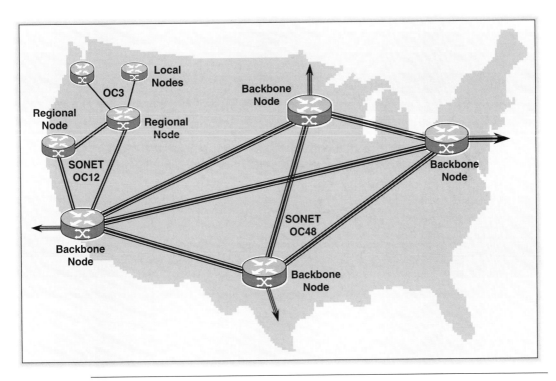

Figure 9.6 Global link network topology.

Mbps (STS-1) to 2.488 Gbps (STS-48) and greater. The Synchronous Digital Hierarchy (SDH) is the corresponding international standard for optical digital transmission at hierarchical rates from 155.520 Mbps (STM-1) to 2.488 Gbps (STM-16) and greater. It is defined by the ITU-T G.707 standard. Table 9-3 [Tech2] lists the hierarchy of the most common SONET/SDH data rates.

The line rate refers to the raw bit rate carried over the optical fiber. A portion of the bits transferred over the line are designated as overhead. The overhead carries information that provides OAM&P (Operations, Administration, Maintenance, and Provisioning) capabilities such as framing, multiplexing, status, trace, and performance monitoring. The line rate minus the overhead rate yields the payload rate which is the bandwidth available for transferring user data such as packets or ATM cells.

Several regional nodes connect to each backbone node using OC12 links running at 622 Mbps. There are also some links directly between regional nodes providing a direct path where traffic between the two nodes is especially heavy.

Several local nodes connect to each regional node using OC3 links running at 155 Mbps. The WAN links from State University, described in the previous section, connect to one or more of these local nodes.

It is possible and even likely that this entire network will not be owned and operated by a single business. For example, one business may own and operate the backbone network. They sell bandwidth connections to other businesses that own some number of regional nodes. Finally, ownership of the local nodes may be spread across a large number of businesses, each of which owns several nodes within some geographic region and purchases connections from the regional companies.

The equipment in a typical local node is shown in Figure 9.7. Each local node serves a variety of customers. Enterprise networks purchase WAN services, content consumers purchase access services, and content providers purchase hosting services.

The gateway router connects to the regional nodes. It also connects to WAN links going to various enterprise networks that purchase their WAN access from Global Link Networks.

Table 9-3   SONET / SDH data rates

Optical Level	Electrical Level	Line Rate (Mbps)	Payload Rate (Mbps)	Overhead Rate (Mbps)	SDH Equivalent
OC-1	STS-1	51.840	50.112	1.728	-
OC-3	STS-3	155.520	150.336	5.184	STM-1
OC-12	STS-12	622.080	601.344	20.736	STM-4
OC-48	STS-48	2488.320	2405.376	82.944	STM-16
OC-192	STS-192	9953.280	9621.504	331.776	STM-64
OC-768	STS-768	39813.120	38486.016	1327.104	STM-256

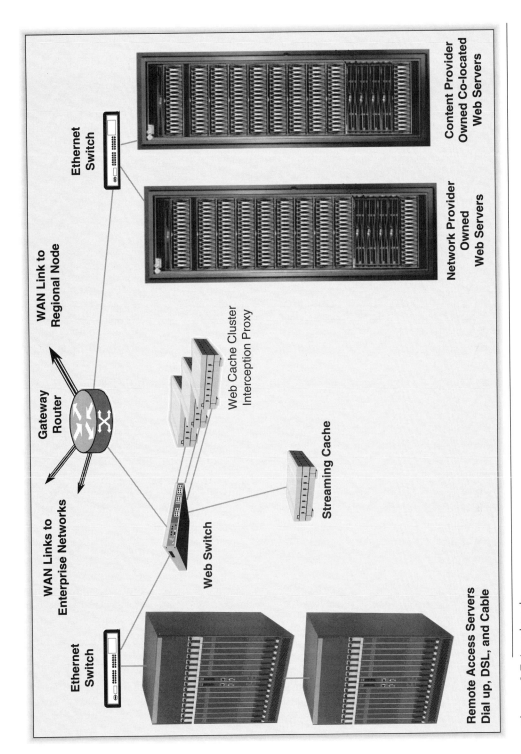

Figure 9.7 Local node.

Content consumers connect through the Remote Access Servers (RAS). Users may choose dial up modem, DSL, or cable-based access, determined by their budgets and access bandwidth needs. Separate remote access servers are dedicated to each type of access. Each RAS is connected through the Web switch directing traffic to the Web cache cluster interception proxy before it connects to the gateway router. This arrangement provides caching services to each content consumer without the users having to configure their browsers to identify the proxy as in the previous State University example. This speeds up their access and reduces the WAN bandwidth needs of the local node. The cache cluster includes both static and streaming caches. Caches are added as needed to increase the capacity and hit ratio.

The hierarchical nature of the network is put to use by implementing hierarchical caching as described in Section 3.6. Large caches are located at each regional node and even larger caches at the backbone nodes. A cache miss at a local node is attempted at the regional node cache. If that fails, the regional node attempts the request at the backbone node cache. If that fails, the request is routed over the backbone to the origin server. The network operators continue to measure performance and tune this configuration to get the best balance between speed and bandwidth savings.

Global Link Networks communicates conscientiously with their customers regarding the benefits and limitations of their services. As part of this communication they describe their use of interception proxies. The overwhelming majority of their customers understand the benefits of the proxy and are pleased to benefit from it. A few are especially concerned about privacy and object to using interception proxies. The network operators respect this choice and program the Web switch to exclude their requests from interception by the proxy.

Content providers host their content on the Web servers located in local nodes. Global Link Networks offers their content provider customers several hosting options. One option is to use the Web servers owned by the network provider. This option appeals to content providers who do not yet own servers, who expect to increase their server needs significantly, or do not want to take on the responsibility of selecting, purchasing, installing, operating, and maintaining the Web servers.

A second option is to co-locate the content provider-owned Web servers within the network provider's local node building. Here the servers are owned and operated by the content provider and the network provider is only supplying bandwidth, along with location services such as physical space, power, and security. Various arrangements for operating the equipment are also available, shifting responsibility toward either the content producer or the network provider.

Fees differ for the various options, so the content provider has their choice of paying the network provider for:

- bandwidth and location services only,
- bandwidth and operations support, or
- bandwidth, operations support, and servers.

In any case, the servers are connected through the gateway router and are accessible across the Internet to any content consumer.

To provide voice services for their customers and to create another revenue opportunity, Global Link Networks decided to offer Voice over IP (VoIP) services. To implement the service they added a SIP proxy to many of their nodes. With this backbone of SIP proxies in place, they then decided to offer SIMPLE-based instant messaging and presence services.

One of their major content provider customers is *New World Times,* a newspaper that has been printed for more that 100 years and is respected around the nation and around the world. The online version of their news service has been successfully hosted by Global Link Networks for many years.

A number of potential readers around the world have complained that the *New World Times* is not available in their native language. The business development group of *New World Times* would like to provide their online service in a large number of natural languages to meet the needs of their global audience. They approached Global Links Networks looking for a solution.

Together they decided the best solution was to enable OPES services from the network. The network providers upgraded their caches to provide OPES processor capabilities and act as the service activation point as previously described in Section 8.2.1. They also installed additional servers to act as OPES callout servers, as is shown in Figure 9.8. The *New World Times* identified a number of content services providers who offer OPES-capable language translation services for a large number of natural languages. They made business arrangements that allow readers to use these translation servers for a fee that is charged in addition to the basic online news subscription fee. They then provided simple instructions on the *New World Times* Web site describing how these translation services can be invoked.

This provides important opportunities for the newspaper, the network provider, and the content services provider. The newspaper is opening its online service to a larger worldwide audience now that it is able to reach readers in their native languages. Now that the network provider has added OPES capability, they are offering a wide range of services to their customers, including access control, virus scanning, anonymous communications services, content personalization and customization, and content adaptation services.

The network providers are also investigating connections to WAP gateways, location services, PSTN gateways, and VoiceXML platforms to provide a wider range of services to their various customers.

In addition to the OPES services, several content providers have been offering Web services, such as those described in Section 8.6, from Web servers located within the local nodes.

9.3 Content Distribution Network Example

A clever group of entrepreneurs are determined to follow the big money in content networking. They recognize that while enterprises and content

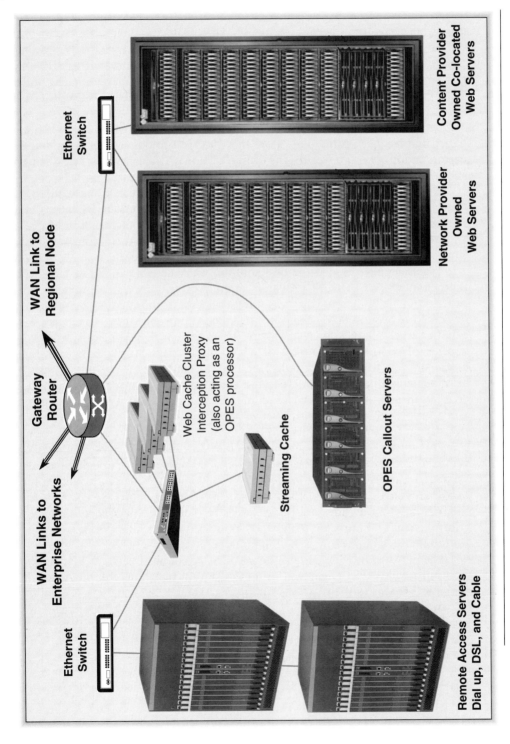

Figure 9.8 Local node offering OPES services.

consumers are willing to pay for network access, the truly deep pockets belong to the large content providers, such as CNN, MSNBC, and others who are making content delivery to very large audiences their core business. They have a plan for shifting content networking payments from the shallow pockets of the content consumers to the deep pockets of content producers. The group named their business *Kala,* which means "money" in Hawaiian.

Their idea is to create a network that provides global request routing and then charge the content providers to use this high capacity content distribution network. The approach they have chosen is to add global request routing capabilities to the existing Global Links Network and either use the existing Web caches or install others within the local nodes to act as service nodes.

The resulting content distribution network is shown in Figure 9.9. Here a Domain Name Server is located in a network node location and configured as a global request router, using the connection monitoring techniques described in Section 5.3.2. Content providers then subscribe with these content distribution network operators for premium service. Sufficient Web caches are then located in each local node and configured as reverse proxies for the content providers

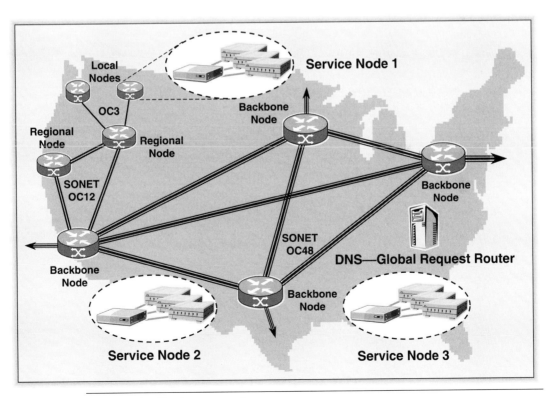

Figure 9.9 Content distribution network.

subscribed to this service. The global request router steers user requests to the service node closest to them, as previously described.

As more content providers subscribe to the Kala services, the network needs more capacity. To obtain this capacity increase, the network is expanded by adding service nodes in more cities around the world. This increases the performance of the network for all the subscribers because the newly added service nodes bring the content of the entire network closer to more content consumers.

To help justify the subscription fee they charge, Kala offers their customers a particular Service Level Agreement (SLA). They measure the response times of the prospective customer's content delivery system before employing the Kala global request routing solution. Services of Keynote systems, described in Chapter 5, are used for these measurements. The response times are then measured after introducing global request routing. Kala guarantees their customers specific response time improvements. Their knowledge of the Keynote system, including the location of their monitoring nodes helps to ensure impressive measured improvements.

CHAPTER 10

Standards Efforts

Standards enable interoperation. Rather than being built as a monolithic, proprietary system, today's networks are typically made up of separate functional components. Each of these components can potentially be provided by a separate supplier. For this to work, however, the interfaces and functions of each component have to be specified. Only then can interoperability between components from different vendors be achieved.

Standards shift power. Because standardized interfaces allow interoperation, control of the system shifts from owners of the proprietary technology to providers of each standardized component. The user and system integrator also gain power, because of the variety of choices they have for each system component [Les00]. The user can choose the best alternative from the class of all products that meet the standard. These components can be compared on the equal basis established by the standard to identify the best in this class of solutions. The final choice may be based on user needs such as cost, availability, aesthetics, convenience, reputation, reliability, performance, or other dimensions beyond those established by the standard.

Open standards are publicly accessible commodities. Anyone can read a standard and work to implement a component, solution, or system meeting that standard. Competition shifts toward creating the best implementation meeting the standard. Over time, this usually leads toward the fastest, most reliable, easiest to use, and most economical solution.

Standards cause controversy. They inevitably represent a compromise between alternative technical and business solutions. Also, because they shift power, various stake holders stand to gain or lose substantially depending on the final form the standard takes.

Most standards are voluntary; standards police are rare. If a provider ignores a standard or fails to meet the requirements of a standard, most often there is no useful recourse to the standards body. If there are no government regulations (e.g., such as for the use of radio spectrum overseen in the United States by the FCC) then avoidance, appeals to the errant provider, or influencing the public opinion may be the only recourse. There are, however, for some standards, various *compliance test suites* or *compliance test services*. These are typically provided by some third party to assess compliance of a system's operation with an identified standard. This may lead to some recognized certification of standards compliance for the system that has been assessed.

Standards evolve. As implementations are created, lessons are learned and standards change to meet emerging needs and technology advances.

Standards are not law and have limited scope. Companies may create proprietary extensions to a standard and thereby create interoperability problems.

This chapter begins by describing the role of standards. It then describes the major standards bodies that are active in the content networking area. Finally, emerging standards forming the technologies described in each of the previous chapters are described.

10.1   The Role of Standards

Broad agreement on the length of a meter and the mass of a kilogram provide *measurement standards* that enable parts built anywhere in the world to fit together and interwork smoothly in complex products and systems. An *interface standard* allows a light bulb purchased from one manufacturer to install easily and operate perfectly in a lighting fixture built, following the same standard, by any other competent manufacturer. The standard protocols, applications, and interfaces discussed throughout this book allow applications and other system elements to interconnect over networks and form distributed systems. The following sections discuss the definition, benefits, evolution, and evaluation of standards for networks and distributed systems.

10.1.1   Definitions

There is no standard definition for the word *standard*. The eleven diverse definitions in one dictionary range from "a flag" to "an acknowledged measure of comparison for quantitative or qualitative value; a criterion" [dict1]. The word is undefined in RFC 1983, the Internet User's Glossary. An ANSI Web site distinguishes and defines each of these standards-related terms: *company standards, industry standard, international standard, mandatory government standard, mandatory standards, national standard, regional standard, standard, standards body, voluntary government standard,* and *voluntary standard* [ANSI1].

A useful definition that is pertinent to the discussion in this chapter and that we will adopt is:

Standard: *Guideline documentation that reflects agreements on products, practices, or operations by nationally or internationally recognized industrial, professional, trade associates or government bodies* [ANS01].

10.1.2 Benefits

Systems built using standards allow interconnection and interoperability of various vendor products. These interchangeable parts increase the number of supply sources, increase competition, increase the choices available to users, reduce the risks of relying on single-source suppliers, and increase efficiencies due to specialization and economies of scale. Standards unleash and focus the massive creative abilities of all the people who build system elements meeting those standards. They also allow systems to be disaggregated so that each component can be provided in a way best suited to its specialized function. In both networks and commerce systems, task specialization often leads to increased productivity.

Figure 10.1 illustrates how standards enable interoperability. A proprietary monolithic system is illustrated in A. Here, some function gets performed; however, the details of how it gets performed are hidden. Also, the interfaces to the application are proprietary. The efforts made to connect to this system and learn to use it are limited to this particular system and cannot be directly extended to similar systems.

In contrast, B shows a distributed system based on standards. Because the application services are standard, connecting to this system and using it is similar to using other systems that meet this standard. Also, some details of the interworking of the system are made visible. Here we can see the overall

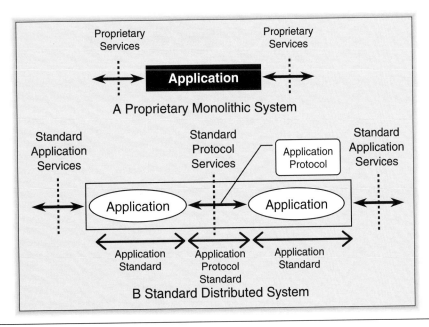

Figure 10.1 Standards enable interoperability.

application is implemented by two other standard applications communicating over a standard application protocol.

Figure 10.2 illustrates this with familiar examples. Here Microsoft Word is chosen as an example of a proprietary monolithic system. The interworkings of this popular word processing application are a closely held secret of the Microsoft Corporation. The file format is mysterious and the display formats are unique to this particular product. In contrast, Web browsing is a distributed system based on several standards. The HTML standard describes the file format and provides display guidelines for documents that make up Web pages. The HTTP standard describes the protocol for transporting information from a Web server to a Web browser. This allows any manufacturer familiar with these standards to create a Web browser that will interwork well with any Web server for any Web page. Similarly any manufacturer can create a Web server that interworks with the system, and any content provider can use any text editor or HTML editor to create content. The standard URL allows content to be uniquely identified and rapidly located in this vast distributed system.

The content provider, the content networking provider, and the content consumer each have a wide choice of vendors that can meet each of their needs. Each member making up the diversity of interests described in Section 1.4 has

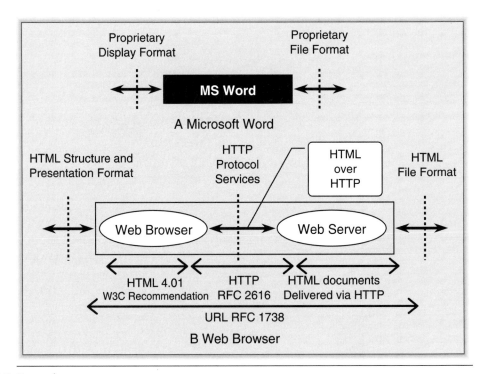

Figure 10.2 Examples.

many alternatives to choose from. Standards provide a basis for the design and evaluation of each component in the system. Regardless of the individual implementation choices they make, the immense distributed system that results will continue to work well *if* each standard is met.

10.1.3 Evolution and Evaluation

Several forces act to create standards and influence their acceptance. These forces generally originate from technical or business problems or opportunities. The brief history of the World Wide Web, told in Section 1.2, illustrates how standards often emerge.

In the late 1980s, CERN faced several business and technical problems, including:

- **Losing information**—People leave the organization, and data and relationships are dynamic or unknown.
- **Diverse databases**—A wide variety of computing systems, file formats, and data structures are used by the organization.
- **Diverse linking relationships**—Trees and keywords are not sufficient to represent the variety of relationships existing between the various types of information.
- **Remote access**—Computers are located in many distant locations.
- **Decentralized information**—Information is created and used by many people in the organization and is not routed through any centralized system.

Tim Berners-Lee proposed using hyperlinks identified by hotspots in text as a solution. He also identified the importance of separating information browsing from storing and serving information [Ber89]. Just as diamonds are cut along natural cleavage lines, it is important to decompose a system into modules along natural boundaries [TPF00]. The Web browser has thrived separately from the Web server ever since.

Several proprietary Web browser implementations followed. These include Berners-Lee's own Nexus browser/editor that featured a GUI and ran on a NeXT computer. Then other platform-specific browsers were developed at CERN. The more widely available Mosaic browser and Microsoft's participation in the technology generated great interest and highlighted compatibility problems. Web pages that worked well with the Netscape browser did not work well with Microsoft's Internet Explorer browser. Also, the original version of HTTP used to transport Web pages from server to browser was undocumented.

The business opportunity provided by the World Wide Web, the technical problems involved in building compatible browsers and servers, and the clear separation of browser functions from server functions resulted in development of standards for HTML, HTTP, and URLs. The technical solutions provided by these standards, along with the many business opportunities created by a reliable World Wide Web, have resulted in wide acceptance of these standards and explosive growth of the Web. The next two sections describe the technical and business factors that tend to make a standard successful.

Technical requirements on standards

Distributed systems consist of several modules interconnected by protocols. Figure 10.3 illustrates several of the criteria used to decompose a distributed system into component modules intercommunicating by protocols. The decisions of where to partition the system into modules and how to design the protocols have a big effect on the success of the overall system. As in cleaving diamonds, system modules are defined so that they have high module strength and loose module coupling [Par72, Mye76].

The criteria for designing effective protocols are more complex. The protocol must be *functional, unambiguous,* and *clean*, as described here:

Functional—The protocol meets the requirements of all of the users. This includes the requirements of the end users, the system architects, the system

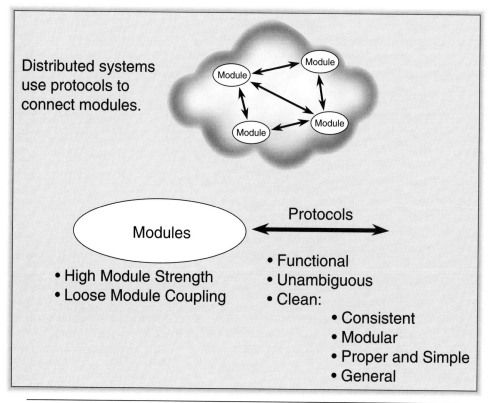

Figure 10.3 Decomposing distributed systems.

implementers, and the system providers. These high level requirements often lead to many lower level requirements, such as preventing endless loops, implementation ease, efficiency, and many others.

Unambiguous—The protocol is unambiguous, consistent, and described at the right level of abstraction. Formal specification notations (such as ABNF, see RFC 2234) and methods (such as state-machine models) are used when they are appropriate. Protocol options and requirements are carefully specified using precise language, such as MUST, MAY, RECOMMENDED or other terms with similar intent to those defined in RFC 2119.

Clean—The protocol specification is well structured, well balanced, modular, simple, correct, general, and maintains conceptual integrity. It has each of the following properties.

- **Consistent**—The protocol has a regular, coherent design that confirms expectations based on previous design choices. A consistent protocol avoids *deadlocks* which are states where protocol processing cannot continue. It also avoids *livelocks* (also know as *endless loops*) which are repeated ineffective execution sequences. It avoids *improper terminations,* which could cause the unexpected end of protocol processing.
- **Modular**—Aspects of the system that are independent of each other are kept separate. The design does not link what is independent and does not separate what is dependent. The system is decomposed into modules that are cohesive and independent.
- **Proper and simple**—The design meets the purpose of the system as simply as possible. Extraneous elements are eliminated. Only the functions that correspond to essential, well understood requirements of the users' and the operating domain are included. Functions are defined exactly once, and the protocol is not over-specified.
- **General**—The protocol design anticipates use in several wide-ranging contexts. The design does not restrict what is inherent in its use, intent, or implementation. This generality allows robustness in many forms, leading to flexibility and adaptability to a variety of environments. Open-endedness allows for future extensions and reuse in other designs and contexts. A well designed general protocol works well even in unexpected conditions. A general protocol is also complete; it considers all that is relevant. It is not under-specified; it specifies a response to all possible inputs. It is bounded, working within system limits for all conditions. The protocol is self-stabilizing, returning to a stable state within a few transitions. The protocol specifies the response to behavior that is outside of the specification. A complete protocol also considers network management, scalability, security, network stability, and internationalization. Finally, protocol implementations should be liberal in what they accept and conservative in what they send [RFC 2360, Sin95,

Hol91]—although interpretation of this controversial suggestion is often debated.

Business requirements on standards

It is widely believed that the BetaMax standard is technically superior to the VHS standard for video tape recorders. Yet throughout the 1980s the greater marketing effort behind VHS steadily displaced BetaMax, and eventually became the universal standard. The network effect created strong forces driving toward a single standard. Adopting a single format enabled friends to share video tapes, allowed studios to produce—and rental shops to stock—a single tape format [Hut1]. This is one of many examples of business conditions playing an essential role in the successful deployment and adoption of a standard.

Because they solve problems and establish new modules, interfaces, and protocols, standards create an arena for developing new products. Successful new products often share a list of know criteria. These criteria help to establish the business conditions that lead to successful new standards.

Standards that solve important problems or create important opportunities for customers in an attractive market have a big advantage. An attractive market has these characteristics [Coo96]:

- The market is large and growing.
- A positive economic climate encourages product purchases.
- The market demand is stable over time rather than cyclical.
- Potential customers in the market are willing to try new products.
- Potential customers are relatively price insensitive.
- Potential customers have money to spend on new solutions. This is often because they run profitable businesses.

In addition, the new standard must provide unique and superior benefits to the available alternatives. Successful standards are likely to result in products that:

- Provide good value for the cost, reduce the users' overall costs of operation, and offer excellent price and performance characteristics.
- Provide a better solution than the previous or existing alternatives. This includes meeting users' needs, offering unique features, or solving a problem existing with the alternative solutions.
- Offer benefits or features that are highly visible and easily seen as useful by the customer.

This requires a good understanding of the many customers' needs and wants throughout the design of the standard. Some features are critical, others are important, and still others are at best "nice to have." The features, performance, security, reliability, and simplicity of the standard must all be balanced to best meet the customers' needs.

Perception, however, is an important reality. Marketing efforts and other techniques for influencing the opinions of decision makers and the buying public can lead to the success or failure of many ideas, including adopting or avoiding new standards [Cia98].

In summary, giving birth to new standards may be nearly as painful and messy as giving birth to infants. However, both creations are full of surprises and potential.

10.2 Content Networking Standards Bodies

The following sections briefly describe several of the standards bodies relevant to content networking. The reader might also want to refer to Chapter 8, which holds some additional information on standards bodies related to content services.

10.2.1 IETF

On April 7, 1969, Steve Crocker of UCLA published a short memo describing work on configuring the host software running in the ARPA Network. Because he was interested in receiving feedback from his peers in the Network Working Group, he titled the memo "Request for Comments." This became the first of more than 3,900 Request for Comments documents published by volunteers interested in contributing their ideas to help shape the Internet [RFC 1, RFC 2555].

In 1986 the Internet Engineering Task Force (IETF) was formed to concentrate on short-to-medium term engineering issues related to the Internet [IETF96].

To briefly describe the operation of the IETF, David Clark, one of the original authors of TCP/IP, famously stated: "We reject: kings, presidents, and voting. We believe in: rough consensus and running code" [Cla92].

The formal statement of the IETF mission is recently expressed in RFC 3935:

"The goal of the IETF is to make the Internet work better. The mission of the IETF is to produce high quality, relevant technical and engineering documents that influence the way people design, use, and manage the Internet in such a way as to make the Internet work better. These documents include protocol standards, best current practices, and informational documents of various kinds."

The RFC identifies these five important operating principals for the IETF:

1. **Open process**—Any interested person can participate in the work, know what is being decided, and make his or her voice heard on the issue. Part of this principle is our commitment to making our documents, our WG

mailing lists, our attendance lists, and our meeting minutes publicly available on the Internet.

2. **Technical competence**—The issues on which the IETF produces its documents are issues where the IETF has the competence needed to speak to them, and that the IETF is willing to listen to technically competent input from any source. Technical competence also means that we expect IETF output to be designed to sound network engineering principles. This is also often referred to as "engineering quality."

3. **Volunteer core**—Our participants and our leadership are people who come to the IETF because they want to do work that furthers the IETF's mission of "making the Internet work better."

4. **Rough consensus and running code**—We make standards based on the combined engineering judgment of our participants and our real-world experience in implementing and deploying our specifications.

5. **Protocol ownership**—When the IETF takes ownership of a protocol or function, it accepts the responsibility for all aspects of the protocol, even though some aspects may rarely or never be seen on the Internet. Conversely, when the IETF is not responsible for a protocol or function, it does not attempt to exert control over it, even though it may at times touch or affect the Internet.

Well over 100 *Working Groups* (WGs) carry out the bulk of the work of the IETF. The current list of Working Groups is available at http://www.ietf.org/html.charters/wg-dir.html. These are presently organized into eight *areas*, with each area overseen by two *Area Directors* (AD). Each group has assigned chairs and technical advisors but, surprisingly, no members. Participation is through the Working Group mailing list and face-to-face meetings. IETF participants are individuals, not organizations—anyone can join any Working Group mailing list [RFC 3160].

The IETF is only one of the several formal organizations that collaborate to make the Internet work. Other closely related organizations include the Internet Architecture Board (IAB), the Internet Society (ISOC), and the Internet Engineering Steering Group (IESG).

The Internet Architecture Board is responsible for defining the overall architecture of the Internet. They provide guidance and broad direction to the IETF. The IAB also serves as the technology advisory group to the Internet Society, and oversees a number of critical activities in support of the Internet.

The Internet Society is a professional membership organization of Internet experts who comment on policies and practices and oversee a number of other boards and task forces dealing with network policy issues.

The Internet Engineering Steering Group is responsible for technical management of IETF activities and the Internet standards process. As part of the ISOC, it administers the process according to the rules and procedures which have been ratified by the ISOC trustees. The IESG is directly responsible for the actions associated with entry into, and movement along, the Internet *standards track,* including final approval of specifications as Internet Standards [IETF2].

The "Request for Comments" (RFC) document series is the official publication channel for Internet standards documents and other publications of the IESG, IAB, and Internet community [RFC 1796]. Much of the work concludes with the publication of RFC documents. There are six distinct types of RFCs:

1. proposed standards,
2. draft standards,
3. internet standards (sometimes called *full standards*),
4. experimental protocols,
5. informational documents, and
6. historic standards.

Only the first three types are intended to become standards. The current list of full standards is available at: http://www.rfc-editor.org/rfcxx00.html.

The goals of the Internet Standards Process are:

- technical excellence,
- prior implementation and testing,
- clear, concise, and easily understood documentation,
- openness and fairness, and
- timeliness.

The relationship of intellectual property rights to published standards can be complex. The intention of the IETF is to benefit the Internet community and the public at large, while respecting the legitimate rights of others.

Specifications that are intended to become Internet Standards evolve through a set of four maturity levels known as the *standards track*. These levels are:

1. **Internet Draft**—During the development of a specification, draft versions of the document are made available for informal review and comment by placing them in the IETF's Internet-Drafts directory. Internet Drafts (ID) have no formal status, and are subject to change or removal at any time. If an ID is referred to at all, it may only be referred to as a *work-in-progress*.
2. **Proposed standard**—This is the entry-level maturity for the standards track. A proposed standard specification is generally stable, has resolved known design choices, is believed to be well-understood, has received significant community review, and appears to enjoy enough community interest to be considered valuable. However, implementers should treat proposed standards as immature specifications.
3. **Draft standard**—A specification from which at least two independent and interoperable implementations from different code bases have been developed, and for which sufficient successful operational experience has been obtained, may be elevated to the draft-standard level.
4. **Internet standard**—A specification for which significant implementation and successful operational experience has been obtained may be elevated to the Internet-standard level [RFC 2026].

However, there often is a disparity between the documented IETF standards process and what is used in practice, which can cause confusion on the part of those people or organizations that use IETF technologies. To address this problem, the IETF has chartered the "New IETF Standards Track Discussion (newtrk)" Working Group to study and resolve this disparity.

Forming a Working Group requires a charter and someone who is able to be Chairperson. This requires work by interested people to help focus the charter and convince an Area Director that the project is worthwhile. Most Working Groups start after a face-to-face Birds of a Feather (BoF) meeting is convened by individuals interested in the topic.

A BOF meeting must be approved by the area director in the relevant area before it can be scheduled. The purpose of a BOF is to make sure that a good charter with good milestones can be created, and that there are enough people willing to do the work needed in order to create standards.

Many BOFs do not turn into WGs for a variety of reasons. A common problem is that not enough people can agree on a focus for the work. Another typical reason is that the work would not end up being a standard, perhaps because the document authors do not really want to relinquish change control to a WG. Officially only two BOFs on a particular subject can take place; either a WG has to form, or the topic is dropped. However, it is not unusual to hold more BOF sessions if progress is continuing toward solving a contentious or difficult problem.

This amorphous process has resulted in publication of more than 3,900 RFCs, adoption of at least 65 full standards, and continued rapid growth of the Internet in many dimensions. These form the basis for most of the technologies described in this book.

10.2.2   ICAP Forum

Sometimes short-term business interests will not wait for rough consensus and running code. For example the ICAP forum formally introduced the ICAP specification in 1999, even though the IETF did not publish RFC 3507 defining the ICAP protocol until nearly four years later in April 2003 [Net01].

The ICAP Forum (www.i-cap.org) was created in 1999–2000 by a group of vendors for the purpose of exchanging and disseminating their ideas and information about ICAP's technical capabilities, improvements, and innovations. The co-hosts of the forum are Network Appliance and Akami, with Webwasher joining later. The Forum consists of a group of companies with a common goal to enable communication between edge devices and network-based applications. The Forum believes that by encouraging vendors to work together it can accelerate the availability of their solutions, understand the problems that need to be addressed, and assist the standards community in developing open standards incorporating concepts Forum members have previously demonstrated. The Forum also acts as an important marketing vehicle. Technical work of the ICAP forum is now limited to discussions of the existing protocol specifications. Other technical work and the development of enhanced protocols have moved into the ITEF OPES Working Group.

10.2.3 **W3C**

The World Wide Web Consortium (W3C) was founded in October 1994 to lead the World Wide Web to its full potential by developing common protocols that promote its evolution and ensure its interoperability. The W3C's goals and operating principles are summarized in the following seven points.

1. **Universal access**—Make the benefits of the World Wide Web available to all people regardless of their hardware, software, network, native language, culture, geographic location, or physical or mental ability.
2. **Semantic Web**—Enable people to express themselves in terms that computers can interpret and exchange.
3. **Trust**—Develop a *web of trust* that provides the confidentiality, confidence, responsibility, and accountability necessary to allow people who may have never met to collaborate safely and reliably.
4. **Interoperability**—Promote use of open computer languages and protocols that allow software components to be interchangeable and avoid market fragmentation.
5. **Evolvability**—Employ the principles of *simplicity, modularity, compatibility,* and *extensibility* in designs so tomorrow's technologies can interwork with today's Web.
6. **Decentralization**—Employ decentralized solutions to create a distributed system free of the bottlenecks caused by centralized elements.
7. **Cooler multimedia**—Continue to enable more interactivity and richer media, including improved flexibility and fidelity of images, sound, video, 3D effects, and animation [W3C7].

Currently 363 organizations are members of the consortium. It does not accept individual members, and their substantial membership fee would discourage individual members even if their policy allowed them. Each W3C Member organization has one Advisory Committee Representative (AC rep).

The AC rep receives official notices from W3C intended for the organization they represent. The AC rep responds directly or delegates response to W3C "Calls for Review," "Calls for Participation," and "Calls for Implementations," as well as other W3C announcements. AC reps come to semi-annual advisory committee meetings where they meet and cooperate with other AC reps. The AC rep also appoints participants in W3C Working Groups.

The W3C presently lists more than 50 topics it is interested in. Work is progressing or has concluded in each of these areas.

Documents published by the W3C progress through these four maturity levels:

1. **Working draft** (WD)—a document that W3C has published for review by the community, including W3C members, the public, and other technical organizations,

2. **Candidate recommendation** (CR)—a document that W3C believes has been widely reviewed and satisfies the Working Group's technical requirements. W3C publishes a candidate recommendation to gather implementation experience.

3. **Proposed recommendation** (PR)—a mature technical report that, after wide review for technical soundness and implementability, is sent to the W3C advisory committee for final endorsement, and

4. **W3C recommendation** (REC)—a specification or set of guidelines that, after extensive consensus-building, has received the endorsement of W3C members and the director. W3C recommends the wide deployment of its Recommendations. W3C Recommendations are similar to the standards published by other organizations [W3C04].

The major standards developed by W3C and described in this book include: HTML, SMIL, XML, and the Web services suite of UDDI, WSDL, and SOAP.

10.3   Content Networking Standards

Each of the Chapters 2 through 8 of this book focuses on a particular technology important for content networking. Each of the following sections describes the technical and business conditions that drive the standards efforts related to the technology of one particular chapter. It also describes the Working Groups and the standards they are developing. Alternative approaches and the characteristics leading to the recommended solutions are also described.

10.3.1   The Early Days

The potential of the Internet attracted increasing interest from a wide variety of users and contributors over a period of more than 30 years. This diverse and widely dispersed group consisting primarily of volunteers organized their efforts in ways that have led to both the rapid evolution of the Internet, and the creation of the various standards bodies and ways of working that have sustained and accelerated this growth.

10.3.2   Content Transport

Chapter 2 describes content transport and the variety of protocols used in the World Wide Web. These protocols include IP, TCP, UDP, FTP, Telnet, and of course, HTTP, used to exchange documents written in HTML.

The evolution of the documents that define the HTTP standard provides an example of the technical and business forces that lead to creating new standards. It also illustrates how the IETF forms Working Groups to solve a problem and concludes the group when the work is completed.

The initial specification of the HTTP protocol was kept in hypertext form and a snapshot circulated as an Internet Draft between November 1993 and

Table 10-1   Evolution of the HTTP protocol standards

Problem	*Solution*
Use of HTTP was increasing; however, the lack of a formal written specification lead to variations in interpretation, implementation, and incompatible systems. Extensions to the protocol were difficult to agree on.	The IETF formed the HTTP Working Group, jointly chartered by the applications area and the transport area. They published RFC 1945 in May 1996 which provided an informational description of HTTP/1.0. In addition to establishing a written description of the common usage of the protocol, this version allows an open-ended set of methods to be used to indicate the purpose of a request. It builds on the discipline of reference provided by the Uniform Resource Identifier (URI), as a location (URL) or name (URN), for indicating the resource on which a method is to be applied. Messages are passed in a format similar to that used by Internet mail and the Multipurpose Internet Mail Extensions (MIME).
RFC 1945 was informational and not a Standards Track document. Also HTTP/1.0 does not sufficiently consider the effects of hierarchical proxies, caching, the need for persistent connections, and virtual hosts. In addition, the proliferation of incompletely implemented applications called HTTP/1.0 made it difficult to determine the actual capabilities of the systems.	RFC 2068 was published in January 1997. This standards track specification defines the protocol referred to as HTTP/1.1. The protocol includes more stringent requirements than HTTP/1.0 to ensure reliable implementation of its features. In addition, it specifies features to support hierarchical proxies, caching and cache control, the need for persistent connections, and virtual hosts.
Widespread use of RFC 2068 identified ambiguities in the language of the specification and several minor difficulties with the defined protocol.	RFC 2616 was published in June 1999. This specification corrected a list of minor problems identified by users of RFC 2068.

May 1994. A revision of the specification by Berners-Lee, Fielding, and Frystyk Nielsen was circulated as an Internet Draft between November 1994 and May 1995. The HTTP Working Group was formed within the IETF to work on the specification of the Hypertext Transfer Protocol [Mas1].

Table 10-1 shows how the IETF responded to address each of the problems that began when use of the HTTP protocol grew rapidly, despite its lack of a formal written specification.

After publishing a total of 12 RFCs, the Working Group concluded in October 2000.

During the same time frame, the HTML specification evolved through the work of the IETF and then the W3C. Table 10-2 describes the pattern of emerging problems and opportunities and the responses the IETF and W3C took to solve these problems.

Table 10-2   Evolution of HTML specifications

Problem or Opportunity	*Solution*
SGML was too complex for the system Tim Berners-Lee described in his 1989 WWW proposal.	The HTML document type was designed by Tim Berners-Lee at CERN as part of the 1990 World Wide Web project. In 1992, Dan Connolly wrote the HTML Document Type Definition (DTD) and a brief HTML specification [W3C2, LC92, W3C3].
No formal specification of HTML was available. Desirable features such as in-line images were not uniformly supported.	RFC 1866 was published by the IETF HTML Working Group in November 1995. This defined HTML version 2.0.
HTML lacked support for tables.	RFC 1942 was published by the IETF HTML Working Group in May 1996. This established an experimental description of a rich set of tables.
The IETF HTML Working Group completed the work of their charter.	After publishing 4 RFCs The IETF HTML Working Group concluded in September 1996.
Several vendors including IBM, Microsoft, Netscape Communications Corporation, Novell, SoftQuad, Spyglass, and Sun Microsystems were facing incompatibility problems because of variation in their approaches used to implement widely deployed features such as tables, applets, and text flow around images.	The HTML 3.2 Reference Specification was published January 14, 1997 as a W3C recommendation. It provides a standard definition for widely deployed features while providing full backward compatibility with the existing standard HTML 2.0.
Vendors wanted to provide an even richer set of features, and improve accessibility for people with disabilities.	The HTML 4.0 Specification was published on December 18, 1997, then revised on April 24, 1998, as a W3C Recommendation. HTML 4.0 extends HTML with mechanisms for style sheets, scripting, frames, embedding objects, and improved support for right-to-left and mixed direction text, richer tables, and enhancements to forms, and offers improved accessibility for people with disabilities.
Minor improvements were suggested and minor errors existed in the HTML 4.0 Recommendation.	The HTML 4.01 Specification was published on December 24, 1999, as a W3C Recommendation.

10.3.3   Caching Techniques for Web Content

The majority of the caching techniques described in Chapter 3 rely on the capabilities defined by the HTTP protocol specification RFC 2616. The caching features of the protocol enabled the development of network caches by a number of vendors.

In 1994 the Harvest project introduced the Internet Cache Protocol (ICP), described in Section 3.6.2. The protocol was primarily designed to facilitate cache hierarchies by locating objects stored in neighbor caches. In 1996 the Harvest cache evolved and split into the Squid project and the NetCache project, which later became NetApp. Minor incompatibilities cropped up in the two implementations of the protocol. Three BOF sessions were held to consider forming an IETF Working Group specific to ICP. No Working Group was formed; however, the primary architects of Squid published RFCs 2186 and 2178 as informational documents describing the protocol in September 1997.

10.3.4 Caching Techniques for Streaming Media

Just as the Web content caching techniques described in Chapter 3 rely on the transport protocol features, the caching techniques for streaming media described in Chapter 4 rely on the features of the streaming protocols.

The Audio/Video Transport Working Group published RFC 1889 as a standards track document in January 1996. This defines RTP, described in Section 4.2.1. The multiparty multimedia session control Working Group published RFC 2326 as a standards track document in April, 1998. This defines RTSP described in Section 4.2.3.

Although these protocols do not include specific caching features, understanding their specification allows development of the streaming caching techniques described in Chapter 4.

Emergence of these standards had another interesting effect. Before they were published, major corporations including Real and Microsoft stressed their proprietary protocols for streaming media. After the standards were published and gained some support, both Real and Microsoft started to show interest in moving to these standard solutions. There seems to be a tipping point where proprietary solutions give way to standard solutions. Factors influencing when this shift occurs include the success of proprietary solutions in capturing and holding market share and the technical and business success of the published standards.

10.3.5 Switching and Routing in Content Networks

The problems of resolving domain names and the growth of the domain name system are described in Section 5.1. A long series of RFCs that describe evolving solutions began in October 1985 with the publication of RFC 952 describing the host table specification. In November 1987, shortly after the formation of the IETF, RFCs 1034 and 1035 were published defining the modern Domain Name System. Since then the DNS Working Group published six RFCs describing the evolution of the Domain Name System before concluding their work in March 1994. The DNS Incremental Transfer, Notification, and Dynamic Update Working Group published 12 RFCs related to *zone transfer, change notification,* and *dynamic update* of the distributed DNS directory before concluding their work in January 2000. The domain name system security Working Group published nine RFCs related to enhancements to the secure DNS protocol designed to protect the dynamic update operation of the DNS before concluding their work in December 1999. Presently the DNS Extensions Working Group is focused on advancing the zone transfer, updating and notifying documents to draft standard, the rewriting the DNSSEC [RFC 2535] proposed standard. They have published 22 RFCs so far [IETF3].

Network Address Translation (see Section 5.2.1), first described by RFC 1631 published in May 1994, predates the formation of the network address translation Working Group. This Working Group provided a forum to discuss applications of NAT operation, limitations to NAT, and the impact of NAT operations on Internet protocols and applications. They published 11 RFCs before concluding their work.

The Virtual Router Redundancy Protocol Working Group is currently active. They published RFC 2338 defining the VRRP Standard in April 1998.

There are no open standards for the Global Routing Systems, described in Section 5.3, other than these basic protocols. If standards were to be developed, the system would have to be decomposed into modules and protocols. Likely modules could include a standard definition of a distance-sensitive DNS server and the associated service nodes. Standard protocols could be defined for communications between this distance-sensitive DNS and the service nodes. Perhaps a standard for explicitly describing the location of clients and service nodes would develop along with standard definitions for various distance metrics. Presently proprietary systems dominate this market and have resisted penetration by standards or suppliers of interchangeable components. This may be motivated by a transient business condition. Because the owner of an effective proprietary global routing system can also bundle the service nodes with that solution, it leads to broader control of this emerging market based on the value of their global routing algorithm.

10.3.6   Peer-to-Peer Content Networks

The peer-to-peer systems described in Chapter 6 (e.g., Gnutella and KaZaA) rely only on informal protocol specifications and ad hoc solutions. Perhaps the lack of a strong business model for these systems is reflected in the lack of standards work in the area.

10.3.7   Interactive Content Delivery—Instant Messaging

Many Working Groups have contributed to the instant messaging solutions described in Chapter 7.

The Instant Messaging and Presence Protocol (IMPP) Working Group published RFCs 2778 and 2779 in February 2000 defining the Presence and Instant Messaging Model. Their several recent RFCs define a Common Profile for Presence (CPP), the Presence Information Data Format (PIDF), Address Resolution for Instant Messaging and Presence, a Common Presence and

Instant Messaging: Messaging Format, and a Common Profile for Instant Messaging (CPIM). They have now concluded their work.

The Multiparty Multimedia Session Control (MUSIC) Working Group published RFC 2327 defining the Session Description Protocol in April 1998. The Session Initiation Protocol (SIP) Working Group has published the many RFCs that define the SIP Protocol.

The SIP for Instant Messaging and Presence Leveraging Extensions (SIMPLE) Working Group has leveraged the work of all of these groups to write many Internet Drafts and RFCs working toward an instant messaging system based on the SIP Protocol that meets the requirements described by the IMPP Working Group.

The Extensible Messaging and Presence Protocol (XMPP) Working Group began with the Jabber Instant Messaging and Presence technology and developed the RFCs that define the XMPP standard.

It will be interesting to see how acceptance of these standards penetrates the popular proprietary instant messaging systems in use today.

10.3.8 Content Services

As described in Chapter 8, two major standardization groups are active in the content services arena today—the IETF and W3C. They can be seen as complementary, but focusing on different approaches.

As described in Chapter 8, the IETF has chartered the Open Pluggable Edge Services (OPES) Working Group to focus on supporting services that operate on data flows between endpoints. So far, the OPES Working Group has developed an architectural framework to authorize, invoke, and trace such application-level services. The framework follows a one-party consent model, which requires that each service be authorized explicitly by at least one of the application-layer endpoints. It further requires that OPES services are reversible by request of the application endpoints.

In particular, the OPES WG has developed a protocol suite for invocation and tracking of OPES services inside the network. The protocol suite includes a generic, application-agnostic protocol core (OCP Core) that is supplemented by profiles specific to the application-layer protocol used between the endpoints. So far, the WG has specified an OCP profile for HTTP, which supports OPES services that operate on HTTP messages. As of this writing, the WG is proposing to continue its work and to specify one or more OCP profiles that will support OPES services operating on SMTP. In particular, the profile to be specified will enable an OPES processor to encapsulate and forward SMTP data and metadata to a callout server for additional processing. In addition, the WG will finalize its work on a rules language to control selection and invocation of services by an OPES processor.

The W3C, in contrast, focuses on specifying mechanisms and protocols in support of traditional business services, such as submitting a purchase order or finding a plumber, in addition to services automatically invoked by software programs. The W3C has created several specifications for announcing, discovering, describing, locating, and exchanging messages to use the services, which include SOAP, WSDL, and UDDI, and are described in Chapter 8.

In the early days of content services, the ICAP Forum was created to develop a first callout protocol for HTTP-based applications. The resulting ICAP specification has now been published as an informal RFC. No further enhancements on ICAP are planned, and the work on future callout protocols moved into the OPES WG of the IETF.

A few more details and a history of the standards groups surrounding content services are also given in Chapter 8.

CHAPTER 11

Summary and Outlook

Innovation creates opportunity. This book has outlined the rapid progress of the Internet over the past 35 years, focusing on the explosion of the World Wide Web over the past decade. This chapter describes that evolution by briefly summarizing the key technologies introduced in each of the previous chapters. Then, by extending each technology forward along its logical path, we suggest future directions of the World Wide Web. Only imagination can limit the opportunities that will result from continued development, integration, and application of these technologies.

11.1 Content Networking Architecture Evolution

Content traverses networks, and Chapter 2 describes how the End-to-End principle guided the original architecture of the Internet. Figure 11.1 shows this End-to-End architecture. The network is relatively simple and the intelligence is moved as much as possible outside the network and into the end hosts.

Routers inside the network implement only protocol layers one through three, realizing a basic, best-effort packet forwarding service through the network, across multiple network links, and multiple network segments. Building on top of IP, hosts implement higher-layer protocols that coordinate the message exchange and organize lower-level network resources to efficiently achieve application-specific design goals. TCP, for example, adds advanced features such as error control, congestion control, and ordered packet delivery on top of the basic IP service. These features enable TCP to provide the underpinning for most application-level protocols such as Telnet, FTP, and HTTP. The Internet architecture allows many different users with different applications to efficiently share common, lower-level network resources.

But closer is better, so Chapter 3 describes how caches are located within clients, the network, and at server farms. Figure 11.2 illustrates how these intermediaries store content within the network. This speeds up responses while

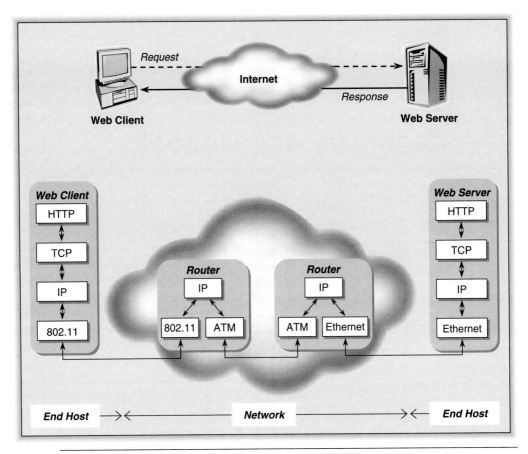

Figure 11.1 The End-to-End model.

reducing network and server loads. These intermediaries diverge from the Internet's original End-to-End principle to provide their benefits. Even though streams are continuous, making them different from Web pages, specialized techniques, explained in Chapter 4, bring the benefits of caching to multimedia streaming content.

Content retrieval requires navigation and Chapter 5 describes how the DNS routes requests to Web servers, Web caches and Web switches. It also describes how Web switches improve operations, and how global request routing connects clients to the best service node. Figure 11.3 illustrates Web switches used to balance server load, and increase the flexibility and reliability of server farms. Web switches are also important for directing network traffic to interception proxies. Global request routing, shown in Figure 11.4, directs client requests to the intermediaries at the service node within the network best able to serve each request. This speeds up responses while further reducing network and server loads.

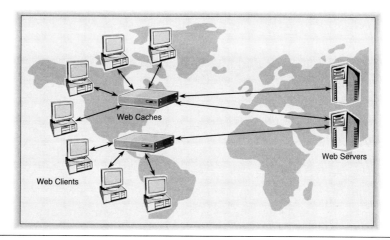

Figure 11.2 Intermediaries store content within the network.

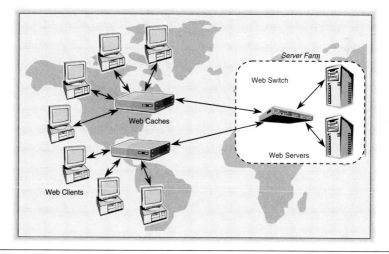

Figure 11.3 Web switches improve operations.

Because peers are equals, Chapter 6 describes how peer-to-peer networks challenge traditional client-server networks, which serve a large number of requests from a relatively small number of high capacity server farms. Figure 11.5 illustrates the symmetric traffic patterns of true peer-to-peer content exchange. This has the potential of improving network reliability and scalability, although practical networks based on a true peer-to-peer architecture are still relatively rare and sparsely deployed.

People enjoy conversing directly with others, and these conversations are a form of interactive content distribution. Figure 11.6 illustrates instant messaging

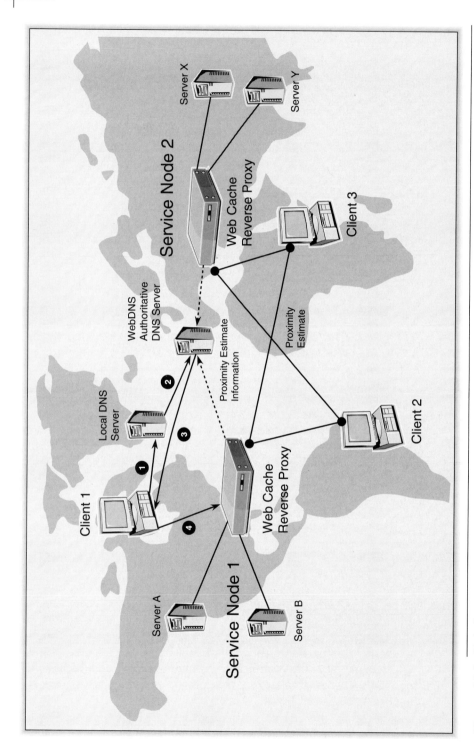

Figure 11.4 Global request routing connects clients to the best service node.

capabilities that allow immediate interaction and dialog with other people who may be using a variety of devices from many different locations, both stationary and mobile. Chapter 7 describes the abstract model for a presence and instant messaging system and then describes a variety of standards-based and proprietary approaches to building such a system. This interactive content delivery presents another challenge for networks that focus traffic or introduce delays.

Service is personal, and value-added services are necessary to make money. People will no longer be satisfied by simply being able to access a Web page on a server in a far away country. They expect far more—instantaneous delivery of information, custom-tailored to their specific needs and preferences. People also expect an integrated solution that converges their various communication needs into a single, easy-to-use system. Content services provide these features by adding value beyond basic content transport. Figure 11.7 shows how content services leverage intermediaries throughout the network, bringing together location information, voice recognition and synthesis, cell phones, wireless PDA, broadband, and databases, transforming the way we live and work. Chapter 8 describes the underpinning technology and architectures. This creates the new arena of the content service provider.

Diverse interests continue to shape these elements into a variety of content networks designed to serve the needs of enterprise users, network operators, content distribution companies, and content service providers. Chapter 9 describes how the various network elements work together to serve the customers' needs.

Standards enable interoperability of modules connected by protocols. The decomposition of a system into separate, well-defined functions has several advantages. First, each of these functions is specialized, which makes them more efficient to implement. Second, they can each be implemented in separate modules, which allows for scalability and flexibility. Such separation

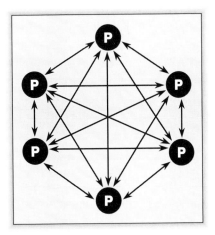

Figure 11.5 Peer-to-peer communication creates symmetric traffic.

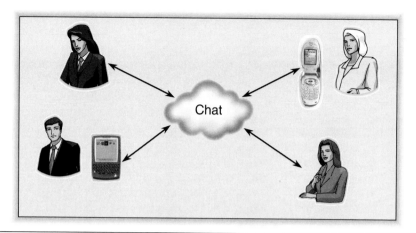

Figure 11.6 Instant messaging enables interactive communication.

requires well-defined interfaces, however. Chapter 10 explains how the creative tension between proprietary solutions and standard solutions continuously energizes Working Groups to identify, describe, and solve more challenging problems.

11.2   The Future of Content Networking

Throughout the evolution of content networking the user requirements have remained constant and are easily stated: *Users want systems that instantly deliver rich relevant content, anytime, anywhere*. Content networking capabilities continue to evolve in both predictable and surprising directions.

Transport continues to get faster and provide substantially greater bandwidth with lower delays, fewer errors, and dramatically lower cost. The transport capabilities available only from wireline connections a short decade ago are now available to wireless devices. This frees users to access richer content anytime and anywhere.

Storage continues to increase dramatically in capacity while access speeds and reliability increase. Cost and the physical size of storage devices continue to drop dramatically. For example, only a decade or so ago, the 40 Gbytes stored by today's pocket-sized iPOD, required rooms full of air-conditioned space filled with banks of expensive disk drives. This increased storage capacity allows richer media types to be stored at Web servers and Web caches throughout the network.

Content will continue to improve until it captures the full richness and intensity of real life and human imagination. Audio will increase in fidelity and video will increase in resolution, depth, and nuance. Text and graphics will allow for

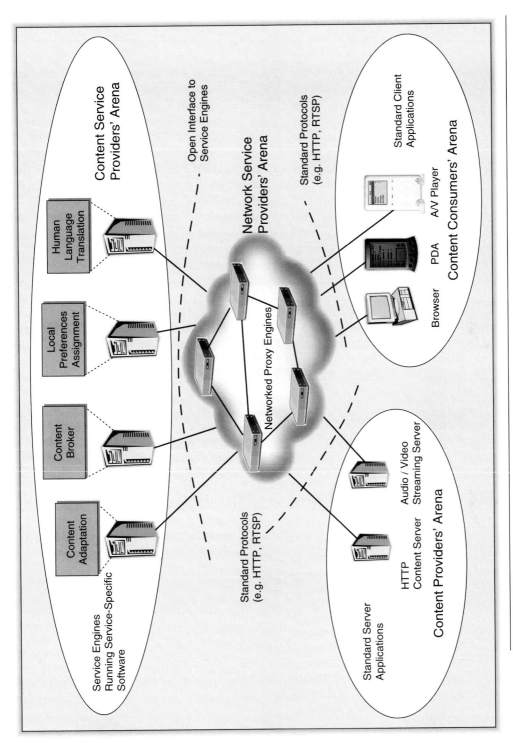

Figure 11.7 Content services add intelligence to the network.

306

better page layout and graphic expression. Intermediate forms such as animation will become easier to create and more realistic. Images, graphics, and video will become more realistic, portraying 3D effects, dramatic lighting, and lifelike movement—as in the movie *Finding Nemo*. Dynamic object types, such as stock quotations and database elements will increase in use and importance. Real-time information such as live Web Cams will increase in utility and usage.

Users at work and play will access this increasingly rich content from a variety of clients. Their clients will become more powerful at home, at work, and on the move wherever users go. Processing power, memory, and display resolution will all increase. Portability, personalization, and specialization will also increase, providing devices such as a portable network-connected MP3 audio player or wearable two-way Web Cam and monitor. User preferences will be communicated that allow the content network to customize semantics, selection, and format. Content directories evolved from today's search engines will become more accurate in identifying content specifically relevant to each user's needs.

Navigation will improve in accuracy, resolution, and speed. Requests will be quickly directed ever more precisely to the network device that can best serve each individual request. Web switches will continue to increase the capacity, reliability, and flexibility of content delivery networks.

Peers will always have good reason to communicate directly. This symmetrical communication creates traffic patterns that are significantly different from client server traffic. Robust peer-to-peer network algorithms, such as the Chord system described in Section 6.3.3 may become popular if an attractive business model for peer-to-peer networks emerges.

People will always want to converse with others. Richer media forms such as graphics, audio, and video will become popular interactive content. Wireless transport mechanisms and adaptation to wireless devices will continue to evolve to bring people closer together. A wide range of alerting signals will convey presence information unobtrusively or with the panache and personal style each user prefers.

The potential of content services is unlimited. Services will become highly differentiated and personalized, as witnessed by the enormous popularity of personalized Web portals such as My Yahoo!. Just as today there are dozens of automobile companies making hundreds of different models, there will be many providers of widely diverse and differentiated content services.

Networks will employ more storage, bandwidth, and processing power while each network element shrinks in physical size. They will become more specialized to meet the needs of increasingly demanding users, while increasing their capacity and variety of service offerings to meet the needs of more users. Integration of wired and mobile access will increase. Convergence and integration of services will also increase. Today's desk telephone, mobile phone, PDA, laptop computer, digital camera, video monitor, movie screen, surround sound system, GPS receiver, DVD player, video recorder, video camera, and portable audio player will be combined into a few well-designed, well-integrated devices for accessing a powerful and ubiquitous content delivery network.

New standards will emerge providing new content delivery functions by allowing interoperability of newly conceived modules interconnected by protocols. These will become more and more specialized as new needs and capabilities are identified and split off into their own modules. The creative tension between proprietary solutions and standard solutions will continuously propel standards work into new areas until delivering rich relevant content is as fast, effortless, satisfying, and personal as pure thought.

Advances in technology will continue to shape the network architecture. Figure 11.8A illustrates how advances in transport technology, such as increased bandwidth, decreased delay, and decreased cost can shift the Internet toward the End-to-End model. If bandwidth is plentiful, then the cost of reaching across the network for content is small in both monetary and performance terms. However, if storage technology improves faster relative to bandwidth, then the "closer is better" Web caching technologies described in Chapters 3 and 4 are most advantageous. Here high capacity, low latency, high reliability, and inexpensive storage can be used in many places throughout the network as a substitute for bandwidth. In this case, the importance of caching intermediaries will continue to increase.

Figure 11.8 B illustrates how improvements in processing power relative to bandwidth may influence the network architecture. Here the alternative approaches considered are the Web-based services, as described in Section 8.6 and services based on intermediaries, such as OPES, described in Section 8.5. If bandwidth is abundant, then reaching across the network to the server for customization is acceptable. If processing is more plentiful than bandwidth, then locally applied services are more satisfactory. This requires that service intermediaries are available, which depends to some extent on the storage costs considerations illustrated in Figure 11.9 A. The problem is three-dimensional, at least. The value of global request routing also depends on the relative abundance of

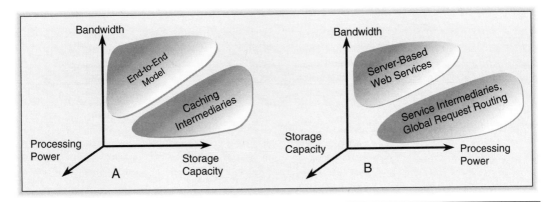

Figure 11.8 Technology advances shape the network architecture.

bandwidth and processing capability. Global request routing uses processing to execute intelligent algorithms to reduce bandwidth needs and transport delays. If bandwidth is abundant, then the savings diminish and routing across the network to the Web server is satisfactory. Other architectural solutions may depend on the relative abundance of processing power and storage capacity, but they are not explored here.

Many powerful forces will continue to drive the evolution of content networks. Figure 11.9 illustrates several of them. Terminals used to run client applications will increase in display resolution, become available instantly after they are powered on, will render images in three dimensions, and will support virtual reality. Terminals we carry with us will become more portable and include higher resolution displays. Terminals we use at home and work will present larger and more lifelike images and higher fidelity sound. Networking will increase in bandwidth and decrease in delay. This allows high speed data transport, fast signaling, and may allow for managing the quality-of-service. Wireless technologies will also increase in bandwidth, availability, and reliability. Finally, new and emerging applications will provide a wide range of useful services, including location-based services, convergence of voice, location, Internet, and wireless services, personal services, integrated and enhanced messaging, and mobile commerce.

Large-scale deployment of high-speed, always-on Internet access, as provided by cable and DSL technology, will also have a significant impact on the future development of content networks. With the availability of broadband connectivity to the Internet, it can be expected that the role of creating and distributing content will no longer be limited to a few well-known content

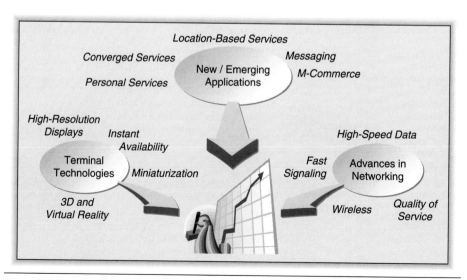

Figure 11.9 Powerful forces are driving the evolution.

providers. Instead, every individual Internet user will potentially become a content source—sharing photos from the backyard BBQ, providing a live image from the local beach, or posting news articles with multimedia content. Constant reduction in costs for the hardware and software needed to produce such content further facilitates this trend. Imagine a world in which every household is a source for many different types of content—live video, recorded videos, audio, images, and news. And anyone in the world—with permission of the content owner—can access this content. New techniques for organizing, identifying, and locating relevant content will be developed. The network infrastructure will change to support the dramatically large number of content sources. New mechanisms will be introduced that protect the privacy of each individual user.

We are still early in the evolution of content networking. The possibilities exceed the imagination. Stay tuned, have fun—and dream on!

Appendix—XML Basics

Several of the topics discussed, including PIDF, XMPP, IRML, SOAP, and WSDL are applications that use XML to exchange data. This appendix provides an introduction to the basic concepts of XML required to understand these XML applications.

XML, the Extensible Markup Language, is a very general and extensible language for identifying the structure of data, including documents. It is defined by Extensible Markup Language (XML) 1.0 (Third Edition) and is a W3C recommendation adopted February 4, 2004 (www.w3.org/TR/REC-xml). XML has been designed for implementation ease and for interoperability with both SGML and HTML. Other design goals are to be easily usable over the Internet, provide support for a wide variety of applications, and make it easy to write programs which process XML documents.

An XML document consists primarily of a collection of *elements*. Elements consist of a pair of start and end *tags*. These tags encapsulate and delimit the data and identify its type. In the following simple example, after declaring the XML version in the first line, the root element `bookinfo` consists of two elements, the `author` and the `title`.

```
<?xml version="1.0"?>
<bookinfo>
    <author>
        Leland R. Beaumont
    </author>
    <title>
        Content Networking: Architecture, Protocols,
            and Practice
    </title>
</bookinfo>
```

Example 1.   bookinfo.xml.

If this example is saved as a file called `bookinfo.xml` and opened using Internet Explorer (version 5.0 or later), or any other XML browser, it will be displayed showing its structure as an XML file.

XML is extensible and flexible because the user is free to define element and tag names. Only a small number of basic element types, such as character string, integer, and date are predefined. XML relies on a separate Document Type Definition (DTD) to provide a grammar specification for a particular document type. Identifying a DTD enables a parser to determine if the corresponding XML document is valid. A valid XML document has the correct nesting of start and end tags and conforms to the rules of the

311

Document Type Definition. Alternatively, the XML Schema Definition (XSD) language can be used to define the structure of an XML document. An XML Schema defines:

- elements and attributes that can appear in a document,
- which elements are child elements along with their order and number,
- whether an element is empty,
- the data types for elements and attributes, and
- the default and value ranges for elements and attributes.

Schema are associated with an XML document by using the `schemaLocation=URL` attribute of the Root element.

When a document is defined by XML, the conventions used in displaying the document are defined using a separate Cascading Style Sheet (CSS) or the more powerful eXtensible Stylesheet Language (XSL) to define display characteristics of each element type. Because the formatting specification is separate from the document content, formats can be chosen to suit the display preferences of the user, or the capabilities of the display device.

Namespaces avoid element name conflicts and allow reuse of predefined element types. Because element names can be chosen freely by the user, element name conflicts can often occur. These are resolved by defining a namespace for each tag. By using the XML namespace attribute `xmlns` in the root element start tag and referring to a unique URL, the prefix b in this example now qualifies each tag as belonging to a unique name space.

```
<?xml version="1.0"?>
<b:bookinfo xmlns:b="http://www.content-
    networking.com/xml/booknamespace" >
    <b:author>
        Leland R. Beaumont
    </b:author>
    <b:title>
        Content Networking: Architecture, Protocols,
            and Practice
    </b:title>
</b:bookinfo>
```

Example 2   bookinfo.xml with namespace declaration.

Predefined element types can be reused by selecting the namespace where they are defined. For example, SOAP is defined as an XML application by the schema at: http://www.w3.org/2003/05/soap-envelope/. Similarly, WDSL is defined as an XML application by the schema at: http://schemas.xmlsoap.org/wsdl/.

Glossary

The special terms used in this book are defined in this glossary. Several of these terms are taken directly from RFCs or other primary references cited. Many terms defined in RFC 1983, the Internet User's Glossary, are not repeated here.

3GPP   The 3rd Generation Partnership Project for wireless. See www.3gpp.org.

AAA   Authorization, Authentication, and Accounting—Services that enable monitoring, logging, accounting, and billing of content usage. This includes mechanisms to ensure the identity and the privileges of all parties involved in a transaction, as well as digital rights management. See RFC 2989.

ABNF   Augmented BNF (Backus-Naur Form) for Syntax Specifications. See RFC 2234.

ADSL   Asymmetric Digital Subscriber Line—A method for very rapidly moving data over regular phone lines. See www.dslforum.org/aboutdsl/adsl_tutorial.html.

AIM   The AOL Instant Messenger service. See www.aim.com/.

AS   Autonomous System—A set of routers under a single technical administration. An AS is a connected group of one or more IP prefixes run by one or more network operators that has a single and clearly defined routing policy. See RFC 1930.

ARIN   The American Registry for Internet Numbers. See www.arin.net/.

ARPA   The Advanced Research Projects Agency, who sponsored the early research work leading to the Internet. See www.arpa.mil.

Bearer Channel   The bearer channel is the primary transmission path and is used to send the data representing the payload of the communication. Contrast with *signaling channel*.

BIND   The Berkeley Internet Name Domain—Is an implementation of the Domain Name System (DNS) protocols and provides an openly redistributable reference implementation of the major components of the Domain Name System. See www.isc.org/index.pl?/sw/bind/.

Binding   Binding is an association between an interface, a concrete protocol, and a data format. A Binding specifies the protocol and data format to be used in transmitting messages defined by the associated Interface.

Callout Server   A server (e.g., within OPES) providing content services that is distinct from the service activation point.

Codec   Short for either compressor/decompressor, or coder/decoder. A codec is any technology for compressing and decompressing data or encoding and decoding a signal.

Codecs can be implemented in software, hardware, or a combination of both. Some popular codecs for multimedia include MPEG, and MP3 audio. Lower fidelity audio formats include PCM, ADPCM, and LPC.

Content   The term content refers to any information that is made available for retrieval from resources on the Internet. This includes, but is not limited to Web pages, images, textual documents, audio and video, as well as software downloads and broadcasts.

Content Adaptation   A content processing service that adapts the format and presentation of content to suit the characteristics of a particular client device or the preferences of a particular content consumer.

Content Consumer   The final destination for the content to be delivered. Content consumers are typically Internet users requesting information through their Web browsers.

Content Creator   The author of content, including Web pages, multimedia files, and other content forums.

Content Distribution Services   Services for moving the content from the source to the destination. These services can comprise Web caches or other devices storing content intermediately on behalf of the origin Web server in the network. The distribution component also covers the actual mechanism and the protocols used for transmitting data over the network.

Content Host   The provider of Web server space.

Content Network   The term content network refers to a communication network that deploys infrastructure components operating at protocol Layers 4 through 7. These components interconnect with each other, creating a virtual network layered on top of an existing network infrastructure.

Content Network Provider   Organizations responsible for helping content providers deliver content to the users. Their resources typically provide caching and replication of data, as well as request-routing and possibly services for content processing.

Content Provider   A general term encompassing the content creator, the content host, or both.

Content Services   Services for creating or adapting content or requests for content to suit user preferences and device capabilities. This includes modification or conversion of both content and requests for content. Examples are content adaptation for wireless devices or adding privacy by making anonymous personal information embedded in user requests. A service engine provides these content services.

CPIM   Common Profile for Instant Messaging. See RFC 3860.

CPP   Common Protocol for Presence. See RFC 3859.

Delegate Services   Content services provided on behalf of the content consumers or by the applications they are running.

DHCP   Dyanamic Host Configuration Protocol. See RFC 2131.

DNS   Domain Name System—The distributed directory used to translate human-friendly hostnames, like www.content-networking.com into the corresponding IP address. The DNS is defined by RFC 1034, RFC 1035, and others.

Digital Millennium Copyright Act   A provision of the U.S. copyright law enacted in 1998 that considers copyright issues in the context of digital media [DMCA98].

Domain   A sub-tree of the domain name space. For example, ".edu", "purdue.edu", and "itap.purdue.edu" are all domains.

Domain Name Space   The set of all domain names and their corresponding IP addresses. This forms a tree-structured name space for the data associated with the names. See RFC 1034.

DTMF   Dual Tone Multi-Frequency is the technical name for touch-tone or push-button dialing. Pushing a button on a telephone keypad generates a sound that is a combination of two tones, one high frequency and the other low frequency.

Elastic Store   An algorithm or device designed to accommodate small timing variations between two devices that need to interwork in real time. It is typically implemented as a double-ended queue, where content is removed from the front while it is added to the back of the queue. The queue is designed to be long enough that timing differences between content arrival and removal never exhausts the queue.

Element   An XML element.

EMS   Enhanced Messaging System—Provides an evolutionary path from SMS to MMS. See www.3gpp.org.

Fetcher   Within the model for Presence and Instant Messaging, a fetcher is a form of watcher that has asked the presence service for the presence information of one or more presentities to be created, but has not asked for a subscription. See RFC 2778.

Forward Proxy   A Web cache working on behalf of content consumers. Traffic is directed to the forward proxy, for example by identifying it as an HTTP proxy in the user's Web browser. Contrast with *Reverse Proxy*.

Grid Computing   Coordinated resource sharing and problem solving in large, multi-institutional virtual organizations [FKe03].

GSLB   Global Server Load Balancing.

HTML   Hyper Text Markup Language. See www.w3c.org/MarkUp/.

HTTP   Hypertext Transfer Protocol—The protocol predominantly used by the World Wide Web as defined in RFC 2616.

IAB   IETF Internet Architecture Board—The IAB is responsible for defining the overall architecture of the Internet, providing guidance and broad direction to the IETF. The IAB also serves as the technology advisory group to the Internet Society, and oversees a number of critical activities in support of the Internet. See www.ietf.org/glossary.html.

IANA   The Internet Assigned Numbers Authority is in charge of all "unique parameters" on the Internet, including IP (Internet Protocol) addresses. Each domain name is associated with a unique IP address, a numerical name consisting of four blocks of up to three digits each (e.g., 204.146.46.8), which systems use to direct information through the network. See www.ietf.org/glossary.html.

ICAP The Internet Content Adaptation Protocol was the first protocol to be defined by an RFC for content service applications. It is defined by RFC 3507.

ICAP Resource Similar to an HTTP resource, but the URI refers to an ICAP service that performs adaptations of HTTP messages. See RFC 3507.

ICAP Server Similar to a callout server, except that the application services ICAP requests. See RFC 3507.

ICAP Client A program that establishes connections to ICAP servers for the purpose of sending requests. An ICAP client is often, but not always, a surrogate acting on behalf of a user. See RFC 3507.

ICAP Forum An industry group formed to advance the use of the ICAP protocol. See www.i-cap.org.

IESG The Internet Engineering Steering Group is responsible for technical management of IETF activities and the Internet standards process. As part of the ISOC, it administers the process according to the rules and procedures which have been ratified by the ISOC Trustees. The IESG is directly responsible for the actions associated with entry into, and movement along, the Internet standards track, including final approval of specifications as Internet Standards. See www.ietf.org/glossary.html.

IETF The Internet Engineering Task Force is the protocol engineering and development arm of the Internet. Though it existed informally for some time, the group was formally established by the IAB in 1986 with Phill Gross as the first Chair. See www.ietf.org/glossary.html.

IMPP The Instant Messaging and Presence Protocol Working Group of the IETF. See www.ietf.org/html.charters/OLD/impp-charter.html.

Inbox User Agent (UA) Within the model for Presence and Instant Messaging, an Inbox UA is the means for a principal to manipulate zero or more instant inboxes controlled by that principal. See RFC 2778.

Instant Inbox Within the model for Presence and Instant Messaging, an Instant Inbox is a receptacle for instant messages intended to be read by the instant inbox's principal. See RFC 2778.

Instant Messaging Real-time, interactive content delivery.

Instant Message Protocol Within the model for Presence and Instant Messaging, the instant message protocol is the messages that can be exchanged between a sender user agent and an instant message service, or between an instant message service and an instant inbox. See RFC 2778.

Interactional Coherence A psychology term referring to the expectation that speakers take turns and their comments "belong together" with each turn intended as a timely response or follow-up to a previous turn [Her99].

Intermediaries The necessary ties between overlaid content networks and the underlying packet network infrastructure is enabled via intermediaries. Intermediaries are application-level devices that are part of a Web transaction, but are neither the originating nor the terminating device in the transaction. The most commonly known and used intermediaries today are probably proxies and Web caches.

ISOC   The Internet Society is a professional membership organization of Internet experts that comments on policies and practices and oversees a number of other boards and task forces dealing with network policy issues. See www.ietf.org/glossary.html.

Jabber   An open source instant messaging system that began the XMPP work. See www.jabber.org.

Jitter   Small quick jumpy movements—any distortion of a signal or image caused by poor synchronization, such as flicker on a display screen or variable frame display rate of a video.

MD5   A message-digest hashing algorithm defined by RFC 1321.

Metcalfe's Law   See Network Effect.

Mixer   In RTP, an intermediate system that receives RTP packets from one or more sources, possibly changes the data format, combines the packets in some manner, and then forwards a new RTP packet. Since the timing among multiple input sources will not generally be synchronized, the mixer will make timing adjustments among the streams and generate its own timing for the combined stream. Thus, all data packets originating from a mixer will be identified as having the mixer as their synchronization source. See RFC 1889.

MRTG   The Multi Router Traffic Grapher is a tool to monitor the traffic load on network links. MRTG generates HTML pages containing graphical images which provide a live visual representation of this traffic. See www.mrtg.org.

MSRP   The Message Session Relay Protocol is used by SIMPLE to send in message mode [CMJ04].

MMS   The Multimedia Messaging Service allow users to send and receive messaging using an array of media types, including text, images, audio, and video while supporting new wireless client types [3GPP1].

Multimedia Content   Content that is represented as a combination of multiple content objects, each of them having a different media type. Examples include video clips with audio or Web pages incorporating text, images, and videos.

MMUSIC   The Multiparty Multimedia Session Control Working Group. See www.ietf.org/html.charters/mmusic-charter.html.

Name Servers   Server programs that hold information about the domain tree's structure and set information. Name servers run the DNS protocol. See RFC 1034.

Namespace   A collection of distinct names represented as strings of characters. Usually the names in a namespace are constructed according to a set of rules given by the definition of the namespace. URIs of various kinds are commonly used to construct the names in namespaces. For example, the namespace for UDDI keys in the recommended keying scheme consists of the URIs in the "uddi" scheme. See RFC 1034.

NAT   Network Address Translation. See RFC 1631.

Navigation   The general problem of locating a destination and determining a path toward it.

Network Effect   Also know as Metcalfe's law, states that the value of a network grows as the square of the number of users.

OCP   The OPES callout protocol, used to invoke a callout server from a data dispatcher.

OPES   Open Pluggable Edge Services. See RFC 3835.

OPES Rules   A set of instructions that specify when, where, and how to execute OPES services.

OPES Service   A process that performs the actual content service transformation. See RFC 3835.

PDA   A Personal Digital Assistant—Provides pocket-sized access to a personal calendar, contacts, notes, games, and other information. Wireless devices allow access to e-mail and Internet content. PDAs became popular with the introduction of the palm pilot, blackberry, and similar devices.

Peer-to-Peer Computing   A set of technologies that enable the direct exchange of services or data between computers [Int01].

Peer-to-Peer Networks   Distributed systems where the software running at each node provides equivalent functions [SKB01].

PIDF   Presence Information Data Format. See RFC 3863.

Poller   Within the model for Presence and Instant Messaging, a poller is a fetcher that requests presence information on a regular basis. See RFC 2778.

Presence Agent   Within the SIMPLE protocols, the presence agent accepts subscriptions, stores subscription state, and generates notifications where there are changes to presence information. See RFC 3856.

Presence Service   Within the model for Presence and Instant Messaging, a Presence service accepts, stores, and distributes presence information. See RFC 2778.

Presence Information   Within the model for Presence and Instant Messaging, presence information consists of one or more presence tuples. See RFC 2778.

Presence Protocol   Within the model for Presence and Instant Messaging, the presence protocol is the messages that can be exchanged between a presentity and a presence service, or a watcher and a presence service. See RFC 2778.

Presence Tuple   Within the model for Presence and Instant Messaging, a presence tuple consists of a status, an optional communication address, and other optional presence markup information. See RFC 2778.

Presence User Agent (UA)   Within the model for Presence and Instant Messaging, a Presence UA is a means for a principal to manipulate zero or more presentities. See RFC 2778.

Presentity (Presence Entity)   Within the model for Presence and Instant Messaging, a presentity provides presence information to a presence service. See RFC 2778.

Principal   Within the model for Presence and Instant Messaging, a principal is a human, program, or collection of humans and/or programs that chooses to appear to the presence service as a single actor, distinct from all other principals. See RFC 2778.

Proxy   In general a proxy is the authority to act for another as an agent or substitute. In this book it refers to a network element that is an intermediary program, which acts as both a server and a client for the purpose of making requests on behalf of other clients. Requests are serviced internally or by passing them on, with possible translation, to other servers. Examples include Web caches and firewalls. See RFC 2616.

PSTN   The Public Switched Telephone Network accesses and interconnects all traditional telephone devices.

RAS   A Remote Access Server—The device in the network that terminates the many access connections coming from each client. This may be a modem pool, terminal server, DSLAM (DSL Access Multiplexer) or the head end of a cable segment.

Render   To convert graphics, audio, video or other multimedia content from a file or any other digital format into visual or audio form, such as on a video display.

Request Routing Services   Services for navigating user requests to a location best suited for retrieving the requested content. User requests can be served, for example, from Web Servers or Web caches. The selection of the most appropriate target location is typically based on network proximity and availability of the systems and the network.

Resolvers   Programs that extract DNS information from name servers in response to client requests. A resolver is typically a system routine that is directly accessible to user programs. See RFC 1034.

Resource   A network data object or service that can be identified by a URI, as defined in Section 3.2 of RFC 2616. Resources may be available in multiple representations (e.g., multiple languages, data formats, size, resolutions) or vary in other ways. See RFC 2616.

Resource Records   The information returned in a primary type of DNS record. These are often A (address), NS (name server), or CNAME (canonical name)-type records. See RFC 1034.

Reverse Proxy   A Web cache working on behalf of content providers. Traffic is directed to the reverse proxy by assigning it the IP address of a Web site. It is also called a server accelerator. Contrast with *forward proxy* and *transparent proxy*.

RFC   The Request for Comments document series is the official publication channel for Internet standards documents and other publications of the IESG, IAB, and Internet community. See RFC 1796.

RIAA   The Recording Industry Association of America is a trade group that represents the U.S. recording industry. See www.riaa.com.

Roster   The term used in XMPP for contact lists. Similar to the "buddy lists" used in AIM.

Routing   Routing is the process of choosing a path over which to send packets. Routing typically refers to path selection at Layer 3.

RTP   The Real-Time Transport Protocol. See RFC 1889.

RTCP   The RTP Control Protocol. See RFC 1889.

RTSP   The Real-Time Streaming Protocol. See RFC 2326.

RTT   Round Trip Time.

Ruleset The collection of individual rules operating within a data dispatcher.

SDP The Session Descriptor Protocol. See RFC 2327.

Sender Within the model for Presence and Instant Messaging, a Sender is the source of instant messages to be delivered by the instant message service. See RFC 2778.

Sender User Agent Within the model for Presence and Instant Messaging, a Sender UA is the means for a principal to manipulate zero or more senders.

Server An application program that accepts connections in order to service requests by sending back responses. Any given program may be capable of being both a client and a server; our use of these terms refers only to the role being performed by the program for a particular connection, rather than to the program's capabilities in general. Likewise, any server may act as an origin server, surrogate, gateway, or tunnel, switching behavior based on the nature of each request. See RFC 2616.

Server Accelerator A synonym for reverse proxy.

Service Activation Point The element in the content services architecture that recognizes requests for content services and dispatches requests for those services. See RFC 3835.

Services Engine An element that provides content services.

SHA-1 A 160-bit message digest that results in consistent hashing [FIPS93, LLP+97].

Signaling Channel The transmission path used to send control information. Contrast with *bearer channel*.

SIMPLE The SIP for Instant Messaging and Presence Leveraging Extensions IETF Working Group. See www.ietf.org/html.charters/simple-charter.html.

SIP The Session Initiation Protocol. See RFC 3261.

SLA Service Level Agreement—an agreement or contract establishing the expected level of service to be provided. This may specify limits on bandwidth, availability, reliability, error rates, delay, transaction rates, and other parameters of the service. As a contract it may specify penalties or other remedies if the service level is not met.

SMPTE The Society of Motion Picture and Television Engineers is a professional organization that creates industry standards. See www.smpte.org.

SMS The Short Messaging System allows text messages no longer than 160 characters to be exchanged between properly equipped wireless clients such as cell phones and PDAs [SMS1].

SMTP The Simple Mail Transfer Protocol is used for sending e-mail messages between servers. See RFC 2821.

SOAP Simple Object Access Protocol is a lightweight protocol intended for exchanging structured information in a decentralized, distributed environment. See www.w3c.org/2000/xp/Group/.

Softphone An application that enables a computer to function as a telephone.

Standard Guideline documentation that reflects agreements on products, practices, or operations by nationally or internationally recognized industrial, professional, trade associates, or government bodies [ANS01].

Subscriber   Within the model for Presence and Instant Messaging, a subscriber is a form of watcher that has asked the presence service to notify it immediately of changes in the presence information of one or more presentities.

Surrogate   A synonym for reverse proxy.

Surrogate Services   Content services provided on behalf of one or more origin servers.

Switching   Choosing among several local endpoints connected to the switch, typically at Layer 2. Also used to describe selection based on Layer 4–7 information.

TLD   Top-Level Domain—the highest level, below the root, of the DNS name space. These are subdivided into ccTLDs (country code top level domains) and gTLDs (generic top level domains). See RFC 1591.

Tragedy of the Commons   The observation that freely available shared resources quickly become exhausted [Har68].

Translator   In RTP, an intermediate system that forwards RTP packets with their synchronization source identifier intact. Examples of translators include devices that convert encodings without mixing, replicators from multicast to unicast, and application-level filters in firewalls. See RFC 1889.

Transparent Proxy   A Web cache working on behalf of network providers. Traffic is directed to the transparent proxy by a Web switch. Contrast with *forward proxy* and *reverse proxy*.

TTL   Time To Live—A method commonly used to expire packets.

UAC   User Agent Client—A logical entity within SIP that creates a new request and then uses the client transaction state machinery to send it. See RFC 3261.

UAS   User Agent Server—A logical entity within SIP that generates a response to a SIP request. See RFC 3261.

UDDI   The Universal Description, Discovery, and Integration specification provides a platform-independent way of discovering and describing Web services and Web service providers. See www.uddi.org/.

UDDI Business Registry   A publicly available UDDI registry. The Web services offered by the UDDI Business Registry's nodes can be found at uddi.org/register.html (for publication of business services) and uddi.org/find.html (for inquiry and discovery of business services).

UUCP   Unix-to-Unix Copy—This was initially a program run under the Unix operating system that allowed one Unix system to send files to another Unix system via dial-up phone lines. Today, the term is more commonly used to describe the large international network which uses the UUCP protocol to forward news and electronic mail. See RFC 1983 and RFC 976.

Vectoring   Directing a request to one of several possible service points based on rules, content, availability, location, or some other criteria.

VIP   Virtual IP address—An IP address that is associated with a pool of real equipment rather than with a specific interface of real network equipment.

VoiceXML   The Voice Extensible Markup Language is designed for creating audio dialogs that feature synthesized speech, digitized audio, recognition of spoken and DTMF key input, recordings of spoken input, telephony, and mixed initiative conversations. Its major goal is to bring the advantages of Web-based development and content delivery to interactive voice response applications. See www.voicexml.org/.

VRRP   The Virtual Router Redundancy Protocol is defined by RFC 2338.

WAP   The Wireless Application Protocol is an industry-wide specification for developing applications that operate over wireless communication networks. See www.openmobile alliance.org/tech/affiliates/wap/wapindex.html.

Watcher   Within the model for Presence and Instant Messaging, a watcher requests presence information about a presentity, or watcher information about a watcher, from the presence service. Special types of watcher are fetcher, poller, and subscriber. See RFC 2778.

Watcher User Agent (UA)   Within the model for Presence and Instant Messaging, a watcher UA is the means for a principal to manipulate zero or more watchers controlled by that principal. See RFC 2778.

W3C   The World Wide Web Consortium—Develops interoperable technologies (specifications, guidelines, software, and tools) to lead the Web to its full potential. W3C is a forum for information, commerce, communication, and collective understanding. See www.w3c.org.

Web Object   Information on the Web is represented in the form of Web Objects. A Web object can be anything from a simple text document to a multimedia presentation or an audio/video clip.

WSDL   Web Services Description Language is an XML format for describing network services as a set of endpoints operating on messages containing either document-oriented or procedure-oriented information. The operations (procedures) and messages (data) are described abstractly, and then bound to a concrete network protocol and message format to define an endpoint. Related concrete endpoints are combined into abstract endpoints (defining services). WSDL is extensible to allow description of endpoints and their messages regardless of what message formats or network protocols are used to communicate; however, the only bindings officially documented describe how to use WSDL in conjunction with SOAP 1.1, HTTP GET/POST, and MIME. See www.w3c.org/2002/ws/desc/.

WSDL Binding   Within WSDL, binding is the process of associating concrete protocol or data format information with an abstract entity like a message, operation, or port type. A binding defines message format and protocol details for operations and messages defined by a particular port type. There may be any number of bindings for a given port type. See www.w3.org/TR/wsdl12-bindings/.

WSDL Message Parts   Message Parts are a flexible mechanism for describing the logical abstract content of a WSDL message. A binding may reference the name of a part to specify binding-specific information about the part. For example, a part may represent a parameter in the message for use with a remote procedure call. However, the bindings must be inspected to determine the actual meaning of the part.

WSDL Ports   A port defines an individual network-accessible endpoint by specifying a single address for a binding. This endpoint is defined as a combination of a WSDL binding and a network address. This establishes an address that provides a single primitive WSDL-defined service. This is analogous to a procedure definition in a procedural programming language.

WSDL Operations   An abstract description of an action supported by the service.

WSDL Port Type   A named set of abstract WSDL operations and the abstract messages involved supported by one or more endpoints.

WSDL Services   A collection of related network endpoints, or WSDL ports.

XML   The eXtensible Markup Language. See the Appendix.

XMPP   The Extensible Messaging and Presence Protocol IETF Working Group. See www.ietf.org/html.charters/OLD/xmpp-charter.html.

Zone   The portion of the domain name space that the name server has complete information about. See RFC 1034.

RFC References

Many of the documents referenced throughout this book are Requests for Comments (RFCs) published by the IETF. To simplify their reference and retrieval, this list of relevant RFCs is presented in numeric order. The full text of any RFC is freely available from the IETF Web site at www.ietf.org/rfc.html.

RFC 1   Crocker, S.: "Host Software," April 7, 1969.

RFC 114   Bhushan, A.: "A File Transfer Protocol," April 1971.

RFC 952   Harrenstien, K., Stahl, M., Feinler, E.: "DoD Internet Host Table Specification," October 1985.

RFC 953   Harrenstien, K., Stahl, M., Feinler, E.: "HOSTNAME Server," October 1985.

RFC 959   Postel, J., Reynolds, J.: "File Transfer Protocol," October 1985.

RFC 976   Horton, M. R.: "UUCP Mail Interchange Format Standard," February 1986.

RFC 1034   Mockapetris, P.: "Domain Names—Concepts and Facilities," November 1987.

RFC 1035   Mockapetris, P.: "Domain Names—Implementation and Specification," November 1987.

RFC 1075   Waitzman, D., Partridge, C., Deering, S.: "Distance Vector Multicast Routing Protocol," November 1988.

RFC 1112   Deering, S.: "Host Extensions for IP Multicasting," August 1989.

RFC 1321   Rivest, R.: "The MD5 Message-Digest Algorithm," April 1992.

RFC 1436   Anklesaria, F., McCahill, M., Lindner, P., Johnson, D., Torrey, D., Alberti, B.: "The Internet Gopher Protocol," March 1993.

RFC 1458   Braudes, R., Zabele, S.: "Requirements for Multicast Protocols," May 1993.

RFC 1459   Oikarinen, J., Reed, D.: "Internet Relay Chat Protocol," May 1993.

RFC 1466   Gerich, E.: "Guidelines for Management of IP Address Space," May 1993.

RFC 1480   Cooper, A., Postel, J.: "The US Domain," June 1993.

RFC 1546   Partridge, C., Mendez, T., Milliken, W.: "Host Anycasting Services," November 1993.

RFC 1591   Postel, J.: "Domain Name System Structure and Delegation," March 1994.

RFC 1597   Rekhter, Y., Moskowitz, B., Karrenberg, D., de Groot, G. J.: "Address Allocation for Private Internets," March 1994.

RFC 1630   Berners-Lee, T.: "Universal Resource Identifiers in WWW," June 1994.

RFC 1631   Egevang, K., Francis, P.: "The IP Network Address Translator (NAT)," May 1994.

RFC 1737   Sollins, K., Masinter, L.: "Functional Requirements for Uniform Resource Names," December 1994.

RFC 1738   Berners-Lee, T., Masinter, L., McCahill, M.: "Uniform Resource Locators (URL)," December 1994.

RFC 1739   Kessler, G., Shepard, S.: "A Primer on Internet and TCP/IP Tools," December 1994.

RFC 1796   Huitema, C., Postel, J., Crocker, S.: "Not All RFCs Are Standards," April 1995.

RFC 1808   Fielding, R.: "Relative Uniform Resource Locators," June 1995.

RFC 1847   Galvin, J., Murphy, S., Crocker, S., Freed, N.: "Security Multiparts for MIME: Multipart/Signed and Multipart/Encrypted," October 1995.

RFC 1866   Berners-Lee, T., Connolly, D.: "Hypertext Markup Language—2.0," November 1995.

RFC 1889   Schulzrinne, H., Casner, S., Frederick, R., Jacobson, V.: "RTP: A Transport Protocol for Real-Time Applications," Audio–Video Transport Working Group, January 1996.

RFC 1890   Schulzrinne, H.: "RTP Profile for Audio and Video Conferences with Minimal Control," January 1996.

RFC 1918   Rekhter, Y., Moskowitz, B., Karrenberg, D., de Groot, G.J., Lear, E.: "Address Allocation for Private Internets," February 1996.

RFC 1928   Leech, M., Ganis, M., Lee, Y., Kuris, R., Koblas, D., Jones, L.: "SOCKS Protocol Version 5," March 1996.

RFC 1942   Raggett, D.: "HTML Tables," May 1996.

RFC 1945   Berners-Lee, T., Fielding, R., Frystyk, H.: "Hypertext Transfer Protocol— HTTP/1.0," May 1996.

RFC 2026   Bradner, S.: "The Internet Standards Process—Revision 3," October 1996.

RFC 2045   Freed, N., Borenstein, N.: "Multipurpose Internet Mail Extensions (MIME) Part One: Format of Internet Message Bodies," November 1996.

RFC 2068   Fielding, R., Gettys, J., Mogul, J., Frystyk, H., Berners-Lee, T.: "Hypertext Transfer Protocol—HTTP/1.1," January 1997.

RFC 2119   Bradner, S.: "Key Words for Use in RFCs to Indicate Requirement Levels," March 1997.

RFC 2141   Moats, R.: "URN Syntax," May 1997.

RFC 2186   Wessels, D., Claffy, K.: "Internet Cache Protocol (ICP), Version 2," September 1997.

RFC 2187   Wessels, D., Claffy, K.: "Application of the Internet Cache Protocol, Version 2," September 1997.

RFC 2222   Myers, J.: "Simple Authentication and Security Layer (SASL)," October 1997.

RFC 2234   Crocker, D., Overell, P.: "Augmented BNF for Syntax Specifications: ABNF," November 1997.

RFC 2246   Dierks, T., Allen, C., Treese, W., Karlton, P., Freier, A., Kocher, P.: "The TLS Protocol Version 1.0," January 1999.

RFC 2326   Schulzrinne, H., Rao, A., Lanphier, R.: "Real Time Streaming Protocol (RTSP)," Network Working Group, April 1998.

RFC 2327   Handley, M., Jacobson, V.: "SDP: Session Description Protocol," April 1998.

RFC 2338   Knight, S., Weaver, D., Whipple, D., Hinden, R., Mitzel, D., Hunt, P., Higginson, P., Shand, M., Lindem A.: "Virtual Router Redundancy Protocol," April 1998.

RFC 2360   Scott, G. (ed): "Guide for Internet Standards Writers," June 1998.

RFC 2396   Berners-Lee, T., Fielding, R., Masinter, L.: "Uniform Resource Identifiers (URI): Generic Syntax," August 1998.

RFC 2535   Eastlake, D.: "Domain Name System Security Extensions," March 1999.

RFC 2543   Handley, M., Schulzrinne, H., Schooler, E., Rosenberg, J.: "SIP: Session Initiation Protocol," March 1999.

RFC 2555   RFC editor, et al: "30 Years of RFCs," April 7, 1999.

RFC 2616   Fielding, R., Gettys, J., Mogul, J., Frystyk, H., Masinter, L., Leach, P., Berners-Lee, T.: "Hypertext Transfer Protocol — HTTP/1.1," RFC 2616, June 1999.

RFC 2617   Frank, J., Hallam-Baker, P., Hostetler, J., Lawrence, S., Leach, P., Luotonen, A., Sink, E., Stewart, L.: "HTTP Authentication: Basic and Digest Access Authentication," RFC 2617, June 1999.

RFC 2775   Carpenter, B.: "Internet Transparency," IETF, February 2000.

RFC 2778   Day, M., Rosenberg, J., Sugano, H.: "A Model for Presence and Instant Messaging," February 2000.

RFC 2779   Day, M., Aggarwal, S., Mohr, G., Vincent, J.: "Instant Messaging/Presence Protocol Requirements," February 2000.

RFC 2822   Resnick, P.: "Internet Message Format," April 2001.

RFC 2914   Floyd, S.: "Congestion Control Principles," September 2000.

RFC 2965   Kristol, D., Montulli, L.: "HTTP State Management Mechanism," October 2000.

RFC 2993   Hain, T.: "Architectural Implications of NAT," November 2000.

RFC 3092   Eastlake 3rd, D., Manros, C., Raymond, E.: "Etymology of 'Foo'," April 1, 2001.

RFC 3160   Malkin, G., Harris, S.: "The Tao of IETF: A Novice's Guide to the Internet Engineering Task Force," August 2001.

RFC 3238   Floyd, S., Daigle, L.: "IAB Architectural and Policy Considerations for Open Pluggable Edge Services," January 2002.

RFC 3261   Rosenberg, J., Schulzrinne, H., Camarillo, G., Johnston, A., Peterson, J., Sparks, R., Handley, M., Schooler, E.: SIP: "Session Initiation Protocol," June 2002.

RFC 3265   Roach, A. B.: "Session Initiation Protocol (SIP)-Specific Event Notification," June 2002.

RFC 3411   Harrington, D., Presuhn, R., Wijun, B.: "An Architecture for Describing Simple Network Management Protocol (SNMP) Management Frameworks," December 2002.

RFC 3466   Day, M., Cain, B., Tomlinson, G., Rzewski, P.: "A Model for Content Internetworking (CDI)," February 2003.

RFC 3490   Faltstrom, P., Hoffman, P., Costello, A.: "Internationalizing Domain Names in Applications (IDNA)," March 2003.

RFC 3507   Elson, J., Cerpa, A.: "Internet Content Adaptation Protocol (ICAP)," April 2003.

RFC 3568   Barbir, A., Cain, B., Nair, R., Spatscheck, O.: "Known Content Network (CN) Request-Routing Mechanisms," July 2003.

RFC 3752   Barbir, A., Burger, E., Chen, R., McHenry, S., Orman, H., Penno, R.: "OPES Use Cases and Deployment Scenarios," Internet Request for Comments, April 2004.

RFC 3835   Barbir, A., Penno, R., Chen, R., Hofmann, M., and Orman, H.: "An Architecture for Open Pluggable Edge Services (OPES)," August 2004.

RFC 3836   Beck, A., Hofmann, M., Orman, H., Penno, R., and Terzis, A.: "Requirements for Open Pluggable Edge Services (OPES) Callout Protocols," August 2004.

RFC 3856   Rosenberg, J.: "A Presence Event Package for the Session Initiation Protocol (SIP)," August 2004.

RFC 3859   Peterson, J.: "Common Profile for Presence (CPP)," August 2004.

RFC 3860   Peterson, J.: "Common Profile for Instant Messaging (CPIM)," August 2004.

RFC 3861   Peterson, J.: "Address Resolution for Instant Messaging and Presence," August 2004

RFC 3862   Atkins, D., Klyne, G.: "Common Presence and Instant Messaging: Message Format," August 2004.

RFC 3863   Sugano, H., Fujimoto, S., Klyne, G., Bateman, A., Carr, W., Peterson, J.: "Presence Information Data Format (PIDF)," August 2004.

RFC 3914   Barbir, A., Rousskov, A.: "Open Pluggable Edge Services (OPES) Treatment of IAB Considerations," October 2004.

RFC 3920   Saint-Andre, P. (ed): "Extensible Messaging and Presence Protocol (XMPP): Core," October 2004.

RFC 3921   Saint-Andre, P. (ed): "Extensible Messaging and Presence Protocol (XMPP): Instant Messaging and Presence," October 2004.

RFC 3922   Saint-Andre, P.: "Mapping the Extensible Messaging and Presence Protocol (XMPP) to Common Presence and Instant Messaging (CPIM)," October 2004.

RFC 3935   Alvestrand, H.: "A Mission Statement for the IETF," October 2004.

References

RFCs are listed in a separate RFC reference section. The reference style used throughout this section is as follows: Author(s) last name, initial(s), title in quotes, publication, and date. If available, the Web site address appears on a separate line. The references are alphabetized according to their tag.

[3GPP1]   3rd Generation Partnership Project: "Technical Specifications Group Services and System Aspects," Multi Media Messaging Service (MS) Stage 1, Release 6, 3GPP TS 22.140.
www.3gpp.org/ftp/specs/html%2Dinfo/22140.htm

[Abl03]   Abley, J.: "Hierarchical Anycast for Global Service Distribution," Internet Systems Consortium, 2003.
www.isc.org/index.pl?/ops/f-root/

[ACK+02]   Anderson, D. P., Cobb, J., Korpela, E., Lebofsky, M., Werthimer, D.: "SETI@home: An Experiment in Public-Resource Computing," Communications of the ACM, 45(11), pp. 56–61, November 2002.
setiathome.ssl.berkeley.edu/cacm/cacm.html

[AHa01]   Aberer, K., Hauswirth, M.: "Peer-to-Peer Information Systems: Concepts and Models, State-of-the-Art, and Future Aystems," Distributed Information Systems Laboratory (LSIR).
lsirwww.epfl.ch/

[AHa02]   Aberer, K., Hauswirth, M.: "An Overview on Peer-to-Peer information Systems," Swiss Federal Institute of Technology (EPFL), Switzerland.
lsirpeople.epfl.ch/hauswirth/papers/WDAS2002.pdf

[AHP+02]   Aberer, K., Hauswirth, M., Punceva, M., Schmidt, R.: "Improving Data Access in P2P Systems." IEEE Internet Computing 6(1), January/February, 2002.

[AHu00]   Adar, E., Huberman, B. A.: "Free Riding on Gnutella," First Monday, 5(10), 2000.
www.firstmonday.org/issues/issue5_10/adar/index.html

[AIM1]   "AIM Terms of Service Agreement."
"You may access AIM Products only through the interfaces and protocols provided or authorized by AOL."
www.aim.com/tos/tos.adp

[Akam1]   Akami Company History.
            www.akami.com/en/html/about/overview.html

[AL01]   Albitz, P., Liu, C.: *DNS and Bind*, O'Reilly, 2001.

[ALT1]   Nortel Networks: "Web OS Switch Software 10.0 Application Guide,"
            Nortel Networks, Part Number 212777, pp. 207–219, February 2002.
            www142.nortelnetworks.com/bvdoc/alteon/webos/webos10.0/212777-A.pdf

[Amb00]   Ambrose, S. E.: *Nothing Like It in the World: The Men Who Built the
            Transcontinental Railroad, 1863–1869,* Simon & Schuster, 2000.

[ANS01]   American National Standard: "Telecom Glossary 2000, American
            National Standard for Telecommunications," T1.523–2001, February 28,
            2001.
            www.atis.org/tg2k/_standard.html

[ANSI1]   ANSI Standards Course Material.
            www.standardslearn.org/courses/wsm/glossary.pdf

[ASW+02]   Andrews, M., Bruce Shepherd, F., Srinivasan, A., Winkler, P., Zane, F.:
            "Cluster and Server Selection Using Passive Monitoring," Infocom, 2002.
            cm.bell-labs.com/cm/ms/who/bshep/PS/infocom02.ps

[Atn99]   atnewyork Staff: "Alley Development Team Readies ICQ for Big Time,"
            atnewyork.com article, February 5, 1999.
            www.atnewyork.com/news/article.php/247731

[Aya01]   Ayars, J., et al: "Synchronized Multimedia Integration Language (SMIL
            2.0)," W3C Recommendation, August 7, 2001.

[BBC02]   BBC News: "Bird Flight Explained," December 16, 2002.
            news.bbc.co.uk/1/hi/sci/tech/1608251.stm

[BCP+98]   Breslau, L., Cao, P., Fan, L., Phillips, G., Shenker, S.: "Web Caching and
            Zipf-Like Distributions: Evidence and Implications." Technical report,
            University of Wisconsin—Madison, Department of Computer Science,
            July 1998.
            www.cs.wisc.edu/~cao/papers/zipf-implications.html

[BDE+00]   Bolosky, W. J., Douceur, J. R., Ely, D., Theimer, M.: "Feasibility of a
            Server-less Distributed File System Deployed on an Existing Set of
            Desktop PCs," In Proceedings of the International Conference on
            Measurement and Modeling of Computer Systems (SIGMETRICS 2000),
            pp. 34–43, 2000.

[Bea01]   Beaumont, L. R.: "Meeting World Wide Demand for your Content,
            Evolving to a Content Delivery Network," A Lucent Technologies White
            Paper, April 25, 2001.
            content-networking.com/papers/world-wide-demand.pdf

[Bea1]   Beaumont, L. R.: "Calculating Web Cache Hit Ratios."
            www.content-networking.com/papers/web-caching-zipf.pdf

[BeH03]   Beck, A., Hofmann, M.: "IRML: A Rule Specification Language for Intermediary Services," June 24, 2003.
papers.mhof.com/draft-beck-opes-irml-03.txt

[Ber89]   Berners-Lee, T.: "Information Management: A Proposal," Proposal to CERN Management, March 1989.
www.w3.org/History/1989/proposal.html

[Ber92]   Berners-Lee, T.: "Re: Is there a paper which describes the www protocol," WWW-Talk Mailing List, January 1992.
lists.w3.org/Archives/Public/www-talk/1992JanFeb/0000.html

[BGH+00]   Bommaiah, E., Guo, K., Hofmann, M., Paul, S.: "Design and Implementation of a Caching System for Streaming Media over the Internet."
papers.mhof.com/rtas2000.pdf

[BHC00]   Beck, A., Hofmann, M., Condry, M.: "Example Services for Network Edge Proxie," November 2000.
papers.mhof.com/draft-beck-opes-esfnep-01.txt

[Bor99]   Borland, J.: "Net Video Not Yet Ready for Prime Time," CNet News, February 5, 1999.
news.cnet.com/news/0-1004-200-338361.html

[Bor02]   Borland, J.: "Roxio Closes Napster Asset Buy," CNET News.com, November 27, 2002.
news.com.com/2100-1023_3-975627.html?tag=mainstry

[Bro04]   Brodsky, A. R.: "Telegraph." World Book Online Reference Center. World Book, Inc. March 3, 2004.
www.worldbookonline.com/wb/Article?id=ar549720

[Brod04]   Brodsky, A. R." "Telephone." World Book Online Reference Center. World Book, Inc. March 3, 2004.
www.worldbookonline.com/wb/Article?id=ar549860

[Bul01]   Bulterman, D. C. A.: "SMIL 2.0, Part 1: Overview, Concepts, and Structure," IEEE Multimedia, October–December 2001.
www.computer.org/multimedia/mu2001/pdf/u4082.pdf

[Bus45]   Bush, V.: "As We May Think," The Atlantic Monthly, July 1945.
www.w3.org/History/1945/vbush/

[CD92]   Casner, S., Deering, S.: "First IETF Internet Audiocast," ACM SIG-COMM, Computer Communications Review, 22(3), July 1992.

[CDK+03]   Castro, M., Druschel, P., Kermarrec, A.-M., Rowstron, A.: "Scalable Application-Level Anycast for Highly Dynamic Groups."
research.microsoft.com/~antr/PAST/anycast.pdf

[CDN+96]   Chankhunthod, A., Danzig, P. B., Neerdaels, C., Sewarts, M. F., Worrell, K. J.: "A Hierarchical Internet Object Cache," Usenix Technical Conference, 1996.

[CEA1]   Consumer Electronics Association, Digital America, History, "Pagers"
                www.ce.org/publications/books_references/digital_america/history/
                pagers.asp

[Chm02]   Chmielewski, D.: "Bertelsmann to Buy Napster for $8 Million,"
                SiliconValley.com News Article, May 17, 2002.
                www.siliconvalley.com/mld/siliconvalley/3284680.htm

[Cia98]   Cialdini, R. B.: *Influence: The Psychology of Persuasion,* Quill, Revised
                edition, October, 1998.

[Cla92]   Clark, D.: "By Popular Demand," Talk given at the IETF Plenary, 1992.

[Clip2]   Clip2 Distributed Search Solutions: "The Gnutella Protocol Specification
                v0.4."
                www.content-networking.com/papers/gnutella-protocol-04.pdf

[CMH+02]   Clarke, I., Miller, S. G., Hong, T. W., Sandberg, O., Wiley, B.: "Protecting
                Free Expression Online with Freenet." IEEE Internet Computing 6(1),
                January/February 2002.

[CMJ04]   Campbell, B., Mahy, R., Jennings, C.: "The Message Session Relay
                Protocol," draft-ietf-simple-message-sessions-09.txt, IETF SIMPLE
                Working Group, Internet Draft, Work in Progress, October 24, 2004.

[CoK03]   Colgrave, J., Januszewski, K.: "Using WSDL in a UDDI Registry,"
                Technical Note, Version 2.0, June 29, 2003.
                www.oasis-open.org/committees/uddi-spec/doc/tn/uddi-spec-tc-tn-wsdl-
                202-20040631.htm

[Com00]   Comer, D.: *Internetworking with TCP/IP—Volume 1: Principles,
                Protocols, and Architecture,* Prentice Hall, 2000.

[Coo96]   Cooper, R.: "New Products, What Separates the Winners from the
                Losers," In Rosenau, M. D.: *The PDMA Handbook of New Product
                Development,* John Wiley & Sons, 1996.

[Copy00]   U. S. Copyright Office: "Copyright Basics (Circular 1)," September 2000.
                www.copyright.gov/circs/circ1.html

[Cou04]   "TheCounter.com: Global Internet Statistics."
                www.thecounter.com/

[CSW+01]   Clarke, I., Sandberg, O., Wiley, B., Hong, T. W.: "Freenet: A Distributed
                Anonymous Information Storage and Retrieval System." In Federrath,
                H. (ed): *Designing Privacy Enhancing Technologies: International
                Workshop on Design Issues in Anonymy and Unobservability* number 2009
                in *Computer Science,* Springer Verlag, Berlin, 2001.
                www.doc.ic.ac.uk/~twh1/academic/papers/icsi-revised.pdf

[Dea03]   Dean, K.: "Schoolgirl Settles With RIAA," Wired News, September 10,
                2003.
                www.wired.com/news/digiwood/0,1412,60366,00.htm

[Dea04]   Dean, K.: "RIAA Strikes Again at Traders," Wired News, January 21,
                2004.
                www.wired.com/news/digiwood/0,1412,61989,00.html

[Dee91]   Deering, S.: "Watching the Waist of the Protocol Hourglass," Presentation at IETF 51 Meeting, London, England, August 2001. www.iab.org/iab/DOCUMENTS/hourglass-london-ietf.pdf

[Dee95]   Deering, S.: "IP Multicast and the MBone: Enabling Live, Multiparty, Multimedia Communication on the Internet." ftp://parcftp.xerox.com/pub/net-research/mbone/mbone-talk-dec95.ps

[Dem03]   Dempsey, J. A.: *A Tale of Two Brothers: The Story of the Wright Brothers,* Trafford, June 2003.

[dict1]   Dictionary.com, entry for "standard." www.dictionary.com

[DMCA98]   "The Digital Millennium Copyright Act of 1998," U. S. Copyright Office Summary, December 1998. www.copyright.gov/legislation/dmca.pdf

[DPT03]   Dvorak, J. C., Pirillo, C., Taylor, W.: *Online! The Book*, Chapter 25 by Matthew Hunt. www.omnipod.com/resources/enterprise_IM_chapter.pdf

[Dup42]   Dupuit, A. J. E. (1842): "On Tolls and Transport Charges," Annales des Ponts et Chausses, trns. 1962.

[ED92]   Emtage, A., P.: "Deutsch: archie—An Electronic Directory Service for the Internet," Proceedings of the Winter USENIX Conference, San Francisco, CA, January 1992.

[EE68]   Engelbart, D. C., English, W. K.: "A Research Center for Augmenting Human Intellect," AFIPS Conference Proceedings of the 1968 Fall Joint Computer Conference, 33, pp. 395–410, San Francisco, CA, December 1968. sloan.stanford.edu/mousesite/Archive/ResearchCenter1968/Research Center1968.html

[Eri94]   Eriksson, H.: "MBONE: The Multicast Backbone," Communications of the ACM, 37(8), pp. 54–60, August 1994.

[Fine1]   Fine, M.: "Soundscan Study on Napster Use and Loss of Sales," Study Submitted in A&M Records, Inc., et al. v. Napster, Inc., No. c 99-05183MHP. www.riaa.com/news/filings/pdf/napster/fine.pdf

[FIPS93]   Federal Information Processing Standards Publication 180–1: "Secure Hash Standard," FIPS PUB 180, May 11, 1993. www.itl.nist.gov/fipspubs/fip180-1.htm

[FKe03]   Foster, I., Kesselman, C.: *The Grid: Blueprint for a New Computing Infrastructure,* Morgan Kaufmann, 2003.

[Fou1]   Foundry Networks: "Global Server Load Balancing with Serveriron," Application Note. www.foundrynet.com/solutions/appNotes/GSLB.html

[Fou2]   Foundry Networks: "Firewall Load Balancing," Application Note. www.foundrynet.com/solutions/appNotes/PDFs/FWLB.pdf

[Fri00]   Fritzler, A.: "AIM/Oscar Protocol Specification," April 8, 2000.

[Gil02]   Gilder, G.: *Telecom: The World After Bandwidth Abundance,* Free Press, May 2002.

[Gre00]   Greenwald, J.: "Instantly Growing Up," Time Magazine, November 6, 2000.

[Har68]   Hardin, G.: "The Tragedy of the Commons," Science, 162: 1243–1248, 1968.

[Her99]   Herring, S.: "Interactional Coherence in CMC," Journal of Computer-Mediated Communication, 4(4), 1999.
             www.ascusc.org/jcmc/vol4/issue4/herring.html

[HHa00]   Hu, J., Hansen, E.: "Record Label Signs Deal with Napster," News.com article, October 31, 2000.
             news.com.com/2100-1023-247859.html?legacy=cnet

[HNG+99]   Hofmann, M., et al: "Caching Techniques for Streaming Multimedia over the Internet" Bell Labs Technical Memorandum, April 1999.
             papers.mhof.com/soccer.pdf

[Hol91]   Holzmann, G. J.: *Design and Validation of Computer Protocols,* Prentice-Hall, 1991.

[Hui95]   Huitema, C.: *Routing in the Internet,* Prentice Hall, 1995.

[Hut1]   Hutchinson Encyclopedia: "Videotape Recorder."
             www.tiscali.co.uk/reference/encyclopaedia/hutchinson/m0005365.html

[IANA1]   "IANA Report on Establishment of the .pro Top-Level Domain," May 6, 2002.
             www.iana.org/reports/pro-report-06may02.htm

[IEC1]   International Engineering Consortium, On-Line Education: "Wireless Short Message Service (SMS)."
             www.iec.org/online/tutorials/wire_sms/topic01.html

[IEN 137]   Cohen, D.: "On Holy Wars and A Plea For Peace," IEN 137, April 1, 1980.
             www.ietf.org/rfc/ien/ien137.txt

[IETF1]   Internet Engineering Task Force: "Homepage."
             www.ietf.org/

[IETF2]   www.ietf.org/glossary.html

[IETF3]   Active IETF Working Groups.
             www.ietf.org/html.charters/wg-dir.html

[IETF96]   Kessler, G. C.: "IETF—History, Background, and Role in Today's Internet," February 1, 1996.
             www.garykessler.net/library/ietf_hx.html

[Int01]   Intel Press Release: "Intel Forms Peer-To-Peer Working Group," August 24, 2000.
             www.intel.com/pressroom/archive/releases/cn082400.htm

[IRI1]   Internationalized Resource Identifiers.
www.w3.org/International/O-URL-and-ident

[ISO86]   International Organization for Standardization: "Information Processing—Text and office systems—Standard Generalized Markup Language (SGML)," ISO 8879, Geneva, 1986.

[ISOC1]   The Internet Society: "History of the Internet."
www.isoc.org/internet/history/

[Jay03]   Jaynes, R.: "Countdown to Kitty Hawk Moments, Wilbur Wins, but Loses," Originally Printed in Flying Magazine, 2003.
www.countdowntokittyhawk.com/news/moments/031126_wilbur_wins.html

[KBC+00] Kubiatowicz, J., Bindel, D., Chen, Y., Czerwinski, S., Eaton, P., Geels, D., Gummadi, R., Rhea, S., Weatherspoon, H., Weimer, W., Wells, C., Zhao, B.: "OceanStore: An Architecture for Global-Scale Persistent Storage," Appears in Proceedings of the Ninth International Conference on Architectural Support for Programming Languages and Operating Systems (ASPLOS 2000), November 2000.
oceanstore.cs.berkeley.edu

[KH95]   Krunz, M., Hughs, H.: "A Traffic Model for MPEG-Coded VBR Streams," 1995 ACM SIGMETRICS Conference on Measurement and Modeling of Computer Systems, Ottawa, May 15–19, 1995.

[Kin02]   King, B.: "Napster's Assets Go for a Song," Wired News, November 28, 2002.
www.wired.com/news/digiwood/0,1412,56633,00.html

[KM91]   Kahle, B., Medlar, A.: "An Information System for Corporate Users: Wide Area Information Servers," ConneXions—The Interoperability Report, 5(11), November 1991.

[Knu73]   Knuth, D. E.: *The Art of Computer Programming,* Volume 3, Sorting and Searching, First Edition, 1973.

[KR01]   Krishnamurthy, B., Rexford, J.: *Web Protocols and Practice,* Addison Wesley, 2001.

[Kub03]   Kubiatowicz, J.: "Extracting Guarantees from Chaos," Communications of the ACM, February 2003.

[Kum95]   Kumar, V.: *Mbone: Interactive Multimedia on the Internet,* New Riders Publishing, Indianapolis, 1995.

[Lau00]   Liquid Audio Press Release: "AOL's Nullsoft Winamp and Liquid Audio Form Multi-Year Digital Music Alliance," January 4, 2000.
www.liquidaudio.com/company/press/2000/archive/01_04_00.asp

[LBK02]   Liben-Nowell, D., Balakrishnan, H., and Karger, D.: "Analysis of the Evolution of Peer-to-Peer Systems." ACM Conference on Principles of Distributed Computing (PODC), Monterey, CA, July 2002.
www.pdos.lcs.mit.edu/chord/papers/podc2002.pdf

[LC92]   Berners-Lee, T., Connolly, D.: "HyperText Mark-up Language, HTML," 1992.
www.w3.org/History/19921103-hypertext/hypertext/WWW/MarkUp/MarkUp.html

[LCL+02]   Lv, Q., Cao, P., Cohen, E., Li, K., Shenker, S.: "Search and Replication in Unstructured Peer-to-Peer Networks." In Proceedings of 16th ACM International Conference on Supercomputing (ICS'02), New York, June 2002.

[Lee03]   Lee, J.: "An End-User Perspective on File-Sharing Systems," Communications of the ACM, February 2003.

[LeG91]   Le Gall, D.: "MPEG: A Video Compression Standard for Multimedia Applications," Communications of the ACM, 34, pp. 47–58, April 1991.

[Les00]   Lessig, L.: *Code and Other Laws of Cyberspace,* Basic Books, June 2000.

[Li99]   Li, W.: "Zipf's Law," Rockefeller University, New York.
www.nslij-genetics.org/wli/zipf/

[LLP+97]   Karger, D., Lehman, E. Leighton, F., Levine, M., Lewin, D., and Panigrahy: "Consistent Hashing and Random Trees: Distributed Caching Protocols for Relieving Hot Spots on the World Wide Web." In Proceedings of the 29th Annual ACM Symposium on Theory of Computing, pp. 645–663, El Paso, TX, May 1997.

[LNB99]   Luotonen, A., Nielsen, H. F., Berners-Lee, T.: "Cern httpd," 1999.
www.w3.org/Daemon/

[Luo97]   Luotonen, A.: *Web proxy Servers*, Prentice Hall, 1997.

[Mar00]   Marsan, C. D.: "Caching Debate Rages," Network World Fusion, April 17, 2000.
www.nwfusion.com/news/2000/0417necp.html

[Mar01]   Marcus, S.: "The History of Napster," Term Paper, University of Tennessee at Knoxville, December 6, 2001.

[Mas1]   Masinter, L.: "HyperText Transfer Protocol (http) Working Group Charter."
www.ietf.org/html.charters/OLD/http-charter.html

[Mcc01]   McCoy, J.: "Mojo Nation Responds," The O'Reilly Network, January 11, 2001.
www.openp2p.com/pub/a/p2p/2001/01/11/mojo.html

[McN99]   McNett, D.: "US Government's Encryption Standard Broken In Less Than A Day," distributed.net Press Release, January 19, 1999.
www.distributed.net/des/release-desiii.txt

[Mer1]   Merit Network, Inc.: "NSFNET History of Usage by Service."
ftp://nic.merit.edu/nsfnet/statistics/history.ports

[MH03]   McCullagh, D., Hu, J.: "FCC Lifts AOL Messaging Limits," CNET News.com, August 20, 2003.
news.com.com/2100-1032_3-5065650.html

[MIME]   "Multipurpose Internet Mail Extensions." See RFC 2045, RFC 2046, RFC 2047, RFC 2048, and RFC 2049.

[MKL+02]   Milojicic, D. S., Kalogeraki, V., Lukose, R., Nagaraja, K., Pruyne, J., Richard, B., Rollins, S., Xu, Z.: "Peer-to-Peer Computing," HP Laboratories, Palo Alto, CA, HPL-2002-57, March 8, 2002. www.hpl.hp.com/techreports/2002/HPL-2002-57.pdf

[Mobi1]   mobilemms.com: "Frequently Asked Questions, How Does MMS Contrast to SMS, EMS and Smart Messaging?" www.mobilemms.com/mmsfaq.asp#3.1

[Moo00]   Moore, K.: "Recommendation against publication of draft-cerpa-necp-02.txt," E-mail Message to the IETF, April 6, 2000. www.mail-archive.com/ietf@ietf.org/msg01333.html

[Moo03]   Moore, C.: "XMPP Rises to Face SIMPLE Standard," InfoWorld, April 18, 2003. www.infoworld.com/article/03/04/18/16imstandards_1.html

[Mye76]   Myers, G. J.: *Software Reliability: Principles and Practices,* John Wiley & Sons, 1976.

[BHL99]   Bray, T., Hollander, D., Layman, A.: "W3C Recommendation: Namespaces in XML," January 14, 1999. www.w3.org/TR/1999/REC-xml-names-19990114/

[Nap03]   Napster Press Release: "Napster's Back," October 29, 2003. www.napster.com/press_releases/pr_031029.html

[Nel67]   Nelson, T. H.: "Getting it Out of Our System," In Schecheter, G. (ed.): *Information Retrieval—A Critical Review,* Thompson Books, Washington, D.C., 1967.

[Net01]   Network Appliance: "Internet Content Adaptation Protocol (ICAP)," White Paper, July 30, 2001.

[Net94]   "Netscape: Persistent Client State HTTP Cookies." www.netscape.com/newsref/std/cookie_spec.html

[NWFE1]   "Network Fusion Encyclopedia" entry for 'Metcalfe's Law." www.nwfusion.com/links/Encyclopedia/M/771.html

[ODF+01]   Dingledine, R., Freedman, M. J., Molnar, D.: "Accountability." In Oram, A.: *Peer-to-Peer: Harnessing the Power of Disruptive Technologies,* O'Reilly & Associates, March 2001.

[OeRa1]   Oetiker, T., and Rand, D.: "The Multi Router Traffic Grapher." www.mrtg.org

[Oika]   Oikarinen, J.: "IRC History by Jarkko Oikarinen." www.irc.org/history_docs/jarkko.html

[OL01]   Lethin, R.: "Reputation." In Oram, A.: *Peer-to-Peer: Harnessing the Power of Disruptive Technologies,* O'Reilly & Associates, March 2001.

[OMH01]   Minar, N., Hedlund, M.: "Peer-to-Peer Models Through the History of the Internet," In Oram, A.: *Peer-to-Peer: Harnessing the Power of Disruptive Technologies,* O'Reilly and Associates, March 2001.

[Ope00]   "Napster Messages," April 7, 2000. opennap.sourceforge.net/napster.txt

[OWC+01]   Waldman, M., Cranor, L. F., Rubin, A.: "Trust," In Oram, A.: *Peer-to-Peer: Harnessing the Power of Disruptive Technologies,* O'Reilly & Associates, March 2001.

[Page]   phone warehouse Web site: "Pager History." www.phonewarehouse.com/pager.htm

[Par72]   Parnas, D. L.: "On the Criteria To Be Used in Decomposing Systems into Modules," Communications of the ACM, Vol. 15, No. 12, December 1972, pp. 1053–1058. www.acm.org/classics/may96/

[Phi03]   Philipkoski, K.: "Battle Not Over for File Sharers," Wired News, December 23, 2003. www.wired.com/news/digiwood/0,1412,61714,00.html

[RDr01]   Rowstron, A., Druschel, P.: "Pastry: Scalable, Decentralized Object Location and Routing for Large-Scale Peer-to-Peer Systems." In Proceedings of the 18th IFIP/ACM International Conference on Distributed Systems Platforms (Middleware 2001), Heidelberg, Germany, November 2001.

[Real1]   RealNetworks: "Introduction To Streaming Media with RealOne Player," 2002. service.real.com/help/library/encoders.html

[RIAA]   Record Industry Association of America, Press Room: "Legal Cases." www.riaa.com/news/filings/default.asp

[RoS04]   Rousskov, A., Stecher, M.: "HTTP Adaptation with OPES," draft-ietf-opes-http-2, Work in Progress, January 2004.

[Rou03]   Beck, A., Rousskov, A.: "P: Message Processing Language," draft-rousskov-opes-rules-01, October 27, 2003. www.measurement-factory.com/tmp/opes/

[Rou04]   Rousskov, A.: "OPES Callout Protocol Core," draft-ietf-opes-core-05, Work in Progress, May 2004.

[RPH+01]   Ratnasamy, S., Francis, P., Handley, M., Karp, R., Shenker, S.: "A Scalable Content-Addressable Network." In Proceedings of the ACM SIGCOMM, 2001.

[RSC98]   Reed, D. P., Saltzer, J. H., Clark, D. D.: "Comment on Active Networking and End-to-End Arguments," IEEE Network, 12(3), May/June 1998. web.mit.edu/Saltzer/www/publications/endtoend/ANe2ecomment.html

[RTSP]   "RTSP Information Portal," Started by RealNetworks. www.rtsp.org

[RWE+01]   Rhea, S., Wells, C., Eaton, P., Geels, D., Zhao, B., Weatherspoon, H., Kubiatowicz, J.: "Maintenance-free Global Data Storage." IEEE Internet Computing 5(5), September/October 2001.

[Sam04]   Samuelson, P.: "What is at Stake in MGM V. Grokster?," Communications of the ACM, 47(2), February 2004.

[Sau04]   Saunders, C.: "VoIP Gets SIMPLE For Avaya," InstantMessagingPlanet. com., February 23, 2004.

[SIMPLE]   "SIP for Instant Messaging and Presence Leveraging Extensions," IETF Working Group.
ietf.org/html.charters/simple-charter.html

[Sin95]   van Sinderen, M. J.: "On the Design of Application Protocols." PhD Thesis, University of Twente, Enschede, The Netherlands, 1995.
wwwhome.cs.utwente.nl/~sinderen/publications/thesis.html

[SKB01]   Stoica, I., Morris, R., Karger, D., Frans Kaashoek, M., and Balakrishnan, H.: "Chord: A Scalable Peer-to-peer Lookup Service for Internet Applications," ACM SIGCOMM, pp. 149–160, San Diego, CA, August 2001.
www.pdos.lcs.mit.edu/papers/chord:sigcomm01/chord_sigcomm.pdf

[SMS1]   smsforum.net/

[Sob95]   Sobel, D.: *Longitude: The True Story of a Lone Genius Who Solved the Greatest Scientific Problem of His Time,* Walker & Co, October 1995.

[SRD84]   Saltzer, J. H., Reed, D. P., Clark, D. D.: "End-to-End Arguments in System Design," ACM Transactions on Communications, 2(4), 1984.
web.mit.edu/Saltzer/www/publications/endtoend/endtoend.pdf

[Sri01]   Sripanidkulchai, K.: "The Popularity of Gnutella Queries and Its Implications on Scalability," Carnegie Mellon University, February 2001.
www-2.cs.cmu.edu/~kunwadee/research/p2p/gnutella.html

[SRL98]   Savetz, K., Randall, N., Lepage, Y.: "MBONE: Multicasting Tomorrow's Internet," 1998.
www.savetz.com/mbone/

[SRT99]   Sen, S., Rexford, J., Towsley, D.: "Proxy Prefix Caching for Multimedia Streams," IEEE Infocom, New York, March 1999.

[SSL96]   Netscape Communications: "The SSL Protocol, Version 3.0," November 1996.
wp.netscape.com/eng/ssl3/

[Ste94]   Stevens, W. R.: *TCP/IP Illustrated—Volume 1: The Protocols,* Addison Wesley, 1994.

[Tar00]   Taro, K.: "Meet the Napster," CNN, September 25, 2000.
www.cnn.com/ALLPOLITICS/time/2000/10/02/napster.html

[Tay03]   Taylor, C.: "Invention of the Year, the 99¢ Solution," Time Magazine, 2003.
www.time.com/time/2003/inventions/invmusic.html

[Tech1]   TechFest Ethernet Technical Summary.
               www.techfest.com/networking/lan/ethernet4.htm

[Tech2]   SONET / SDH Technical Summary.
               www.techfest.com/networking/wan/sonet.htm

[TellA]   Tellme Networks, Inc.: "Our Clients."
               www.tellme.com/clients.html

[TellB]   Tellme Networks, Inc.: "Tellme Studio VoiceXML 2.0 Essentials."
               studio.tellme.com/vxml2/ovw/essentials.html

[Tha]   Thawte Certification Authority. www.thawte.com

[TPC]   TruePosition Corporation: "The Location Equations: Sub-50M
               Accuracy, Any Phone, Anywhere."

[TPF00]   Telling, R. H., Pickard, C. J., Payne, M. C., Field, J. D.: "Theoretical
               Strength and Cleavage of Diamond," Physical Review Letters, 84(22),
               May 29, 2000.
               www.tcm.phy.cam.ac.uk/~cjp20/publications/PRL84_5160.pdf

[TSS97]   Tennenhouse, D. L., Smith, J. M., Sincoskie, W. D., Wetherall, D. J.,
               Minden, G. J.: "A Survey of Active Network Research." IEEE
               Communications Magazine, 35(1), January 1997.

[UDD00]   uddi.org: "UDDI Technical White Paper," September 6, 2000.

[UDDI V3]   uddi.org: "UDDI version 3.0, UDDI Spec Technical Committee
               Specification," 19 July 2002.

[Ver03]   VeriSign,,Inc.: "VeriSign Trusted Web Transactions Solution," 2003.
               www.verisign.com/products/trustedTransaction/trustedTransaction.pdf

[Vich1]   Vichinsky, J. H.: "Napster and the Law," Course Notes, Thomas M.
               Cooley Law School.
               www.doylepc.com/cyberlaw/napsteressay.html

[VoiceXML]   McGlashan, S., et al: "Voice Extensible Markup Language
               (VoiceXML) Version 2.0," W3C Candidate Recommendation,
               February 20, 2003.

[W3C CCPP]   "Composite Capability/Preference Profiles (CC/PP): Structure and
               Vocabularies," W3C Working Draft, July 28, 2003.
               www.w3.org/TR/CCPP-struct-vocab/

[W3C04]   World Wide Web Consortium: "World Wide Web Consortium Process
               Document," February 5, 2004.
               www.w3.org/2004/02/Process-20040205

[W3C1]   World Wide Web Consortium: "Homepage."
               www.w3.org/

[W3C2]   W3C: "Some Early Ideas for HTML."
               www.w3.org/MarkUp/historical

[W3C3]   W3C: "HTML Home Page."
               www.w3.org/MarkUp/

[W3C7]   W3C in 7 points: "World Wide Web Consortium."
               www.w3.org/Consortium/Points/

[W3S04]   W3Schools.com: "Browser Statistics."
               www.w3schools.com/browsers/browsers_stats.asp

[WAP00]   Wireless Application Protocol Forum, Ltd.: "Wireless Application
               Protocol, Architecture Specification," WAP-210-WAPArch-20010712,
               July 12, 2000.

[WAP01]   Wireless Application Protocol Forum, Ltd.: "WAP Pictogram
               Specification" version April 6, 2001, Wireless Application Protocol,
               WAP-213-WAPInterPic-20010406-a

[WAP02]   Wireless Application Protocol Forum, Ltd.: "WAP 2.0 Technical White
               Paper," January 2002.

[WAP UA]   Wireless Application Protocol Forum, Ltd.: "WAG UAProf," version
               October 20, 2001. Wireless Application Protocol, WAP-248-UAPROF-
               20011020-a.
               www.wapforum.org/

[WDNS]   imminet: "WebDNS 100, Building Smarter Faster Networks to Satisfy
               Global Users," Product Description, Lucent Technologies, 2001.
               content-networking.com/papers/brochure-webdns.pdf

[Wes01]   Wessels, D.: *Web Caching,* O'Reilly, 2001.

[Wes02]   Wessels, D.: "Squid Web Proxy Cache," 2001.
               www.squid-cache.org/

[WF03]   Wessels, D., Fomenkov, M.: "Wow, That's a Lot of Packets,"
               Proceedings of Passive and Active Measurement Workshop (PAM),
               April 2003.

[WiZ01]   Witmann, R., Zitterbart, M.: *Multicast Communication—Protocols and
               Applications,* Morgan Kaufmann Publishing, 2001.

[Woo02]   Woods, B.: "Review—AOL's AIM," atnewyork.com, May 24, 2002.
               www.atnewyork.com/news/article.php/1144451

[WRC00]   Waldman, M., Rubin, A., Cranor, L.: "Publius: A Robust, Tamper-
               Evident, Censorship-Resistant Web Publishing System," Proceedings of
               the 9th USENIX Security Symposium, August 2000.
               publius.cdt.org/publius.pdf

[BHM+04]   Booth, D. et al: "Web Services Architecture," W3C Working Draft,
               February 11, 2004.
               www.w3.org/TR/ws-arch/

[XMPP1]   "IETF Text Conferencing."
               xmpp.org/ietf-chat.html

[ZYF02]   Zeinalipour-Yazti, D., Folias, T.: "A Quantitative Analysis of the Gnutella Network Traffic," University of California, Department of Computer Science, Riverside, CA, June 17, 2002. www.cs.ucr.edu/~csyiazti/cs204.html

Index

Page numbers in italics denote illustrations and tables.